NEVER

A

LOVELY

SO

REAL

NEVER A LOVELY SO REAL

The Life and Work of **NELSON ALGREN**

Colin Asher

W. W. NORTON & COMPANY

Independent Publishers Since 1923

New York | London

For information about permission to reproduce selections from this book, write to
Permissions, W. W. Norton & Company, Inc., 500 Fifth Avenue, New York, NY 10110

For information about special discounts for bulk purchases, please contact
W. W. Norton Special Sales at specialsales@wwnorton.com or 800-233-4830

Manufacturing by LSC Communications Harrisonburg
Book design by Chris Welch
Production manager: Lauren Abbate

Library of Congress Cataloging-in-Publication Data

Names: Asher, C., author.
Title: Never a lovely so real : the life and work of Nelson Algren / Colin Asher.
Description: First edition. | New York : W. W. Norton & Company, [2019] |
Includes bibliographical references and index.
Identifiers: LCCN 2018049775 | ISBN 9780393244519 (hardcover)
Subjects: LCSH: Algren, Nelson, 1909–1981. | Authors, American—
20th century—Biography.
Classification: LCC PS3501.L4625 Z55 2019 | DDC 813/.52 [B]—dc23
LC record available at https://lccn.loc.gov/2018049775

W. W. Norton & Company, Inc., 500 Fifth Avenue, New York, N.Y. 10110
www.wwnorton.com

W. W. Norton & Company Ltd., 15 Carlisle Street, London W1D 3BS

1 2 3 4 5 6 7 8 9 0

To Nora and Dante—for keeps and a single day

A certain ruthlessness and a sense of alienation from society is as essential to creative writing as it is to armed robbery. The strong-armer isn't out merely to turn a fast buck any more than the poet is out solely to see his name on the cover of a book, whatever satisfaction that event may afford him. What both need most deeply is to get even.

—*Nelson Algren, writing in* Nonconformity

I have said that nothing factual that I write or say will be as truthful as my fiction. The life, the opinions, are not the work, for it is in the tension between standing apart and being involved that the imagination transforms both.

—*Nadine Gordimer, accepting the Nobel Prize in literature*

The world's so big yet so small. It's one block.

—*Nasir Jones, on Olu Dara's "Jungle Jay"*

CONTENTS

III.   EVERY DAY IS D-DAY UNDER THE EL

IV.   WANDER YEARS

V.   EXILE

INTRODUCTION

Nelson Algren in the early 1960s. Chicago History Museum, ICHi-068778;
Stephen Deutch, photographer

The first thing you should know about Nelson Algren is that he wrote like this:

> The captain never drank. Yet, toward nightfall in that smoke-colored season between Indian summer and December's first true snow, he would sometimes feel half drunken. He would hang his coat neatly over the back of his chair in the leaden station-house twilight, say he was beat from lack of sleep and lay his head across his arms upon the query-room desk.

Yet it wasn't work that wearied him so and his sleep was harassed by more than a smoke-colored rain. The city had filled him with the guilt of others; he was numbed by his charge sheet's accusations. For twenty years, upon the same scarred desk, he had been recording larceny and arson, sodomy and simony, boosting, hijacking and shootings in sudden affray: blackmail and terrorism, incest and pauperism, embezzlement and horse theft, tampering and procuring, abduction and quackery, adultery and mackery. Till the finger of guilt, pointed so sternly for so long across the query-room blotter, had grown bored with it all at last and turned, capriciously, to touch the fibers of the dark gray muscle behind the captain's light gray eyes.

Algren went to great lengths to seem tough. He favored dark suits, affected a limp, and acted brashly when he had an audience—but he could write about romantic relationships with uncommon nuance and insight:

> Those first hours together had been no more than those of any side-street solitary, any bar-wise, woman-wise bookie falling in love with any brash young chick from the suburbs wearing white batiste.
>
> It was autumn, but summer came back, a full week, just for them . . .
>
> Marriage was a bit he had never regarded seriously, one bit in which he had never seen himself. Marriage, he had always felt, was a standing joke. He had mocked it. She had slipped onto her finger a ring that he might have found in a box of Crackerjacks. Its stones, as it were, were plastic dice. He had slipped it onto her finger intending mockery, a mock marriage; instead she had put her lips to it. The mockery failed. The summer air had married them.

Algren wrote nonfiction as well—essays, reviews, and articles—and when he turned his attention to social critique he produced insights so trenchant they remain relevant decades after they were written. He wrote these lines describing the United States, for instance, in 1953:

> Never has any people possessed such a superfluity of physical luxuries companioned by such a dearth of emotional necessities. In no other country is such great wealth, acquired so purposefully, put to such small purpose. Never has any people driven itself so resolutely toward such diverse goals, to derive so little satisfaction from attainment of any.

Thanks to all that talent, Algren became very famous. He wrote eleven books, and millions of people bought them. His masterpiece, *The Man with the Golden Arm*, received the first National Book Award, earned a record sum when its paperback rights were sold, and was adapted for stage and screen—its protagonist was played by Robert Loggia and Frank Sinatra, respectively. Algren also received the *Time* magazine award for the novel, three Pushcart Prizes, an O. Henry Award, and the American Academy of Arts (later the American Academy and National Institute of Arts and Letters) Award of Merit. His fourth novel was adapted into a film starring Jane Fonda, and a musical, and inspired the Lou Reed song "Walk on the Wild Side."

Algren was influential as well, and if you're a fan of American literature there's a good chance he earned the respect of or inspired your favorite author. In 1940, Richard Wright called Algren "the best writer of good prose in the U.S.A." Ernest Hemingway once said Algren was the second-greatest living American author, after William Faulkner—and later said Algren had topped Faulkner. Ross Macdonald, Martha Gellhorn, Kay Boyle, Jimmy Breslin, Thomas Pynchon, Russell Banks, Betty Friedan, Rachel Kushner, and Don DeLillo have all expressed their admiration for Algren's work, and Cormac McCarthy told Algren, "You were one of the people who influenced me to become a writer." Simone de Beauvoir wrote Algren into four of her books, and Hunter S. Thompson once told an interviewer, "I admired Algren and still do. I thought at the time [1956] that no living American had written any two books better than *The Man with the Golden Arm* and *A Walk on the Wild Side.*"

But despite Algren's talent, sales, and influence, his name has been obscure for decades because he forswore writing novels a few years after he became famous—that fact is tragic in its own right, but it's doubly so because the cause of Algren's disillusionment and decline is being revealed in full only now.

The Man with the Golden Arm was published in 1949, near the height of the Red Scare, and Algren—a member of the Communist Party in the 1930s—used it to insult a pair of former party members who had begun selling information about their erstwhile comrades to the FBI. Those men were named Louis Budenz and Howard Rushmore, and Nelson considered them traitors, so he mocked them in his novel. He reimagined each man as a cheap salesman, and on page 219 of *Arm* he had his protagonist look up at a pair of billboards that read:

BUDINTZ Coal
One Price to All

RUSHMOORE COAL
Fastest Delivery
Cheapest in Years

No critic mentioned that slight when *Arm* was released, and no one has in the years since. It's likely few readers ever noticed it, but unfortunately, it seems Budenz and Rushmore did. A few days after Algren received the National Book Award, Budenz, without being prompted, told an FBI agent that Algren had once been a member of the Communist Party. Rushmore did the same a few months later, and because

Algren had also publicly supported the Hollywood Ten and Julius and Ethel Rosenberg, the FBI launched an investigation into his activities that included surveilling his home, opening his correspondence, recruiting his neighbors and landlords as informants, and requesting information on his activities from family members, friends, publishers, agents, the secretary at the YMCA he frequented, business associates, lawyers, the editor of his local newspaper, former political allies, and a psychiatrist who treated him.

As a result of the FBI's campaign, Algren was subpoenaed by the House Un-American Activities Committee, barred from obtaining a passport, and investigated—and nearly prosecuted—for perjury and defrauding the government. His publisher suppressed one of his books and then dropped him, and afterward he had a breakdown, attempted suicide, and committed himself to a psychiatric clinic. But though the FBI's scrutiny had profound effects on his life, Algren remained largely ignorant of their activities. They operated in secret, so Algren blamed himself when his life began falling apart. He presumed the paranoia and depression that began to cripple him in the 1950s were the result of personal weakness, and decided his books were not being published because no one wanted to read them. Eventually, he recovered and returned to form, but by then too much time had passed and he was unable to reclaim his former eminence.

Though it has long been known that the FBI was interested in Algren, the full extent of their involvement in his life has not previously been revealed. And in the absence of a clear explanation for the foreshortening of Algren's career, people—critics, academics, and fans alike—have relied on speculation to explain it. Some said Algren had writer's block. Others said he drank and gambled his talent away. A few, based on nothing but the fact that he once wrote a book about morphine addicts, claimed he was a drug abuser. And a select group— distrustful of the fact that Algren's characters were often inmates, vagabonds, and petty criminals—attacked the merit of his work and diminished the great intellect that had guided its composition. He's the "bard of the stumblebum," they said. "An underworld groupie." A man soaked in "puerile sentimentality."

But none of that is true, and it is my hope that people will reevaluate his character and work now that a full account of his life is available. It is my desire that readers of this book will come to see Algren as his friends saw him—a man whose death "was a tragic loss to the world of laughter, to the spirit and example of generosity and courage, and an irremediable aching blow" to everyone he was close to. And it is my ambition that people will then seek out his best work and read it in the same spirit in which it was read when it was published: a time when critics compared Algren to Dostoyevsky, Dickens, and Sandburg, and said his books deserved to be "read, remembered, and admired"; when he was considered "a writer of parables" capable of suggesting "the whole contour of a human life in a few terse pages"; and when his stories were celebrated for their ability to convey "the dramatic sense of right against wrong and everkindled hopefulness."

Part I

BECOMING SOMEONE IS A SOLITARY PROCESS

From city to city he went now; there was no standing still and there was no turning back. No place to go, and no place to rest. No time to be idling and nothing to do. He moved, moved, everything moved; men either kept moving or went to jail.

—Somebody in Boots, *1935*

The Story of Isaac

(1820–1911)

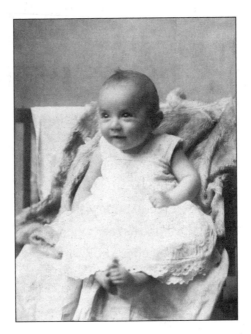

Nelson Algren—then, Nelson Algren Abraham—about 1909.

Nelson Algren was fifty-three years old in the spring of 1962. Five foot eleven, maybe 185 pounds—famous, but not wealthy. He lived alone in a third-floor walk-up on Chicago's West Evergreen Avenue, and his lifestyle was idiosyncratic.

Nelson's apartment was a canvas—an unmediated expression of his psyche. The air smelled of smoke, and blues records spun on the turntable. There were pictures of Fyodor Dostoyevsky, Charles Dickens, and Joan Baez on display in the living room—as well as a German

Mauser, and a blue helmet that had been recovered from the corpse of a soldier who died during the Ardennes Counteroffensive in 1944. Huge collages composed of newspaper and magazine images depicting boxers, racehorses, and baseball players covered the walls, and there were books everywhere—thousands and thousands of them. Their weight made the shelves lining the apartment's walls sag, and piles of them had taken root in the wood floors and started growing toward the ceiling like stalagmites. There was boxing equipment lying around as well, a blue Schwinn, and a metal bread box stuffed with love letters written by Simone de Beauvoir.

Time meant little to Nelson, so he enforced no structure on his days. He sat down at his typewriter when he felt the urge to write, and rose when he felt like stopping. Sometimes he worked just long enough to string together a pair of clauses. Other times he wrote in manic bursts that kept him up through the night—typing, smoking, and slashing at his manuscripts with a felt-tipped pen. He visited the Luxor Turkish Baths on North Avenue when he wanted to relax, and swam at the YMCA on Division Street when he needed exercise. He dropped by Jazz Ltd. and sat near the bandstand when he wanted company, and when his phone rang, he lifted the receiver and waited. He didn't speak until he was certain the person on the other end of the line was not an FBI agent.

Nelson had once been among the most renowned writers in America, but that time had passed. His last novel was six years old and he swore he would never write another because he had been too badly used. "No, no novel," he said. "I'd as soon attempt that as I would to open a pizza joint on Chicago's Westside without getting protection first." He wrote whatever he wanted now, or for whoever was paying—short pieces, for the most part, and that was fine. Even if his work never appeared between hard covers again, he would always be the author of *Never Come Morning*, *The Neon Wilderness*, *The Man with the Golden Arm*, *Chicago: City on the Make*, and *A Walk on the Wild Side*. Millions of people had read his books. He had done enough.

Even though Nelson's fortunes were in decline, interviewers still sought him out. They were young writers, mostly—aspirants bearing dog-eared paperbacks and sheepish looks—and when they arrived, Nelson invited them into his front room and offered them bourbon. He signed their books, raked his fingers through his hair, and waited for their questions.

Is it true Hollywood cheated you out of millions? they asked. Did Hemingway *really* say you were the second-greatest American writer? When were you in jail? What is Simone de Beauvoir like? And what do you think of Saul Bellow's work?

Interviewing Nelson was tough, but rewarding. He chewed on a cigar while he spoke, and he used its stump to punctuate his remarks. His hands danced, his brown eyes twinkled mischievously, and he regularly broke into belly laughs that left him gasping. He frequently responded to direct questions with bawdy jokes or long, loping stories that never concluded, but he always loaded his guests down with the sort of spiky quotes editors love.

Chicago is a "great gray sub-civilization," he said.

"I'm not second best to anybody. Either I've lapped the field or I'm nowhere."

"The American way isn't living for the moment," he pronounced. "It is to be insured for twenty years, and then when you are forty or fifty to retire. But by that time you can't enjoy anything."

"I don't know of one writer who has taken a university job who is able to continue to write seriously," he said about Bellow.

Nelson would indulge any question asked respectfully, but as he settled into the long twilight of his career, he began taking charge of his interviews. Legacy was on his mind, so he brushed past questions about Beauvoir and Hemingway and dragged his interviewers into the past—through his childhood, and his father's, and his grandfather's.

He had spent his life telling other peoples' stories, and now it was time to tell his own.

"My mother had a candy store," Nelson said. My father "was a machinist. He worked at the screw works," and later, he worked for the Packard Motor Car Company. Everyone thinks I'm Polish, Nelson said, but I'm not. "My father's father" was a Swede.

Nelson's paternal grandfather was named Nils Ahlgren, and he was born in Sweden around 1820. His parents were merchants, and the family lived in Stockholm—then a city of seventy-five thousand, built on fourteen islands surrounded by the Baltic Sea. A Gothic cathedral dominated the skyline at the time, and stone buildings with peaked roofs faced each other across narrow alleys that sliced through the city like cracks spider-webbing across old porcelain. The air smelled of salt, and ships bobbed in the harbor: three-masted clippers, and dinghies heavy with the weight of lumber, fish, and people.

Sweden was in decline when Nils was young—an empire on the dark side of its meridian. There was a recession, and peasants were fleeing the countryside and overwhelming the cities. But despite the country's turmoil, Nils enjoyed a privileged childhood. His eyes were blue as a cloudless sky, and he was healthy, and curious. He worked for the family business and had enough leisure time to read, dream, and develop respect for the power of words.

The Ahlgrens belonged to the Church of Sweden, a Lutheran denomination, because it was the state religion. Nils became a member at birth and remained one through his teens and into his twenties, but near the end of his third decade he became a skeptic.

The church taught that the Old Testament and the New were both the word of God, but only the wild, apocalyptic majesty of the Hebrew Bible attracted Nils. The vengeful Lord of Genesis spoke to him when He proclaimed, "I will wipe from the face of the earth the human race

I have created." And Nils could feel the power of God's wrath when he read that fire rained on Sodom and Gomorrah from the heavens, leaving nothing behind but "dense smoke rising from the land." The story of Abraham—a man so devout he was willing to kill his only son when God commanded it—taught Nils about faith and sacrifice.

Nils read Deuteronomy as well, and learned that God chose the Israelites "out of all the peoples on the face of the earth to be his people, his treasured possession." And afterward, he began to question the Church of Sweden's theology. The Old Testament's message seemed clear to Nils—the Jews were God's chosen people, not the Christians—so he relinquished his ties to the church, announced he had become a Jew, and renamed himself to show the depth of his new faith.

At some point near his thirtieth birthday, Nils Ahlgren became Isaac Ben Abraham—or, Isaac, son of Abraham.

Conversion wasn't uncommon in Sweden at the time, but it always went the other way. What Nils did was a sign either of true piety or pure madness. There were about three thousand Jews in the country, and they had few rights. A law called the *judereglement* prohibited them from marrying Christians, converting Christians, or living outside the country's three largest cities. The Swedish Parliament eased those restrictions in 1838—and people rioted in response. The law was soon restored.

In that context, it's no surprise that Isaac boarded a ship bound for America.

Isaac arrived in New York City alone.* He was thirty-three, maybe thirty-four. The manifest of the boat that brought him to America said

* Readers should begin inserting adverbs such as *maybe* and *possibly* and *likely* into everything they read about Isaac. He left many stories behind when he died, but few documents. The shipping manifest of a boat called the *White Falcon* recorded the immigration of a Swede who called himself Abraham Abraham in 1854—this is *probably* Isaac. Rabbi Felsenthal of Chicago's Sinai congregation made a note about

he was a laborer, but he looked more like a prophet—Moses reborn as a Swede. He moved through the world with the swaggering confidence of a zealot, his eyes shone like turquoise spotlights through a thicket of hair and a full beard, and his speech was inflected with brimstone.

Isaac was beyond the reach of his country's bigotry and his family's judgment in America, so he embraced his new identity. He began attending synagogue in New York, and introduced himself as a scholar. There were German Jews in the city then, and Poles, and Prussians—people who had been born into their faith and suffered for their bloodlines in Europe—and Isaac, a convert, chided them for lapses in their orthodoxy. He tried to debate rabbis, and stood on street corners and hollered about the Lord's wrath like a harbinger of the end of days.

Soon, though, Isaac realized the city was no place for a true believer and he went looking for wide-open spaces and greater freedom. He headed west, following a path that had been blazed by an earlier wave of Swedish immigrants. He passed through Pennsylvania, Ohio, and Indiana, and then traveled north until he entered the Minnesota Territory, where people lived in log cabins and the government ruled from forts built at the edge of the Dakota Nation. Europeans were free to settle on any plot of land they cared to there, chase vice where it led, and worship any God they chose.

So, Isaac decided to stay. He became a trader, and for seven years he earned his living buying and selling pelts.

Then the Dakota Sioux started a war. The tribe's territory had been shrinking for years as settlers claimed pieces of it in violation of a treaty, and tribe members were starving because the United States gov-

---

marrying Isaac to Jette Scheuer on March 29, 1863, and a census taker found him on a farm in Indiana in 1880. The Chicago voter registration rolls from 1890 mention a Swedish Isaac Ben Abraham—but aside from that, there's nothing. The version of events presented here represents the most believable story I could piece together from those documents, several contradictory and embellished interviews, and a handful of Nelson's contradictory, and often fictionalized, memoirs.

ernment had failed to pay for land it had agreed to purchase, and had taken control of. So the Sioux began attacking settlements and raiding forts. They defeated the territory's militia in the Battle of Redwood Ferry, and afterward civilians fled along wagon trails en masse—their belongings piled on horse-drawn carts, bonnets or wide-brimmed hats on their heads to protect them from the August sun.

Isaac was among them. He traveled south after the Dakota Uprising, and didn't stop until he reached Chicago—a young city growing up and out along the shore of Lake Michigan. Twenty years earlier, there had only been four thousand settlers in the area, and they had spent their nights hiding inside a fort they built on land they had snatched from the Pottawatomi nation. But when Isaac arrived, there were twenty-five times that many. New residents were arriving every day, and the city was simultaneously expanding to accommodate them and crumbling beneath their weight—brick buildings were rising as high as five stories, but the Rush Street Bridge collapsed when cowboys drove a herd of cattle across it.

Within a year of arriving in Chicago, Isaac met a woman named Jette Scheuer and began to court her. She was a German-born Jew who worked as a servant, and she was only twenty-seven years old. Isaac was forty-three by then, but she agreed to marry him anyway. Rabbi Bernhard Felsenthal of the Sinai Congregation made them husband and wife on March 29, 1863, and after the ketubah was signed and the Torah reading concluded, the newlyweds abandoned the city.

Isaac and Jette moved thirty miles south and east, to Indiana and the relative stillness of Lake County—close enough to Chicago to see the city's lights shimmer on the horizon at night, but distant enough to ensure they would have clean air and potable water. They found a bit of unclaimed land near the tip of the Little Calumet River in an area that would later be called Black Oak, and squatted it. Isaac opened a country store, and he and Jette began farming. They decided to start a

family, and soon Jette gave birth to a child. She had another the following year, and another the year after that.

When Isaac settled into fatherhood and married life, his name began
to seem ironic. The fault was all his. He had cursed himself by selecting
one that promised much more than he could deliver. The biblical Abraham had been a man willing to sacrifice everything for his faith. His
son, the biblical Isaac, had been a settled family man who eschewed
concubines and never left Canaan. But Isaac Ben Abraham—the man
born Nils Ahlgren—had no taste for labor or suffering, and he was no
patriarch.

Isaac had a convert's desire to seem righteous and act righteously,
but he also had the instincts of a grifter. He quoted from the Old Testament fluidly and often, but experimented with perpetual motion when
he should have been working, and minted his own coins and used them
in place of legal tender. It's said he once tried to place his country store
on wheels so he could roll it across the county line when tax collectors
approached. And he held destiny in higher regard than family.

Isaac was a Zionist, and a socialist, and he believed he had a religious obligation to move to Jerusalem and build an egalitarian society there. When he pictured the future, he saw himself studying the
Torah in the Holy Land, not farming a scrap of dirt in Indiana. In
1866, the power of that vision overwhelmed him, and he abandoned
his family and traveled west alone—through the territories, and then
Nevada, and finally into California. He stopped when he reached San
Francisco, where he began preaching on street corners, the way he
had when he arrived in America twelve years earlier.

Then Jette caught up to him. She had placed her two eldest children
in someone's care and chased Isaac across the country carrying her
youngest son, Moses.* She reconciled with Isaac when she found him,

---

* It's unclear what happened to these children.

and they made a new home by the San Francisco Bay and began saving money so they could sail for the Holy Land. They had a son the following year and named him Gershom, after the son of the biblical Moses. Next, they had a daughter and named her Hanna, after the mother of Samuel—last of the Hebrew judges.

The Abraham family crossed the Pacific and the Red Sea in 1868, and then proceeded toward Jerusalem by land. They must have seen the city for the first time when they crested the Mount of Olives. The glittering Al-Aqsa Mosque would have been visible, as would the Temple Mount and the white crenulated wall encasing the Old City. If it was the right time of day, they would have seen men and women filing through the Mughrabi Gate while wind riffled their long robes, and heard muezzin calling from the minarets of the city's mosques—*Hayya 'alas-salāh / Hayya 'alal-falāh.*

Isaac and Jette found an apartment in the Old City, and then Isaac began recruiting adherents. He introduced himself as a rabbi, and before long he attracted a following and the family's apartment became a gathering place for pious men eager to learn about the promise of Socialist Zionism. He spoke, and people listened. It was the life he had been dreaming of since he left Indiana to pursue his destiny.

Jette was not so lucky. While Isaac parsed God's will, she cooked, cleaned, and cared for their children. She watched her husband hold court, noticed that every step he took toward the Lord was a step away from his family, and decided to leave him.

About a year after the family settled in Jerusalem, Jette told Isaac she was taking their children back to Indiana. Then she told Moses, Gershom, and Hanna to pack, and to say goodbye to their father. Isaac didn't interfere because he did not believe they would leave. He watched as they filed out of the apartment and walked away. Then he stepped outside so he could continue watching. He expected them to turn back, but they never did.

Finally, just before the family passed out of sight, Isaac yelled, "Hey! I'm coming with you!"

The Abrahams returned to America together, made their way back to Black Oak, and moved into their old house. Isaac was in his fifties by then, and diminished—by age, but also by the thousands of miles he had traveled and by his wife's defiance. He and Jette had two more children together, but each received a German name like hers instead of a biblical one like their father's. Their sixth child was Rosa; their seventh was Adolph.

Isaac walked out on his family for the second time in 1884. He was bent and gray by then, and the faith that had propelled him across both the world's great oceans and the width of a continent, in an age when most people never left the village they were born in, had abandoned him. He still knew every word in the Bible, but they no longer meant much to him. He became an itinerant preacher after he left the farm, and kept himself fed by serving his audiences any flavor of gospel they requested. Hebrew, Baptist, Lutheran—it had all become the same to him.

Isaac's fourth child, Gershom Abraham, was seventeen years old when his father abandoned him, and twenty-six in 1893, when he moved away from the Black Oak farm. Even at that age, he left only because he had no choice. Banks were failing by the hundreds that year, and businesses by the thousands. Small farms were going bankrupt because they couldn't borrow money for seed, and unemployment had quadrupled. The financial crisis was called "The Panic," and that's what people did—they walked away from their homes and families and went looking for work.*

---

* Nelson sometimes claimed his father went to Chicago in 1886 to work as a scab during the McCormick Harvesting Machine Company strike. I doubt this. More often, Nelson said his father left the farm to work at the World's Fair, and that lines up with other statements from family and friends.

In the Midwest, most found their way to Chicago, where six hundred acres of parkland were being developed for the World's Columbian Exposition—an international fair so ambitious it promised to be the largest event in the region's history. Forty-six nations were expected to participate, millions of people were expected to attend, and two hundred buildings had to be created to accommodate them.

Gershom and his older brother Moses applied for work at the exposition, and they were hired. They became laborers and, along with several thousand other men, they worked tirelessly for months to achieve a seemingly impossible goal: building a city within a city in less than a year.

They erected buildings, covered them with white stucco, and strung electric lights along their sides and eaves. They laid out the Midway Plaisance and a Court of Honor with a pool at its center that was presided over by a bronze statue holding a plaque that read LIBERTy. They built a Ferris wheel that could carry eleven hundred people at once, and a moving sidewalk that ran down a pier and ended at a casino. Then, just before their task was complete, Buffalo Bill Cody set up his Wild West show across from the exposition's gates, and twelve Norwegian men docked a facsimile Viking ship they had sailed across the Atlantic. Spaniards arrived in replicas of the *Niña*, the *Pinta*, and the *Santa María*, and workers from Japan built a pavilion on a wooded island.

After all the streets had been paved and all the buildings painted, President Grover Cleveland traveled west from Washington, DC, to inaugurate the fairgrounds everyone had begun calling the "White City." He was an egg-shaped man with a droopy mustache, and when he mounted the podium he had been instructed to mount at the appointed moment, he found himself facing a crowd of nearly half a million people. There was a golden button in front of him, and when he depressed it, hundreds of thousands of bulbs flickered to life and set the fair ablaze like a signal fire on the plains. Three giant spotlights began darting across the sky. The casino opened its doors, and the Ferris Wheel spun.

Gershom and Moses continued working at the exposition after it opened, and for months their days were a blend of futurism and retrograde spectacle—a moving sidewalk, an electric kitchen, and Calamity Jane spinning yarns. But then the fairgrounds closed and the aseptic promise of its whitewashed walls began to fade. Buildings were torn down, and the remaining structures collected soot from Chicago's polluted air and turned gray. People without homes began camping inside them and cooking over open fires they fed through the night to keep warm.

Eventually, White City burned, and when it was gone, Gershom and Moses were unmoored. Their agrarian childhoods had taught them nothing about surviving in an industrial metropolis, but somehow they managed. Moses became a brass finisher, and Gershom became a machinist. He hired on at Otis Elevator, and then went to work for the Chicago Screw Company, where his shifts were long and tiring and he never received vacation. He began to suspect that leaving the farm had been a mistake, and he never stopped.

After settling in Chicago, Gershom made a study of his father's character. He thought about Isaac's rambling, his shirking, and his zealotry. He remembered the distance Isaac's faith imposed between himself and the world, and reflected on the way Isaac left people behind when they became inconvenient. And when it was time for Gershom to decide what sort of man he wanted to become, he used his father's life as his guide—whatever Isaac Ben Abraham was, Gershom Abraham refused to be.

Because Isaac was a believer, Gershom was not. He preferred the predictability of rubber and steel to the changeable nature of gods and ideas, and he believed only in the value of his labor. The American

Dream was his faith—work hard, he told himself, and you will be rewarded. He never claimed atheism, but he never entered a house of worship either—temple, church, or mosque. It's said he once referred to God as a son of a bitch, and blamed him for starting "all our wars."

And because Isaac was an aesthete, Gershom was incurious but physically powerful. He never touched books, his lips moved when he read the newspaper, and he fought as a semiprofessional boxer. When he was in the ring, he faced his opponents dead-on, cantilevered his head back beyond their reach, and extended his hands so he could parry their punches. It was the stance used by Gentleman Jim Corbett, and it made Gershom look like a man whose fists were running toward a fight his body was trying to flee.

Gershom rejected Isaac's legacy most poignantly by dedicating himself to family. He and Moses shared an apartment just north of the West Chicago railroad shops for years, and when the Black Oak farm failed, they moved their mother and a sister in with them as well. Gershom even agreed to help Isaac when he reappeared suddenly.

Isaac had not been in touch with his wife or his children for more than a decade when he tracked them down in Chicago, but they allowed him to move in with them anyway. It was winter, and they agreed to shelter him until it was warm enough for him to go back on the road. He wouldn't have survived the season if they turned him away. He was in rough shape by then, and his faith had abandoned him completely. "There is no truth," he supposedly said. "There is no religion, no truth. It is all nothing."

Isaac left in the spring, just as he had promised. "I don't have any right to live on you," he said, "because I deserted you."

Gershom showed his father out, walked him to Madison Street, and gave him fifty cents. He waited until a streetcar arrived, and then he watched Isaac climb on board and shuffle down the aisle—bent, bearded, and frail. It was the last time they saw each other.

Isaac died a few years later, and afterward Gershom erased the last trace of his father's legacy by anglicizing his name and removing the Old Testament reference.* At some point near his thirty-fifth birthday, Gershom Abraham became Gerson Abraham.

Gerson met a woman named Golda Kalisher in the late 1890s, and began courting her. He brought her to Lincoln Park to see the electrified fountain, and wooed her at a beer hall called Bismarck Gardens, where you could sit beneath trees and rest your stein on a white tablecloth. Soon, they were engaged.

Golda went by "Goldie," and she was a blunt-faced woman with a sharp tongue. Discipline was her watchword. She and Gerson shared that, but not much more—they were both secular Jews who had been raised in large families. Their mothers had nearly identical names, and they were getting too old to be single. The list ends there.

If Gerson was attracted to anything about Goldie, it was her family, and the idea they represented. Her parents—Louis and Gette—were American archetypes. They had emigrated from Prussia with their sights set on assimilation, and achieved it. Louis was a cigar maker and a stern, attentive family man. He was proud that his children were citizens, and proud too that he had been able to move them out of the Jewish ghetto along Milwaukee Avenue within his lifetime. He allowed them to speak German at home, but insisted they speak English in public. He encouraged them to marry gentiles, and most of them took his advice.

Goldie was the exception. She married Gerson on July 2, 1899, and then moved into the flat on North Crawford Avenue with him, Hanna, Moses, and Jette. Nine months later, she gave birth to a daughter and named her Irene.

The family scattered afterward. The Packard Motor Car Company offered Gerson a job in Detroit, and he accepted. Rosa moved to Ham-

* This chronology of Isaac's life contradicts other published chronologies. You'll find an explanation for the discrepancy when you reach chapter 27.

mond, Indiana—near the old Black Oak farm—and brought Jette with her. She worked as a seamstress, and her wages supported them both. Moses stayed in Chicago.

Gerson settled into the long middle of life when he reached Detroit. His talents developed, and over time he became a great craftsman—a master of the caliper and the lathe—but he remained the quiet, humble man he had always been. He rarely spoke about himself and never complained, and eventually he was rewarded for his skill and his stoicism. Packard gave him a promotion and a raise, and he and Goldie took advantage of their rising fortunes. They had another daughter, and named her Bernice. They bought a house at 867 Mack Avenue, and they opened a candy store that Goldie operated. Then they had a third child.

Goldie brought a son into the world seven years after she gave birth to her second daughter, and when it was time to name him, she and Gerson did so in honor of his deceased grandfather Nils Ahlgren—the man who had transformed himself into Isaac Ben Abraham, the rambler, zealot, and teller of wild tales who died a pauper. It was a prophetic choice.

That child was born on March 28, 1909, and his birth certificate reads: Nelson Algren Abraham—third legitimate child of Gerson Abraham, Jewish, age 41, born in California, occupation: machinist. And Golda Abraham, Jewish, age 31, born in Chicago.

Between St. Columbanus and the Wrought-Iron Gate of Oak Woods Cemetery

(1912–August 1920)

Nelson Algren Abraham mugging for the camera, July 1920.

erson Abraham lost faith in the automobile industry in 1912 and resolved to get his family out of Detroit. Horses were faster and more reliable than cars at the time, dray wagons could haul heavier loads than trucks, and trains moved people with unrivaled efficiency. There is "no future" in cars, Gerson believed. They "are not going to go." Soon, he reasoned, everyone would come to their senses and stop driving, and when they did, Motor City would collapse. He didn't want to be around when that happened, so he left the Packard Motor Car Company and moved his family back to Chicago. It seemed like a provident move.

The Abrahams decided to settle on the South Side when they returned, and they began searching for somewhere to live. Before long, they found an inexpensive two-family home in a quiet residential neighborhood, and took out a mortgage and purchased it. The house they left behind in Detroit had faced a busy street and a high school, the view through its windows was marred by smokestacks, and soot clung to its walls like black mold. But their new home at 7139 South Park Avenue was near Chicago's quiet southern border, and downtown was a jagged line on the horizon.

The Abrahams' new neighborhood was called Park Manor, and it was working-class, Catholic, and had the feel of a small town. One- and two-family homes lined its side streets, and the main drag boasted a movie theater with a white tile facade and a soda shop with a player piano. A teenager delivered milk from a local dairy to people's doorsteps every morning, and the iceman guided his horse-drawn cart through the area in the afternoons. On occasion, an organ grinder meandered through the streets in search of an audience with money to spend. When he found one, he turned the crank of his music box and his capuchin monkey—in bespoke vest and cap—danced for the spectators surrounding him, and then extended a paw and collected their pennies.

Sixty years earlier, Park Manor had been swamp, prairie, and freight tracks. Then a developer named Cornell recognized its potential and began buying up large swaths of land. He divided the tracts he purchased into small plots, and then he sold them to immigrants from Europe who built themselves homes and businesses.

Almost every inch of the area had been leveled and developed since, but somehow, amid all that industry and ambition, a swatch of grassland had been overlooked, allowed to grow wild, and then ceded to the neighborhood's children. It was their exclusive domain by the time the Abrahams arrived, and on warm afternoons they stalked each other across its expanse, or flew kites, while tall grasses swayed drunkenly around them. After sunset, they lit bonfires to guard against the night and gathered around the flames they conjured. Then they rested potatoes on the ruby and alabaster coals that formed on the ground, and waited for them to blacken and char while soot swirled into the air, cooled, and fell like gray snow.

A church called St. Columbanus dominated the western edge of the field, and loomed above the children while they cavorted. It was an intimidating building that was at once a house of worship, a school, and the cultural center of the neighborhood. A large, unadorned cross pierced the sky at the peak of its roof, and there was a rabbit hutch at the base of its front steps that the Right Reverend Monsignor Dennis P. O'Brien tended to. The doors of the church school were heavy and double-wide, and when they opened on weekday mornings, nuns emerged wearing dark habits. They lingered in the entryway's shadow while their charges filed past, and then they stepped back inside and sealed the building tightly.

The Abraham family home faced the field and the church beyond it, and contrasted each sharply. It was as tame as the first was wild, and as unobtrusive as the second was regal—nothing but red bricks, a flat roof, a narrow backyard, a patch of grass out front the size of a postage stamp, and a set of steps that ended at the sidewalk. The walls inside were bare, and the furniture was mismatched. There was a couch in the living room, and a piano, and when the family gathered there and looked through their front windows, they saw a big Midwestern sky, Ford Model Ts with wooden wheels, gas-burning street lamps, and, if they timed it just right, the cross on the church's roof ringed by crimson light as the sun, descending toward the horizon, slipped behind it and set it ablaze.

Gerson transitioned into his new life in Park Manor smoothly, and soon he had distinguished himself with his capacity for industry and labor. He built a garage in his backyard, filled it with tools, and began fixing his neighbors' cars, furniture, and appliances for nominal fees. He planted a vegetable garden across the street from his house at the edge of the field the neighborhood's children had claimed, and began tending it on Sunday mornings, when most other husbands were in church. He rented out the second floor of the family home to a widow with a young daughter, and then he hired on as a mechanic for the Yellow Cab Company.

Gerson worked "bell to bell" from that point forward—dawn to dusk, six days out of every week. He left the house carrying a metal lunch pail each morning, and walked a few blocks to the last stop on the streetcar line that ran along Cottage Grove Avenue. He waited there for his train, and when it arrived, he rode ten miles north to the Loop. He retraced his steps at the end of his shift, carrying an empty lunch pail, each evening, and then opened the front door of his house and greeted his wife and children.

The family assembled for dinner when Gerson returned home, and took their places around the dining room table. They spent little time together most days, so their nightly meal should have been a joyful occasion, but it rarely was. As a rule, the atmosphere in the house was tense and dolorous—mostly as a result of Goldie's presence.

Unlike her husband, Goldie felt diminished by the family's relocation. Her mind took a dark turn when she left Detroit, and afterward she was a disconsolate and heedless character. She dropped things, walked into walls, and burned meals. She mixed up her *M*s and *N*s when she spoke so that *moon* sounded like *noon*, and *soon* was *soom*—and she compensated for her lack of grace and eloquence with volume, and violence.

Dissatisfaction was Goldie's favorite topic of conversation, and she never lacked material. The way she explained it each evening, everything about life in Chicago was disappointing—her house, her Irish neighbors, her children, and, most especially, her husband.

Gerson was a tall, taciturn man. His hands were thick with calluses that had been packed with grease, and he had broad, powerful shoulders.

Men deferred to him in the street or on the job because of his size, but he was timid and hapless at home—tender, adoring, and quiet in a manner that projected weakness rather than strength. He never understood jokes the first time he heard them—or the second, or the third. Movies were just light and sound for him, and he relied on his children to explain their plots. Sometimes their father's simplicity embarrassed them, but mostly they found it endearing.

Goldie did not. She blamed Gerson's mild nature for her discontent, and shortly after moving to Park Manor, she launched a campaign designed to transform him into the sort of man who gave orders instead of following them. Her methods were not benign. She called him a failure in front of their children; she called him stupid; she yelled.

Gerson adopted a defensive stance when Goldie confronted him. He fanned a newspaper out in front of his face when she became upset in the evenings, or retreated to his garage, and sometimes he left the house in the morning even earlier than necessary in order to avoid her. He rarely responded directly to her provocations, and it was always a mistake when he did.

You need to let me rest if you want me to succeed, he'd say. And Goldie would reply with curses, smashed dishes, and slammed doors.

Irene and Bernice were also targets for Goldie, but neither suffered the way their father did. Irene turned twelve the year the family returned to Chicago, and Bernice turned ten—they were close in age, but very different temperamentally. Irene was rigid and uncompromising. She looked and argued like her mother, but she had more talent and bigger dreams. She was an accomplished piano player, and she planned to leave her family behind and travel east when she was old enough. Bernice was athletic and buoyant—a movie buff, a devoted reader, and an aspiring actress who survived her mother by avoiding the house. She was a member of the theater club, and she swam. When World War I casualties began arriving in Chicago hospitals, she visited them as a Red Cross volunteer.

Nelson, however, was a nuisance of a higher order in his mother's eyes. Goldie could tolerate her daughters because each had qualities she admired. When Irene played the piano in the living room, she was a perfect manifestation of her mother's middle-class aspirations. Bernice brightened the house with her movie-star smile and sang while she washed the dishes. But there was nothing about Nelson that Goldie enjoyed. His list of sins was simply too long to be ignored, or forgiven. He was born when she was thirty-one years old and ready to be finished with motherhood, and he had too much energy. Worse yet, he looked like his father—tall and thin, angular features, fair hair.

The most generous thing that can be said about Goldie's relationship to Nelson is this: She tolerated him. She expected him to abide by her rules and occupy himself, and when he did those things, she left him alone. When he did not, she beat him. At an early age, he learned that giving his mother a wide berth was the safest course of action.

Nelson began attending the Park Manor School at Seventy-first Street and Rhodes Avenue in the fall of 1915, and afterward he spent very little time at home.

When the last bell of the school day rang each afternoon, Nelson and his classmates met outside and began making their rounds through the neighborhood. They visited their homes to steal potatoes and root beer from their parents' basements, or stalked the iceman's cart so they could attack his cargo when he stopped to make deliveries. They played cops and robbers in the field by St. Columbanus until World War I broke out—and afterward they played Allies and Huns. They sorted themselves into teams when the game began, and then dispersed across their battlefield and fought using bombs made from garbage wrapped in the pages of tabloid newspapers, and guns fashioned from sunflower stalks. They were the children of Irish, German, English, and Scottish immigrants, and they were keen to display their patriotism, so the brave Allies charged forward confidently each afternoon while the Huns skulked and schemed. They clashed violently when they met, and the Huns, who always lost, died with theatrical flourish—with a leap to imitate the blast of a grenade, or writhing in agony after catching a bullet.

On weekend days, Nelson explored Park Manor alone. He left home early and walked toward Grand Crossing, the freight junction that ran along the neighborhood's eastern border. When he reached the berm its tracks rested on, he began moving north in a snaking line—up the embankment, down to the street, up again. Older boys haunted the tracks as well. They collected coal and grain that had fallen to the ground, and sold their spoils to a hermit who lived in a shack built from discarded wood. But Nelson spent his time hunting empty cigarette packs and beer corks. He removed the foil linings from the packs when he found them, pressed them between his palms, and molded them into balls. The beer corks were as good as cash at school. The most prized were dyed bright colors and emblazoned with intricate designs, and they could be traded for dozens of less desirable Schlitz corks, or candy.

Nelson turned west when he reached Sixty-third Street, and walked toward White City—one of the largest amusement parks in the country, and Park Manor's northern border. It was a mass of white buildings encircled by a white fence, and it was visible from any direction for blocks and blocks. Roller coaster tracks peeked above the roofline of the surrounding buildings, a large American flag fluttered in the wind, and a three-hundred-foot monolith called White Tower pricked the sky and blazed like a sun when the half million lights encircling it flickered to life at night. At its base, a sprawling saturnalia unfurled— there was a restaurant that sat twenty-five hundred, a ballroom where a thousand people could dance at once, a miniature railroad, and a carousel. At an exhibit called Midget City, people could pay to jeer at dwarves who had been hired to act out the functions of family and government. And any white person with change to spare could visit African Dip, and pay to dunk a black man into a tank of water.

When Nelson reached the fence surrounding White City, he headed for the trash heap behind the park's casino. Bags of refuse were often piled so high in the bins there that they towered above his head, and he spent hours digging through them—searching for a "lucky cork or two" the way "country boys might seek four leaf clovers."

Nelson knew Goldie would send him back outside if he returned before she was ready to see him, so he rarely began walking home before dusk. Sometimes he miscalculated, though, and arrived early.

You need air, Goldie said on those occasions. Go back outside. It was not a suggestion.

Nelson went to his backyard when that happened. There was a wooden piano crate on the porch, and if he had nowhere else to go, he hid inside it until he thought it was safe to reenter the house. Occasionally, on winter days, he spent hours huddled there—watching snow fall, or feeling his body grow stiff while vapor from his breath billowed around him, and then condensed and froze.

Nelson and Gerson discovered each other in 1918, when Nelson was nine years old. Their relationship had been loving before then, but distant. Gerson had no idea what a father should do with a son until Nelson became interested in the adult world, but afterward they became close.

Gerson spent Sunday mornings tending his garden that spring and summer, and when he finished, he and Nelson headed toward the Warshawsky Company—a junkyard on South State Street. They visited with a purpose in mind each time, and then forgot it. They went looking for a furnace, or gears for a cuckoo clock Gerson was trying to fix, but after perusing Warshawsky's maze of tires, metal dashboards, pipes, and piles of bolts, they would leave with something else entirely.

One afternoon, Nelson spotted the top of a wagon in a pile of trash. It had no wheels and no handle, but he had to have it anyway, so Gerson bought it. They lugged it back to Park Manor, and when they reached their home they dug through the junk in their basement until they found Nelson's baby carriage. They removed its wheels and bolted them onto the wagon. Nelson found a post and a handlebar next, and attached them as well. Then he found an empty can of tomatoes, removed its label, perforated its sides, placed a candle inside, and hung it from the handlebar he had just installed. Gerson gave him a bell.

For the remainder of the summer, Nelson rode his pushcart to the streetcar stop on Seventy-first Street each day and met Gerson at the end of his commute. He was a whippet-thin child with tousled hair that stopped just above his jug ears, and he peered out at the world through big, watchful eyes as he rolled through the streets—the ding, ding of his bell announcing him, and the lantern's crenulated light showing him the way.

Gerson handed his empty lunch pail to Nelson when he stepped off the trolley, and then they headed home—eight blocks west, one block south. Gerson took long, weary strides. Nelson coasted beside him, eager and attentive.

Gerson rarely talked about himself, but when he and Nelson were alone, he sometimes did. He spoke in a bemused, confessional tone, and the stories he selected suggest he was so guileless, he had never learned that he should, at the least, pretend to understand the world.

My very first memory, Gerson told Nelson, is of camels. I saw them in Jerusalem, and I saw men wearing turbans there as well. I remember the Great Chicago Fire too. It was October 1871, and I had just returned to the Black Oak farm with my family. I was very young, but I can still recall the way the horizon turned red after the sunset. The fire burned for days, and when it was extinguished, Chicago was gone.

I helped build the World's Columbian Exposition, Gerson said, and when it opened I walked the Midway until I reached the Street in Cairo so I could watch Little Egypt perform. She went on stage wearing a skirt and leggings, but not much of a top. She had a thin scarf, and she wrapped it around her body, and then unwrapped it. She rocked her hips and a band stomped. It was called a belly dance.

I found work as a machinist when the Exposition ended, Gerson said, and afterward I rarely saw the city at night. There were a few exceptions though. Once, I visited the Columbia Ballroom on North Clark Street and saw McGuire's Ice Cream Kings. They wore white suits on stage, and women danced the speedy three-step while they played. Another time, I visited a saloon owned by Heinie Kabibbler. I ordered a drink, the bartender handed me a mug, and I raised it to my lips. A thin vertical slit had been cut into the glass, but I didn't notice, so beer poured down the front of my shirt when I took a sip.

B aseball commanded Nelson's attention the following year. The game was life in Park Manor then, and the White Sox were the gods who determined its course. The team was winding its way toward the World Series, and everyone said they couldn't be stopped. After all, they were tougher than ordinary men, and quicker, smarter, and cagier.

Every boy in the neighborhood identified himself with one of the team's players. Some favored the college boys on the White Sox roster—Eddie Collins, and Red Faber. Others looked up to veterans like Eddie Cicotte, and Shoeless Joe Jackson—men who returned to the ballpark year after year, the way working stiffs reported to factory jobs. But Nelson idolized a wild character named Charles August "Swede" Risberg.

The Swede was a thin Californian with a long face and a permanent scowl. He played shortstop and he could throw, but he was better known for the persona he cultivated off the field. He claimed that he had been kicked out of third grade, and he drank, fought, and womanized. He told reporters he didn't have a care in the world, and they believed him—at least enough to print his claims. "He would gleefully toss up his chances for fame and lucre and take the first train back to the Pacific Coast," one wrote, "where he knows everybody and is known by everybody."

Nelson carried a Swede Risberg bat around Park Manor that summer, and when he wanted to broadcast his casual attitude toward life, he leaned on it heavily. He began telling people to call him Swede, and he taught himself to walk pigeon-toed, because that was the way Risberg walked.

Nelson's best friend at the time was Jake Somerhaus—a baseball prodigy who carried a clay pipe that he packed with tobacco scrounged from discarded cigarettes. He and Nelson prowled the freight tracks together on the weekends and scavenged in the trash heap behind White City Casino. They pitched baseball cards for a while as well, and then they discovered brewery trucks.

The trucks passed through Park Manor regularly, loaded with barrels of trub—a thick, treacly, alcoholic mixture of dead yeast and fermented malt. They were headed toward the stockyards on the West Side, where their cargo would become slop for pigs, and as they bounced along the neighborhood's roads, the trub sloshed around, spilled, and poured into the street.

Every time the boys spotted a truck, they began jogging. When they closed in on their target, they extended their arms and used empty cans to catch some of the trub before it reached the pavement. Then they returned to the sidewalk and drank—swallowing, and retching, until their throats were numb and their eyelids heavy.

They enjoyed their buzz, and then they left Park Manor and visited the printing room of the *Saturday Blade*. One of Gerson's brothers worked on the presses, and every week he gave Nelson a stack of papers to sell.

The *Blade* was a five-cent broadsheet that called itself "America's Greatest Weekly" and sold hundreds of thousands of copies with every print run. A pair of American flags graced its cover, and a three-color comic dominated the center of the front page. The paper had a respectable veneer and a populist sensibility, but its DNA was all tabloid and its headlines screamed. MAN SELLS WIFE, THEN SHOOTS BUYER, they announced. SMALL WOMAN 'BEANS' BIG HUBBY WITH HARD SAUSAGE AND RAW LIVER, proclaimed another. LOWLY PEANUT HAS HOUR OF TRIUMPH.

William D. Boyce owned the *Blade*. He was a bootstraps man, and his life story doubled as his faith. He worked as a coal miner when he was young, but eventually he saved some money, invested it, and became a multimillionaire. He founded the Boy Scouts of America and believed that the paperboys who distributed his tabloid were a pure expression of the country's entrepreneurial spirit. They had names like Raymond Gamble and Lawrence Eagle and Carl Ray, and their pictures appeared in every issue of the paper—hair neatly combed, chaste smiles on their faces. They lived in places like Black Lick, Pennsylvania, and London, Ohio, and they were the image of Middle American rectitude.

But Nelson and Somerhaus were not. Selling papers was a mercenary enterprise for them, not a moral crusade. They worked the corner of Seventy-first Street and Cottage Grove Avenue, where two train lines crossed—one running north and south, to the Loop and back, and the other heading west toward Halsted Street. They announced the *Blade*'s blood-red headlines while flitting from train to train, sipped from their cans of trub, and swelled with pride when they succeeded in cheating their customers.

Nelson timed his sales to the streetcars' movements when he could. If a customer paid him with a dime, he accepted their money and began digging in his pockets for coins. It was an act. When the car began rolling, Nelson found what he was looking for. He raised a hand to display his customer's change, and began stumbling. He lunged melodramatically, and made himself cough. He stopped to catch his breath, and began running again after the trolley had pulled so far ahead that he had no chance of catching it. Then he watched his mark recede into the distance and mimed disappointment.

He pled poverty when someone paid with a quarter. I don't have enough change, he'd say, and ask his customer to wait while he got some. Then he'd run across the street toward the saloon on the corner opposite the trolley stop, enter through the front door, and disappear through the women's entrance on the side of the building. He would hide there until his customer tired of waiting and walked away.

After the boys sold through their papers, they sat on the corner. The Oak Woods cemetery fence was at their back—thick wrought-iron bars wrapped around 180 acres of rolling green. The sidewalk beneath them radiated heat from the day's sun, and the neighborhood saloon, the focus of their attention, was directly across the street.

Somerhaus's uncle Johnson was the neighborhood brawler—the "white hope" of the corner of Seventy-first Street and Cottage Grove Avenue. He drank his days away in the bar and fought on the sidewalk out front on Saturday nights. The flickering blue-green flames of the gas lamps were his floodlights, and his ring was a circle of bodies.

Johnson usually picked his own fights, but when he neglected to, someone inside the bar arranged one. Words would be exchanged; threats made. The pretense didn't matter, only the promise of blood.

The boys had to watch Johnson's fights from across the street because the barkeep chased them off when they got too close, but even from a distance they could see the action—men pouring out of the bar, a ring of bodies forming on the sidewalk; Johnson swaying drunkenly and crooning like a man whose mouth was full of marbles.

Oh sweet Dardanella, he bellowed, *I love your harem eyes / I'm a lucky fellow*—a thick rope of spittle dangling from his lips, the crowd laughing.

No one ever taught Johnson to fight, and he never learned. When an opponent approached, he raised his hands to guard his face, but that was all. He didn't parry, and he didn't dance. Instead, he lurched like a toy ship in a toddler's bath and swung his fists wildly. Size was his only advantage. He was tall and thick, and he used his weight to tire his opponents—he leaned on them, shoved them, and absorbed flurries of punches with the resignation of a penitent paying down a mortal sin. Most weeks, that strategy served him well, but not always.

Once, the boys saw Johnson face a real fighter—a small, trim, muscular man who wore a cap that cast a shadow across his face and kept a lit cigarette in his mouth to show how little he feared his opponent. Its cherry glowed in the night like a taunt while they fought.

He approached Johnson casually and feigned a low punch. When Johnson dropped his hands to block it, the thin man smashed a fist into his teeth. Blood hit the sidewalk. The crowd cheered.

Then the thin man went to work. His feet scraped across the pavement, and he landed punches at will—to Johnson's head, to his body, and to the head again—*thunk, thunk, thunk.*

Johnson tried to run, but his friends hooked their arms and tightened their grips so he couldn't get free.

"You've got him now, Johnson!" they yelled.

"He's on his last legs, Johnson," someone lied. "Finish him."

Johnson regarded the thin man—a shadow flitting lightly, a will-o'-the-wisp dancing in the night. He took a breath and raised his arm and pointed an accusatory finger. Then he advanced—six feet of bloody rage moving with the grace of an ox.

The thin man slammed a fist into Johnson's chest when he got within reach. It landed where the ribs are most flexible and a good hit can force them against the heart and disrupt its rhythm. *Commotio cordis*, it's called. The punch staggered Johnson, and the fight ended. The crowd returned to the bar. Someone wiped blood off Johnson's face with a towel, and everyone resumed drinking.

"It's just a case of a good little man lickin' a good big man," Somerhaus said, unconcerned. He often rooted for Johnson's opponents. Nelson did not. He watched the fights intently without understanding why. They didn't make him laugh, and he never cheered for either side. He walked away from each one feeling a "sort of city-wide sorrow," he wrote later, and worried that "something had suddenly gone horrible wrong between St. Columbanus and the Oakwoods [sic] Cemetery gate." But he kept returning, week after week.

There were two poles in Nelson's life by 1920, and they were pulling him in opposite directions: Gerson was one; Bernice, the younger of Nelson's two sisters, was the other. He encouraged Nelson to make peace with the fact that he would spend his life laboring. She counseled Nelson to explore the world outside of Park Manor, and endeavor to live a more rewarding life than their father's.

Bernice was athletic, and precocious—an excellent student, and, even in her adolescence, an iconoclast. At approximately the same time as the pastor of the Park Manor Congregationalist Church was using his pulpit to decry "feminine modernists, who wink at the practice of drinking and smoking in women, or deny the alarming spread of these filthy habits," she was delivering the valedictory speech at her grammar school graduation.

By the time Bernice entered high school, she had become charming, erudite, and confident. She continued to excel academically, but embraced her nonconformist instincts as well. Over the next three years, she received top scores in physics, wrote poetry, and proclaimed herself an atheist. She had aspired to become an actress when she was a child, but theater had since lost its appeal. Instead, she decided to become the first person in the Abraham family to earn a degree. In 1918, she took the entrance exam for Chicago Normal College, passed with high marks, and enrolled. It was her ambition to become a teacher.

Gerson and Bernice both had influence over Nelson for a while, but his standing diminished over time and hers grew in proportion. Nelson realized how naïve his father was when they grew close, and soon afterward he began looking to Bernice for direction. Luckily, she was an ideal role model—outspoken, full of ideas, and excited about living. She told Nelson there was more to life than baseball, fixing cars, and watching grown men beat each other in front of the corner saloon. She said he could become something more than a mechanic's son if he wanted.

Bernice told Nelson to read Robert Louis Stevenson's *A Child's Garden of Verses*, so he did. He got the book from the library and read its sixty-five rhyming poems—then he read them again, and again, until he knew them by heart. He studied them so closely that he could quote them from memory for decades afterward.

Bernice also encouraged Nelson to write, and he tried to do so just after he absorbed Stevenson's poems. His first composition was a broadsheet newspaper patterned after the *Saturday Blade*. He called it the *Chicago Evening News*, and he created only a single copy of a single issue by writing on butcher paper with a well-sharpened pencil.

The dateline at the top of the front page of the *News* says March 6, 1920—three weeks before Nelson's eleventh birthday—but there is no way it was written in a day. The paper has eight vertical columns of text that include political satire, fictional sports news, gossip, and employment listings. It reads like the end result of a long process of drafting, erasure, and revision—the work of an ambitious child with a focused mind and a creative impulse linked inextricably to his talent for observation.

The center of the front page of the *News* is dominated by a comic entitled "The Lonesome Hermit." It shows a man standing at the side of a cliff, looking down at a ladder below his reach. Above his head are the words "Bolshevism Cave." The ladder is marked "Intercourse with World," and the man is thinking, "I wish I could get that ladder." The columns surrounding the comic scissor freely between fact and fiction, but they all take their inspiration from current events. One is dedicated to a common 1920 fantasy: JACK JOHNSON TO FIGHT DEMPSEY. MARY PICKFORD GETS DIVORCE, another reads, and at the bottom of the page, qualified dishwashers are encouraged to apply for work at 2728 N. Clark Street.

Nelson folded the *Chicago Evening News* when it was complete, and put it away. Then he kept it safe for more than forty years.

The Abrahams left Park Manor a few months after Nelson created the *News*. They moved to a Jewish neighborhood on the North Side called Albany Park, and bought another small house with a porch and a tiny yard. Irene went to work as a secretary then, and Bernice started college. Nelson entered Hibbard Middle School. Goldie fulminated, and Gerson opened a tire and battery shop on Kedzie Avenue. He finally joined the owning class, but he did not become a boss—he worked six days a week, sometimes seven, and he had no employees.

Nelson spent eight years in Park Manor, and when he felt nostalgic as an adult, his mind lingered there. He wrote about his old neighborhood at length near the end of his career, but when he did so, he bent its story to shape the dark and cynical cast his mind had taken by then. In his telling, Park Manor was a synecdoche for a world that bends toward entropy—a place where people make a show of being conformist so they can lead sinful private lives, where good men kill themselves, and heroes are destined for villainy.

I sent a Valentine's Day card to the only black girl in my class one year, Nelson wrote later, and my childhood sweetheart was enraged when she found out. "*You* send Valentines to niggers," she swore. I took that girl to the neighborhood soda shop every Sunday for months before we split, he said, but our visits stopped suddenly when the shop's owner died. He hung himself from the ceiling above the counter, and his body dangled above a jar of maraschino cherries for days before it was discovered.

Violence was the neighborhood's common tongue, according to Nelson. There was a local bully, he said, and he was a terror. His name was Baldy Costello, and he punched me every time we crossed paths. After I moved, he raped and killed a sixteen-year-old girl. The Chicago race riots passed just north of my house, Nelson said. "Thousands of whites" were involved, and one afternoon my sister Bernice saw six of them drag a black man into a doorway. She heard a shot a moment later, and then she saw the white men stroll away casually.

Even baseball, by Nelson's telling, was a farce. The month after he left Park Manor, the White Sox were indicted for fixing the 1919 World Series with the help of the gambler Arnold Rothstein, and Swede Risberg was accused of playing a central role in the scheme. My love for the game and my friends' love for the game "was not shaken" by the indictments and trial, Nelson wrote later. "But we stopped pitching baseball cards and took to shooting dice. The men whose pictures we had cherished were no longer gods."

"Tell Your Tire Troubles to Nelson Abraham"

(September 1920–June 1927)

Lopsided cars pulled out of the traffic on Kedzie Avenue, rolled into Gerson Abraham's garage riding their rims, lurched, and stopped. Their drivers stepped out of their vehicles, and then Gerson went to work.

He raised the car with a jack, unbolted the wheel with the flat tire, and pulled it off its axle. He removed the inner tube, pumped air into it, submerged it in a trough of water, and rotated it. Bubbles appeared at the site of the puncture, and Gerson removed the tube from the water when he spotted them, marked the area with a pencil, rubbed gasoline on it, and cut a rubber patch to size. Then he clamped the tube and the patch together with an electric iron, and waited. Acrid smoke rose; his eyes watered.

When the patch fused with the tube, Gerson removed the iron, filled the tube with air, and returned it to the trough. If no bubbles appeared, he fitted the tube inside the tire, hefted the wheel back onto the car's axle, tightened the lug nuts, and lowered the jack. Then he collected a dollar from his customer, sometimes a dollar fifty—the cost of his labor added to the price he paid for supplies.

Nelson worked in the garage too. He joined his father after school occasionally, helped out on Saturdays, and opened the shop by himself on Sunday mornings. He studied Gerson's technique when they worked together, and tried to match his father's talent, and speed. Customers sometimes complimented Nelson's work, and when they did, he felt proud.

After they closed the shop for the evening, Gerson and Nelson walked down Kedzie Avenue toward home. Gerson wore slacks and a jacket; Nelson wore short pants. Their hands were speckled with globs of rubber, and their throats stung. The day's earnings clinked in Gerson's pockets. Trolleys passed them, heading south toward the Loop or north toward Skokie as they walked, and so did horses, Stephens Roadsters with spoked wooden wheels and canvas tops, and Jordans with sensuous body lines and chromed headlights.

Their neighborhood, Albany Park, was semi-suburban and mannered. Its avenues were lined by department stores, restaurants, and theaters, and its residential streets were a postcard scene of economy and aspiration—two-family homes and neatly spaced trees. The area's thirty thousand residents commuted to the Loop each morning on the Ravenswood El line together, filled the pews of the neighborhood's synagogues and churches every weekend, and worried about the value of their homes. Most, like Goldie, had spent their childhoods crowded into tenements near the center of the city and lived for the day they could afford to move farther north, to Hollywood Park, or maybe Rosehill.

Nelson and Gerson reached their home at 4834 North Troy Street a few minutes after leaving the tire shop, and entered. The air was heavy and still inside, and the light was dim. It was a dreary house, but more peaceful than the one in Park Manor had been—less crowded, quieter.

Irene was gone. She had moved to New York City shortly after Nelson entered high school, and found work as a secretary for a sheet music company. She rented an apartment on Creston Avenue, in the Bronx, and avoided marriage as if it were a communicable disease. Bernice came and went—brightening the house, and then disappearing. She was working as a substitute teacher, and her income liberated her. She attended the symphony and the opera regularly, and co-owned a cottage on the sand dunes in Gary, Indiana, with several other teachers. When it was warm, she spent weekends there. She swam competitively in college, and she could still walk down the beach in Gary, slip into the water, and swim a mile with ease.

Gerson and Goldie had reached détente. They were getting too old to fight the way they once had. He was fifty-four years old when Nelson entered high school; she was forty-four. They had been married for a quarter century, and their relationship had finally settled into a tolerable rhythm. She made soup twice a day because it was his favorite food, and he held his tongue while she rambled. On Sundays, his only day off, she left him in peace while he sat on the back porch and logged the week's earnings in a little notebook smeared with rubber.

Goldie no longer bothered Nelson either. He was nearly six feet tall, and athletic in a rangy, undisciplined way. He ran track and played basketball, but he weighed less than 135 pounds, so he looked like a willow branch draped in a jersey when he did. He was too scrawny to be a fighter, but too big for Goldie to beat, so she preserved the idea of her authority by avoiding confrontation.

Nelson's friends were Benton Curtis, Ralph Zwick, and Jerome Hanock, and they were as tame as the neighborhood that raised them. "We were the kind who did as we were told," Curtis said. He was a mechanic's son, like Nelson. Zwick's father owned a hardware store, and Hanock worked at Sears, Roebuck every summer to prepare for a career as a purchaser.

The boys met when they entered Hibbard High School in 1923, and for the next three years they considered themselves brothers. When classes dismissed on weekday afternoons, everyone not working that day would gather at Nelson's house to play penny-ante poker, or visit a boy named Sidney Yates who lived nearby. He had invented a game that used playing cards as avatars for professional baseball players, and the boys could lose hours imagining their way into the big leagues.* They studied together, too, pitched pennies along the sidewalk, or, if there was nothing else to do, bounced a ball off the steps of their school.

More than once, Nelson, Curtis, Zwick, and Hanock pooled their money and bought cars. They saved until they had twenty or twenty-five dollars, and then they went looking for a wreck—maybe a Model T with a sheet-metal body and a straight-four engine that idled roughly. Then they fixed it. Nelson knew tires, and Curtis understood engines. He could drive, too, and when the brothers got their first car running, he taught the rest of them. They were fourteen or fifteen years old, but when they rolled through Albany Park, seeing and being seen, they felt like men. Sometimes, they drove south to Gary on weekends and spent a night in Bernice's cottage, beyond the reach of their parents' authority.

The boys had humble ambitions. They planned to graduate, and then follow their fathers into the working world. They could see their futures clearly in the distance, and as they plodded toward them, they indulged only one fantasy: basketball stardom. It was "our great aim in life," Curtis said.

Chicago youths were enraptured by the game. It was mostly amateur at the time, and fully segregated—a sport for gangly teenagers who dribbled slowly and shot from deep court. College and high school teams dominated; professionals were an afterthought. The biggest event of the year was a national interscholastic tournament hosted by the University of Chicago, but there were dozens of independent teams in the city as well—churches, sports clubs, and settlement houses sponsored them, and they had their own tournaments, champions, and bragging rights.

The boys thought they played well enough to compete in one of those local leagues, so late in 1925, they decided to form a team. Their goal was to qualify for the Chicago Boys' Tournament—a citywide compe-

---

* This Sidney Yates is *the* Sidney Yates in Chicago—he became a member of the US House of Representatives later, and remained one for decades.

tition scheduled to begin early the following year. If they won, or came close, they would get their names in the local papers and earn a bit of glory they could cherish after they entered the adult world.

They spread word of their plan through Albany Park, and scheduled a meeting to discuss it on October 25. Seven people attended that first night, including the brothers, and Curtis was elected team captain. They met again the following day, decided their colors would be red and white, and voted to call themselves the Uptown Arrows. Training began immediately.

The team was a serious enterprise for the boys. They gathered at a community center called the Herman Beardsley Butler House every Monday and Thursday that fall, and played for an hour and a half—shooting, passing, and racing across court while their sweat dappled the gym's waxed floors. Between practice sessions, they held team meetings.

The Arrows stepped on the court for their first league game in early winter looking like winners. They were confident, and their custom red and white jerseys were clean and new. Nelson was a guard. It was his job to linger by the basket, snatch rebounds, run, and shoot. He had the right physique for the position, but he learned that day that he needed more than height and energy to be a ball player. He never scored, and the team lost, 26–9.

The Uptown Arrows picked up some momentum when they defeated a squad from Christ Lutheran their second time out, but couldn't maintain it. Their enthusiasm was no substitute for talent. They kept a detailed record of their team's history in a thin notebook. It begins as a breathless chronicle of selecting players, electing officers, and debating names, but quickly devolves into a spare and depressing chronicle. One item from January reads, "[Nelson] Abraham continues in his slump, again failing to register a point."

The Uptown Arrows made it to the Chicago Boys' Tournament the way they had planned, but just barely. Their record was ten wins, seventeen losses, and one tie. They played their first tournament game on

February 10, 1926, and lost. They were eliminated from the competition, and the team disbanded afterward.

Nelson was upset by the Arrows' defeat, but his disappointment was soon eclipsed by a more profound loss. Months earlier, his sister Bernice had agreed to marry a man named Morris Joffe, and their wedding—an event Nelson interpreted as a betrayal—had finally been scheduled.

Bernice and Joffe had met on the beach in Gary about three years earlier. She was picnicking with friends from work on the day in question. He was visiting with a fraternity from the University of Illinois at Urbana-Champaign (their guest, not a member—he couldn't join because he was Jewish). He was paying his way through school by cleaning their house, and they showed their gratitude by allowing him to accompany them on trips. Some people would be offended by that arrangement, but not Morris. There was a mercenary aspect to his character. He was engaged to marry a different woman the day he met Bernice, but he called off the wedding when Bernice agreed to date him.

No one understood what Bernice saw in Morris, Nelson least of all. He hated the man from the moment they were introduced. At first, his distaste was instinctual, but in time he found cause.

Nelson admired and respected Bernice, and Morris was her antithesis in every way that mattered. She was an atheist with a vivid intelligence and a deep appreciation for art. He was a striver's striver—a conservative man who wore expensive clothes and never read for pleasure. He grew up poor, but became a chemical engineer after graduating college, registered a few patents, and began amassing a small fortune. He attended synagogue and kept kosher, but only because it was expected. He was no believer, and the people who knew him best said he was only truly interested in himself.

Bernice and Morris married in 1926, and moved into an apartment on Ainslie Street. It was only a few blocks from Gerson and Goldie's house, but Nelson rarely visited. He felt Bernice had rejected him when she wed Morris, and rejected the values they shared as well. She had introduced him to books, taught him to think critically, and told him to ignore the example their parents set with their loveless marriage. But when it was her turn to be bold, she accepted the consort of a man whose only virtue was his steady income.

That summer, Nelson and Curtis drove to Gary so they could spend their last long break before the end of high school on the beach. Zwick and Hanock remained in Chicago to work. The boys moved into the cottage Bernice co-owned with her teaching colleagues and lingered there for weeks, walking on the sand and watching the fall approach like a storm cloud on the horizon. Flames from the blast furnaces of the Gary Works steel mill licked the sky to the north, water lapped at their feet, and they worried about the future.

"We felt life was passing us by," Curtis said. He thought there was a civil service job in his future, but the prospect brought him no joy. Nelson talked about becoming a journalist, but talk was all he did. He had been feeling cynical and lonely since Bernice married Joffe and moved away, and he dwelled on her perceived betrayal throughout the summer. He felt that he had suffered a great loss, and he nurtured that sensation until it opened a fissure in his life that divided his adolescence into a "before" and an "after"—a time when he had brothers, and the solitary years that followed; the era when he claimed heroes, and the period when he defined people by their shortcomings.

Chicago meant freight lines and slaughterhouses when Nelson was young—factories that spit steel, and stoic men who worked until their bodies gave out. But it had changed since. Gangland figures captured the public's imagination in the early 1920s, and by the middle of the decade the city was more closely associated with the names O'Banion, Torrio, and Capone than it was with International Harvester or Union Stock Yards.

Chicago's new archetypes were audacious characters. They wore wide-lapelled suits instead of coveralls, carried guns, drank, and operated on pure id. They fought each other for territory like warring European kings, paid off police officers, and manufactured liquor at industrial scale despite Prohibition. They filled the papers with headlines like GANGSTER FOUND SHOT TO DEATH, BURIED IN ASHES, and they operated brothels and gambling parlors even in the city's quietest neighborhoods.

One of those operations was located in the building next to Gerson's tire shop. It was called Johnson's, and it was an open secret in Albany Park. Armed guards stood out front, and young men came and went at all hours, wearing pretty women on their arms. There was another club on the other side of Kedzie—a sister organization—and large men regularly drove trucks down the street, parked in front of one of the clubs, and then went inside and began emptying it. They loaded cases of liquor, tables, and chairs into the trucks, and then drove to the other club and unloaded while the neighborhood watched. An hour or so later, the police would raid the building that had just been emptied and find nothing.

Johnson's had been tempting Nelson for years. He and Curtis had ogled the cars parked out front, and watched police disappear inside and emerge hours later. But he didn't try to visit until after he returned from his trip to Gary.*

The first time Nelson visited Johnson's, he entered the building alone, passed an armed guard who scrutinized him, walked through a restaurant on the ground floor, and climbed a flight of stairs. He entered a closed room at the top, where a second guard frisked him, and then he was allowed into the club.

Dice clacked and roulette wheels spun inside Johnson's. Playing cards riffled as dealers shuffled them, and money was scattered on

---

* Nelson claimed he began visiting Johnson's in his junior year of high school, but Curtis said Nelson drifted away from his friends in favor of the club in their senior year, and I defer to him here.

tables like scrap paper. A bartender stood behind a bar shaped like a horseshoe and served liquor to confident, loose-limbed men.

Nelson took in the scene, and recognized a few faces. He had patched tires for some of the club's regulars, and maybe that connection gave him the nerve to approach one of the tables. He had money from working at the garage and he understood poker, so he placed a wager—then another, and another.

Johnson's was a revelation for Nelson—a new paradigm for understanding the world. The Albany Park he knew was a maze of routine and obligation, where plans were made in units of years and decades. But inside the club, the future was an abstraction, and people were emancipated from the concerns he had been inculcated with. They abided no schedules and obeyed no laws they could circumvent. They rode waves of endorphins and liquor wherever they led—peaking when they hit their numbers, and plunging into the trough when they crapped out, but always, even in their darkest moments, giving the impression they were members of a species so high on the food chain, it made its own rules.

Johnson's had a narcotic appeal for Nelson. He returned soon after his first visit, and by winter he was a club regular and the brothers had lost track of him. The four of them never had a falling-out, or fought, but every time Curtis, Zwick, and Hanock tried to make plans with Nelson during senior year, he told them he was busy. In his absence, they gossiped about him. They traded stories about speakeasies with armed guards, and big wagers, but in truth they knew little about how Nelson was spending his time.

Nelson was still working in Gerson's garage in early 1927, but by then his attitude had changed. He could see what other people saw when they looked at his father—a meek old man whose callused hands would never be clean—and when he watched Gerson kneel down to peer beneath a young customer's car, and heard that customer tell Gerson to hurry up, he felt a "pang of shame."

Nelson made no attempt to conceal his scorn. He adopted a condescending attitude toward his father that winter, and began offering him unsolicited advice.

Gerson didn't mark up the price of the supplies he used when he charged customers, so he only profited from his labor, and Nelson thought that was foolish.

You have to mark up the prices if you want to make real money, he insisted.

Gerson refused. "I can't charge *more* than what I paid for it, can I?" he demanded.

"Of course," Nelson replied. The grocer charges more for his products than he pays to buy them, doesn't he?

"That's different," Gerson said. "He's a *business* man."

Gerson was scandalized by Johnson's and mystified by the fact that the club was able to operate openly, so Nelson antagonized him by flaunting his connections there. He told Gerson about the horseshoe-shaped bar, the liquor, and the police who visited to collect bribes. But Gerson refused to listen. "Well, that's crazy," he said. "A cop can't do that; they'd put him in jail. That would be dishonest."

"Cops, Pa, cops take money, cops steal," Nelson said.

"I don't want to listen to crazy talk like that," Gerson said. "A cop, a policeman is made to defend the law! That is why he is a policeman."

"Don't act like that, Pa," Nelson said, almost pleading.

Months passed that way. Nelson sniped, Gerson sputtered defensively, and tension built between them. Their conflict finally reached a breaking point early on a Sunday morning. Nelson had gone out the night before, won forty dollars shooting craps, and got home late. He was still in bed a little before nine o' clock when he heard Goldie say it was time for him to get up and open the garage. He ignored her. He didn't need the few dollars he would earn patching tires for a day, so he went back to sleep.

Gerson walked into the room about half an hour later.

"Are you going to open the shop?" he asked.

"Open it yourself," Nelson said.

And Gerson did. He worked seven days that week, and seven days the next, and the one after it. Nelson never went back to the garage, and his father never had another day off.

Nelson was nearly estranged from his father by the end of his senior year, and still distant from his friends. He was moody, listless—nervous about the future, but unwilling to admit it. Gerson was pressing him to decide what he would do next, but Nelson resisted. They argued more.

Gerson wanted Nelson to join a union and become someone's apprentice, or maybe enter a trade school. "Now it's time for you to be a draftsman," he said, "to be something."

Nelson responded with calculated nonchalance. "I'll get by," he told his father, but he didn't say how.

Their argument dragged on without either side conceding, until Bernice intervened. She and Nelson hadn't been seeing each other much, but she still felt obliged to speak on his behalf. "He's going to college," she told her parents. She said she and Morris would pay Nelson's tuition at the University of Illinois, if he agreed to two conditions: he had to pay for his own books, food, and housing, and he had to pursue a practical degree.

Nelson accepted; he had no other options.

Gerson was stunned by the idea. He never finished grade school, and he couldn't understand the purpose of college, but he didn't argue. He held Bernice's opinions in high regard, and at least college would get Nelson out of the house.

Nelson graduated from high school in June 1927, and when he did, Curtis, Zwick, and Hanock realized he had been living a more divided life than they imagined.[*] While it was true that he had been drinking

---

[*] Their school had changed buildings and names since they enrolled. It was called Roosevelt High School when they graduated.

and gambling throughout senior year as they suspected, he had also earned the highest grades of his high school career, become a member of the Civics Club, and helped the varsity basketball team win a city championship.

Nelson had even joined the yearbook committee and been appointed Class Prophet. It was his job to write satirical articles about his class-mates' futures, and he used his position to bid a tender farewell to the friends he had been drifting away from. In a series of news briefs, he predicted each of them would achieve more than they believed them-selves capable of. "Benton Charles Curtis has been appointed chief caretaker at the Lincoln Park Zoo," one story reads. "It is the con-tractor's conclusion that the 106-story all-steel structure now under construction . . . will be completed by Oct. 1," another announces. "Wireless lighting systems are placed exclusively by the Zwick Sys-tems of Lighting." Jerry Hanock is showing "exceptional ability" in his new position with the Chicago Cubs, another says.

Nelson prophesied a more pedestrian future for himself. Instead of penning an article claiming that he was destined for greatness, he inserted a small, self-effacing advertisement into the yearbook that reads:

TELL YOUR TIRE
TROUBLES
-TO-
Nelson Abraham
VULCANIZING
RETREADING

Stoic. Academic.
Ink-Stained Wretch.

(July 1927–June 17, 1931)

An ROTC inspection at the University of Illinois, Urbana-Champaign in 1927—the year Nelson was a member. ROTC Inspection, courtesy of the University of Illinois Archives

The air was heavy when Nelson reached the University of Illinois at Urbana-Champaign in mid-September, and the sun was deadly. It was unbearably hot the week he arrived, but then a storm raged across campus, thunder shook the ground, lightning lit the plains with evanescent sparks, and the temperature plunged. The first frost of the season fell after the storm passed, and by the time it melted, Nelson was alone. He had fifty dollars in his possession—the cost of tuition—and he knew no one.

Nelson agreed to enroll in college when Bernice suggested it because he had no alternative to offer. But there was another reason as well. He had been harboring a secret ambition to transcend his class for years, and he knew that moving to Urbana-Champaign was his best chance of realizing it. In college, no one would know him as the solicitous child who patched tires in his father's garage, or the gangly teen who feigned apathy and posed as a gangster. He would be anonymous, and free to reintroduce himself as the person he believed he was capable of becoming.

Nelson made a clean break with his past that year. He stopped walking pigeon-toed and calling himself Swede. He cut off contact with his "brothers" in Chicago, and avoided speaking to his parents. Then he isolated himself on campus, and scheduled his days tightly.* He moved into a single room that cost ten dollars a month, began working—odd jobs at first, then waiting tables and washing dishes—and registered for a heavy load of classes. He took European history, Spanish literature, zoology, fencing, artillery drill, and organic chemistry—and he lived the harried, sleep-deprived life of a working student.

There weren't many hours remaining in the day after Nelson met his obligations, but he spent what time he had searching for new ideas, and for heroes who could replace the laborers, ballplayers, and gun-toting men he admired as a child.

Marcus Aurelius was Nelson's first college role model. Aurelius ruled the Roman Empire for almost twenty years and led one of its most successful military campaigns. Machiavelli called him the last of the Five Good Emperors, but Aurelius was also a philosopher who recorded his ideas in a series of essays. He died near modern-day Vienna in 180 AD, and afterward his writings were published under the title *Meditations*. Seventeen hundred years later, Nelson discovered a translation of that book in southern Illinois and read it in a trance.

Aurelius was a Stoic. He claimed that abstention and physical dis-

---

* This was not entirely a matter of choice. Nelson would have had a hard time assembling a social life on campus. Student life revolved around fraternities at the time, and most of them disallowed Jews.

cipline are virtuous qualities, and argued that personal integrity is more important than social standing or physical comfort. He believed thoughts engender actions, and reasoned that a person who distracts themselves with trivialities will necessarily lead a trivial life. Conversely, he said, anyone who focuses on meaningful subjects has the potential to affect the world in profound ways.

His ideas are simple, powerful, and—within their own context— irrefutable. They thrilled Nelson. He had been raised in a place where labor and violence were the wellsprings of self-respect for men, and intellectual curiosity was suspect. But Aurelius reversed that logic. He argued that every idea is worthy of evaluation, and people should act according to their principles, even when doing so seems irrational. "Do your duty," he wrote, "—and never mind whether you are shivering or warm . . . dying or doing something else."

Nelson read and reread *Meditations*, and then remade himself in Aurelius's image. He began by forsaking indulgences. He abstained from sex and avoided masturbation. Wood alcohol was sometimes available on campus, but he declined to drink it. He believed that he did not deserve to consume more calories than his body required, so he never touched sweets. He limited his sleep, and remained silent when possible to encourage the formation of profound thoughts.

Then he gave form to Aurelius's ideas by imposing structure on his life. He woke at six o'clock every morning and took a cold shower. Breakfast was oatmeal flavored with a dash of salt, and when it was time to leave for work or class, he traveled from his room to his destination along the most efficient route possible. He was reading Chaucer, Shakespeare, and Byron at the time, and he forced himself to dwell on their ideas in his idle moments—"Life is short, and art long," he might have thought on his way to work. "Sweet are the uses of adversity," and "Man marks the earth with ruin."

The Urbana-Champaign campus had a feel that was both majestic and jocular. Brick buildings with white-framed windows surrounded a large quad laced with walking paths, and tall oaks provided shade when the school's twenty thousand students traveled between classes. But at the beginning of the school year, crowds gathered around bonfires fueled by wood that freshmen had scavenged from the neighborhoods surrounding the university. Fraternity pledges raced each other around a city block wearing pajamas, and hundreds of students draped themselves in rags and meandered through the streets, banging drums and playing fiddles—the "Hobo Parade," they called it.

But Nelson was immune to his classmates' boisterous attitudes. He chose to move about campus like a phantom—quiet and expressionless. He avoided student gatherings, made no friends, and refused to observe social niceties. When people greeted him, he responded using the fewest number of words possible. "Good morning," he said, or "Good afternoon." But that was all. If someone tried to engage him in small talk after saying hello, he paused to weigh the worthiness of their comment. If it deserved an answer, he provided one; if it was trivial, he said nothing.

Soon, Nelson developed a reputation for being aloof and superior. Students rolled their eyes when he approached. They whispered, and he distracted himself from their judgment by parsing the ideas of dead men. When people snickered, perhaps Byron's lament for the fates of great thinkers comforted him:

> With the sad usage of all sorts of sages,
> Who in his lifetime each was deemed a bore.
> The loftiest minds outrun their tardy ages;
> This they must bear with and perhaps much more.

Nelson was famously gregarious later in life. In Chicago, in the 1960s, he hung out at a bar called O'Rourke's with Studs Terkel and Roger Ebert, and drank at Riccardo's with a progressive councilman named Len Despres. He was a familiar face at every racetrack within easy reach of the city, and his apartment was a landmark. Visiting was a rite of passage for local artists, and for writers from across the country. When William Styron and Terry Southern visited in 1964, Nelson met them at O'Hare, brought them back to his flat, and kept them up drinking and talking until Southern passed out on a cot, clutching a glass of bourbon. The next morning, Nelson put his visitors in a cab and directed it to the Cook County Jail. The warden was a friend of his, so they were invited inside and offered a tour.

Nelson's abstemious college regime seemed bizarre and out of character to everyone who knew him afterward, so when it came up, he felt obliged to explain himself. He claimed that Stoicism appealed to him for two reasons, and the first was the parallel between Aurelius's ideas and the lifestyle of his namesake, Nils Ahlgren—the man who became Isaac Ben Abraham.

Most of what Nelson knew about Isaac came from Goldie. Gerson rarely spoke about his father, but Goldie often did. She saw Isaac's life as one long cautionary tale, and she employed anecdotes from his travels like cudgels to beat her children into line when she feared they were beginning to indulge bohemian notions.

Goldie's favorite story about Isaac took place on the ship that carried the Abraham family from Jerusalem to America.* By her telling, Isaac grew restless at sea. He was accustomed to the adoration of crowds, but on the boat, only his family knew him and they were no longer interested in his pontifications. Before long, he became desperate for distractions and began digging through his family's belongings. Eventually, he found some cash Jette had hidden in her bags, removed the bills, and studied them. He looked at George Washington's portrait, and thought about Exodus. He remembered that God told Israel, "Thou shalt not make unto thee any graven image. Thou shalt not bow down thyself to them . . ." And then he realized what his faith demanded.

Isaac carried Jette's money to the ship's deck, walked to the railing

---

* It's likely that this story—like all stories about Isaac—is partly apocryphal. That said, Goldie told it for at least twenty years without Gerson contradicting her.

facing the sea, and began to preach. He was a bearded old man with a fistful of bills, and he was ranting into the wind. "Man is made in the image of God . . . so it's a crime to have money," he said.

Passengers gathered to listen. They watched expectantly.

Isaac rambled until his audience was large and eager, and then he threw the bills overboard. They flitted through the air toward the surface of the water, landed, and then sank into the ocean. When they disappeared, the Abraham family was destitute.

The moral of the sea-voyage story was obvious to Goldie: If you allow ideas to get in the way of common sense, they will ruin you, and they will ruin your family. But after Nelson discovered *Meditations*, his grandfather's life took on new meaning. He saw virtue and idealism in Isaac's actions, and felt a strong connection to his legacy.

The year Nelson remade himself as a Stoic, he also began signing his writing assignments "Nelson ben Algren" in Isaac's honor. And later, he told an interviewer, "For the first time I understood my father was not my father: my grandfather was my father. A sense of identity with him became so strong that it dawned on me: I was him."

The standard Nelson set for himself in college was impossibly high, and that was the second reason he found Stoicism appealing. "It was an interesting kind of struggle," he said. He regularly fell short of his ascetic ideal, but the challenge of trying to achieve it reframed an unremarkable stretch of life into an extended contest between sin and virtue. "It wasn't a passive thing," he said. "I was always perpetually falling off this grand plane that I had arranged."

The Urbana-Champaign campus didn't advertise any tempting vices. There was a movie theater, but the law required it to close on Sundays. Liquor was hard to find, and student life was tightly regulated by the Dean of Men, Thomas Arkle Clark—a celebrated paternalist who wrote a cliché-laden column for the student paper. "You can't build a structure of any importance without giving attention to the foundation," he proclaimed. "[I]t is a tendency of human nature to follow the leader."

Clark advocated celibacy, religiosity, and prohibition, and he maintained a network of student informers who helped him enforce the college's code of discipline. Expulsions were common under his tenure, and even automobiles were controversial—"The parlor sofa isn't what it used to be," one student editorial cautioned. "It's made of black leather now, and it's set right behind the steering wheel."

But ten blocks west of campus, in Champaign, none of those prohibitions existed. There was a red-light district on that side of town that boasted speakeasies, gambling parlors, and a network of brothels, all operating with the consent of the city's political infrastructure. A madam named Bess Maxwell owned one of those establishments, and after she left the trade, she told a reporter that she had remained in business by making payments to a local law firm. The firm handed a portion of her money to a man named Herman "Blue" Klemick, and he delivered it to the mayor. She received protection in return, and so did all of the other brothels in the area. They had so little fear of prosecution that they operated a free shuttle service that ran between Walnut Street—the heart of the red-light district—and the campus's fraternities.* On any given night, seventy percent of the johns in Champaign were university students.

Gambling and liquor didn't appeal to Nelson the way they had in Chicago, but women did. After he learned about the brothels along Walnut Street, resisting the urge to visit became a nightly struggle. He told himself to stay in his room and read. He tried to "think of nothing but Marcus Aurelius," but sometimes his resistance crumbled and he rose in the early hours of the morning and began walking toward Champaign.

Once, he left his room and headed west. He was alone, and lustful,

* Credit for reporting this story belongs to Ed Borman, a *Daily Illini* reporter who wrote a series of articles in 1939 that detailed the arrangements Champaign's brothel operators reached with the city's mayors and police between 1925 and 1939.

and he moved furtively. He entered an unfamiliar part of town, passed several warehouses, and continued. When he reached a dimly lit house, he told himself he had found the place he was looking for, and he stopped. He stood outside for a while, and then knocked at the door.

A woman answered. What do you want? she asked.

"Well, I've got a couple dollars to spend," Nelson said.

The woman turned and hollered to a man inside the building. Before the man appeared, Nelson ran away.

It wasn't the last time Nelson visited Walnut Street, but every trip ended the same. He never entered a brothel in the district, but each attempt gave him "a very oppressive sense of sin," and he judged himself as harshly for his failures as he would have if he had succeeded.

Nelson didn't abandon Stoicism because he fell short of his ideals. He held faith with Aurelius's ideas as well as he could, though it pained him to do so, until he found new ones to replace them.

In the spring semester of his sophomore year, Nelson took a class taught by a criminologist named Donald R. Taft. It was called Social Control, and it forced Nelson to reevaluate everything *Meditations* had taught him.

Taft was a handsome man with progressive politics, and a tight smile. He wore eyeglasses with thick round frames, and he spoke in metaphor. "Crime is an art which society has made punishable by law," he told a group of students the year Nelson met him. "As educated people, we should not lose our perspective. If we hastily think of murderers and robbers as our most dangerous foes, we may overlook other people who really threaten us more."

That point of view was novel for Nelson, and so were the other ideas Taft exposed him to in class. William Ogburn's writing, in particular, forced Nelson to reevaluate the way he thought about sin and personal responsibility.

Ogburn's most famous book is *Social Change with Respect to Culture and Original Nature*, and in it he argues that human behavior can only be explained by considering biological inheritance, economics, and political factors. "[S]ocial conditions may become so rigorous in their impositions or effects upon human nature that behavior we call crime will be resorted to," he wrote. "In periods of economic desperation there is more temptation to violate laws regarding property."

Nelson decided to become a sociologist after taking Taft's class. He was excited to discover a system of thought that acknowledged the power that institutions had to influence individuals, and tried to understand antisocial behavior instead of simply condemning it. But he still saw value in the Stoic ideal, and Aurelius's ideas continued to influence him for the rest of his life. They played a role in shaping his lifestyle and personality, and they informed his writing as well.

Nelson's fiction is often diminished because of his obvious sympathy for the poor, prisoners, prostitutes, and addicts. Critics sometimes bowdlerize it as apologia.* But in truth, Nelson was a moralist, and his characters are a complex mix of discipline and resignation. They feel constrained by society and unfairly used, but they maintain what Carl Sandburg called "a strange midnight dignity." There is no self-pity in them, and when they are accused of breaking the law, they question the moral authority of the people who condemn them instead of begging for forgiveness.

"I fulfill my obligations even if I have to rob a warehouse to do it," one of Nelson's most memorable characters says in *The Man with the Golden Arm*. His name is Sparrow. He makes his money stealing dogs, shoplifting, and running drugs, but he thinks of himself as a businessman.

Sparrow sometimes plays the clown, but he was speaking earnestly about his sense of obligation. His best friend, Frankie Machine,

---

* "What he wants to say is that we live in a society whose bums and tramps are better men than the preachers and the politicians and the otherwise respectables," Norman Podhoretz wrote in 1956. "Nelson was basically an underworld groupie," William Styron wrote forty years later.

doesn't pick up on his tone though. The conversation bores Frankie, so he responds lightly.

"That's the problem with the whole country, all you businessmen cheatin' the peoples so fast 'n hard there's nothin' left for an honest hustler to steal," he jokes.

"I don't think there's any difference," Sparrow responds evenly, "a businessman is a hustler with the dough to hustle on the legit 'n a hustler is a businessman who's either gone broke or never had it. Back me up with five grand tonight 'n tomorrow mornin' I get an invitation to join the Chamber of Commerce 'n no questions asked."

Frankie and Sparrow are speaking in Chicago a few years after the conclusion of World War II. They can sense the social order realigning around them, and they know virtue has become fungible—less meaningful than it once was, but harder to claim; as tangible as five thousand dollars, and just as difficult to get your hands on. Sparrow is stuck on the wrong side of that divide, but instead of resigning himself to his fate, or embracing a nihilistic view of the world, he adheres to his own personal code and rejects the idea that wealth and virtue are synonymous.

Nelson's discipline began "sliding off" after he took Taft's course. Like an alcoholic returning to the bottle, first he tried a little, and then he tried a lot. He started eating more, stopped taking cold showers, and began responding when people spoke to him. Then, in the spring of 1930, he moved into a boardinghouse at 714 Iowa Street and began sleeping with his landlady. "I think I began to recognize that pleasure wasn't necessarily evil," he said.

That was around the time Nelson decided to become a journalist. It was a compromise position—it promised neither the aesthete's life he envisioned after discovering *Meditations*, nor the prestige of becoming a sociologist, but it was a realistic option. He couldn't afford to stay in school long enough to earn a graduate degree, and he had realized that asceticism wasn't a career. Whatever journalism's shortcomings were, it was better than retreading tires for a living.

After Nelson made his choice, he pursued his new trade with the same energy he showed when he transformed himself into a Stoic. He took nine journalism courses in his last three semesters of college, and worked as a court reporter for the student paper, the *Daily Illini*. He earned a spot on the banquet committee of the Illinois State Press Convention in November 1930, and the next month he stayed on campus through the winter break and served as the *Illini*'s assistant editor for the holidays.

Nelson was well positioned for a job by the spring of 1931. He had been writing for the paper for at least a year, and his grades were good—in his last two semesters, he earned seven As, four Bs, and a C in headline writing. He joined the Journalism Alumni Association after he took his finals, and sat for a test the Illinois Press Association offered to graduating seniors. He passed, and received a wallet card that could be presented to potential employers. It said: Nelson Abraham is a capable "editor, columnist, foreign correspondent, copywriter."

Nelson received his BSJ—Bachelor of Science in Journalism—on June 16, 1931, and then prepared to return to Chicago and launch his career. His future seemed certain, and when he pictured it, he conjured a bucolic scene—a steady job with a little newspaper, collared shirts, and a comfortable retirement. "I had tremendous faith" in the "little card" the Press Association gave me, he said. It meant "I could be whatever I wanted to be."

The Past Receded Like
a Wave Just Spent

(June 18, 1931–January 1933)

Nelson entered the City News Bureau of Chicago wearing a dark
suit and walked toward the general manager's office. Glasses
framed his brown eyes, and a conservative tie hung down the front of
his high-collared dress shirt.

The bureau, a local wire service, was a proving ground for young journalists. Its office was notoriously filthy, and its staff was known for being
unruly and tenacious—they kept a bottle of Scotch hidden in the flush
tank of the toilet in the bathroom, and they approached their work the
way soldiers would. They covered every corpse that reached the morgue,
every news conference downtown, and every serious court case in the
city with no expectation of gratitude or glory. They made duplicates of
every story they filed, placed the copies inside canisters, inserted those
canisters into pneumatic tubes, and sent them flying toward the city's
six largest papers at twenty feet per second. Editors skimmed those stories when they reached their destinations, and if they had merit, they
appeared in the paper later that day beneath someone else's byline.

Nelson waited to be acknowledged when he reached the general
manager's office. The man's name was Isaac Gershman, and he had
been with the bureau for fourteen years. He had a head shaped like an
egg, and he spoke in staccato bursts.

I'm looking for a job, Nelson said when he had Gershman's attention.

There's no reason to even ask for your name, Gershman replied. Too many people need work now.

He wasn't exaggerating. It was the spring of 1931, and the economic crisis that would later be called the Great Depression was a year and a half old. Chicago's unemployment rate was twenty-five percent.

Nelson must have persisted, or begun to look desperate, because Gershman reversed himself immediately.

OK, he said, tell me your name. Then he turned and told his secretary, "Add this young man's name to our list of applicants!"

"I'll phone you as soon as we have an opening," the secretary told Nelson. Then she went back to her work.

Nelson took a seat and resolved to remain in the office until he had been hired. He didn't realize Gershman had been placating him, or that he was never going to receive a call. He waited, maybe for hours, until the secretary told him to leave, and then he limped back to his parents' house at 4834 North Troy Street.

The Abraham family home was a crowded, despairing place that spring—thick with regret and frustrated ambition. Gerson's garage was failing and his savings had vanished. He had invested his retirement money in swampy Florida land a few years earlier, and now it was gone. Bernice and her husband, Morris Joffe, were living on the second floor with their two-year-old son, Robert, but they weren't paying rent. Morris lost his job after the stock market crash in 1929, and when the Albany Park Bank closed a year later, he lost five thousand dollars—every cent he had saved. Bernice was still working as a substitute teacher with the Chicago school district, but the city was paying her in scrip that had no cash value.

Nelson's family hid their struggles from him while he was away at college, so returning home was like entering a funhouse version of his old life. Gerson had been earning a steady income when Nelson left for Urbana-Champaign. Joffe had been setting money aside to buy a house, and Bernice had been receiving checks regularly. Nelson had not been expected to shoulder any responsibilities then, but now his family was relying on him.

Nelson was confident the News Bureau would hire him at first, but he expanded his job search when he realized they never would. Chicago was home to the *American*, the *Daily News*, the *Evening Post*, the *Herald Examiner*, the *Tribune*, the *Southtown Economist*, and the *Citizen*, among others, and he intended to apply to every one of them.

Nelson had been only vaguely aware of the country's economic crisis while he was in college. The *Daily Illini* ran stories about unemployment, emergency relief, and the Dow's fluctuations while he was on staff, but those things seemed distant and abstract on campus.* Stock prices fell, rose, and fell again, but life in Urbana-Champaign was not much affected and it wasn't clear there was any reason to worry. Recovery was announced more than once, and President Herbert Hoover kept insisting the dawn was about to break on the horizon. "I am convinced we have now passed the worst," he said, "and with continued unity of effort we shall rapidly recover."

But Nelson felt the Depression's impact acutely when he returned to Chicago. He sensed its presence in his home, read about its casualties in the papers, and saw its victims in the streets. The city was a purgatory that year, he wrote later—the past had receded "like a wave just spent," the future was unknowable, and millions were trapped in "the slough of the waters," waiting helplessly for the next wave in the set to thunder up the beach and scatter them like grains of sand.

Chicago's social fabric was already badly frayed by the time Nelson began looking for work in June. Three-quarters of the city's banks had

---

* It seems incredible, but Nelson claimed he was unaware of the Depression until graduation. "I didn't even know when I got out of school in thirty-one that there was a depression," he told an interviewer. "You found out then?" the man asked. "Yeah, I found that out," Nelson replied. "It was sort of a bring-down."

closed and left their depositors penniless. The sidewalks were clogged with panhandlers, and the daily papers were filled with news of violence and desperation that grew more ominous by the day. A homeless child, no more than five or six years old, was discovered sleeping outside the St. Clair Hotel with a dog standing guard over him near the end of the month, and five days later a nightclub singer named Clementine McHugh shoved a chloroform soaked rag down her throat after being fired. When the police investigated her death, they found eighty-eight cents in her hotel room, and a note that read, "I'm tired of it all. I have made a failure of everything."

Then a heat wave settled over the city and lingered for weeks. Hundreds of thousands of people jammed the Lake Michigan shore to cool off, and those who couldn't afford train fare stayed home and baked. "Suffering was general," the *Tribune* reported. Dozens died from the heat; a few drowned in scrums on the beaches. The parks became campgrounds in July as hundreds of women, turned away by the city's overburdened shelters, took up residence in them. The government began defaulting on its payrolls that month as well, and Communist Party activists led marches through the streets every day to demand emergency relief, a moratorium on evictions, and the end of capitalism.*

By August, Chicago was a puddle of gasoline waiting for a match—and on the third day of the month, the police struck one.

Two officers, a real estate agent, and two bailiffs visited the 5000 block of South Dearborn Street that afternoon to evict a seventy-two-year-old woman named Diana Gross. They entered her apartment when she answered their knock, and they began to empty it. They carried her furniture outside and piled it on the sidewalk, and then did the same with her clothes, dishes, and keepsakes.

Gross's neighbors watched them work. Then a few left the block to find representatives of the local Unemployment Council—a Communist

---

* The numbers are breathtaking, actually. There were 408 Communist Party demonstrations in Chicago in 1931, and 566 in 1932.

Party front group. They found them leading a march nearby, and spread news of Gross's eviction through the crowd. A few minutes later, five thousand activists wearing buttoned shirts and fedoras flooded Dearborn Street, surrounded the bailiffs and the police, and began carrying Gross's possessions back inside her apartment.

Police reinforcements arrived on the scene before the activists were finished, and forced their way into the crowd. They were outnumbered, so they seized a few of the group's leaders, threw them in a van, and drove away. Three officers arrived on foot then, and found themselves facing an angry crowd. They expected to find other police on the scene, but there were none. They drew their pistols in fear, and the crowd surged.

Twenty-five additional officers mobbed the block then, and found the three men who preceded them "bleeding from knife cuts and blows with bricks, stones, and sticks." They began shooting, and a protestor returned fire from a doorway. The crowd fractured, and the police took cover inside a storefront and fired into the street blindly until it cleared.

By nightfall, three black protesters were dead. One was a Communist Party activist who arrived on the scene expecting to become a target. Before he reached Gross's apartment, he told a friend, "If there is shooting I expect to be killed because I shall be on the front rank." He was unarmed, but the police shot him five times. The second man to die had joined the protest on a whim. He panicked when the police began firing into the crowd, grabbed an officer's gun, and was shot immediately. The last man to die, another activist, suffered the worst fate. The police abducted him during the melee in front of Gross's house, threw him in a van, shot him in the head, mutilated his body, and then dumped it in Washington Park, where the Communist Party gathered before marches.

Mayor Anton Cermak was vacationing on a yacht during the fighting, but he came ashore to be briefed by an aide and issue a statement. "A ruthless policy of suppression would, in the present situation, only incite further disorders," he said. ". . . [A] policy of conciliation must be adopted." He urged people to remain calm, and he temporarily suspended all evictions. It was a prudent decision.

Sixty thousand activists marched down State Street five days later, carrying the bodies of the two activists who had been killed by the police. A red flag fluttered at the head of the procession, and banners reading JOIN THE FIGHTING PARTY OF YOUR CLASS moved through the crowd. Forty thousand people gathered on the sidewalks to watch the parade, and Communist Party members solicited them for donations.

By the end of summer, signs reading WE DO NOT PAY RENTS had begun to appear in apartment windows throughout the city. Serious people were talking about the possibility of a second American revolution, and Nelson was preparing to leave town. He had been searching for work for three months with no luck, and figured he would face less competition outside Chicago.

Nelson left home in the fall wearing his only suit. He was twenty-two—baby-faced, broke, maybe half as tough as he imagined himself to be.

He traveled alone, and his route was haphazard—sometimes north, and sometimes west. Occasionally, drivers noticed him walking along the shoulder of the road, spotted his high-collared shirt, mistook him for a priest, and pulled over to offer him a ride. But more often he walked, or rode in empty freight cars. He slept in homeless shelters when he was lucky enough to find one, and slept outside when he wasn't. His life was as joyless as it had been while he was a Stoic, but far less dignified—he went where his rides carried him, and ate what he was given or nothing at all.

Every time Nelson entered a new town, he visited the office of the local newspaper, presented his Press Association card, and asked for a job. But the answer was always some version of no. When he stopped in small towns, they told him to look for work in the cities. And city papers invariably told him to try finding work at a small-town paper.

After a month or so, Nelson reached Minneapolis. He was four hundred miles from home, and it was getting cold. He went to Fourth Street, found the *Journal*'s office, went inside, and asked for work.

Their answer surprised him. "Well, sit down and try your hand," an editor said. So Nelson did. He spent the day writing headlines, and at the end of his shift he was encouraged to return the next morning.

The Depression had hit Minneapolis just as hard as it hit Chicago. Tens of thousands of people were unemployed, and earlier that year a few hundred of them mobbed a grocery store and began emptying its shelves. The store's owner tried to scare them off with a pistol, but to no avail. The crowd attacked when they saw the gun, broke the owner's arm, and continued about their business.

But the city felt like an oasis to Nelson. First, the *Journal* put him behind a desk. Then a grocer gave him food, and a hotel offered him a room with a view of the Foshay Tower—a thirty-two-story slate building modeled after the Washington Monument. Both extended him credit.*

Nelson settled in at the paper and began to feel his life was finally coming together. Then, at the end of his first week, he saw people lining up for their checks and took his place in the queue. When he reached the front of the line, he asked for his.

"We can't pay you," the man in charge said. "You're just getting experience. There's a man out of town and you're just filling in for him."

This came as a surprise. "Well, then I have to leave," Nelson said.

"Well, thanks for coming around," the man said.

Nelson was still in Minneapolis when it began to snow. He had sixty cents and a half-empty bottle of liquor to his name, and he spent his days in bed, eavesdropping on the rooms below his.

Most of them were occupied by prostitutes. Nelson hadn't realized that when he moved in, but when he stopped working and began to spend more time in the hotel, it became obvious. The sound of their

---

* Nelson sometimes said he stayed at the YMCA in Minneapolis, but in the story this account is based on—an unpublished piece of first-person prose, unlabeled except for a title, but apparently a memoir—he describes his housing situation as I describe it here.

commerce seeped through the floor, and he spent hours imagining himself into their lives. They must be miserable, he thought—piteous, sickly. "I began fancying the very wallpaper to be crawling with disease," he wrote later.

One night, while Nelson was watching the snow fall outside his window, someone knocked on his door. The sound startled him. He opened it and found a young Swedish woman standing in the hallway, smiling. She was wearing flimsy pajamas, and there was a sweater draped over her shoulders.

Nelson stepped aside to let her in.

"Somebody told me you were drinkin' Rock an' Rye up here all by yourself," she said.* "Ain't you lonesome? I thought you'd give me a drink."

Nelson handed her his bottle of liquor, and she took a slug. He saw her lips encircle the opening, and told himself to throw the bottle away when she left.

"I bet you're from out of town," she said. Her tone was part flirtation, part business. "Have you got any change?"

Nelson showed her his sixty cents. It was a meager offering, but she didn't take offense. She didn't accept, either.

"It aint [sic] enough there," she said. "Haven't you got no *folding* money?"

Nelson did not. "Let's finish the bottle," he offered. He was repulsed by her, but lonely too—desirous. He placed his lips gingerly on the bottle of Rock and Rye and took a swig. Then he passed it to the woman, and she emptied it.

He began talking because he didn't want her to leave. "It's a tiresome kind of game, isn't it?" he asked.

"O-you mean downstairs," she said. "Yeh, it gets you down after a while. Well, just like everything else."

---

* Rock and Rye is a treacly mixture of rock candy syrup and rye whiskey that was popular during Prohibition because doctors could prescribe it as a tonic.

"Does everything get you down?" Nelson asked.

"Well, you know what I mean," she said. "What's the diff if you come to work here at seven and stay till five in the morning taking care of guys, or whether you stand on your pins from nine to five-thirty runnin' a elevator? Here at least you get a chance to have a cigarette when you want it. You're all punched out when it's time to go home anyhow. And this pays a little better."

The woman's confidence surprised Nelson. He had assumed she would be ashamed of her profession. "Do you go home?" he asked.

"I live home and my folks think I'm a real nice girl," she snapped.

"Well you are," Nelson said. "I think you're a nice girl—I don't have sympathy with people who just start condemning before understanding—preachers you know—"

The woman's face went blank when Nelson said "condemning." His voice trailed off when he noticed her reaction. "I had been overly eager to prove I had no contempt for her," he wrote later, "while she had never once assumed I would be contemptuous."

The woman moved toward the door. "You aren't preaching at me now, are you?" she asked with her hand on the knob. Nelson mumbled an apology, and the woman obliged him with a few minutes of small talk. Then she left him alone with his sixty cents, his empty bottle, and his view of the Foshay Tower.

Nelson contacted his sister Irene in New York after that conversation and asked her to wire money so he could leave Minneapolis. He paid his debts when it arrived, and returned to Chicago. Then he hunkered down at home.

He left town again in the spring to search for work, and headed south—through southern Illinois and Kentucky, then farther.

This time, he traveled mostly by train. When he needed a ride, he found a freight yard, hid just beyond its boundary line, and scrutinized every train that approached. When he spotted one moving slowly and pulling empty boxcars or uncovered gondolas, he emerged from his hiding place and started jogging. He adjusted his pace to match the train's, and when he pulled even with something he could grasp—a ladder, or a handhold near an open door—he grabbed it, leapt, and allowed the train to pull him into the air as it galloped down the tracks.

It was a perilous way to travel. When the railroad police, known to everyone as "bulls," spotted free riders, they arrested them, or worse. Some riders claimed they had witnessed killings, or been beaten severely—and the trains were lethal in their own right. Men sometimes leapt into hopper cars without looking, slid down a sloping inside wall, fell through an open hatch at the bottom, and landed on the rail ties beneath the moving train. If a rider closed the top of a tank car they were hiding inside and sealed themselves in, they were likely to starve. And boarding was dangerous as well. It was easy to stumble while running alongside a train and fall beneath the wheels. Once, Nelson saw a man lying near the tracks and bleeding to death after being mangled that way.

There were two million people on the road that year, chasing the promise of work or fleeing chaos, and before long Nelson was anonymous among them—a shadow flitting through the trees at the edge of the road, a hint of menace sleeping in the weeds on the outskirts of town. He traveled by night to avoid being arrested for vagrancy, begged, and stood in line at relief missions to wait for his turn to shower, eat putrid meat, and drink weak coffee.

Weeks passed, and then months. Pounds melted off Nelson's thin frame, and his suit became threadbare. His Press Association card tattered around the edges, and his expectations withered. He rolled through Tennessee without finding work, and then Virginia. He passed through North Carolina, headed toward the Atlantic coast, then caught a ride on the South Pacific line outside Greenville and jogged south—through South Carolina, Georgia, Alabama, and Mississippi, and then into Louisiana.

Nelson's train pulled into New Orleans early one morning in August, and he hopped off near the Mississippi River and walked along its bank until he reached the French Market on North Peters Street. Vendors were raising their curtains for the day when he arrived, stocking their shelves, and beginning to cook. He had a little money, maybe a nickel, so he went inside, bought a po' boy sandwich, and sat down. He spotted a man at work near where he was eating, and decided to watch him. The man was large, shirtless, and thickly muscled, and he was using a large knife to decapitate turtles—*thwunk . . . thwunk . . . thwunk*.

Nelson wandered after he ate. He walked through the city until he found a soup kitchen distributing chicory coffee and bananas, and then he lay down on a park bench and went to sleep.

Nelson had traveled at least three thousand miles since he began looking for work the year before, and the ambition that drove him after he graduated from college had diminished over their course. He no longer expected to become a journalist, and he made his plans for the future in units of hours and days instead of years. He wanted enough money to eat and rent a room, and he wasn't particular about how he earned it.

Not long after Nelson arrived in New Orleans, the Standard Coffee Service Company offered him a job selling delivery subscriptions door to door. He had never been in sales, and didn't like the idea of spending hours on his feet under the Louisiana sun, but he accepted anyway. It was the only work he could find.

Nelson's days began early. He was still sleeping on a park bench, so he woke when the sun rose. He tried to find some food, and then he walked to Magazine Street and waited for a truck from Standard Coffee to pull up. He climbed in the back when it arrived, along with a dozen other men, and then the driver ferried him to the neighborhood he had been assigned to canvass that day.

When the truck stopped, Nelson went to work. He climbed porch steps, his body dripping with sweat, and knocked on doors. Women usually answered, and when they did he held up a red tin percolator and began his pitch.

A coffeepot just like this one could be yours for free, he said. All you have to do is agree to buy your coffee from Standard.

He carried a stack of subscription forms, and when someone looked interested, he held one out for their signature. Speed was an important part of his sales strategy. If he allowed potential customers to deliberate, they were likely to realize that buying two pounds of coffee from Standard every week for six months would cost them more than a new coffeepot.

Nelson met the other salesmen on a street corner at the end of his shift, and when the Standard Coffee truck arrived, he handed his sales slips to the driver. He had been promised one dollar for every two the company received from the customers he signed up, but he rarely saw it. The drivers distributed the commissions, and they skimmed freely. Discontent was widespread among the crew, but no one complained too bitterly—a fraction of a commission was better than nothing.

One day, a man from the sales crew approached Nelson and asked if he needed a place to stay. He called himself Luther, and said he was renting a room on Camp Street for seven dollars a week. He had one roommate already, but there was space on the floor for another body and Nelson was welcome to it so long as he agreed to pay a third of the rent.

Luther was a pigeon-chested man who said he came from Florida. He wore cowboy hats, chain-smoked hand-rolled cigarettes, and had a sociopath's way with words. He dissembled mellifluously and was full of schemes that couldn't possibly fail.

Nelson accepted Luther's proposal and followed him back to Camp Street. That's when he met the other roommate—a rangy Texan with a steel plate in his skull. This man introduced himself as Luther as well, and told Nelson his head had been injured while he was fighting in World War I. It was not the most likely explanation. He had a violent temper, carried a gun, and had been to prison.

Luther, Luther, and Nelson Abraham were a bizarre trio—two Southerners in their late thirties or early forties, and a twenty-three-year-old secular Jew from Chicago. Poverty was the only thing they had in common, but for a time it was enough to bind them. They slept shoulder to shoulder in their tiny room. They shared meals, and Nelson declined to question either of his roommates about their names, or their past, to avoid confrontation. He was convinced that neither man was really named Luther, but didn't press the issue. He called the smooth talker from Florida "Luther Luther" to prevent confusion. The violent Texan was just "Luther."

One evening, Luther returned home with a stack of certificates the size of high school diplomas. They had been printed by a chain of beauty salons, and each one promised the bearer a free shampoo and a marcel wave. The fine print stipulated that "free" was a term of art. The five-dollar wave was really being offered for three fifty, as a promotion, but Luther said no one would notice that caveat. The way he figured it, the three of them could make their rent in a day if they distributed the certificates and collected tips as they went.

Nelson and Luther Luther agreed to the plan, and the next morning all three men left home together and began scouting for likely targets. They walked until they found a block of apartments that looked promising, and then they checked each building to see if there were phone lines running between it and the poles on the corner. When they found one with no connection, they approached.

Nelson selected doors at random and knocked. If a woman answered, he held up a certificate and congratulated her. He explained that he had been instructed to give away one free marcel wave on every block he visited that day. The salon that hired him was trying to develop its business, and she was her block's lucky recipient. If the woman looked at Nelson suspiciously, he urged her to call the salon. He knew she couldn't do so without going to the pay phone on the corner, but he played the innocent.

Almost every woman Nelson spoke to that day accepted the certificate and gave him the twenty-five-cent "courtesy charge" he asked for.

Nelson and the Luthers made ten dollars that day. They went out again the next morning, and by the evening they had ten more—a small fortune. A sandwich cost a nickel at the time, steak cost a quarter, and you could buy sex for a dollar in the city's red-light district.

They felt rich, so they doubled down. They worked their scheme a third time the following day, but by then their luck was gone. Nelson and Luther Luther did well, but Luther did not. He returned to the room on Camp Street at the end of the day looking like tenderized meat. He had been jumped by a group of men whose wives had been scammed by the trio earlier in the week, and beaten severely.

N elson and the Luthers left New Orleans the next morning in Luther Luther's car—a 1928 Studebaker with running boards, a boxy top, and bug-eye headlights. They had no destination in mind.

They went north first—past Baton Rouge and Alexandria, Natchitoches and Shreveport. They entered Texas after three hundred miles, and pulled into a boomtown called Gladewater, where oil rigs encircled Main Street like mechanical giants closing in for a kill. Nelson asked for work, but he was turned away.

Then they went south—past Houston, Corpus Christi, and Baffin Bay. The landscape emptied as they drove, and the air became heavy with moisture blowing off the Gulf of Mexico. Eventually, they entered the floodplain speculators had begun calling Magic Valley, saw thousands of trees dripping with brightly colored fruit lined up neatly on both sides of the road, and decided to stop.

They rented a cabin using Nelson's wristwatch as collateral, and found a grapefruit orchard that needed pickers. Then they went to work—climbing ladders, pulling ripe fruit from sagging limbs and placing it in bags, descending to the ground, and then sprinting to the next tree.

Nelson was soon covered with bruises, and scratches that festered in the damp heat, but he was grateful for the work despite its hardship. On a good day, he earned seventy-five cents.

Luther was not. He had no interest in laboring under the Texas sun for a starvation wage, so one afternoon he took out his pistol when the trio returned to their cabin. He told Nelson and Luther Luther that he had been watching the local convenience store, a Jitney Jungle, and thought it would be easy to rob. They had a car and a gun, and if they planned everything well, they could make it out of the valley before the police began chasing them.

Nelson and Luther Luther agreed, but they had no intention of following through. When Luther fell asleep that night, they snuck out of the cabin and drove away in the Studebaker. They raced south again, and didn't stop until they spotted an abandoned Sinclair station twenty miles north of the Mexican border. They were on a quiet stretch of highway between Rio Hondo and Harlingen when they pulled over, and there was no one around. There was a grapefruit orchard on one side of the road, abandoned and gone to seed, and a mesquite forest on the other. Lizards and snakes sunned themselves on stones and tree stumps, and buzzards circled in the sky.

Nelson and Luther Luther examined the station. The pumps were dry, but the building was intact. They peered through its windows to make sure no one was living inside, and then they drove to Harlingen to find out who owned it.

Benton Curtis, Nelson's childhood friend, never left Chicago. He continued to live with his parents after he graduated from high school, and when the Depression hit, he resigned himself to a long tenure. "Jobs were absolutely unavailable," he said. He and Nelson had only seen each other a few times since Nelson left for college, but they still enjoyed each other's company. They got together after Nelson returned from Urbana-Champaign at least twice, went dancing, and visited a speakeasy.

Those visits had been the only bright spots in an otherwise bleak year for Curtis, so he got excited when he received an envelope bearing a Texas return address, and Nelson's name.

There was a letter from Nelson inside, and a proposal.

I found an abandoned gas station on a "thoroughfare" in Texas, Nelson wrote. It's a Sinclair station, and the local agent says I can have it for nothing as long as I fill the tanks with his gas. We can run the station together if you come down here. The building needs work, but it's livable, and gas is cheap. If you can provide some cash, we can open the station as soon as our gas arrives. You should come; after all, "you've got nothing better to do."

Curtis wrote back and said he liked the idea of running a gas station in Texas. Then he bought a bus ticket.

Nelson met Curtis in Harlingen when he arrived. They caught up, and then they visited the local Sinclair agent. Curtis had twenty dollars with him, and he used fifteen to buy about 150 gallons of gas. The agent promised to have it delivered soon.

Nelson wanted to go to the station then, but Curtis was hungry.

I still have five dollars, he said. Let's get something to eat.

Nelson recoiled. "Don't ever show me that money and don't ever show anybody that," he snapped. "If anyone ever discovers you have any money, they'll kill you for it."

Nelson's reaction worried Curtis, but he didn't understand the depth of his predicament until he saw the station. That's when he realized that the "thoroughfare" Nelson mentioned in his letter was really a sleepy road stretching between two poor, sleepy towns. And the money-making opportunity he'd spoken of was really a chance to sleep in an unheated garage and sell gas for two cents more per gallon than it cost to purchase.

Curtis realized Nelson's plan was ill-fated when he arrived, but he stayed anyway, and soon he and Nelson slipped into a daily routine the way they had when they became friends in Albany Park.

They took turns lugging a five-gallon jug to a nearby creek to collect drinking water each morning, and then they sat in the station's shadow to avoid the Texas sun and waited for customers. There was a red-lettered sign that read SINCLAIR—SE HABLA ESPAÑOL—SINCLAIR above their heads, and a Spanish–English dictionary rested on the ground by their feet. They staved off boredom by reading out-of-date newspapers, and occasionally they sold some gas—two gallons on an average day, three when they were lucky.

They bunked down near each other inside the station each night, and slept lightly. That was the only time they saw Luther Luther. He spent his days puttering up and down the valley in the Studebaker, burning gas. He returned after dark each night and claimed a cot, but never seemed to sleep. Curtis often woke several times before dawn, and every time he opened his eyes he saw Luther Luther chain-smoking in silence across the room—his body obscured by shadow, but his face lit by the crimson glow of the cherry burning at the tip of his cigarette.

Luther Luther approached Curtis and Nelson with a plan a few weeks after they got the station running. He had been spending his days making arrangements with local farmers, he said, and several of them had agreed to give him black-eyed peas on consignment. In exchange, he had agreed to shell them, package them, sell them to stores, and pass on a share of the profits.

There was a fortune to be made in black-eyed peas, Luther Luther said, and if Nelson and Curtis wanted a piece of it, they could supply the labor. If they did the shelling and packaging, he said, they were welcome to eat as many of the beans as they wanted. They would get paid as well, when money started coming in.

Nelson and Curtis had been eating nothing but raw tomatoes for some time, so they agreed and went to work. They spent the next several days shelling beans and pouring them into Mason jars. They sealed the jars when they were full, stacked them neatly, grabbed an empty jar, and then repeated the process. They kept at their task until they ran out of beans one day and Luther Luther failed to return with a fresh load.

That night, Nelson and Curtis heard an unfamiliar sound and got out of their cots. It seemed to be coming from the pumps, but it was too dark to tell. Nelson called out, but heard no reply, so he and Curtis closed the station door and went back to sleep.

They realized what had happened the next morning. Luther Luther had returned in the dark, siphoned off as much gas as the Studebaker's tank would hold, and driven away. He was not coming back. He had been selling the black-eyed peas at a ridiculously low price to ensure they sold quickly, and pocketing all of the money. He hadn't been paying the farmers, and when they began looking for him, he ran off.*

"We're known to be with him," Nelson said. We need to leave. If we don't, "we'll wake up with a knife in our backs."

Curtis agreed and returned to Chicago, but Nelson remained on the road.

Nelson followed the freight lines north and west after leaving the station, and began to write long, winding letters about his time on the road. It was a form of catharsis. He wrote about sleeping outside, going hungry, all the prostitutes he saw working the streets in New Orleans, the Luthers, the beauty parlor racket, the Sinclair station, and the black-eyed peas. "I gave the whole Confederacy hell" in those letters, he said.

---

* A note for Algren fans: If you think the version of events presented here contradicts one you have read in the past, you are correct. Nelson discussed these events in "So Help Me," "The Last Carousel," the introduction to the 1965 edition of *Somebody in Boots*, and "The Art of Fiction No. 11" published in *Paris Review*—as well as *Conversations with Nelson Algren*, *Nelson Algren* by Martha Heasley Cox and Wayne Chatterton, and unpublished writings held in his archive. He altered his account of the time he spent on the road during the Great Depression each time he told it—often drastically—so this account does not align perfectly with any of its antecedents. I composed it by checking Algren's writings and interviews against the historical and archival record, comparing them to an interview with Benton Curtis, and then creating the most reliable composite possible. In some cases, obviously, Nelson is the only possible source. I rely on him in those instances, but omit contradictory details. For instance: in one account, Nelson claimed that black butterflies descended on the Sinclair station. Elsewhere, he said they were white. Those accounts can't be reconciled, so I (reluctantly) left the butterflies out. Also, when Curtis's version of events contradicts Nelson's, I defer to Curtis. As it happens, Nelson never acknowledged that Curtis traveled to Texas.

And as Nelson wrote, he drifted toward home.

In La Feria, Texas, a traveling carnival hired Nelson to be a shill. It was his job to linger by a crooked roulette wheel and lure suckers by pretending to win and broadcasting his triumphs. He was paid in hot dogs, and when he spotted an opportunity, he ran away with some of the carnival's money and hopped a train.

In El Paso, Nelson played craps with the cash he stole, and went bust. The police arrested him for vagrancy, and he spent a few days in jail. When he was released, he continued moving north, and by December he had made it as far as Oklahoma—seven hundred miles from the gas station outside Rio Hondo where he started running, but still seven hundred miles from home. "I remember going through Tulsa around the first of the year and it was cold," he said later. "It was snowing. I remember eating at a kind of home—I don't think it was a Salvation Army home . . . but a smaller outfit—Army Veterans' God's Blessing Station, or something like that. I remember. I remember it must have been around Christmas and that it was awful cold."

"So Help Me"

(February 1933—January 26, 1934)

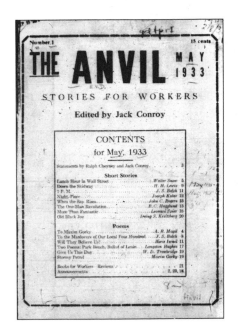

The first issue of Jack Conroy's magazine, The Anvil,
published in May 1933.

The only things Nelson possessed when he returned to Chicago were the story of his time on the road and a consuming desire to tell it. He witnessed "thousands of little scenes" during his travels, and when he moved back into his parents' house, those moments "piled up into something" that made him "not just want to write," he said, "but to really say it."

The urge Nelson felt was creative—but evangelistic too. He had been raised to believe America was a place where men like him could earn degrees, find steady jobs, and buy homes using loans at reasonable rates. But by the winter of 1933, he had become convinced the meritocratic ideal was a fraud, that everyone who placed their faith in it had been fooled, and that he was obliged to reveal that deception. "Everything I'd been told was wrong," he said. "... I'd been assured that it was a strive-and-succeed world ... But this was not what America was. America was not socialized and I resented very deeply that I'd been lied to."

Nelson had decided the American archetype was not a man who reports to work at a family-owned newspaper for twenty years and then enjoys a comfortable retirement—it was the teenager he met along the Southern Railroad, begging for soap. The youth had an outfielder's mitt attached to the waist of his pants, and a contract in his pocket promising him a position with the Tallahassee Grays. The league he expected to play in had been disbanded, but no one had told the boy. He would learn when he reached Florida, but until then he carried himself with a threadbare sort of pride.

And if that boy wasn't America, then it was a woman sitting "before a whiskey glass with a false bottom" and pleading for her dignity in the same breath she used to offer her company. "Don't get the wrong idea, Mister. I'm no whoo-er," she insisted. "But at the moment I don't have a place to sleep."

It was "the tens of thousands of Americans literally milling around ... trying to survive," Nelson said, and "all the whores in New Orleans." It was four hungry people "sitting around a little kitchen" holding empty bowls, waiting to receive thin soup that was being ladled from a common pot. They saw that there was only one piece of ham floating in the broth, and every one of them prayed the other three would go hungry. It was the boy Nelson saw fall beneath the wheels of a moving train—and a gaunt man chain-smoking through black Texas nights while plotting against his bunkmates.

Nelson had never read a story or a book that described the America he had experienced over the past year and a half, so he felt compelled to commit his stories to the page. The problem he had to confront was how. He could write, but didn't know anyone else who could, and had no idea where to send his work. He didn't even own a typewriter.

The advertisement appeared in a small magazine, maybe the *Saturday Review of Literature*, and Nelson read it eagerly.

The Writers' Circle is looking for new members, it said, and anyone interested should bring their work to the Jewish People's Institute in Lawndale and ask for Murray Gitlin.

Nelson boarded a Kedzie Avenue trolley car one day that winter, rode it eight miles south, and then walked west until he arrived at a sturdy four-story building clad in tan bricks. He went inside, found Murray Gitlin's office, and addressed him deferentially.

I would like to join your group, he said.

Gitlin was a kind, avuncular man. The Writers' Circle was a sideline for him. He earned his living as a social worker at the institute, but he took both roles seriously. He wrote seriously too. He had just completed a play called *There Are 87 Million*, and a few years later his work would appear in *Scribner's* and *Esquire*.

Gitlin listened to Nelson and thought, This is a nice young man. I like him. "Well," he said, "let me see some of your things."

Nelson produced one of the letters he had written after the fiasco at the gas station in Texas. Gitlin read while Nelson waited, and was impressed. He thought Nelson had a natural talent for composition and a keen ear for dialogue.

"You don't need my help," Gitlin said when he finished the letter. "You're a writer already, just go do it." You should turn this letter into a story and begin submitting it, he said. "If one magazine turns it down just go to another one, that's all there is to it."

Nelson appreciated the encouragement, but eventually confessed that he needed more tangible help. He had nowhere to write, and no typewriter, so Gitlin found an unused room at the institute and told Nelson he could come and go as he pleased.

Afterward, the two men barely spoke. Sometimes, Nelson dropped by Gitlin's office to say hello, but mostly he kept to himself and worked.

Nelson wrote four stories that winter, and the best was based on a letter he composed after leaving the Sinclair station in Texas. It began as a faithful account of events, but transformed into a work of fiction as Nelson revised. He made Luther Luther the story's protagonist, renamed his own fictional counterpart "the Jew kid," and wrote himself into a supporting role. He brought Luther's plan to rob the Jitney Jungle to the foreground, and then imagined what would have happened if he and Luther Luther had participated. The robbery gets botched in the fictional version, the trio flees in a Chrysler they carjacked, and the police chase them into an orange grove. They hide there, and then they board a train. Eventually, one of the Luthers shoots the "Jew kid" with a sawed-off shotgun.

Nelson's decision to have his antagonist narrate the story of his time in the South was an inspired choice. It transformed a self-pitying account of unemployment and homelessness into the portrait of a man who has abandoned any hope of conventional success. And it allowed Nelson to use Luther Luther's sociopathic perspective to communicate the corrosive effect poverty has on morality without preaching to his readers or condescending to his characters.

"A dollar woman come by and give us the eye . . . ," Nelson wrote. "We all three of us went down to the Mex bootlegger an' give him three bucks for the long cut short." And "the moonlight was on his face like I seen it on the dead faces at Cantigny."

Nelson's story was a gorgeous, plotless thing when he finished revising—a study of atmosphere and character written in a voice with no literary precedent. Luther Luther is the only person who speaks. He has been arrested for robbing the Jitney Jungle and killing the "Jew kid," and the story's narrative is the self-serving version of events he offers to his attorney. His account begins with this rangy sentence and continues in the same vein for twelve pages.

> Now perhaps you will think that I am just lying to you and maybe you will even think that Fort really wanted to get rid of the Jew kid so's we would oney have two ways to split instead of three, but you know, Mr. Breckenridge, guys like me can't never get away with bull like that to big-league lawyers like yourself, so you can just take my word for it Fort didn't really mean to hurt the Jew kid a-tall, and that's the truth so help me.

Nelson brought his story to Murray Gitlin when it was finished, and asked for feedback. Gitlin loved it. You should start submitting this around, he said, begin with *Story* magazine. Nelson gave his manuscript the title "So Help Me," and then he put a copy in the mail the way Gitlin suggested.*

While Nelson waited to hear back from *Story*, he read. The last time he'd studied literature seriously, he was a college freshman, and enamored with English writers like Byron and Chaucer. Now he was interested in orienting himself within the current scene, and discovering writers who had something to say about the Depression.

He found what he was looking for that spring when he bought the first issue of *The Anvil: Stories for Workers*—a twenty-four-page magazine that sold for fifteen cents. He opened its cover and found an editorial that promised the magazine would publish only "vital, vigorous material drawn from the farms, mines, mills, factories and offices of

---

* The letter this story was based on has been lost, unfortunately, as have all the others Nelson wrote while train hopping home from Texas.

America." Then he continued reading, and discovered stories by obscure figures named H. H. Lewis and Joseph Kalar and B. C. Hagglund that described unemployment, homelessness, and plowing fields.* The prose in them was chunky and turgid, but they excited Nelson because they were brash and confrontational.

"The hunger beast pounced upon me, chewed me up, digested the sweet juices of my egotism, and dumped me *down and out*, phew, to reek on the social veldt," Nelson read. And "Our throats were raw with cursing the world and our minds were sick with buffoonery and we ached painfully for a cold clean wind to come hurtling upon us like an invisible broom, sweeping out cobwebs of despair."

On page 15, Nelson read, "I saw millions of farmers forced to the last ditch, mortgage holders fighting them with a piece of paper and a sheriff, in the name of law and order," and then he set the magazine aside, composed a letter to its editor, and mailed it to:

Jack Conroy
Rural Route Four
Moberly, Mo.

Conroy was a tall, broad-chested man whose biography included everything that should be expected of the founder of a magazine like *The Anvil*. He had been raised near the coal mine his father worked and died in. He became an apprentice in a railroad shop when he was thirteen, stayed on the job for nine years, tried college, and then dropped out. He married a farmer's daughter named Gladys Kelly, had children, and went to work in an automobile factory. Then he resumed his education using correspondence courses, and transformed himself into a writer. By the time Nelson's letter reached him, he was about to com-

---

* These men were, respectively: a farmer, a mill worker, and a farmer who moonlighted as a publisher.

plete his first novel, and had already edited two previous magazines—
Unrest and *Rebel Poet*.

Nelson wrote to Conroy looking for a publisher, but he found
a mentor instead. Conroy didn't accept any of Nelson's stories, but
through their correspondence, and the material he published in *The
Anvil*, he introduced Nelson to the proletarian literature movement—
the milieu that defined the beginning of Nelson's career.

The proletarian writers were an idiosyncratic group. Herman Spector was one. He was a shipping clerk who bragged that he had never
been farther west than Tenth Avenue in Manhattan, and he used
verse to document his poverty and discontent. "I am the bastard in
the ragged suit," he wrote, "who spits, with bitterness and malice to
all." Josephine Herbst was another. She was raised in Iowa, spent time
with Ernest Hemingway in Europe, and wrote about the privations of
farm life. Another one of their number composed terse sentences like
this: "I was a little savage and lover of the street." His name was Mike
Gold, and he was famous for writing a best-selling bildungsroman
about life in a Lower East Side tenement called *Jews without Money*.
James T. Farrell was one of the youngest authors on the scene. He
recently made his mark with a novel called *Young Lonigan* that was set
just north of Nelson's childhood home in Chicago.

Spector, a high school dropout, wrote with the fiercely competitive
spirit of a man intent on wresting accolades from an ambivalent world.
Herbst devoted three novels to chronicling her family's economic
struggles and eventual ruin. Gold was proud that his book helped
"hundreds of thousands of people" understand "that not all Jews are
millionaire bankers." And Farrell said he wanted to document the life
of a "normal American boy of Irish-Catholic extraction" who lived
and was educated in "spiritual poverty."

There wasn't much connecting the motivations of the proletarian
writers, but they had a unifying goal: they wrote to broaden the scope
of American literature so that working-class characters could assume

prominent roles, and most understood that effort as part of a larger struggle. They believed their writing had the potential to change the world, and the Communist Party USA—the proletarian literature movement's greatest benefactor—encouraged them to embrace that possibility.

The party had been quick to understand the Depression's potential. They began organizing among the unemployed and within labor unions soon after the crash, but also invested in a cultural offensive. They opened the pages of their largest magazine, *New Masses*, to working-class writers, and funded a national arts organization called the John Reed Club—so named for an American journalist who witnessed the Russian Revolution, wrote about it, and then founded a Communist organization. They paid to create new proletarian magazines, supported independent projects like *The Anvil* by distributing them, and managed to buy a significant amount of influence among young, disaffected creative types.*

Authors are revered in the Soviet Union, the party said. The state pays them salaries and publishes their work. "Art is a class weapon," and authors are agents of history. Your lives are the proper focus of culture, they said. The Depression isn't your problem—capitalism is.

Nelson was attracted to the party's ideas, and its aggressive tactics. They had spilled blood the year before while fighting Adolph Hitler in Germany, and fought with the police in Chicago and forced the mayor to issue a moratorium on evictions. No other group could say the same, so Nelson joined the movement.

He began corresponding with members of the Communist Party that summer, and soon he was referring to himself as a "proletarian writer" and a "revolutionary artist." He said that America's slums had to be destroyed, and only a revolution could destroy them.

---

* Joining the Communist Party was a source of pride for writers at the time. Malcolm Cowley, then the literary editor of *The New Republic* and later a respected critic, remembered the party's appeal this way: "There was an enormous prestige at that time for people who belonged to the party. They were listened to as if they had received advice straight from God."

"I believed the world was changing," he said later, "and I wanted to help change it."

Story magazine accepted "So Help Me" in July 1934 and published it as their lead feature in August. Nelson's name appeared on the cover below Zora Neale Hurston's and above William Faulkner's. It was a bold way to arrive, and people noticed.

A few days after *Story* went on sale, Nelson received a letter from a New York publisher called the Vanguard Press. He opened it, and read: "We are interested in a novel on the basis of this piece in *Story* magazine." Then he left home. He grabbed an extra shirt, some notepads and pencils, and started walking. He found a spot along one of the highways that ran east from Chicago, stuck out his thumb, and got lucky. Two young guys with a bunch of extra bedding piled in the back seat of their car pulled over for him. They were headed for New York City by way of Niagara Falls, and told Nelson he could ride with them.

Nelson reached Manhattan on September 13. He looked at the return address on the letter he received from Vanguard—100 Fifth Avenue—and went looking for it. He found the building near Union Square Park, went inside, and said he wanted to speak to the person in charge.

He was twenty-four-years old, disheveled, and baggy-eyed. He had one published story to his credit—no appointment, no agent, no manuscript.

Vanguard's owner agreed to meet anyway. His name was James Henle, and he had been a journalist before he became a publisher. He signed muckrakers after taking over Vanguard, and championed the work of James T. Farrell. The press had published Karl Marx in the past, jeremiads like *People vs. Wall Street*, and a memoir called *I Am a Fugitive from a Georgia Chain Gang!* A scruffy kid from Chicago was a stretch for them, but not much of one.

Henle invited Nelson into his office and let him talk.

Someone from Vanguard sent me a letter, Nelson explained. And I'm here to answer. I don't have a book, but I want to write one.

Henle played along. What would you write about? he asked.

I spent last year on the road, Nelson said. I train hopped from Chicago to New Orleans, then spent time in Texas. If I write a book, it will be about drifting. I'll hop freight trains back to the Rio Grande Valley, sleep in hobo jungles, and write about what I see.

Henle liked the idea. The Depression was lumbering into its fourth year, but no one had written an account of the economic crisis like the one Nelson described.

I'll give you two hundred dollars to write that book, Henle said. Half in advance.*

Nelson agreed. He had never been paid so much.

What will it cost you to travel south and begin working? Henle asked.

Nelson considered the question. He calculated the price in his head and began to answer, but then checked himself. He figured it would cost less than three dollars, but he decided to set his price high so he could negotiate from a position of strength.

Ten dollars, Nelson said finally. It will cost me ten dollars to get to Texas and start writing. Then he watched in disbelief as Henle reached into his wallet and removed some cash.

Henle sat at his desk after paying Nelson, and typed up a letter identifying its bearer as a Vanguard Press author. He figured it would be an effective defense against a vagrancy charge. He gave Nelson the letter, wished him luck, and showed him the door.

Henle had a formal publishing contract typed up the next day and mailed it to Creston Avenue, in the Bronx, where Nelson was staying with his sister Irene. It read: "This letter will confirm the agreement we reached verbally yesterday afternoon. The Vanguard Press has advanced you $10.00 to finance you in writing your novel tentatively entitled THE GODS GATHER." Another thirty dollars will be issued

---

* That's a bit less than four thousand dollars in today's dollars.

when you sign this contract, thirty more will be sent to you in October, and a final installment will arrive in November. We expect you to send us everything you have written in December. "If we feel that we then want to publish your novel when completed, we are to advance you an additional hundred dollars." Your completed manuscript will be due "on or before March 15, 1934."

Nelson hopped a freight train after he signed his contract, headed for New Orleans along the Southern Pacific line, and began eavesdropping on the men riding with him. As his train rattled down the rails, Nelson transcribed their conversations on the pages of his notebook in script that peaks awkwardly, fades, and jots off the page.

"At the Mexican line eat at Two Joe's restaurant," he scrawled.

"For fools and the unfeeling this is all well enough."

"I did not deny drinking when asked by the Salvation Army."

Nelson's plan was simple. He was going to retrace the route he traveled the year before—New Orleans first, then west into the Rio Grande Valley. The boxcars he rode in and the towns his trains cut through would become the setting for his novel. Dialogue would flit to him on the wind as miles flew past. Characters would emerge fully realized. Scenes would appear. He figured the book would practically write itself, but that's not the way it worked out.

Nelson made it to New Orleans and caught a westbound train the way he planned, but then he stumbled. He headed toward the Magic Valley, but kept moving when he should have stopped—through the part of southern Texas he knew, then north until he reached El Paso a thousand miles later. He stopped there to reassess, and visited Ciudad Juárez to watch a bullfight because the border was so close.

A toreador fluttered his flag and slashed with his sword inside the arena. A drunken American yelled, "He'll toss 'em all. This the bes' ol' bull ever was in these parts." The crowd cheered, and the bull died a gory death.

Nelson was as lost when the carnage ended as he had been when it began, so he decided to fall back on what he knew. He returned to El Paso, hopped on a freight rolling east, and headed toward the setting of the novel he promised Henle. He didn't make it far. Railroad bulls stopped Nelson's train outside Sanderson, Texas, and walked the snaking line of its cars. They found him inside one, pulled him out, and left him by the side of the tracks.

Nelson was stranded then. He was in the high desert and it was early October. It would be cold when the sun set behind the hills encircling the town, so he started walking. He found US Route 90 and stuck out his thumb. He had been on the road for three weeks, and hadn't written a word. If he didn't complete a draft of his novel in two and a half months, he was at risk of losing his contract.

Someone spotted Nelson by the side of the road, pulled over, offered him a ride, drove eighty miles west, and dropped him off in a small city that had been built at the junction of two rail lines. The town was called Alpine. It had three thousand residents, one paved road, a department store, a barbershop, a hotel, two restaurants, and three churches—one Catholic, one Baptist, and one Methodist. There was a small college at the base of a hill on the east side of town.

Nelson decided to stay. He found a rundown ranch at 909 West Avenue that rented rooms to railroad workers, and approached the owner. Her name was Nettleton, and she promised Nelson a clean place to sleep and one hot meal a day for ten dollars a month.

Nelson agreed to her terms and paid her. Then he went to his room. There was a bed inside, a dresser, and a small desk. Light was provided by a bulb attached to a wire dangling from the wood ceiling.

Nelson unpacked his things: pads, pencils, one extra shirt. Then he began writing. First, he created a protagonist—a young, naïve boy from a poor, violent home in Texas. Then he conjured a world so bleak it reads more like an outer circle of hell than a human environment. Finally, he led his protagonist along a narrative path that closely tracks the one he followed himself the year before—away from home in search of work, in and out of relief missions and traumas, through New Orleans and Texas.

Nelson had adopted a dispassionate tone when he wrote "So Help Me," and his style was almost ethnographic—closely observed and free of judgment. But by the time he began *The Gods Gather*, he was a revolutionary endeavoring to expose capitalism as a violent and predacious system, and his methods were blunt and fervent. At the beginning of the book, Nelson's protagonist discovers a child's mangled body lying near some train tracks where they had been scavenging coal, and notices an eye hanging "by one long thin wet thread." Another character is decapitated by a train a few pages later, and then the protagonist, whose face had recently been slashed with a knife, and whose brother had been beaten bloody by their father, leaves home hoping to find safety outside of Texas—and fails.

"From city to city he went now; there was no standing still and there was no turning back," Nelson wrote. "No place to go, no place to rest. No time to be idling and nothing to do. He moved, moved, everything moved; men either kept moving or went to jail. . . .

"A summer passed, suns passed, clouds passed, rain fell; he begged, he cringed; he lived with a ragged throng."

Alpine was watching Nelson. The town was accustomed to drifters coming through on the trains, but they had never had one stay so long or adopt such odd habits. People saw Nelson walk through downtown carrying a stack of papers every morning, make his way to the campus of Sul Ross State Teachers College, disappear inside for hours, and then retrace his route in the evening and return to the Nettleton house.

Nelson had approached the school's president, asked for permission to use the typewriters on campus, and received it. To seal the deal, he flashed the letter Henle had given him, and afterward rumors spread. Students heard that the drifter hanging around campus was really a writer under contract with a New York publisher, and their curiosity was piqued. They watched Nelson more closely than anyone, and the more they scrutinized him, the more interesting he seemed—he rarely took breaks from writing, and wore the same pair of khaki pants every day. He bought tobacco and coffee in town, but ate sandwiches he scrounged from campus trash cans for lunch.

Eventually, a redhead named Paul Forchheimer found the courage to approach Nelson. He wanted to become a writer, so he went to the Nettleton house and knocked at the door. He was surprised when Nelson greeted him warmly and welcomed him inside.

Nelson and Forchheimer were only a few years apart in age, but a world of experience separated them. Forchheimer had lived in Alpine his entire life, and was in awe of his host. They spent a long time discussing life and literature the night they met. Nelson said writing had the power to change the world, and talked about the months he spent on the road and the role they played in his work. He explained that he was under pressure to finish his book so he could collect the rest of his advance, and said he wouldn't be in Alpine much longer.

Forchheimer returned later with friends, and soon Nelson had his first taste of fame. He offered his visitors tea when they came to the boardinghouse, and began meeting with them in a café downtown. He read some of his work to them, and spun yarns while they drank Coca-Cola and coffee. He claimed to be Theodore Dreiser's nephew, and said his work had appeared in "various eastern magazines." I've been a "truck driver, a dough-mixer, a hobo, a court-reporter, and a coffee salesman," he said. They believed every word.

Nelson was running out of money and time, and knew he wasn't going to finish his book by his December deadline. He had written maybe two hundred pages, but he didn't want to send them to Henle because they needed work. "I didn't have a novel," he said. "I had a heap of typing."

Nelson told Jack Conroy that he was heading north, and Conroy advised him to join the Chicago chapter of the John Reed Club so he would have somewhere to write when he arrived. Nelson thought it was a good idea, so he applied. He wrote a story about a man who lacks the courage to tell his wife he has been laid off, and gave it the title "American Diary." He wrote "submitted for adm. to club" in pencil at the top of the cover page when he finished his manuscript, and put the story in the mail.

Then he worked on his novel through the holidays.

The Sul Ross Writers' Club invited Nelson to speak on January 15, and he agreed. His rent was only paid through the end of the month, and it would be a nice way to say goodbye to Alpine.

The meeting was held in the home of a woman named Audrey Lewis, and fifteen people attended. Sandwiches, cookies, cocoa, and coffee were served. A reporter was on hand to cover the event.

Nelson had never given a speech before, but he acquitted himself with the confidence of a zealous convert. The title of his talk was "The Culture of the Proletariat," and he held forth like a man who had been immersed in his subject for years.

"The literature of the proletariat originated just prior to the World War, and has gradually gained recognition since that time," he said. Then he explained that every other form of literature—everything popular at the time—was trivial in comparison. When the history of American letters was written, he predicted, Jack Conroy's writing would be held in higher regard than Sinclair Lewis's, or any other contemporary.

Then he discussed style, and censorship. "If I'm writing a story about a railroad construction gang, and a man gets hit hard with a hammer," Nelson said, "he's not going to say, 'Goodness gracious.' He's going to say, 'Son of a bitch!'"

Nelson returned to his room after his speech, and a few days later he wrote a poem that begins "All night one night I heard your voice, my city." It was time for him to go home.

———

Nelson walked up the hill toward Sul Ross at about 6 p.m. on January 25. The sun had already set, and the school was closed. He walked through the building's south entrance and headed for the typing room. He tried the knob, but it wouldn't turn. Then he noticed an office. He gave the door a push, and it opened.

He sat down at a desk behind a typewriter and pecked out a few words. He felt nervous, shaky. He wasn't sure why he was there. He typed for about fifteen minutes, then stopped. He found the machine's dust cover and slipped it on. Then he opened a drawer and lifted the typewriter. He had intended to put it away, but instead he slipped it under his arm and carried it back to the Nettleton house.

Nelson packed the typewriter in a crate that night, brought it to Alpine's freight depot in the morning, and mailed it to his parents, charges reversed. Then he walked to the edge of town and waited for the train, which was scheduled to arrive at 10:15.

Nelson hopped aboard when it rumbled past and rode east—toward San Antonio, and eventually a ride north toward home. The freight took on water in Sanderson about an hour later, and Nelson hopped off and rolled a cigarette. He had a chill, so he leaned against a wall a few yards from the tracks, basked in the sun, and smoked.

He was the image of repose when the police spotted him. They were close by the time he noticed them, so he didn't bother running.

"Good morning," he said when they were within earshot.

They asked his name. He replied: Nelson Abraham.

The sheriff took Nelson into custody then, brought him back to Alpine, and delivered him to the Brewster County courthouse. The sheriff there told Nelson he was being charged with a felony, and before the day was over, Nelson had written and signed a full confession.

"I wanted a typewriter very bad because I am a writer by profession," he wrote. I need one but don't own one, and never have, so I took one from the college. "There is nothing that is more vital to my mere existence as a typewriter, it is the only means I have to earn a living."

"What Is a Carpenter without His Tools?"

(January 27–February 1934)

The Brewster County jail comprised four cells on the second floor of a red brick building, a common toilet that was flushed using a bucket, and thin vertical windows. The sheriff and his family lived in an apartment beneath the lockup. There was a porch outside their door, and chairs for sitting and entertaining. They left the inmates alone, and expected the same in return.

The jail provided no distractions, so each man inside killed time in his own way. A rodeo rider named Jess spent hours pacing and singing—*I kissed her and I named the day*, he crooned, *that I would marry sweet Kitty Wells.* He was a shrewd sociopath. He killed a Mexican man in Texas, and fled south before being arrested. Then he killed a Mexican woman in Mexico, recrossed the border, and turned himself in. He knew he would be punished less harshly for killing a Mexican in America than he would in Mexico.

A one-handed drifter spent his days bragging and bullying. He talked about his sexual conquests, and claimed to be the actor Art Acord's brother. They looked alike, so it wasn't the worst lie. When he had nothing else to do, the drifter thickened the callus on the stump where his hand had been. He used it like a pommel to bend tobacco tins, and he used it to fight. The inmates had devised their own set of rules, independent of the sheriff, and the drifter enforced them. "Every man must wash his face and hands before handling food," they said. "Any man found guilty of marking on the wall will be given 20 licks on rectum west."

Nelson wrote and drew. He sketched the cowboy and the drifter, and recorded the cowboy's song. He had been allowed to keep his notebook, and he used a page to write to Jack Conroy. "I'm on my way to Huntsville," he said.* He sent a letter to his family as well, but didn't tell them he had been arrested. Near the back of his pad, he began a note to James Henle, but never finished. "I've gotten myself into an unholy scrape down here," it said.

Weeks passed, but they felt like months. Prisoners watched trees sway in the wind outside their windows, studied clouds, and played checkers. When they saw someone approaching the building, they pressed their faces to the bars and hollered. Sometimes, they waved. "It was a big event if the sheriff brought in somebody, a federal prisoner, overnight," Nelson said. "Once they brought in a guy who had been shot—they shot him somewhere—he'd been shot in the back. We killed that day watching him die."

Paul Forchheimer, the Sul Ross student Nelson befriended, visited. He stood in the runaround between the stairs and the cells, looked through the bars, and thought, "I don't think there's anything worse than being in a jail in Alpine, Texas." He asked Nelson if he needed food, books, or money, and Nelson said, "No."

Nelson walked from the Brewster County Jail to the Brewster County Courthouse on February 21 and met his attorney. The man's name was Wigfall Van Sickle, and he was a southern gentleman of the old school—polite, verbose, and bearded. He was a lush as well, but no one in Alpine held it against him. Locals called him Judge to show their respect.

---

* Huntsville is a Texas prison.

Nelson's trial began that morning. He and Van Sickle took seats behind the defense table. C. R. Sutton, the judge, presided from the bench. Twelve male jurors sat in the box, and the gallery seats were filled. A local reporter had been assigned to cover the trial, and a Sul Ross professor brought his class. Paul Forchheimer was there.

There were five names on the docket for the day, so Sutton brought the court to order. Van Sickle entered Nelson's plea—not guilty—and the district attorney presented his case.

His name was Roy R. Priest, and his job was easy because the evidence favored him. He had a typed and signed confession, he had witnesses, and he had Nelson's reputation. Priest heard about the speech Nelson gave before his arrest—the one advocating profanity, and praising radical writers—and used it against him during the trial. Nelson Abraham is guilty, Priest told the jury, but he's no mere thief. He is a "militant, defiant man" who deserves to be punished harshly.

When Priest took his seat, Van Sickle rose.

The jury, the judge, the students in the gallery, and the reporter with the deadline waited to hear Nelson's defense, but it's hard to imagine Nelson following along. He knew what he had done, and thought he knew where he was headed. I'm on my way to hell, he told Conroy— he saw prison in his future. A chain gang. The end of a career that had never begun.

This man is an artist, Van Sickle began, "a youth with a mysterious brain," not a militant. He was "not stealing because of any criminal intent. In these troubled times of economic depression this man was stealing for the same reason Jean Valjean stole a loaf of bread," he said, "to survive."*

"You would not be hard on a carpenter or a craftsman if he stole the tools necessary to his livelihood. This man before you stole the means of work to earn his loaf of bread."

---

*   This reference is to the convict in Victor Hugo's classic, *Les Misérables*.

"What is a carpenter without his tools?" Van Sickle asked at one point. "What is a craftsman without his means and implements of work? What is a writer without the use of a typewriter?"

Van Sickle's speech gained momentum as it approached its conclusion, and Nelson, who entered the courtroom expecting conviction, must have been heartened by its eloquence.

"This young man claims to be a writer," Van Sickle told the jury. "Whether he is a good one or a poor one rests undiscovered in the lap of the future. Should he become famous in his chosen craft, there would be disgrace to Alpine and Brewster County to be known as the place which lodged in prison the novelist Abraham."

Van Sickle finished then, and rested.

Judge Sutton instructed the jury. "The defendant," he said, "stands charged by indictment with the offense of theft, to wit: the taking of one typewriter." If you find him guilty, the judge said, you may impose a penalty of "not less than two nor more than ten years."

The jurors didn't deliberate long because the court was scheduled for a second trial that afternoon. They filed back into the room as one, and then their foreman addressed the court.

His name was Cas Edwards. "We, the jury," he said, "find the defendant guilty as charged in the indictment and for his punishment a confinement in the penitentiary for a term of two years." Any hope that Van Sickle's eloquence might have inspired in Nelson must have died with those words, but before he could lament his fate, Edwards continued. "We further find that the defendant has never before been convicted of a felony in this state or in any other state, and recommend that the sentence be suspended during the good behavior of the defendant."

Nelson was confused, so he turned to Sutton for an explanation.

You're free to go, the judge explained. He said it wasn't necessary for Nelson to serve his time in Texas. He had to leave the state immediately, but if he returned to Alpine in two years and swore that he had not been in any trouble since his trial, they would consider his sentence complete.

Nelson was a felon, but he wasn't going to prison. He walked into the Texas afternoon alone then, and in the morning he went to Holland Avenue and waited by the tracks. A gondola car approached around 10 a.m., and Nelson grabbed onto it as it passed, and hoisted himself aboard.

Paul Forchheimer watched from the sidewalk. He waved, and Nelson waved back. The train rumbled away from Alpine into the high desert, and before he was out of earshot, Nelson yelled above the din of its passage.

"So long," he said. "I'm really leaving this time."

Somebody in Boots

(March 1934–April 1935)

An author photo taken to accompany the release of Nelson's first novel.

When Nelson returned from Texas, Gerson Abraham was sixty-six or sixty-seven years old—unemployed, and deeply depressed.

He had never been out of work, and he had no idea how to fill all the hours in a day. He had farmed his family's land in Indiana as a child and helped build the Columbian Exposition in 1893. He had worked for Otis Elevator, the Chicago Screw Company, Packard Motor Car, and Yellow Cab. He owned his own garage for fourteen years, and after the economy and his haplessness conspired to shut it down, he felt lost. He ate soup twice a day and read the newspaper. He taught his grandson how to box like the bare-knuckled fighters he'd faced in the ring as a young man, and when he saw his wife, Goldie, he flinched.

Time had distilled their relationship to its purest form by then. She was the gloved fist, and he was the heavy bag—when she swung, he swayed. "Get out of my sight," she hollered when she saw him. "You just get downstairs." And Gerson went. There was a rocking chair near the furnace in the basement, and a bottle of Rock and Rye, and sometimes he spent entire days down there, rocking and drinking, rocking and drinking.

Nelson couldn't write at home. It was painful to see his father so diminished, and the house was chaotic and tense. His sister Bernice and her husband, Morris, had moved down to the first floor so that Gerson could rent out the upstairs flat. They had recently had a daughter named Ruth, and their son, Robert, was five and precocious. He regularly agitated Goldie so much she beat him with the handle of a broom, and with Nelson's encouragement he had begun raising a fist during family meals and chanting, "Long live the proletarian revolution."

Nelson sent Jack Conroy a few stories and some verse he wrote in Texas, explained his plight, and asked for advice.

"You are going to turn out a good book," Conroy replied. "I am certainly glad to hear you are okay in Chicago." His first novel, *The Disinherited*, had just been released, and he promised to send a copy. He asked Nelson to promote it through word of mouth, and reminded him about the application he submitted when he was in Texas. "Ankle around to 1475 S Michigan Ave," he wrote, "and call on Bill Jordan of Left Front and the John Reed Club."*

* Some published chronologies date Nelson's membership with the John Reed Club to 1933, not 1934. The mistake is understandable. The letter quoted here—which definitively establishes his introduction to the club—is not held among Nelson's correspondence at his archive because he pasted it into a scrapbook that was placed in a box of uncatalogued material.

Nelson said he would, and one day in late winter, he followed through. The World's Fair had returned to Chicago, forty years after the Columbian Exposition lured Gerson to the city, and Nelson entered its shadow when he reached Michigan Avenue. One of the steel towers suspending the Sky Ride loomed sixty stories above him to the east, and a stadium, Soldier Field, sprawled at its base. The monolithic Hall of Science building sat like a sentry at rest in the distance, and a pair of oversized flags whiffled in front of the Swedish pavilion. The first Chicago Fair was dignified and austere—the White City. But the second was a riot of colorful buildings that spanned more than four hundred acres of land. It was shuttered for the winter, but some said it would bring enough money into Chicago to end the Depression when it reopened. Others said it already had.

Nelson entered a building just north of the rail bridge that crosses Michigan Avenue, climbed a dimly lit flight of stairs, and found a door bearing the words: THE CHICAGO JOHN REED CLUB. He entered and saw a large, dingy room encircled by benches. The floor was littered with cigarette butts and crumpled papers. Copies of *New Masses*, the country's largest proletarian magazine, were available, and so was a Soviet publication called *International Literature*. The walls were covered with murals, and they were as brash as the rest of the space was drab. One depicted working people—stern, powerful, idealized figures— dominating a huge metropolis. Another showed thousands marching behind red banners, their mouths open in screams or chants.[*]

The room filled to capacity most Saturdays for public events, and guest speakers took the stage. John Strachey, the British anti-fascist and future Secretary of State for War, spoke once. So did the sociologists Louis Wirth and Ernest Burgess. Maxwell Bodenheim, a bohemian novelist and former Chicago newspaperman, appeared as well.

---

[*] This description draws from Richard Wright's memoir *American Hunger*, and so does the description of club activities that follows.

He read some poetry while sipping from his flask, and stopped when he got too soused to stand.

Members filled the room on Tuesdays, and held meetings where they organized art exhibits and drafted political statements. A proletarian magazine called *Left Front* was edited on site, and sometimes people were recruited from the audience to join demonstrations or visit labor unions to advocate for revolutionary politics and art.

Meetings adjourned with a rendition of "The Internationale."

"Arise, ye prisoners of starvation!" members sang. "Arise, ye wretched of the earth! For justice thunders condemnation: A better world's in birth!"

The World's Fair was visible through the room's east-facing windows, and if club members were so inclined, they could gaze on the fairgrounds while they sang, and marvel at the power and ingenuity of the system they hoped to dismantle.

The Brewster County jail was Nelson's crucible. He entered the lockup a dispirited child who dabbled in radical ideas and indulged literary dreams, but he emerged a committed revolutionary—and like his father and his grandfather before him, he renamed himself to celebrate his transformation.*

Nelson introduced himself as Nelson Algren when he joined the John Reed Club—not Nelson Abraham, Swede, or Nelson ben Algren—and when people asked about his family or his past, he claimed to be an orphan. "I don't have any parents," he said. Most club members doubted Nelson's story, but they accepted him on his own terms and celebrated his membership. Jack Conroy's friend Bill Jordan read "So

---

* It's true that Nelson used the name Nelson Algren when "So Help Me" appeared in *Story* magazine, but he continued using Abraham afterward—that name appears on his Vanguard contract, and it's how he introduced himself in Texas. He didn't drop Abraham entirely until he was released from jail.

Help Me" during a meeting, and a short notice announcing Nelson's involvement with the club appeared in the May/June issue of *Left Front*.

People thought of Nelson as a mysterious figure, but he did little to nurture their curiosity. He was "shy, inarticulate, diffident" and "modest in outward expression," one member said. He had a "gangling, shuffling" way of walking, another remembered, and he chuckled about the world's ironies and contradictions under his breath. One perceptive woman suspected Nelson had suffered some kind of trauma, but she didn't take the matter to heart because, at the time, it seemed everyone had. We were all "on the verge of suicide," she said. "We had no jobs. We had no food."

Nelson stood out at the club for his talent as a writer and the depth of his political convictions. "He had a very conscious political orientation," someone said—he was a Communist, pro-Soviet—and he had unmitigated disdain for anyone who was not. Some club members said they intended to get rich by writing, not to foment a revolution, and in response, Nelson spread word that he had no respect for them. "Nelson was death on anyone who regarded literature in terms so impure," someone said.

Nelson hadn't made a close friend since he moved to Albany Park in 1923 and met the "brothers" he attended high school with, but he ended that lonely streak at the John Reed Club. Two young writers named Abraham Aaron and Richard Wright were soon his confidants.

Aaron was from a little town in Pennsylvania called North Butler, where his family owned a general store. There was a porch attached to the front of their shop, where customers—coal miners and steelworkers, mostly—ate, and talked. It would have been a bucolic scene if the family hadn't been so poor, or the area so homogeneous. The Aarons were the only Jews in town, and by the 1930s, locals had begun harassing their only daughter and painting swastikas on their windows in the night.

Aaron was an aloof and impassive character. He wore crisp shirts and well-pressed pants even when money was tight, and he spoke in confident tones. Some people thought he could be condescending, but his siblings felt he had earned the right to act superior. He had always been bright, and he worked hard to get an education. He hired on at a tire factory after high school, and then at Jones and Laughlin Steel. It took three years, but eventually he saved enough money to move to Illinois and begin attending the University of Chicago.

Chemistry was Aaron's major, but it couldn't hold his attention. He took on part-time jobs to cover the cost of tuition, and wrote fiction in his free time when he should have been studying. His characters were based on the miners and factory workers he'd met growing up in North Butler, but only because they were all he knew. "I was a proletarian writer without meaning to be," he said.

Aaron discovered an early copy of *The Anvil* in the university library, read it eagerly, and then wrote to Jack Conroy. When Conroy accepted one of his stories, Aaron dropped out of college so he would have more time to write, joined the John Reed Club, and picked up a copy of Karl Marx's *Das Kapital*.

"Nature does not produce on the one side owners of money or commodities, and on the other men possessing nothing but their own labour-power. This relation has no natural basis . . . ," he read. "[T]he labourer belongs to capital before he has sold himself to capital. His economic bondage is both brought about and concealed by the periodic sale of himself."

When Aaron finished reading Marx, he joined the Communist Party. He believed the workers' revolution was nigh, and wanted to establish himself on the right side of history. He planned to lash the bourgeoisie with his pen and send the masses flooding into the streets with his metaphors. But it didn't work out that way because the party had more use for him as a propagandist and foot soldier. They sent him to the stockyards to write profiles of the men who worked there, and sent him to South Chicago, where he squared off against the police during eviction protests—and he complied, but grudgingly.

Nelson resisted that kind of pressure, and Aaron admired him for that. Soon after they met, they began spending nights at a cafeteria called Pixley & Ehlers, where they debated politics and literature over bowls of baked beans and mugs of burnt coffee.

They shared a core set of beliefs, but disagreed about the relationship between art and ideology. Aaron wrote with a political purpose in mind that dictated the content of his stories—a "directive image," he called it. Nelson thought that was a mistake. If "you write something and it works and it's whole then it's a story," he said. He argued that the unadorned truth serves the revolutionary cause better than propaganda. "He wanted to depict what he saw as he saw it, let the chips fall as they may," Aaron said.

Aaron and Nelson each believed writing was the best chance they had to find meaning in their lives, and they bonded with Richard Wright over their common lack of prospects.

Wright was born on John Rucker's plantation, in Mississippi—the same piece of land his grandfather worked as a slave two generations earlier. His family relocated to Memphis when he was three, and things began falling apart soon afterward. His father stopped coming home, his mother went to work, and Wright and his brother Leon went unsupervised during the day. When he was five, Wright began venturing out alone. He wandered into a bar and cadged drinks, and went into the streets and begged. His mother told him to stop rambling—then she beat him, and prayed.

Wright finished eighth grade at the top of his class, but then dropped out of school and went to work. He was hired as a laborer, a porter in a clothing store, and then a messenger for an optical company. In 1927, he fled north and moved into a tenement apartment in Chicago with his aunt. Then he went back to work. He washed dishes in a diner, dug ditches, and cleaned animal cages for a medical center. When he had free time, he tried to write.

Wright met Aaron when they were both working for the post office as temporary clerks. Aaron invited Wright to his hotel room when he

learned they shared an interest in literature, and soon they were meeting there every week. Other writers came as well, and they stayed up
late, smoking, drinking, and eating latkes.

Wright followed Aaron to the John Reed Club in 1933. He was shy
when he first visited—quiet, round-faced, skeptical. "What on earth
of importance could transpire in so dingy a place?" he thought. He
wondered why the mostly white audience welcomed him, and he
never stopped. "In the end I had to admit that they were glad to have
me . . . ," he wrote. "But I still doubted their motives." Nevertheless,
he continued attending. There was no other integrated organization
in the city that would admit him, or entrust him with authority. He
became executive secretary of the Chicago chapter a few months after
he first attended, and then he joined the Communist Party.

Nelson and Wright became friends soon after they met, and then
became coeditors of *Left Front*.* They were poor, untried writers, trying to balance their politics and their art, and bound by their desire to
succeed. Eventually, they became two of the greatest authors who ever
emerged from Chicago, but at the time it wasn't clear either of them
would have a career.

N elson began dating a soft-spoken woman with dark hair, and by spring
he had moved himself into her apartment. It was a cynical arrangement
on both sides. The woman was engaged to marry a literature professor,
and she wanted a fling before taking her vows. Nelson needed a place to
work and access to a typewriter, and he was willing to pay for both with
self-esteem. His girlfriend said she enjoyed sleeping with him because
he was more sexually naïve than her fiancé, and he laughed it off.†

---

* Wright never mentioned Nelson in his memoirs by name, but in *American Hunger*
he refers to Nelson anonymously as "a writer who was to create some of the best
novels of his generation."
† This woman is one of the few true mysteries in Nelson's life. He never spoke
about her after 1935, and later, none of his friends could remember her name.

The girlfriend worked during the day, and while she was gone Nelson squatted in her apartment and wrestled with his novel. He revised the chapters he wrote in Texas and advanced his narrative, and as he did, the book became more autobiographical. He wrote the Brewster County jail into the story, and described it precisely. Then he sent his narrator to Chicago, and had him visit the World's Fair. He brought politics to the foreground, and meditated on race. His friendship with Richard Wright and the Communist Party's message about racial equality had affected him deeply, and their influence is evident in the text. He gave his white protagonist two black friends, and then had him marry a black woman.

As he worked, Nelson's method changed. He was no longer content to describe the predation he had seen on the road the way he had imagined he would when he pitched his novel to James Henle. Now he wanted to diagnose causes and suggest solutions as well, so he reframed the book's early chapters as the preamble to an argument for revolution, and inserted propagandistic phrases to make his intention clear.

Chicago is "trying with noise and flags to hide the corruption that private ownership had brought it," he wrote. And then he warned the wealthy: "Get all you can while yet you may. For the red day will come for your kind, be assured."

Nelson mailed his manuscript to New York in two installments—the first in June, the next in July. Then he waited.

Vanguard's response arrived quickly, but wasn't encouraging. James Henle sent Nelson's book to James Farrell when he received it and asked for a reader's report. He was the only other Chicago author on the publisher's list, so it was a reasonable but unfortunate decision. The two men corresponded about the novel, and then Farrell distilled their concerns into sixteen pages worth of feedback. Collectively, they took issue with everything from the book's title to its prose and ideas.

Nelson had submitted his manuscript as *Native Son*, a phrase lifted from a traditional song that begins:

The miners came in '49
The whores in '51
They jungled up in Texas
And begot the Native Son.

He thought it suited the novel's protagonist, and its setting, but Henle rejected it. A California politician was running for office as a "native son" of the state at the time, and he didn't want to confuse readers.

Henle and Farrell were even more critical of the book's racial politics. Henle thought it was a mistake for Nelson's protagonist to marry a "negress." Farrell agreed. He was a proletarian writer, but not a member of the Communist Party. He had started a riotous argument at the John Reed Club earlier that year by speaking in defense of Joseph Stalin's main political opponent, Leon Trotsky, and he associated Nelson with his antagonists. He thought the interracial marriage was just a way for Nelson to write "the Party line" into his book.

Nelson resented Vanguard's feedback, but he ceded to all of their demands. He needed the book to go to print, so he removed the interracial marriage, made the political rhetoric more subdued, and polished the prose.

Nelson's novel occupied him through the summer, and while he was distracted, the political scene shifted dramatically.

The Chicago John Reed Club hosted the Midwest Writers' Congress in August, and party members dominated the proceedings. They arrived with an agenda provided by the leadership in New York and Moscow, and *Left Front* was near the top. They argued that the magazine should be eliminated because it was a waste of resources. They said artists should be more focused on serving the revolution and less concerned with their careers. Writing and painting were fine, they said, but painters should be creating propaganda posters, and writers should focus on leaflets.

Richard Wright fought the proposal. He argued that culture was a necessary component of the class struggle, and that *Left Front* was an important part of the club's work. His objections made no difference, though, and when he realized he was going to lose the argument, he decided to end with a rhetorical jab.

If you kill the magazine, he asked, why not get rid of the John Reed Club entirely?

The party faithful gave Wright a tongue-lashing for his insolence and accused him of "defeatism." But the next month, at the Second National John Reed Club Congress, they did precisely what he suggested.

The club had twelve hundred members nationwide by then, but the party leadership had decided it no longer served the movement's interests. They were looking toward Hitler's rise in Germany with apprehension, and preparing for war. They needed organizers in America, and high-profile supporters—not unpublished bohemians—so they announced that the club was going to be dissolved, and that a new organization called the League of American Writers would replace it. The move was presented as a means of making writers more relevant to the cause, but it was imposed by fiat and most members resented the change.

Wright was devastated. "The club was my first contact with the modern world," he wrote later. "I had lived so utterly isolated a life that the club filled me with a need that could not be imagined by the white members." He tried to keep the club and *Left Front* going without the party's support, but couldn't raise the funds. Bills piled up, and rent came due. He lost the meeting space, and the magazine folded.

Nelson resubmitted his manuscript to Vanguard in November, and emerged from his seclusion. That's when he realized that there was no club for him to return to, no magazine to edit. He had no other obligations, so he directed all of his energy toward promoting his book. Vanguard entitled the novel *Somebody in Boots*, and scheduled its release for the third week of March 1935—four months after the manuscript was accepted, and within days of Nelson's twenty-sixth birthday. That didn't leave much time for promotion, but Nelson managed to place excerpts in *American Mercury*, *The Anvil*, *Calithump*, *Masses*, *Partisan Review*, the *Windsor Quarterly*, and *Sanctuary*.

The book's augury seemed bright, but then a troubling omen appeared. The *Windsor Quarterly* had accepted a section of the novel set in a jail cell and entitled "Thundermug." They slotted it into their winter issue and printed it, but the college that sponsored the publication seized the edition and destroyed it before it could be distributed. Then they printed a second run. Nelson's name is listed in the index of that version, but when readers turned to the page where his story was supposed to appear, they found only four words:

Censored by
Commonwealth College

A note at the end of the magazine explained the blank page. "Thundermug" was removed, it said, because it "violates ancient taboos"—a reference, presumably, to the story's description of sexual predation in the jail where it is set.

Commonwealth's censorship should have lowered Nelson's expectations for his novel, but it didn't. He began telling people he had written a sensation—a singular account of American poverty, and a piece of gospel truth that was bound to become a best seller. He was half right.

Somebody in Boots is the story of Cass McKay, a "sickly" semi-literate who was raised in a Texas shack without a mother. His father, Stuart "Stub" McKay, is a Bible-thumping teetotaler whose only passions are "fighting and hymning." His brother Bryan was disabled by gas while fighting at St. Mihiel during World War I, and his sister Nancy is feral. She lives in a "sloping windowless cavern" separated from the shack's common room by a strip of cheesecloth, and brawls in the streets. "She grew in light, unattended," Nelson wrote.

Poverty and ignorance define Cass's life. He's underfed, slouches badly, and doesn't attend school because his father won't allow him to be taught by a Mexican woman. His mind is plodding and inflexible, but occasionally something catches his eye and he has a spark of inspiration. "A sudden light would flash within his brain," Nelson wrote, "illuminating earth and sky." Those moments only sharpen the despair he feels for the balance of his days, though, because he is regularly confronted by gruesome images—the sight of a mangled body lying beside the freight tracks, Bryan tearing a cat's head off, or Stub beating Bryan until his features run "together like water."

Cass enters a trance after Bryan's beating and walks away from home with escape on his mind. He boards a boxcar when a train passes, and rides out of town perched on its roof. "He was going somewhere now where men were somehow less cruel," Nelson wrote.

Boots meanders along without a plot for 150 pages, and during that time Cass is more witness than protagonist—a camera turned toward Depression-era America and set to record. He goes to New Orleans and gets slashed by a knife, then returns home to find fires raging through town, nearly starves, goes back on the road, and becomes anonymous. He sells discarded newspapers in Brooklyn, sleeps on the street in Chicago, participates in a gang rape, and eats unidentifiable meat swimming in "diarrheal brown gravy" at a relief mission in San Antonio.

But then Cass gets arrested, and *Somebody in Boots* transforms into an extended examination of the constraints poverty imposes on character and morality. Freed, by his incarceration, from the need to feed himself and find shelter each night, Cass realizes he can decide what type of man he wants to become and begins experimenting with the archetypes available to him.*

---

* The jail that appears in *Boots* is, basically, the Brewster County jail. The layout is the same, and the characters in the novel are based on the people Nelson met there. The jail in *Boots* has "rules" just like Brewster County did, and they are nearly identical—an easy trick because Nelson stole the "Rules of the Court" posted in the Brewster County lockup before he was released.

First, Cass embraces nihilism, and criminality. In jail, he meets an inmate named Nubby O'Neill—a one-handed bigot who claims to hate black men so much his "left nut gets tight" when he sees one. O'Neill threatens to whip Cass for betraying his race when he learns Cass was arrested along with a black man he had befriended on the road. But Cass saves himself by betraying his friend, and becomes O'Neill's acolyte. "Why, ah *hates* them ugly black sonsabitches," he lies.

Cass and O'Neill are released from jail around the same time, and they meet in Chicago. They share a room in a flophouse, go dancing, and drink heavily. Then, when they run out of money, they break into a butcher shop. The burglary goes awry, and Cass runs off with the money he stole and goes into hiding.

Next, Cass tries love. He falls for a prostitute named Norah Egan, and they manage to build something approximating a life together. She teaches him to read, and her affection transforms him. "He realized now that heretofore he had been ill. He had been ill and he had not known. His head had been clogged with darkness, and now it was clear." The couple lives together for two blissful seasons, but their lives are always tenuous. Neither can find legitimate work, so they commit robberies as a team, and eventually Cass is arrested and sent to Cook County Jail.

When Cass is released, he can't find Norah. He's too scared to commit another robbery, so he goes to work for a burlesque called Hauser's Little Rialto Theater. Then he rents a single room and begins saving money so he'll be able to take care of Norah when they reunite.

Cass is a pitiful creature when he hires on at the theater. He has a sallow complexion, an unruly shock of ginger hair, and a Texas drawl that marks him as an outsider. But work has a positive effect on him, and over time he becomes healthier and more confident.

Cass spends his days pacing in front of the Little Rialto Theater wearing a red cardboard hat and carrying a blue megaphone. An endless trickle of pedestrians flows past, and he advertises the theater's offerings to them. It's a demeaning job, but he enjoys being useful and finds small pleasures in his daily tasks.

Occasionally, a speaker mounted above Cass's head comes to life and threatens to drown out his voice. The World's Fair is in town, and the mayor and the president each use the speaker to make announcements intended to boost attendance. "I am fully convinced that this exposition will aid in the strengthening of national morale," the president says.

Cass is neither intelligent nor curious, but even he feels insulted by the pablum coming out of the speaker, so he raises his voice to compete with the president's. "All she wears is sleeves an' two beads o' perspiration," he hollers. "She got the stuff that makes the young men old an' the old men young!" His protest is ineffectual, of course, but he finds it thrilling to yell at a more powerful man without fear of consequence.

The Little Rialto Theater is also where Cass meets Dill Doak—a shrewd showman, a reader, a revolutionary, and a black man who refuses to speak to white men "with servility." Doak begins walking Cass home after work, and talking to him about politics and world events. "To hell with humility, meekness—I believe in *fighting*," he says. He invites Cass to join him for a rally in Washington Park, and when Cass agrees, they recline on the grass together and watch men and women mount a stage to address a large interracial crowd.

"Ah've worked in sweat-shops since ah been twelve," one says. "Africa or America," another proclaims, "it doesn't matter where the Negro lives, he will be exploited."

Joining the Communist movement is Cass's last, and most promising, option. Among the paths available to him, becoming an activist and fighting to change the political system seems like the safest bet. He attends more rallies with Doak, and for a time it seems the movement will give him direction and purpose. But then the world imposes its will on him.

Nubby O'Neill reappears near the end of the book and beats Cass savagely for befriending "a nigger so black he looks like a raincloud comin' down the street." Then Norah returns, and rejects him. She has become a prostitute again, and no longer trusts any man. Cass begs her to take him back, but she shakes him off with the news that she's ill. "I'm sick, Red," she says. "Bad sick. You'd catch something from me."

Cass is as miserable when the book ends as he was when it began. He decides to rejoin Nubby, and they plan to leave Chicago together. "Ah reck'n ah'll take out o' this pesthole direc'ly," he tells himself. By then, all of his ambitions have died but one—he wants the words "Hell-Blazer" tattooed across his chest.

The purpose of *Boots* is clear only after the last of Cass's dignity is stripped away. The book is a self-consciously futile act of protest, not a celebration of the outlaw's life, a homily for the redemptive power of love, or a call to arms. It's Nelson's version of pacing the sidewalk with a blue megaphone in hand, trying to shout loudly enough to drown out the voices of the president and mayor.

This country is uncivilized, he says. The railroad tracks are lined with bodies. The American Dream is dead, and the World's Fair has as much chance of ending the Depression as a stripper has of reversing the aging process. The city is "a whore, selling a tin souvenir."

Nelson's mother never read *Somebody in Boots*, but she said it was a piece of trash. Other reviewers were kinder.

Jack Conroy praised the novel in *New Masses*, and the *New York Sun* called it a "powerful, disturbing book." The *Washington Post* said it had "narcotic beauty" and proclaimed it "an important social document and a frankly brutal mirror of our time and people." The *Washington Herald* said it should be "read, reread, and studied."

But the best notice was written by H. W. Boynton, and it appeared in the *New York Times*. He was turned off by McKay and the book's political content, but he accorded both a grudging sort of respect. "Like it or not, one must take this book as in many ways a book of the hour," he wrote.

Boynton found much more merit in Nelson's craft, and he was perceptive enough to see through the radical patina of his writing. "There is a creative impulse at work here that declines to be subdued," he wrote. "The book as a whole has the bitterness not of revolutionary zealotry but of disillusioned youth, of a sensitive soul which has visited the seventh circle of the damned and aches with a pity for the shapeless and hopeless creatures it has found there."

That review was a coup for Nelson, but it wasn't enough—he needed the book to sell, and it never did. Some readers thought it was too violent; others too sexual. Its political passages scared away the mainstream, but radicals felt Nelson didn't go far enough. The book suggests poverty and racism may have foreclosed any chance of a revolution in America, and that felt like betrayal to true believers.

Five hundred people bought *Boots*, then six, then seven hundred. Sixty more, then no one. It didn't even earn back its advance.

Nelson's friends began to worry about him when they learned about the book's sales. They knew how badly he needed money, and soon after *Boots* was released, they began to hear distressing rumors about his mental state. People said he was barely functioning, and Bill Jordan, the head of the John Reed Club, heard that Nelson had hiked into the woods alone and tried to get lost so he would starve to death.

Abe Aaron was visiting his family in Pennsylvania when he began to suspect something was wrong, and he wrote to Jack Conroy to express his concern. "Had a letter from the guy [Nelson] about two weeks ago," he wrote. "He's not feeling so hot; feels he hasn't done as good a job as he ought, I guess. He's a fine fellow. . . . [I]f you know him at all you know that he's damn serious about his work, and there aren't too many such. I hope he has some luck."

The Crack-Up

(April 1935–May 25, 1935)

New York City May Day parade, 1935. Though he is not pictured here, it seems Nelson joined this contingent of writers for a portion of the march. Photo by Ben Shahn, courtesy of the Harvard Art Museums/ Fogg Museum

Lawrence Lipton's phone rang at 3 a.m. in early April, and a woman's voice came through the line when he picked it up. She was upset.

"You don't know me," she said, "but I'm the girlfriend of Nelson Algren, and I've just come, just discovered, coming home, I find he has a gas pipe in his mouth." Nelson was barely conscious, she said, and babbling, "The only one, the only one, the only one." She wanted to take him to the hospital, but he wouldn't go. "I wanted to get in touch with his parents, but who knows who his parents are? Nobody, none of his friends seem to know he ever had any parents."

Nelson can't be left alone, she said. "I'm afraid that he'll, the minute I turn my back and walk out of the house, he'll do it again."

"He doesn't want anybody over. He says the only one he'll talk to is you."

The call was a surprise. Lipton had met Nelson but didn't know him—they had spoken once, maybe twice. Lipton was a gregarious man, though, a magnet for strays. He lived in a four-story building at 737 Rush Street on the Near North Side. It had been a boarding-house before he rented it, and not much changed when he took it over. Friends crashed when they felt like it, friends of friends dropped in, strangers slept off their binges. There were parties and readings every week, and a writers' group met there on Wednesdays. It was the kind of house people went to when they had nowhere else to go, so Lipton told Nelson's girlfriend to send him over.

"Put him in a cab," he said. "I'll pay for the cab."

Nelson arrived in a dark mood—still suicidal—and spent the morning telling Lipton his story. My book was stillborn, he said. The magazines I care about ignored it. Others reviewed it poorly. It isn't selling, and it isn't going to. I put too much of myself into it, and now I feel like a fool. My relationship is breaking up, and I can't make anything of my sex life.

When Nelson exhausted himself, Lipton offered him a place to sleep. They resumed their conversation the next day.

Lipton was a round-faced, bespectacled man who spoke with volume and force. He was about ten years older than Nelson, and thought of himself as many things—a writer, a guru, a muse, an amateur therapist. He had read Sigmund Freud, and felt he had a "good deal of knowledge" about psychology because he had been in analysis for years. He believed he could help Nelson, so he kept him talking—first for one night, then many more. He called it "therapy." He called himself a "healer."

A week passed, maybe two, and Nelson's depression deepened. He ruminated over the events of the last few years and tried to find some reason to feel hopeful about the future, but failed. He had applied for hundreds of jobs since he graduated from college, and been rejected by every one—he had slept outside and nearly frozen, traveled thousands of miles, gone hungry, and been incarcerated twice. Becoming an author had been his last hope, but he had failed at that as well.

Nelson's mood was labile. He was often sad, but he could become angry as well. Sometimes, he raged at Lipton, and other times he withdrew into himself.

When Nelson stopped speaking, Lipton conceded he was out of his depth and decided to find help. Nelson had claimed, when asked, that he had no family, but Lipton discovered that was a lie. He questioned some of their mutual friends, learned that Nelson's parents were alive, and then went to Troy Street and told Gerson and Goldie everything he knew—the girlfriend, the suicide attempt, the long-simmering rage.

"Your son has been living with me," he said. He needs your help.

Gerson and Goldie agreed to move Nelson back into their house, but they never had the chance. The following day, Lipton became convinced Nelson was going to attempt suicide again, and he brought him to a psychiatric hospital. The staff took Nelson into custody when he arrived, and locked him inside a padded room with barred windows.

Lipton watched, and then spoke to Nelson through the bars. His voice was pleading, regretful.

I'll get you into outpatient treatment, he swore. You only have to stay here for a little while.

Nelson just stared at the floor. The hospital released him three days later, and he returned to his parents' house and moved into his childhood bedroom. His girlfriend tried to visit, but Goldie called her "whore" and chased her away. Lipton stopped by as well, but Nelson refused to speak to him.

At the end of April, Nelson traveled to Manhattan to attend the First American Writers' Congress. He had been released from the hospital no more than a week earlier, and he was still unstable, but his attendance was expected and he didn't want to cancel.

After the John Reed Clubs were disbanded the year before, Nelson had agreed to sign an open letter calling for a congress to convene, and a new organization called the League of American Writers to be created. Jack Conroy signed too—so did Langston Hughes, Lincoln Steffens, Theodore Dreiser, and fifty-nine other "established" writers.

It began, "The capitalist system crumbles so rapidly before our eyes that, whereas ten years ago scarcely more than a handful of writers were sufficiently far-sighted and courageous to take a stand for proletarian revolution, today hundreds of poets, novelists, dramatists, critics, short story writers and journalists recognize the necessity of personally helping to accelerate the destruction of capitalism and the establishment of workers' government."

It took almost a year to organize the congress, but when it finally came together at the Mecca Temple on West Fifty-fifth Street, no one complained about the wait. Two hundred and sixteen writers from twenty-six states were arranged on the main stage when the proceedings began on April 26. Another 150 looked on from the floor, and an audience of four thousand sat beneath the arabesque tile mosaic covering the ceiling, and watched. The room was lit by chandeliers.

A German writer named Friedrich Wolf had been selected to speak first. When the appointed time arrived, he walked to the lectern and began.

I have traveled all the way from Europe, he said, because "we felt that in the capitalist world, the American writers are one of the most important outposts in the battle against war and fascism, determined as our comrade Anatole France said, 'to be the conscience of the world.'"

The congress should have been a vindication for Nelson—of his politics, his writing, and his choices since college—but he didn't feel that way. He was there, but not present.

Nelson sat on a panel with Jack Conroy and a young Midwestern writer named Meridel Le Sueur on the first day of sessions. The subject was the proletarian novel, the room was full, and Mike Gold, author of *Jews without Money*, was moderating. He began to introduce the speakers arranged on the stage, and while he spoke, Le Sueur looked at Nelson and thought, "He's going to vomit."

Nelson rose slowly when Gold finished, and moved toward center stage. He was shaking as he walked, and shaking when he reached the lectern. He looked at Gold, and Gold looked at him. The room was silent. Le Sueur thought Nelson was about to collapse, so she ran up and put a hand on him. Gold caught on. He put an arm around Nelson, and began prompting him with questions.

Nelson mumbled his responses. His voice was so low no one could hear him when he began, but it rose and steadied as he spoke. Sam Ross, a writer who knew Nelson from Chicago, was in the audience, and after a few minutes he could hear what Nelson was saying.

My book was a failure, Nelson said. Please, buy my book.

How embarrassing, Ross thought.

Eventually, Jack Conroy stepped in. He walked to the lectern, moved Nelson aside, pulled a speech out of his pocket, and began to read it without introducing himself.

The congress ended on April 28, and during the final plenary, Richard Wright spoke from the floor. The audience was mostly white, and he wanted them to know how isolated he felt as a black writer. How hurt he had been when the John Reed Clubs were shuttered. "You may not understand it. I don't think you can unless you feel it. You can understand the causes, and oppose them, but the human results are tragic in peculiar ways," he said. "Some of the more obvious results are lack of contact with other writers, a lack of personal culture, a tendency toward escape mechanisms of ingenious, insidious kinds."

The League of American Writers was officially founded after Wright finished, and Nelson was elected to its national council. As the congress closed, someone on the floor yelled, "Everything remains to be said. Everything remains to be done. Let us get to work." The audience responded with riotous applause, and when it died down, James Farrell spoke.

We should sing the "The Internationale," he said. So everyone did.

"Arise, ye prisoners of starvation!" they sang. "Arise, ye wretched of the earth!"

New York City hosted two May Day parades in 1935—one socialist, and one Communist. Nelson joined the Communists. He marched along Fifth Avenue from Madison Square Park to Thirty-second Street, then across town and down.

The crowd was pocked with banners. FIGHT AGAINST IMPERIALIST WAR, one said. EVERY ARTIST AN ORGANIZED ARTIST, another proclaimed. Sailors visiting from the Soviet Union marched in uniform. The Irish Workers Clubs carried shillelaghs and shouted "Free Tom Mooney and the Scottsboro Boys." And a two-story-tall papier-mâché giant carrying a massive copy of the *Daily Worker* coasted down the street on a float.

Nelson marched with a group of writers that included Conroy, Mike Gold, and James Farrell. They were walking behind a Harlem spiritual leader called the Reverend Major Jealous Divine, who was seated in a white limousine, flanked by young women banging tambourines, and someone in Nelson's group raised his fist and hollered, "We write for the working class." The atmosphere was festive, but Nelson was not. At one point, he spotted a writer named Jack Balch and glared at him. He looked "malevolent," Conroy said. Balch had made a comment at the congress that Nelson resented, and the year before, in Chicago, he called Nelson's writing "dark and gloomy." Nelson approached Balch at the march and said, "How does it feel to be a dirty rat, Jack?" The two never spoke again.

Richard Wright thought Nelson was losing his mind, so he went to James Farrell for help. Farrell agreed to see if there was anything he could do, and he met Nelson on May 5. They spent the day wandering the city, and as they walked, Nelson rambled. *Boots* was on his mind, the end of his relationship, the future. He ruminated on those subjects for hours, but they all seemed beside the point to Farrell. Whatever Nelson's problem is, he thought, it started years ago. It's deep seated.

That night, Farrell wrote in his diary, "A going almost insane." The next day, he made some calls. James Henle at Vanguard Press offered some money, and Elizabeth Ames, the director of the Yaddo artists' colony, offered Nelson a place to stay. Farrell's ex-wife Dorothy was working at the colony, so she could act as a caretaker.

Farrell put Nelson on a northbound train that afternoon. A Polish writer named Nathan Asch was also headed to the colony, and he served as an escort. Dorothy Farrell met the men at the Saratoga Springs station and drove them to a bar owned by the gangster Lucky Luciano. The three of them shared a drink, and then Dorothy delivered the men to Yaddo—a four-hundred-acre estate of manicured lawns, fountains, and gardens, organized around a mansion.

Nelson moved into a studio, and Dorothy brought him his meals. "He wasn't doing anything," she said later. "He was just alive."

Elizabeth Ames dictated a letter to James Farrell the day after Nelson arrived. "I have not had the chance to see young Algren," she said, "but Dorothy . . . seems satisfied that he will find himself at home, and probably get from Yaddo what you had hoped he might."

Ames set the letter aside when it was finished. She planned to mail it in the morning, but Nelson was gone before she did.

He tried to sneak away in the night, but Dorothy Farrell caught him. She begged him to stay, but he refused.

I got some bad news from home, he said. I have to leave. Then he walked out, made his way to Albany, and caught a bus to Chicago. He never returned to Yaddo.

Part II

THE
CHICAGO
SCHOOL

The 26-girl and the handsome drummer
Will be sleeping in separate beds come summer
The checkroom nifty has quit to knit lisle
The bouncer's bad eye will defer him a while—
So let's hear the *How Long Blues* once again,
Play it over and over while stirring your gin—

—"*How Long Blues*," Poetry *magazine,*

September 1941

Two Forlorn Children

(May 26–December 1935)

Amanda Leocadia Kontowicz had what was once called a "diffi-cult" childhood. Her father emigrated from Poland when he was an infant, grew up in Milwaukee, married young, and had children—a boy, and then, two years later, a girl. He was a striver of the classic American type, a factory worker who owned a plot of land where he planned to build his family a home when he could afford to. Then he went to work one day, joined some friends for a game of baseball on his lunch break, and was hit in the head. His head still hurt the next morning, and a month later he was dead.

Amanda was six months old when her father died, and afterward she lived with her mother, her older brother, and her maternal grand-mother. Her mother worked as a seamstress. Her grandmother spent her days reading the Bible.

Amanda's mother remarried thirteen years after her first husband died, and chose a drunk who moved the family to Chicago. Amanda was fourteen at the time, and lonesome. Her brother played in the street with other young boys, but never invited her to join them. She wasn't allowed to bring friends to the house, either, so words became her life. She bought the *New Republic* at department stores in the Loop, and read Conan Doyle and J. S. Fletcher at the library. Solitude wasn't a choice, but she owned it without shame and used it like a shield. I prefer being alone, she said. "I'm an observer."

Amanda's stepfather lost his job eventually, but kept his routine. He left the house each morning, drank the day away, and then returned home at night. The family's money didn't last.

When Amanda graduated from high school, she wore a white dress and posed for a photograph holding her diploma. Then she found a job, rented a room in a boardinghouse near the Biograph Theater, said goodbye to her mother, and dipped her toes into the adult world. She spent her wages on movie tickets and expensive clothes, and she began smoking heavily, drinking lightly, and dating widely.

Amanda was a beauty—dark, quiet, and mysterious—so she had no trouble attracting suitors. She had her first kiss when she was nineteen, and the following year she fell in love with a charming older man named Richard Leekley. He was married and had a child, but he lived alone and told Amanda he intended to get a divorce as soon as he could afford to. She believed him.

Amanda was attracted to Leekley mainly because he was a poet. Writers gathered in his apartment each week to discuss their work, and she often attended as well, to eavesdrop and play host. She met Richard Wright there, and babysat for Meridel Le Sueur. Late one night, she and Leekley went to the offices of *Poetry* magazine and slipped some of his verse under their door. When it was published a few months later, she felt very proud.

Amanda got pregnant in 1935, and Leekley pressured her to get an abortion. She did, but reluctantly. The relationship ended with the pregnancy, but Leekley wouldn't let it go. He said he would kill himself if Amanda left him, so she stayed—even when "I was attached to someone else," she reflected later. "I was alone."

Summer started early in Chicago that year. Amanda was working in a General Electric factory at the time, and by May it was an oven. A few of her coworkers collapsed from the heat, and she avoided their fate by wearing silk summer dresses and light shoes. She was a remarkable sight—an indomitable woman, blossoming as the city wilted—and Leekley knew it. He begged her not to leave him, took her on dates to regain her favor, and invited her to join him at the Workers' Center on Kedzie Avenue to hear a young writer named Nelson Algren read from his first novel.*

Amanda and Leekley arrived at Nelson's reading together on May 26. They chatted for a while, and then she drifted off with a friend and found a quiet spot where they could watch the room without being conspicuous. They heard Eugene Bechtold give a lecture entitled "Ten Years of Workers' Literature" and listened to a band.

The Workers' Center was crowded, but eventually Amanda and her friend spotted Nelson standing by himself near a table stacked with copies of *Somebody in Boots*. Rumors about his breakdown were swirling through the audience, but he seemed oblivious. He sold a few books, and signed a few—perked up when people spoke to him, and slumped when they walked away.

"Why," Amanda's friend asked, "would an attractive guy like that want to take his life?" Amanda said she didn't know. Then she added, "He has such a lost look in his eye."

Nelson walked out alone before the event ended and left an unsold copy of *Boots* sitting on a table. Amanda and Leekley noticed the book as they were leaving, and brought it home. Then Leekley got Nelson's number from a friend and called him.

I have your book, Leekley said. You should come get it.

When Nelson returned from Yaddo, Gerson and Goldie were living in a dank basement apartment on Kedzie Avenue and surviving on emer-

---

* Amanda claimed she first saw Nelson when he read from his novel at the John Reed Club in May 1935, but that is impossible—the JRCs had been closed for a year by then. I am confident she really saw him at the Workers' Center. The timing is right, and this is the only documented appearance Nelson made in relation to the publication of *Somebody in Boots*.

gency relief. Their house had been foreclosed on while he was away, and they were destitute—they had no business, no savings, no home.*

They had lost everything, and the weight of that fact had crushed Gerson. He had finally become the failure Goldie had always insisted he was, and his mind was not able to reconcile itself to that fact. After moving to Kedzie, he spent his days pacing and clutching a newspaper he never seemed to read. Like a boxer who has been hit so hard he saw black lights, it was clear he would never be the same. Sometimes when he thought no one could hear, he muttered to himself, "It's hard to die. It's hard to die."

Nelson moved in with his parents because he had nowhere else to go, but he avoided their apartment whenever possible. He visited friends that spring, read history books, looked for a job, and made his appearance at the Workers' Center. Then he received a call from Richard Leekley, and went to retrieve his misplaced copy of *Boots*.

When Nelson arrived at Leekley's apartment, he noticed a woman there. She had milky white skin, and dark, inquisitive eyes. She never spoke, but he could feel her watching him, and that piqued his interest.

Nelson left with his book, but called the apartment later and tried to reach the woman. When she didn't respond, he called again—and again.

Eventually, she replied. Leekley is out of town, she said. We can meet.

Amanda was twenty-three at the time and Nelson was twenty-six, but they courted like teenagers, furtively. They held hands on double-decker buses and visited the Lincoln Park Zoo. Amanda cracked jokes, and Nelson laughed. They spent warm nights walking along the shore of Lake Michigan, and Nelson made his confession in the small hours of the morning. He told Amanda about the crate he huddled inside as a

---

* A brief tragic aside—the Workers' Center was one street over from the home Nelson's family had just lost. It would have been possible for him to see his old backyard from the center's roof.

child when he needed to hide from Goldie, taking cold showers in college, and his time on the road.

My real name is Abraham, he told her. I'm Jewish, and I was recently released from a padded room.

Amanda listened, and thought: He was a lonely child, he still is, and he needs to be loved. Then she gave up her room at the boardinghouse, dumped Leekley, and stopped working.

That summer, Nelson and Amanda visited Gary, Indiana. They hitchhiked south from Chicago and reached the city in the dead of night. The sky was ink-black and starless, and Nelson played the gentleman. He led Amanda through empty streets, down paths, and through a bog.

Nelson's sister Bernice and her husband, Morris, owned a small cabin on the beach that they had purchased before the stock market crash. They spent summers there with their children, and that year they invited Nelson and Amanda to join them. The family shared meals most days, and then Nelson and Amanda wandered off. They sat on the sand dunes, read, chain-smoked, and went running in hiking boots. Nelson plinked the keys of Bernice's typewriter occasionally, and when he did, his young nephew became excited.

"Unk," Robert Joffe said, your next novel is "going to be a best seller."

"Yeah, right," Nelson replied.

Bernice and Morris returned to Chicago with their children when summer ended, but Nelson and Amanda stayed on in the cabin. Amanda strolled naked along the edge of the water when no one was watching, and Nelson tried to write. They ate pancakes for a week because there was a sack of flour in the cabin, and when they ran out of food, they hitchhiked back to Chicago. Nelson stole salami from Goldie, and Amanda's mother gave them potatoes and onions.

They lived in languor as paupers and felt content, but then winter approached and their idyll faded. They had decisions to make. The cabin wasn't insulated, and there were no jobs in Gary, so they left. They found a basement room in Chicago with a single narrow window high on a street-facing wall. The rent was six dollars a week and they paid it using Amanda's savings. Years earlier, her mother had given her one hundred dollars, and it was still in the bank. The money would cover their rent through the end of the year if they bought nothing else.

Nelson stole so that they could eat. He slipped into the street each morning around five thirty—before dawn, but after the milkman made his rounds—and filled his arms with bottles of milk and tomato juice that had been delivered to his neighbors. Amanda often woke to the sight of him standing over his haul, looking delighted. In those moments, she saw a man thinking, "You're trying to do me in, but look; I've got the better of you. So you've got a Depression. Well, OK, I'm going to get by anyhow."

Nelson finally found work at a gymnasium. It was his responsibility to hose sweat from the bodies of the gym's wealthy members when they finished exercising, and though it was a demeaning job, he was glad to have it. The unemployment rate was still north of twenty percent.

I "felt obliged to abandon further pursuit of literature as a means of subsistence," Nelson wrote later. But that didn't mean he wasn't writing. When he had energy after work, he lingered on street corners with a notepad, watched people, and started conversations with strangers. Then, when he went home, he created character sketches that are reminiscent of "So Help Me" and the time when he first thought he knew something about the world no one else did.

"Frank Mears turned south down Dearborn Street, and no face turned to follow," one begins. "He went into a tavern where music was, and he'd been drinking four straight days. He banged on a table till they threw him out, and he walked south down Dearborn. On Harrison he stood and swayed: a dollar was all he possessed, and he waved it like a flag."

Nelson was recovering at the end of 1935, but Amanda was struggling. She sank as he rose. A year earlier, she had had a job, money to spare, and a room of her own. Now she was living in a basement and drinking stolen milk. She needed to feel she was better than her circumstances, so she withdrew the last twenty-five dollars in her bank account, took it downtown, and bought a pair of suede oxfords.

Nelson was incredulous. They were unable to pay their rent in December and had to move as a result, but Amanda was not contrite. She displayed her oxfords proudly on the windowsill, and when she was feeling low she brought her nose close to the suede and took a deep breath.

Nelson and Amanda's next apartment was smaller and cheaper—a single room on the third floor of a narrow building on Ontario Street. It came with a bed and a chair, but no table. There was one window, a burner for heating food in the closet, and the bathroom was down the hall. The man living in the room next to theirs was an alcoholic whose floor was carpeted with cigarette butts that had been adhered in place by vomit, and the building's lower floors were occupied by male sex workers who leaned out their front windows to solicit passersby.

"We're here," they said in a singsong lilt, "and we're gay."

It was a bacchanal, Amanda said later, and Nelson loved it.

Nelson quit the gymnasium, became a laborer for a freight company, and wrote less and less each week. Amanda cleaned houses on occasion, but mostly she just sat home alone because they couldn't afford for her to do anything else. Once, Richard Wright visited and found them in a sorry state. They tried to be good hosts, but had little they could offer him. Amanda was embarrassed, and when Wright sensed her discomfort, he put her at ease with a joke. "Jeezus," he teased, "just like home, beans and spinach."

Nelson rarely drank, but he returned from work on Christmas Day with a bottle of liquor, a tree, and a gift for Amanda. They opened the bottle, poured, and toasted their first holiday. They laughed, and when their neighbor heard them through their shared wall, he rapped at the door with an empty cup. Nelson invited him inside, filled it, and then they drank to the end of a bleak and dispiriting year.

Trotskyists, Council Communists, and Mattickites

(January 1936–September 1937)

Nelson spent his days loading trucks in early 1936, and his afternoons wandering the city in search of people he could interview or eavesdrop on. He went home after dark, and tried to write while Amanda read. Sometimes, he perused the daily papers, looking for material he could use in his stories, but he was often disappointed because most of the news that spring and summer was news of war.

Left-wing political parties took power in Spain in March, and 150,000 of their supporters stormed Madrid, waving red flags in celebration. Hitler sent troops into the Rhineland in violation of a peace treaty, and Italy tried to snatch Ethiopia from Emperor Haile Selassie. When the League of Nations called for peace, Prime Minister Benito Mussolini—a bullet-headed fascist who called himself Il Duce—responded coolly. "Equality" between Italy and Ethiopia, he said, "does not exist in the Italian lexicon." The Italian Army crushed Selassie's at Maychew before the end of the month, and then followed the battle's survivors to Lake Ashenge and gassed them.

The German government announced that every German child was required to enroll in Nazi Youth organizations in April, and the following month, Emilio Mola began laying the groundwork for a fascist coup in Spain. In June, on German Day, fifty thousand people gathered in

Soldier Field in Chicago to watch children march behind swastika flags while giving stiff-armed Nazi salutes, and Spain was cleaved by civil war in July.

Nelson retreated from the world when he met Amanda, and he had been living a quiet life since. But he reforged his ties to the Communist Party when wars began breaking out. He marched in protest when Italy invaded Ethiopia, and again when the Spanish Civil War began. Then he and Richard Wright founded the Chicago chapter of the League of American Writers and used it to raise money for the fighters opposing the fascist coup.

When Nelson returned to the political fold, he discovered, again, that the landscape had shifted since he was last involved. Energy that had once gone into reversing evictions and marching to demand full employment was being directed instead toward Spain, and toward challenging fascists in America. The Communist Party was forging alliances with liberals and progressives, and proletarian literature was an afterthought. Leaflets and pamphlets hold the power to "strike a blow, hammer against the minds of the workers," Jack Conroy proclaimed in 1935. It was a powerful idea, but its shelf life was short—only a year later, it felt hopelessly naïve. Words could not save Madrid or keep Hitler from marching on Stalingrad, so the proletarian writers' movement lost momentum and coasted back toward the margins of the literary world.*

That last change was the most significant for Nelson. It liberated him. He had published in proletariat journals, and benefited from his connection to the John Reed Club, but his work never fit the genre—he wrote about the poor, not the working class—and his accommodations to the form were clumsy and insincere. Two sections of *Somebody in Boots* are introduced by quotations from the *Communist Manifesto*, and in one of his early short stories a character sings, *Rise up, workers,*

---

* Fifteen proletarian novels were published in the United States in 1935—in 1936, there were six, and in 1937, only five.

farmers / To battle! Those feints embarrassed him later, and when the party lost interest in literature, he accepted their disregard as a gift—from that point forward, he was a Communist at protests and political meetings, but he wrote on his own terms.

When Nelson wasn't working, organizing, or marching that spring, he was reading. His taste was omnivorous. He read and reread Dostoevsky, Aleksandr Kuprin, and Stephen Crane—and discovered new levels of meaning each time. He admired the way Dostoevsky claimed all of St. Petersburg as his subject, and was in awe of Kuprin's dedication to accuracy. Kuprin's most controversial novel was a detailed account of life inside a Russian brothel entitled *Yama*. The research took years, and Kuprin conducted it by living among the women he wrote about. Stephen Crane's novella *Maggie: A Girl of the Streets* also became a touchstone for Nelson. It's a brutal thing—as unsparing in its depiction of poverty as *Somebody in Boots*, but free of rhetoric. Crane paid to print the book himself because no publisher would touch the material, and Nelson admired him for that.

Nelson also read through the works of the generation of Chicago writers who preceded him, and drank in their mash of naturalistic observation and lyricism. Theodore Dreiser achieved something lasting with *Sister Carrie* because he was brave enough to write "without fear of public censure," Nelson thought. Carl Sandburg's poetry entranced him. It was so beautiful, it could reverse the natural order of things. *Stormy, husky, brawling / City of the Big Shoulders*, Sandburg wrote. *Laughing even as an ignorant fighter laughs who has never lost a battle.* And afterward, Chicago raced to become the place he described.

"Life is in ourselves and not in the external. To be a human being among human beings, and remain one forever, no matter what misfortunes befall, not to become depressed, and not to falter—this is what life is, herein lies its task," Dostoevsky wrote. Crane said, "Environment is a tremendous thing in the world and frequently shapes lives." The chasm between those positions echoes the conflict Nelson first wrestled with in college—Stoicism and personal responsibility to the right, the constraints of society to the left. Kuprin wrote to persuade. He hoped *Yama* would hasten the abolition of prostitution, a trade he described as "a worse evil than war or famine." Sandburg made no grand pronouncements.

Nelson decided the single thread connecting his literary heroes' work was perspective—each had discovered the truth about their society among the "born-to-be-doomed." That insight raised novel questions for Nelson, and he answered them, in time, using a vernacular of his own construction. Good writing comes from the gut, he began saying, and the greatest literary works open "a wedge for the inarticulate of the world."

How to write, Nelson began to think, is a less meaningful question than *why*. Literature must challenge authority and defy demagoguery, he decided. It is born in fidelity to the truth and crumbles into incoherence in its absence. The writer's job, he wrote, is to put down the "world of reality" by working "without haste, as the story grows within, regardless of all social and moral ideas, regardless of whom your report may please or offend, regardless of whether the critics stand up and cheer for a month or take hammer and tongs after you, or simply ignore you—regardless of all forms, of all institutions, of all set ways of conduct and thought. Regardless, chiefly, of what the writer himself prefers to believe, know, think or feel."

The emphasis of Nelson's work changed again that year. His first publications are largely autobiographical—"So Help Me" is the story of the Luthers; *Boots* is, loosely, the chronicle of his vagabondage, imprisonment, and politicization—but in 1936, Nelson began following Kuprin's lead by immersing himself in unfamiliar parts of the city.

"I was just going around Chicago," he said later—watching, listening, recording. Property owners demolished buildings by the hundreds to avoid paying taxes that year, and scab-kneed children played in debris-strewn lots. Squatters occupied condemned buildings along South State Street, and families slept in parks. The Illinois Workers Alliance marched on City Hall to demand jobs. A union leader was shotgunned in the street. Three women were beaten to death with hammers in their hotel rooms. A man walked into Humboldt Park, shot himself in the head, and had his pocket picked before his body cooled—and Nelson tried to absorb it all.

"I went to a Walkathon, one of these three-day, I mean everlasting dance marathons. I spent a couple days there," he said, and "started a whole series of stories about the cheap hotels on South State Street." He visited brothels and flophouses, walked through the parks, listened to barkers calling outside dime burlesques, and by summer he had formed the genesis of the idea that eventually defined his career: He was going to write a series of books that would provide an "accurate description of" the city. The first would be set in Chicago's Near Northwest Side, close to the neighborhood where Amanda was raised. Three more would follow.

He described his plan in a fellowship application a few years later:

> This project would attempt to relate the economy of a representative cultural pocket to incidence of delinquency therein. It would attempt presentation of economic and political factors making toward juvenile criminality among 300,000 Poles inhabiting a clearly-defined-geographic area. . . .
>
> Its presentation would be through the methods of naturalism, and its scope confined to a fictionalized portrayal of some forty-five case histories. . . .
>
> Volume two [will deal] with the Italian areas centering around Halsted and Taylor Streets, volume three with the Negro belt between 47th and 35th Streets, and the final volume with the Mexican section of East Chicago and Gary.

Nelson left his job at the shipping company a few weeks after he settled on the idea of writing a tetralogy, and signed up for emergency relief. His plan was to secure a job with the Illinois Writers' Project, and he knew they would only hire him if he was indigent.

The project was a make-work program created by the federal Works Progress Administration the year before. There was one in each state, and any writer who needed a job was guaranteed employment. Even "near writers" were welcome, and by the time Nelson was hired in September, it seemed every burned-out journalist and struggling novelist in Chicago was on staff. Richard Wright was working there, and so were Abe Aaron and Larry Lipton.

The project was housed in a converted warehouse at 433 East Erie Street, and its main room was large, undivided, and cacophonous. The sound of fingers tapping keys, phones ringing, and pens scratching across sheets of cheap paper stock combined to form a thrum of white noise that drifted toward the high ceiling and then returned as an echo. More than a hundred writers shared the room, and they were a motley crew. Some had never been employed. Others could boast illustrious careers and humiliating layoffs. Hacks who had managed to falsify a record of publications sat next to aspiring sociologists, and John Reed Club alumni and Communist Party organizers spent their work hours trying to form a union.

The writers' project had one main task—the creation of a travel guide for the state of Illinois—but its mandate was loose. The year before, the head of the Federal Writers' Project told the *New York Times* he wanted to give young writers "an education in the American scene," and in Illinois, his pronouncement was interpreted liberally. Project workers were assigned to collect oral histories, slave narratives, even recipes, and the savviest among them got themselves assigned to tasks they would have undertaken on their own. Richard Wright spent his time writing short stories, and essays about Chicago's Black Belt. Abe Aaron interviewed postal workers.

Nelson wasn't given the same leeway, at least not at the beginning. He was hired as a "field worker"—the lowest rung on the ladder—and his first assignment was a travel guide for Galena, a small city 160 miles west of Chicago. Local interviewers performed the research, and Nelson did the writing. It was grunt work, but he took it seriously. During his first months on the job, he wrote a sixty-seven-page narrative of Galena's history that doesn't contain a hint of the style he employed in his stories or his novel.

"Galena, nestling against steep hills in the quiet valley of the Galena River, is the oldest city of northern Illinois," he wrote. "It lies in the northwestern corner of Jo Daviess County six miles below the Illinois–Wisconsin line and four miles from the Mississippi. In 1826, while Chicago still was a swamp village, Galena was a bustling outpost swarming with miners, gamblers, traders, rivermen, and trappers."

There's irony to be found in the image of the young firebrand author of *Somebody in Boots* bent over a typewriter to turn out a bland account of a minor city he would never visit, but Nelson chose to ignore it. He saw the Writers' Project as a second chance—and felt heartened when he looked around at work and saw dozens of writers who had spent the grimmest years of the Great Depression feeling the "world was against them," blinking themselves out of a long, depressive slumber.

If it weren't for this place, Nelson thought, "The suicide rate would" be "much higher."

Nelson and Amanda were not getting along. For the first year of their relationship, they were so poor, survival was the best they could hope for. But then Amanda started working, Nelson was hired by the Writers' Project, the remainder of their lives unfurled into the distance, and they were forced to discuss the future. The conversation never ended well.

Amanda had specific ideas about where her life was headed. She had middle-class aspirations and wore them proudly. She wanted a house, nice clothes, children, and a husband who provided for her— the kind of man her father would have been if he hadn't died so young, or her stepfather could have been if he didn't drink.

Nelson's ideal life was a photo negative of Amanda's. His parents had spent their lives working, having children, buying homes, and starting businesses. But they had nothing to show for their decades of provident labor, not even tenderness, and Nelson wanted a different lifestyle. He intended to make writing his priority—and he wanted a partner, not a housewife. He insisted that he and Amanda share their domestic responsibilities, and offered to pay their rent and bills if she agreed to buy groceries and pay for her own clothes. He thought it was an equitable suggestion, but she was offended by it. "He refused to pay for anything," she said.

Nelson and Amanda each tried to wring a piece of the life they wanted from the other's stubbornness in early 1937, but mostly they tried in vain. They exchanged bitter looks across their single room, and their conversations became cool and impersonal. They shared a tiny bed without touching, and Nelson's absences became pronounced. He watched boxers maul each other beneath a cloud of cigarette smoke each week at the Marigold Gardens, visited White City when it hosted fights, and bet on horses at Maywood Park. He conducted interviews for his books whenever he found willing subjects, and he worked to raise support for the Spanish Republicans.

By then, the civil war in Spain had become an international conflict. Adolph Hitler was sending planes, tanks, and soldiers to fight alongside the Nationalists and stop "Communist barbarism." So was Benito Mussolini. The USSR and Mexico were backing the Republican government, and Nelson and Wright were raising money for their cause through the League of American Writers. The United States was neutral in the conflict, but hundreds of individuals, including friends of Wright's and Nelson's, had volunteered to fight in the International Brigades that were opposing the fascist coup. Oscar Hunter, a John Reed Club alumni, sailed for Spain and enlisted—and so did Oliver Law and Harry Haywood, members of the local Communist Party.[*]

Amanda was always home when Nelson drifted back to Ontario Street after a meeting, an interview, or a boxing match, and when he came in,

---

[*] Nelson claimed people were surprised that he didn't volunteer to fight in Spain. "My defense when asked why aren't you there was that I don't want to get killed," he said.

they chatted about the news or traded book recommendations. Neither of them was satisfied with the state of their relationship, but they weren't miserable either—there was something comforting about the predictability of the rhythm they had slipped into. They rarely kissed, and sex was unheard of, but they never fought or raised their voices either.

It would be a stretch to call the feeling they shared love, but they married anyway. Nelson took a few hours off work on March 1, 1937, and met Amanda at City Hall. He brought two dollars to pay for the marriage license, but no ring. A young prostitute he had been interviewing accompanied him and served as their witness. Amanda had never seen the woman before, and never saw her again.

Nelson didn't tell his parents about the ceremony, and Amanda didn't tell hers. He returned to work after the judge presiding over their union declared them man and wife, and she visited her mother. That night, she saw an old friend, and announced casually, "I got married today."

Friends flitted through the single room on Ontario Street in the spring to see the newlyweds, and even at its beginning, 1937 felt swollen with endings.

Abe Aaron visited, and brought the news that he was thinking about letting his Communist Party responsibilities slide so he could write more. He published under the pen name Tom Butler, but he wasn't publishing much. There was a long short story on his desk that wanted to become a novel, but never did because he had no time to work on it.

Richard Wright visited, too, and the three old friends read letters that Aaron's little brother Chester mailed from North Butler, Pennsylvania, and sent back edits. Good paragraph, they wrote. Move that sentence. You should be a writer, they told him.[*]

---

[*]   I should note that Chester Aaron took their advice. After a stint in World War II, he wrote a novel called *About Us* that was published in 1967 to rave reviews. Twenty-three more books followed.

Wright's visits were part of an extended goodbye. "Most of the young artists and writers with a tinge of talent flee this city as if it were on fire," he said the year before—and now it was his turn to join them. One of his stories, "Big Boy Leaves Home," had recently been selected for an anthology, and he was planning to use the attention it brought him to establish himself in New York City. He knew few people there, and had no job or apartment waiting, but he still believed moving east would improve his prospects.

Wright left Chicago on the last Friday in May with forty dollars in his pocket, and made it to New York just in time for the Second American Writers' Congress—a much different event than the one he attended two years earlier, and a sad coda to the idealistic and creative period that began when he, Aaron, and Nelson became close.

The congress was being held at Carnegie Hall that year, and the audience's mood was grim. Attendance was one-eighth what it had been the first time, and the Spanish Civil War, not the workers' revolution, was the main topic of conversation.

When the congress opened on June 4, a statement written by Albert Einstein was read aloud. Then portions of a film shot on the front lines of the fighting in Spain were screened, and Ernest Hemingway took the stage. He had just returned from the war, and the speech he had prepared was his first. He was thirty-six years old, and his wide Midwestern face looked too wholesome for his subject.

"Every time [the fascists] are beaten in the field they salvage that strange thing they call their honor by murdering civilians," he said. "If I described it, it would only make you vomit. It might make you hate. But we do not want hate. We want a reasoned understanding of the criminality of fascism and how it should be opposed. We must realize that these murders are the gestures of a bully, the great bully of fascism. There is only one way to quell a bully, and that is to thrash him."

Hemingway was trying to rouse the audience, but they were too scared to be inspired—most knew people who were fighting in Spain at the time, and some had already lost friends to the war. Other speakers followed Hemingway, but their message was so uniform the *Times* didn't distinguish between them. "Directly or by implication," the paper reported, "the speakers, themselves writers, exhorted their fellow craftsmen to join the 'fight against fascism' as a matter of self-preservation."

The single message of the congress was unity, but in the years that followed it was remembered instead as the moment when the literary establishment's long flirtation with the Communist Party soured.

On the final day of sessions, a group of writers interrupted a meeting to announce they were breaking with the party and siding with a dissident. We are "for Trotsky,"* they said. As they spoke, Joseph Stalin was dispatching his political rivals in Moscow. A trial at the beginning of the year had ended with thirteen executions—another was under way, and more were expected.[†]

The protest was a small thing—just six people standing up in a room—but it set the terms for a conflict that divided the Left for years. It was the moment when dreams about the glorious Soviet homeland and global revolution gave way to flat, calculated declarations about the need for discipline, compromise, and sacrifice.

News of the protest reached Chicago in a letter from Richard Wright, and its arrival fractured both the Writers' Project and the League of American Writers—the Stalinists in each group lined up on one side, everyone else lined up against them. "It was a quarrelsome situation," one local writer said.

Abe Aaron found Wright's account hard to believe. He remained unconvinced the protest would have any effect until the party dismissed

---

*   This group included Mary McCarthy, Dwight Macdonald, Fred Dupee, Eleanor Clark, and Philip Rahv and William Phillips, the editors of the *Partisan Review*.

†   This period is now called "The Great Purge," but at the time it wasn't yet clear to most Americans that Stalin was killing innocents. Even the United States government thought the trials were fair. Ambassador Joseph Davies reported, "It is generally accepted by members of the Diplomatic Corps that the accused must have been guilty of an offense which in the Soviet Union would merit the death penalty."

a friend of his for having Trotskyist "tendencies" a few weeks later. His faith died then. "I'm letting my Party membership slide and mean to do no more organizational work—at all," he wrote.

Wright was more sanguine. If the Soviet Union needed to cleanse the party's ranks in order to remain strong, he felt, then so be it.

Nelson sided with Wright and continued to back the party. He wrote to Howard Rushmore, the editor of the *Daily Worker*, and asked for information he could use to defend the Moscow trials to his coworkers. When Rushmore responded with several articles, Nelson thanked him.

These will become "part of my arsenal of arguments for use against the guys who are 'more left than the Communists,'" Nelson wrote. "Incidentally, we have a flock of such in the office of the fed. writers project where I work. . . . In fact, we have about one of every variety: Trotskyists, Mattickite, Council Communists, United Worker's Party, one National Socialist."

At Home in Rat Alley

(October 1937–February 1940)

Nelson, Jack Conroy, and their friends distributed these fliers to advertise the inaugural Chicago performance of The Drunkard's Warning.

Nelson and Amanda had been living in their single room for nearly two years when they decided to move. He had become a supervisor at the Writers' Project, and she had been hired to take a census of the homeless population in Lincoln Park. They could finally afford more space, so they visited the South Side to look at some storefronts people had begun converting into studios.

The buildings faced each other across an unnamed alley behind Cottage Grove Avenue. They were constructed for the 1893 World's Fair and designed so that men wearing bowlers could parade the gauntlet of their display windows in the company of corseted women, but time had degraded them. Businesses had struggled, and closed. Paint had peeled, wood floors had warped, rats had moved in, and the surrounding neighborhood had developed a lawless feel. Police cruisers began screaming down the avenue past abandoned buildings, and a pair of bars called Jolly John's and The Old Bowery began serving sugary wine into the small hours of the morning.

Then bohemians and radicals christened the area Rat Alley and claimed it for themselves. Gilbert Rocke, a painter and John Reed Club alumnus, rented one of the storefronts, and a muralist named Mitchell Siporin moved into another. The poet Frank Marshall Davis had an apartment around the corner, and young Marxists established a commune at the end of the block where they lived along utopian lines and installed petty tyrants to oversee chores—the kitchen commissar, comrade commissar for the second-floor bathroom, czar of trash disposal, and so on. A writer named Frankie Lemon lived there, and so did the actor Lou "Gigi" Gilbert. Nelson knew both from work, and he knew their upstairs neighbors, Neal and Christine Rowland, because they raised money for the fight in Spain.

Two adjacent storefronts were unoccupied. They were connected by a door through their shared wall and the cost for both was only twenty-five dollars a month, but they were rundown and unlivable.

Nelson and Amanda rented them anyway. They paid to have a toilet, a sink, and a stove installed, and then bought drapes to cover the seven-foot-tall display windows, and painted their floors Copen blue. They put a bed in one unit and filled the other with used couches and chairs. Nelson bought a maple writing desk. Amanda bought a dining-room set. Then they built benches by the windows and hung a punching bag from the ceiling so Nelson had something to hit when his writing was not going well.

When they finished, they had their first comfortable home, and Nelson had a suitable base for the next act of his career. He was moving in several distinct circles at the time, and the storefronts put him near the center of each.

The Writers' Project was a short trolley ride north, and by then Nelson was a fixture in the office. After he completed the Galena guide, he wrote an economic history of Illinois and a regional cookbook.* They were inglorious assignments, but he submitted them without complaint, and in the process he earned the respect of the aspiring authors on staff. Saul Bellow had begun admiring Nelson from afar, though Nelson never noticed him, and Margaret Walker, the youngest writer in the office, began asking Nelson for feedback on her poetry.

Nelson was secretary of the Chicago chapter of the League of American Writers as well, and the storefronts allowed him to host meetings. During his tenure, an impressive list of literary figures gathered in them. Two editors from *Esquire* and an associate editor at the *New Republic* visited. So did George Dillon and Peter DeVries from *Poetry* magazine, and the black writers Margaret Walker, Frank Marshall Davis, and Ted Ward. The league was Nelson's primary contact with the political world by then, but he also maintained a working relationship with the Communist Party. The party regulated the league's membership, so Nelson remained a public supporter long after he began expressing misgivings in private.† He spoke at a party fundraiser in 1937, and later he signed a statement defending the worst Moscow show trial—the one that inspired Arthur Koestler to write *Darkness at Noon*.

Living in Rat Alley also put Nelson at the center of a social scene. He commuted north with his neighbors in the mornings, worked his shift at the Writers' Project surrounded by friends, and clocked out alongside comrades while debating Stalin's Popular Front strategy. He might host

---

* This book was part of a project called America Eats. The FWP shelved it at some point, and Nelson's manuscript died a merciful death. Then, in the 1970s, Nelson sold his copy of the cookbook to a friend, who convinced the University of Iowa to publish it under the title *America Eats*. Now, any Algren fan interested in cooking sixty gallons of Flemish booya using thirty pounds of oxtails and four fat hens can buy a copy, and turn to page 82.

† In a letter dated January 14, 1938, Nelson criticized the party's stewardship of its magazine *New Masses*. "All I can see is that these things are due to editorial slovenliness ... and it occurs to me to wonder how people who feel perfectly capable of running an entire nation at a moment's notice, can reconcile to themselves their inability to run a small magazine with efficiency."

a meeting or drop into a benefit at the commune afterward, and when it ended, he could rejoin the afternoon's debate at Jolly John's and keep it going until the bartender hit the lights and cleared the room.

Writing was the one thing the storefronts didn't facilitate. Nelson only worked on his novel after his other obligations were satisfied, so progress was slow. He wrote at night, mostly, and sometimes Amanda lay in bed and listened to him struggle. She could hear music seeping beneath the door separating their rooms, and the thick, percussive sound of fists pounding a heavy bag, the crunch of paper being wadded up and discarded, and the whisper of fresh sheets curling around the typewriter's platen.

Nelson couldn't afford any more distractions, but that winter he took on a new project anyway. He, Abe Aaron, and Richard Wright had been talking about starting a magazine like the old *Left Front*. They thought the literary scene was strong enough to support one, but none of them was interested in becoming its editor, so Nelson sent Jack Conroy a letter and asked if he would.

It was a calculated offer. Conroy had fallen a long way since Nelson and Aaron first sought him out for counsel and encouragement, and they thought he needed rescuing.

Conroy was thirty-eight years old by then, and married with three children—he had a home, a penchant for bear hugs, and a warm smile, but no money, not much of a career, and too much fondness for hard drink.

He had spent years as an object of reverence on the literary left. People called him The Sage from Moberly after his first novel was published in 1934, and it was commonly accepted that his life's experiences gave him an intimate understanding of the country's troubles. His talent, and the cachet his life story bestowed on him, even catapulted him into the mainstream for a while. The *New York Post* made the first Writers' Congress seem important by reporting that people had clustered around "such famed novelists as Jack Conroy." The *Herald Tribune* interviewed him at the event, and the conference's organizers gave him prominent placement on the agenda because they knew he could draw a crowd.

But then Conroy rushed out a second novel to chase the success of his first, and it was panned. Next, he agreed to merge *The Anvil* and *Partisan Review*, and lost control of his magazine. The Guggenheim Foundation awarded him a fellowship, and the prestige that accompanied it lifted his prospects for a while, but by the summer of 1937 it was clear the headiest days of his career were past. He was a "wounded gorilla," Meridel Le Sueur said, and no one "struggled for him." When the Second American Writers' Congress convened that year, he drew no crowds and delivered no speeches because he hadn't been invited.

That was a dark time for Conroy. He wasn't earning much by writing, and his wife, Gladys, was working in a shoe factory and drawing a meager wage. They owned a home outright, but there was a chance their children could go hungry.

Conroy needed money desperately, so he went to St. Louis and applied for a job with the Missouri Writers' Project. He was qualified to become its director, but they offered him a position as a staff writer instead—a great insult, to his mind. He accepted because he had no other options, but after he left his family behind in Moberly and rented a small apartment near his new workplace, his mood soured. He became angry about his circumstances, and sought comfort in a bottle, and in company that reflected his state of mind.

One day, at a union meeting, Conroy met a wild young man with pale blue eyes. His name was Lawrence "Bud" Fallon, and he was a laborer at an aluminum mill who dreamed of becoming a writer. He said he admired Conroy's first novel, and began calling him "the great arthur" as a sign of respect. Soon, they were inseparable.

Fallon never published any of his writing, but he was famous in the St. Louis area nevertheless. He organized for the Congress of Industrial Organizations before he hired on at the aluminum mill, and people still chanted, "C-I-O, C-I-O, C-I-O" when he entered bars. Then they

braced themselves. His rages were legendary, and nothing was sacro-
sanct when he was in their grip. One morning, he woke in a stranger's
car, naked except for a pair of pants and covered with dried blood. On
another occasion, he broke up a party by smashing forty bottles of beer.
He became so violent one evening that he left a veteran bartender shaking his head in disbelief. "One man'd go down and the winner would
take on somebody else," the man said later. "Fightin', fightin', all night."

Fallon traveled at the head of a pack, and that added to his mys-
tique. His coworkers Russell Finch, Bill Walker, and Otto "Doc Otty
Ollie Snake" Schaefer trailed behind him most nights, and so did a
thickly built man named Jesse Blue who carried a gun and sold narcotics. Conroy became a member of Fallon's retinue as well, and he
recruited a man named Wallie Wharton to become the group's bard.
Wharton was a chubby poet with a head full of angelic curls who lived
to sully the innocent promise of his face. He cursed creatively, had
sex promiscuously though he was married, and recited satirical poems
when he went out carousing.

"I've got a leanin' toward Lenin these days," he declaimed. "They
tell me a leanin' like that really pays."

Conroy dubbed the group the Fallonites and accepted their friendship
gratefully while he was in St. Louis. Their esteem was a timid replace-
ment for his once-upon-a-time fame, but it was a welcome alternative
to loneliness, so he met up with them after leaving work most evenings.
When they started fighting, he returned to his apartment, but when
they stuck to drink, he kept up. "I often reeled into the palatial offices
of the Writers' Project," he wrote, "without having been to bed at all."

Conroy passed a year that way, and more. He put on weight and his
features thickened. He stopped writing, and eventually he slunk home
to Moberly, Missouri—a town he described as "just a lot of boxes set
on the prairie." Then he slipped back into poverty in the two-story
wood-framed house he shared with his wife and three children. Gladys
had been laid off by the shoe factory, and he couldn't find work.

That's when Nelson's letter arrived. You should move to Chicago, it said. You can live with me and Amanda until you get established. The Writers' Project will hire you, and when we launch our magazine, you can be the editor. We'll call it the *New Anvil*.

It was the best offer Conroy had received in a long time, so he accepted.

Jack Conroy boarded a northbound bus in Missouri near the end of March, and looked around for a fellow drinker. He spotted a likely candidate traveling alone, sat down next to him, began talking, and didn't stop for hours. I rambled like "an old, sad faithful lecher . . . ," he boasted later. And with my encouragement, my new friend "reeled from the vehicle" every time it paused to take on passengers and "returned with a half-pint of Golden Wedding, of which I contrived to consume three-quarters."*

Conroy was drunk from Moberly to Chicago, and he was drunk still when he reached Rat Alley and introduced himself to Amanda. They had never met, and he made a poor first impression. He was in a "bad way," she said—I thought he was a "pathetic character," "an alcoholic."

Nelson was more forgiving. He knew what it was like to despair over the failure of a book, so he greeted his friend warmly and moved him into the apartment's only bedroom. For the next several months, he and Amanda slept on benches in the living space so Conroy could have the bed.

Conroy was a large presence, and after he moved in, the storefronts began to feel crowded and tense. He spoke to Amanda as though she were his audience, not his host, and when she cooked a meal intended to keep the household fed all week, he finished it in days. Sometimes, she bought herself candies on payday, as an indulgence, and when she forgot to hide them, he ate those too. Nelson was often busy with work or meetings, and in his absence Conroy caroused. The Writers' Project

---

* Golden Wedding was a cheap brand of rye whiskey whose label featured a drawing of two elderly men wearing tuxedos.

hired him, and when he began bringing home a salary, he redoubled his drinking. He started an affair with a coworker named Theodora Pikowsky a few weeks into his tenure, and afterward he came and went at unpredictable times. Once, he returned home late, passed out on the living room floor, and woke with coins resting on his eyelids— passage across the River Styx, paid by Nelson and Amanda.

But Nelson and Conroy moved forward with the *New Anvil* despite Conroy's drinking. Nelson requested that the League of American Writers sponsor the magazine, but they didn't reply. He asked a second time, and when that request went unanswered, he and Conroy realized they would have to raise money themselves.

They decided to stage a play and charge admission. Theodora Pikowsky offered the loft she rented near the Writers' Project as a performance space, and friends offered to provide musical accompaniment and act. When all the logistical details of the performance were settled, Nelson and Conroy drew advertisements for the event and distributed them around town. They said: *The Drunkard's Warning*, by Jack Conroy, will be performed by "an all-star cast" so " 'the anvil' can ring forth again." Line drawings of overflowing beer mugs framed the announcement, and a single five-pointed star hovered above one playfully.

Pikowsky opened the doors of her fourth-floor loft at 8 p.m. on May 16. The room filled quickly, and soon everyone was warm and drunk. Nelson spotted his dark-haired ex-girlfriend in the crowd, and introduced her to Amanda. Then he worked the room while the two women chatted. He saw project employees drinking and becoming convivial, and league members chatting with bohemians from Rat Alley. A blues guitarist named Oscar White mingled, and Maxwell Bodenheim stumbled around. He was supposed to read some poems before the play began, but he was too drunk to stand, so Amanda took him to an empty bedroom and forced coffee on him.

The Drunkard's Warning was written as a satire of the temperance movement, but it took on new dimensions each time it was staged. It was more a happening than a play, and Conroy used its Chicago debut to advance his long-standing assault on the person and career of James T. Farrell—one of the only writers to give his first novel a bad review.

Conroy stepped onto the makeshift stage in Pikowsky's loft when the crowd quieted, and announced he was playing the role of James T. Barrelhouse—a mawkish drunk. There was an actress on stage as well, but when he tried to engage her in dialogue, she forgot her lines and wandered off. A man named Red Kruck added a farcical touch to the performance when he entered the drama wearing a skirt that was too short to conceal his hairy legs. Someone struck a sheet of metal to simulate thunder—*thoom, thoom, thoom*—and Nelson meandered around the stage, mumbling nonsense. "You Goldblatt," he proclaimed, "bargain in a Marshall Field topcoat!"

The performance wasn't professional, but it was a good time, and everyone was high and happy for a while. Then a Trotskyist arrived.

The conflict that had begun when six dissidents spoke out against Stalin at the Second American Writers' Congress the year before was still raging in Chicago. The Stalinists Nelson associated with saw Trotsky's supporters as heretics, so Red Kruck stopped performing when he saw the man, and attacked. The stage emptied then, and the fight spread through the crowded room. Nelson beat someone in the head with a broom handle, and then a gun went off and people ran.

The police arrived a few minutes later. They asked who was in charge, and arrested Nelson, Conroy, and Pikowsky.

Nelson was released the next morning, but the night had other consequences. Amanda confronted him about his recklessness, and so did the party. A few days after his arrest, he received a letter from Franklin Folsom, the executive secretary of the League of American Writers. It said: "I have heard very distressing rumors about your conduct and Conroy's about which I should have complete and official information so that no injustice will be done as a result of having doubts raised by rumors. I am sure you know that I am referring to charges of drunkenness and disorderly conduct."

Folsom instructed Nelson and Conroy to meet with a local party leader to discuss the fundraiser and provide "proper information" about the melee at Pikowsky's. It wasn't a suggestion. A man named Frank Meyer got in touch next, and ordered them to report to his office in downtown Chicago.

Nelson and Conroy arrived for their meeting on time, but Meyer left them sitting in his waiting room. He emerged from his office after an hour, invited them inside, and then told them to take a seat. He was a severe-looking man with high cheekbones and a tight smile, and he spoke using the tone of a principal scolding wayward students. You are casting "bad reflections on the radical movement," he said.

Nelson didn't take it well. He resented Folsom and Meyer, but in the weeks that followed, he developed real loathing for the snitch. Someone had seen him drunk and written to New York to report him, and he was disgusted by that idea. He was willing to defend Stalin and the Moscow show trials because the Soviet government sent guns and money into Spain to fight fascism, but he couldn't abide being told how to act. I thought that's what "we were fighting the war against," he said.

Nelson didn't split with the party after that interview, at least not immediately. He continued working with the League of American Writers until 1940, but he was more mutineer than soldier after Frank Meyer lectured him. He defended dissidents when he attended meetings, spoke up when he disagreed, and made writing his priority.

Two years before Jack Conroy moved to the city, Nelson had decided to write a series of novels that provided an "accurate description" of Chicago, but he had not been focused on the project for most of that time. He changed his priorities that spring though. He freed up time by neglecting his obligations to the League of American Writers, and used it to collect material by wandering around with a notebook in hand. This time, though, he traveled with company.

First, he attached himself to Jack Conroy, and used his friend's charisma to gain entrance to spaces he was too shy to visit alone. They had

been assigned to collect oral histories for the Writers' Project, so they
spent their days in bars on North Clark Street, interviewing inebriates,
prostitutes, and unemployed laborers. Their evenings were more of the
same. They shot dice in the back rooms of saloons, and became the
only white members of the True American Business and Social Club—
a black organization on the South Side where Nelson played cards and
mooned over a waitress named Zenobia Gibson.

Nelson thought of the weeks he spent carousing with Conroy as
research, but they were also more enjoyable than any since his childhood. His life had been defined by abstention, poverty, and political
convictions since college, and he had been hiding behind a stern and
over-serious mask for just as long, but there was no chance of maintaining that pretense with Conroy, and no reason to—the force of
Conroy's personality was too strong to resist, and submitting to his
will was reliably rewarding.

One night, they left the True American Business and Social Club
early in the morning and began walking north toward the Cottage
Grove storefronts. On the corner of Thirty-fifth Street, they spotted a
street preacher hollering above the din of passing cars, and stopped to
listen. When the man paused for breath, Conroy requested a wedding.

Marry me and my friend, he demanded in his well-lubricated Missouri drawl.

The man refused. He said he was saving souls, not damning them,
and quoted Leviticus 18:22: "Do not have sexual relations with a man
as one does with a woman; that is detestable."

Conroy would not be denied, though, and eventually the preacher
relented and proclaimed Nelson and Conroy husband and husband.
Passing cars sanctified the occasion by strafing the new couple with
their headlights, and the moon was their witness.

Then the Fallonites arrived. They swept into Chicago a few months
after Conroy relocated, and soon they were as notorious as they had

been in St. Louis. They proclaimed themselves "hipsters in artistic revolt against the establishment," and tried to lay claim to a leadership role within the cultural left—but in truth, they were just clever, violent drunks, and people were drawn to them for their novelty, not their intellectual pretensions.

Chicago had never experienced anything like the Fallonites. They were mill workers who claimed to be writers, and brawlers who followed the Communist Party's internal debates and mocked its leaders. They moved by dusk to the sound of breaking bottles and epithets, and dark rumors swirled around them. They called themselves "lost" men because they had once stolen a slot machine from a Mafia-owned gambling parlor, and one of them claimed he had raped a dog. They took pride in riding roughly through the home of anyone foolish enough to permit them entrance, and despite their ties to the political left, they treated women with open disdain. "Tell all them kunts [sic] to rinch [sic] out good before I come up," Fallon wrote before visiting Chicago. Then, during a party, he led his gang into a back room of Meyer Levin's house, where they had group sex with a woman named Rose. He left when they finished, bought an armload of ice cream cones, and passed out on a sidewalk while clutching them to his chest.*

Conroy and Fallon had a complicated and symbiotic relationship, and when Fallon began visiting Chicago, they revived and deepened it. They rehashed their escapades in St. Louis endlessly, and developed a unique patois that allowed them to make reference to liquors, political figures, and the female anatomy without being understood. Each of them had constructed an image of himself that relied on his relationship to the other, and as a result they clung to each other more tightly all the time. Conroy still felt like a star because Fallon said he was, and Fallon flattered himself with the notion that he was something more than a violent drunk because his best friend was a once-famous writer.

---

* Amanda, who knew Rose, claimed that this encounter was consensual—but added that Rose regretted it afterward.

Nelson also began hanging around Fallon that year, but their relationship was much simpler. Nelson was fascinated by Fallon, and thought of him as a valuable source—a man whose biography was both unique and emblematic of their generation. He was a union man who disdained labor, a utopian who had slathered himself with a high-proof veneer of cynicism rather than hold fast to his ideals, and a frustrated man-child who insisted, a bit too stridently, that the world was against him.

Nelson spent a fall, a winter, and a spring following the Fallonites around with a notebook in hand. He trailed them when they visited Chicago, and then back to Missouri when he could. He transcribed their drunken babble, transformed their meanderings into scenes, and went to great lengths to fit in with them. He wore black suits when they were around, talked out the side of his mouth, and made a spectacle of himself. Whenever music began playing, he swung his arms in wide arcs, spun on his toes, and convulsed off beat. There was something balletic about his dancing, something pained—he looked like a man toe-stepping his way across an electrified floor, or a blind boxer swinging haymakers at threatening shadows.

Nelson's act was entertaining, but it didn't withstand close scrutiny— "It got a little ridiculous the poses he would put on," Frankie Lemon said—and the Fallonites never accepted him because, bluster aside, he was far more reserved than they were. "He was smart as a shit house rat," Conroy said later. "He didn't drink much, he was too cautious."

Bud Fallon could see the situation clearly. He tolerated Nelson's presence because it lent his gang prestige, but he resented being the object of Nelson's curiosity, so he set the price of access high, and raised it steadily. At first, he mocked Nelson. "I don't have a Pulitzare but I'm not the type to care," he recited once in a packed bar. "'Cause I got a pocketful of notes." Then he attacked Nelson's reputation by mailing anti-Semitic letters to Meyer Levin and Henry Alsberg—the head of the Federal Writers' Project—and signing them with Nelson's name. Finally, in December, he sent an abusive letter directly to Nelson.

"I . . . know you for what you are," it read, "the flash in the pan, the mediocrity, the almost-but-not-quite-Algren. The Communist Ass Kisser unparalleled, the fawning, vapid, favor courter. . . .

"Better be content to sink into your greasykike [sic] obscurity . . ."[*]

Nelson accepted Fallon's provocations as the price of collecting material, but eventually he realized he was paying for the time he spent with the Fallonites in more painful ways as well. He never had enough time to write, his friends were beginning to surpass him, and his personal life was a shambles.

Richard Wright, who was living a more focused and austere life in New York, had just published a collection of short stories to great acclaim. Nelson wrote to congratulate him, but his circumstances also required him to mention an old loan in the same note. "I hate to knock down that $500, needing it as I know you do," he wrote to Wright, "but you will recall that you intended to send along a couple bucks I loaned you, when you could spare it. . . . we live here on the grim verge ourselves."

Nelson was the up-and-comer when he met Wright five years earlier, so the reversal of their fortunes was impossible to ignore—and so was the state of Nelson's marriage. By the spring of 1939, it was nothing but silence and jagged edges.

Amanda rarely saw Nelson, so she found other ways to fill her time. She had recently begun attending a weekly painting class where she focused on abstracts and still lifes. She liked the idea of being an artist, like Nelson, and coveted his approval, so once she brought a watercolor back to Rat Alley and asked him what he thought of it.

---

[*] This letter has a complicated history. Fallon actually signed it with the name Wallie Wharton—one of his acolytes. He misspelled Wharton's name, though, and Nelson learned Fallon was its author. Conroy confronted Fallon on Nelson's behalf eventually, and somehow the letter made its way into Wharton's possession. Now, it lives in his archive at the State Historical Society of Missouri.

"It's very nice," Nelson said, "but what does it mean?" His reaction made Amanda feel fragile and discouraged. She resented the idea that all art had to have social significance, so she quit. "I never really did anything after that," she said—no more classes, no more painting.

Amanda had a new job by then. She had stopped counting the homeless population in Lincoln Park and accepted a less conventional position selling erotic books on the sidewalk outside a porn theater on Michigan Avenue. It was not as physically demanding as her last job, but still trying. She had to stand for hours, and look charming while she solicited.

One day at work, a tall Armenian man named Ed Cazarian approached Amanda. He was an old friend of Richard Leekley's, so they spent a few minutes catching up. Before he left, Cazarian asked Amanda if she'd like to have dinner sometime. His implication was clear, so she took a moment to consider the proposal's merits. He's "ugly," she thought, but he's very nice.

"Yes," she replied then. I would.

Cazarian passed by regularly after that. They ate dinner together several times, and then they began visiting hotels to have sex.

Amanda could have hidden the relationship, but didn't. Conroy was having an affair, and she suspected—but never had proof—that Nelson was, too, so she flaunted hers. She told Cazarian to call the Rat Alley apartment when he wanted to see her, and took his calls without shame. Sometimes, Nelson answered the phone, heard a man's voice, and handed the receiver to Amanda.

"I'll see you at eight thirty," she'd say. Then she went out for the night.

Amanda expected Nelson to confront her about the relationship, but he never did. Instead, he watched her leave, and brooded until she returned home.

Once, she and Cazarian spent a weekend together. They drove to Peoria, Illinois, where he lived, and played house. On the second evening, they had sex several times and then went to sleep. That night, Amanda dreamed about Nelson and woke up screaming his name.

Cazarian ended the relationship the next day. He said he wanted to marry Amanda, but suspected she would never leave Nelson, so there was no reason for them to see each other again.

Amanda returned to Rat Alley feeling chastened and lonely then, and slipped back into whatever was left of her marriage. She had been seeing Cazarian for months, but she and Nelson never spoke about him.

Nelson's sister Bernice had been sick for some time by then. Her stomach was swollen, and she was lethargic. She was in constant pain as well, so in early 1939 she agreed to have exploratory surgery. When the doctors cut her open, they found cancer in her intestines. It was a death sentence.

Bernice's husband, Morris, had recently gone back to work, and he spent lavishly to make her happy and comfortable. He took her to California that summer for a vacation, and bought a large house in North Park when they returned. Then the family gathered. Gerson and Goldie moved in so they could care for Bernice and her children, Robert and Ruth, and Morris stayed close to home.

Nelson's reaction was different. Bernice had introduced him to the written word when he was young, encouraged him to write, and made it possible for him to go to college. Without her, he would have become a mechanic or maybe ended up in jail after getting too involved with the scene at Johnson's. He was in her debt, and he decided to honor her life with labor instead of grief. After her diagnosis, he cut back on the amount of time he spent with Fallon and Conroy and began writing like a man on deadline.

The first novel in Nelson's planned series was going to be set in the Near Northwest Side—the Triangle, the heart of Chicago Polonia. So he began spending his free time there, collecting material.

The neighborhood had a fascinating history. A hundred years earlier, a few Polish immigrants fled the Polish–Russian War and settled in the area with the intention of establishing a state called New Poland. They failed politically, but succeeded in every other regard. Waves of immigrants followed, and created a neighborhood that was both part of the city and separate from it.

The Polish community in the Northwest was the largest ethnic enclave in Chicago when Nelson began his research, and among the most powerful. It produced millionaires, policeman, teachers, politicians, and priests. The *Dziennik Chicagoski*, *Zgoda*, the *Dziennik Zwiazkowy*, and a handful of other newspapers kept people informed. St. Stanislaus Kostka, St. Boniface, and Holy Trinity tended to their souls, and the Catholic Union and the National Alliance told everyone how to vote. It was possible to live in the area without ever finding a reason to leave, and it was possible to thrive without knowing English.

But the Triangle was changing. New immigrants were pouring in from Europe and competing with native-born residents for jobs and space, and the American-born generation that came of age during the Depression was faltering. Their ethnicity prevented them from joining the city's mainstream, but their American childhoods created an unbridgeable distance between themselves and their parents. They spoke broken Polish, bowed their heads in church without praying, and looked toward the future with apprehension. There weren't enough civil service positions to go around anymore, and political posts were only available to the people with the deepest roots and the most friends.

The Triangle's insularity made those children feel like orphans. They were the product of a city that never wanted them and a neighborhood that couldn't afford to provide—so they became toughs and boxers, stick-up men, prostitutes, and madams. They hung around school yards, gathered under the El tracks, and kept themselves out of jail by paying off the police and ward politicians who had come of age a generation ahead of them.

When Nelson began spending time in the neighborhood, he focused his attention on those youths because their lives captured the area's shortcomings and contradictions. He started haunting street carnivals, juvenile court, poolrooms, and a juvenile detention home. He began corresponding with prisoners who had been convicted of street crimes in the area, and a former alderman of the Twenty-sixth Ward who had been indicted for selling civil service jobs. And he wandered around the Triangle, interviewing people and writing down snippets of dialogue as they floated past.

In the evenings, after he returned home, he typed up the best material he had collected:*

"I used to go by taverns; I was fourteen."

"In 1937 I was lyin' til 1938, then I seen it didn't do no good."

"The boys rolled a Jew on Division Street for $6 and his topcoat. A few days later they were picked up on suspicion. After they were thrown in a cell awhile the same Jew was thrown in with them, drunk. They rolled him again."

After a four-year absence, Nelson's writing finally returned to print in 1939. He and Conroy had released three issues of the *New Anvil*, and his poetry appeared in each one. Then *Poetry* magazine accepted a piece of his, and published it in November.

That poem is called "Home and Goodnight," and it's a beautiful thing—fifty-seven lines of closely observed atmosphere and lament that offer the first clear indication of the direction Nelson's work was taking. Its tone is lyrical, and its sensibility political; it speaks directly about race, but there isn't a hint of sanctimony or bitterness in it.

The boys in the three-piece orchestra can go home now,
And the come-on girl fingering a pink paper gardenia and saying,

---

* In a grant application Nelson submitted that year, he listed the locales mentioned above, and also: "churches . . . taverns, bookies, amusement parks," and "private homes . . . police show ups . . . the Illinois State training school and . . . meeting-places of gangs functioning as 'social and athletic clubs.'" He also used his position with the Writers' Project to interview a boxer named Davey "Human String Bean" Day and a prostitute. Material from both interviews later appeared verbatim in his second novel.

"My feet is killen me but I'm still dancen"—
Can walk two blocks east and have breakfast No. 9 at the Greek's
    with her best boyfriend
And be back dancing in bed; all in twenty-five minutes flat.
But the brown boy who gets an indifferent hand for imitating
    Stepin Fetchit,
Saying in a studied drawl while kneeling for pennies,
"Thank yo' all fo' de neckbones, suh,"
Will have to ride out to 47th and Prairie,
The longest ride of all.

"Home and Goodnight" was the high point of Nelson's year—and
the weeks that followed its publication were the low. The Writers' Project fired everyone who had been on staff for more than eighteen months
in December, and Nelson, Conroy, and most of their friends got the ax.
Almost everyone living in Rat Alley was unemployed and in need of distraction by the end of the year, so one night they walked south in a pack
and found a black and tan club where they could drink and hear good
jazz. Nelson and Amanda went, and so did Conroy and the Fallonites.

When they arrived, John Barrymore, a movie star and notorious
lush was making a scene, and a band was laying down a beat. Nelson
found a seat off to the side of the room, started a conversation, and
took in the music. Amanda danced and partied. "I must have been
drinking as much as Barrymore," she said later. Eventually, a young
Fallonite named Russ Finch offered her his hand, and they pressed
together closely and moved with the music.

The sky was pitch black when the group left the club and began moving north in a long snaking line toward Thirty-fifth and Cottage Grove.
Nelson and Conroy chatted in the lead. Amanda and Finch brought
up the rear. The group cut through Washington Park to save time, and
before Amanda reached its northern edge, she began to feel sick.

I drank too much, she said. I need to throw up.

Finch had just enrolled in the University of Chicago and rented an apartment nearby, and he told Amanda she could use his bathroom. Nelson was more than a block ahead and home was three miles away, so Amanda agreed. Then she spent the night.

The next morning, Finch walked Amanda home. When they opened the door to 3569, they found Nelson sitting alone and looking grim.

Finch said hello, but Nelson didn't respond. He was staring at the floor and wouldn't look up. Finch considered Nelson for a few minutes in silence, and then left.

"I'm leaving," Nelson told Amanda when Finch was gone. He didn't raise his voice or curse, but he looked angry.

Nothing happened with Finch, Amanda insisted, but she didn't have much credibility. Her affair with Cazarian had ended only a few months earlier. She saw Nelson wasn't convinced, so she answered his challenge.

"No," she said. "I will."

Amanda moved in with Theodora Pikowsky that afternoon, and over the next few weeks Nelson fell apart. He rattled around the storefronts, obsessed, and became violent. He and Conroy ran into Finch and Amanda at Pikowsky's loft once, and Nelson attacked Finch with a knife. Then Amanda moved into Finch's apartment, and Nelson smashed a window in their building's lobby.

Nelson spread word that he intended to kill Finch, and then he spent several weeks drinking himself stupid. He stumbled through the neighborhood with a bottle in hand, and once he was spotted slumped against a wall, nearly insensate, singing "Three Little Fishes."

"Boop boop dit-tem dat-tem what-tem chu," he crooned. "And they swam and they swam all over the dam."

Morning

(March 1940–September 1942)

Richard Wright's second book, *Native Son*, was released in March, and it created a sensation. It became the first Book of the Month Club selection by a black author, and an immediate best seller. Reviews appeared everywhere, and most praised it effusively. "The finest novel as yet written by an American Negro," one review said. "A rare and special thing," added another.

Wright's former coworkers at the Writers' Project in Chicago were proud of his success, but not surprised by it. They had always respected him for his talent and work ethic, so they celebrated his accomplishment by cutting his reviews out of newspapers and magazines and pinning them to the large bulletin board near the front of their office, where they were visible to everyone, Nelson included. He had recently been rehired by the project, so he walked past Wright's reviews several times a day, and each time they caught his eye, he must have experienced a confusing mixture of pride and envy.

Despite constant reminders of its release, Nelson resisted the urge to buy a copy of *Native Son* for weeks. Wright had promised to send one to him, and he was waiting for it to arrive.* The book finally reached Rat

---

* Wright never said it in so many words, but I interpret this gift as a thank you. *Native Son* had been the title of *Somebody in Boots* until Nelson's publisher objected.

Alley on a Saturday morning, and when Nelson opened it, he found an inscription inside its cover that was so touching it must have erased any resentment Wright's success had created.

"To my old friend Nelson," it read. "Who I believe is still the best writer of good prose in the U.S.A."

Nelson grabbed a postcard then, and typed, "I haven't begun it [*Native Son*] yet because I can't get past the autograph. I hope you meant it all the way, because it did something to me . . . I'm now hoping I can do something—just a little—toward earning that inscription."

Then he began reading.

Native Son is the story of Bigger Thomas, a twenty-year-old black man who lives in a rat-infested room on the South Side of Chicago with his mother, his sister, and his younger brother Buddy. He is angry and listless, and wastes his days "trying to defeat or gratify powerful impulses." He leans against walls and smokes cigarettes, shoots pool, fights, and plans a robbery he doesn't follow through on.

When *Native Son* begins, Bigger is trying to change his life. He breaks with his gang and ventures into the white world—a "cold and distant place" with large homes and "secrets carefully guarded"—to accept a job as a chauffeur. The position is a coup for Bigger, but he derives no satisfaction from it. He is anxious and on edge. He feels scrutinized, and though he can't articulate it, he understands, subconsciously, that his fate has been predetermined by his race. The world expects him to disappoint, and the pressure of their expectation builds inside him.

Bigger's employer has a spoiled and reckless daughter, and it's Bigger's job to drive her around. She tries to convert him to communism the first time he does so, drinks heavily, and has sex with her boyfriend in the back of the car. She's too drunk to walk by the time Bigger brings her home, so he carries her to her room and lays her on the bed. He steals a kiss, and before he can slip away, her blind mother approaches. Bigger knows he'll be accused of rape if he's found alone

---

Wright remembered the original title, though, and asked Nelson if he could use it. Nelson agreed.

with a white woman, so he places his hand over the girl's mouth to keep her quiet. She squirms when he touches her, so he presses harder, and suffocates her by mistake.

The police catch Bigger eventually—the courts try him, a jury convicts, and a judge sentences him to death. "They wouldn't let me live and I killed," Bigger says before his execution. "I didn't know I was really alive in this world until I felt things hard enough to kill for 'em."

Nelson spent two days reading *Native Son*, and when he reached the final page he was sure he had just finished an American classic. The book had the sociological heft of great proletarian writing, and the psychological nuance of the best Russian novels. It transcended politics, trampled over the bounds of polite discourse, and challenged authority the way Nelson believed literature should.

Nelson typed a letter to Wright when he set the book down.

> *I really hadn't planned on writing you about NATIVE SON, because I'd assumed it was just one more good book in America. I assumed it would deal almost wholly with external situations, would prove, competently, the need for change, would be well-written and get good reviews and be half-forgotten by the time your next appeared. But I'm honestly hit so hard I have to get it off my chest. This isn't by any means a letter of congratulation. I don't feel any need to tell you how well-thought out or how well-sustained it is and all that, you'll hear that all over.*

The most striking thing about the book, Nelson said, was that the story and characters were "such a threat."

> *I mean a personal threat. At first I felt it was just a challenge but it's more. You've done a very, very smart thing. I don't think any white person could read it without being either frightened or angry at the end. My own reaction happened to be anger more than anything else. I mean when someone's threatened out of a clear blue sky, he*

starts getting sore. I don't mean I'm angry now. I don't see how anyone could stay angry, assuming he's got a notion of what it's all about, because, of course, you're right, sociologically and psychologically and you can't stay angry at patent truth.

Nelson typed until he had filled three pages. When he finished, he folded them, slipped them into an envelope, and dropped it in the mail. Then he prepared to leave Rat Alley. *Native Son*'s reception made him more confident in the direction of his own work, and emboldened him to abandon the storefronts in favor of a place where he could write without distraction.

Nelson moved to Chicago's Northwest Side three weeks after he wrote to Wright, renting two rooms at 1907 West Evergreen Avenue—a quiet building near the heart of Polish Chicago.

Nelson's new apartment was smaller and more austere than his last home, but it provided everything he needed: solitude and easy access to sources. None of his friends lived nearby, so it was easier for him to focus. He spent most of his free time in front of a typewriter after he moved, and when he needed a break, he stepped onto the wooden porch attached to the back of his building and watched the city breathe. He could see laundry hanging limp on backyard clotheslines from there, children playing on rooftops, and steam rising from factories. The setting of his novel was just outside his door, so when he needed material, he descended his front stoop. The southern corner of Wicker Park jutted toward his building like the tip of a spear, and the El tracks crossed his street at the end of the block. He regularly spoke with the young toughs who lingered in the crenulated shadows cast by the overhead tracks, and if none of them was around when he visited, he turned down Milwaukee Avenue and walked a few blocks to the Triangle.

Nelson thought he could complete his novel in ten months if he focused, so he simplified his life. He chose not to have a phone line installed in his apartment, and rarely invited anyone to visit. He even stopped cooking for himself. Instead, he kept a pot on his stove that he never emptied or cleaned. When he got hungry, he added food to whatever remained of his last meal—vegetables, meat, or beans— then poured some water in, turned on the burner, returned to his manuscript, and waited for his concoction to boil.

Richard Wright visited Chicago two months after Nelson moved, and found his friend happy and hard at work. The two of them discussed Nelson's novel, wandered around the city to snap pictures for a photo essay Wright was developing, and then convened a meeting of their old crowd.

Wright's visit was a triumphant homecoming. He had published two books since moving away, and had married. *Native Son* had already sold a quarter of a million copies and Orson Welles had made an offer for the stage rights, but when Wright, Nelson, Aaron, and Conroy got together in a saloon, their conversation focused on the war, not Wright's accomplishments.

Germany had been emboldened when Spain fell to Franco the year before, and had invaded Poland, Denmark, and Norway since. France was being carved up as Nelson and his friends talked and drank—one piece to the Germans, one to the Italians, and one to a German puppet regime in Vichy—and everyone knew Britain was next. The only question was how America would respond.

Wright didn't think the war would reach the United States, and he had no intention of fighting if it did. He grew up in the Jim Crow south and didn't feel he owed the country a thing. He planned to run if he got drafted, probably to Mexico, and told his friends America should let the Germans have England. The British Empire would crumble if London fell, he argued, thus freeing large portions of Africa, the Middle East, and Asia. It wasn't clear to him that German expansion in Europe would be worse than allowing the British to retain control of most of the Southern Hemisphere, and he couldn't forgive Britain's refusal to support the Republicans in Spain.

When bombs began sailing across the English Channel, Wright hoped everyone tracking their approach would remember the fall of Madrid. "I think the English will make damn good Nazis," he told Nelson.

Abe Aaron wasn't as cavalier. He didn't think there was any chance Hitler would stop after London, and he reasoned that it would be better to fight the German army on European soil than the American coast. Everyone gathered that day had reason to worry about a fascist invasion, but Aaron's fear was a living thing. He came from a long line of European Jews, and the terror of pogroms was part of his genetic inheritance. Before his family emigrated, a Russian cossack gutted one of his aunts, and—according to family legend—stuffed her abdomen with sawdust while her younger brother watched.

Aaron said he planned to enlist in the army if America entered the war, and to ask for a combat posting.

Nelson was more concerned about his own government than the German Reich. Paranoia ends lives more slowly than bullets, but just as surely, and it had already begun taking hold in America. The House Committee on Un-American Activities—known as the Dies Committee—had been investigating radicals and subversives for the past two years, and had already forced the leaders of the Communist Party and the League of American Writers to testify.

"I'm on the books," Nelson told Wright—meaning he was a subversive in the government's eyes. It was only a suspicion on his part, but he was right. His name had already been mentioned to the Dies Committee five times. A letter he signed had been entered into the Congressional record, and someone told the committee Nelson was part of a Communist "antiseptic squad." Soon, J. Edgar Hoover, the head of the FBI, learned about the testimony and ordered his agents to investigate Nelson as a threat to internal security.

Wright, Nelson, Aaron and Conroy had been supporting and competing against each other for six years by then, but their lives began moving along different trajectories when Wright's visit ended, and they never met again as a group.

Aaron turned inward that year and became paranoid. He left Chicago a few months after Wright's visit, and tried, and failed, to enlist in the army. Then he cut ties with his friends. He was convinced the FBI was spying on him, and didn't want to put anyone he loved at risk. He burned most of his papers, and he signed correspondence with "Better destroy this letter. Best luck." He moved to New York and then California, married, became an accountant, and had three children who grew up believing their father was a reticent, apolitical man. He never told them about the years he spent in Chicago, or his famous friends Richard Wright and Nelson Algren.

Conroy slipped into obscurity. He never wrote another novel, and for the next several years, he drank ever harder. "I feel pretty goddamn bad looking at Jack," Aaron wrote, "for it's a sad thing to see a man like him breaking up." Conroy and Nelson remained friends, but they were never competitors again. He spent the next forty years writing children's books, editing an encyclopedia, and rehashing his glory days.

Wright settled into his fame, and built on it. He was working on a photo essay and a piece about developing *Native Son*, and over the course of the next few years, he married a second time, had two children, took up residence in Paris, and transformed himself into an international figure. By the time he died, his work was an acknowledged tenet of the American literary canon.

And, for the first time, Nelson dedicated himself solely to his writing. He stopped editing the *New Anvil*,* cut his ties with the League

---

* I have given the *New Anvil* short shrift—I know it, and regret it. In brief: The magazine was notable for remaining independent when most small magazines were being absorbed into college English departments. It was also the first nationally distributed magazine to publish two important black writers—Margaret Walker and Frank Yerby. Nelson and Conroy rented office space for the magazine from the Insti-

of American Writers, and avoided Rat Alley. He kept Conroy at a distance—there are "too many parties" in his life, he said, "too many pals"—and he finally accepted help that Wright had been offering for months.

Wright was signed to Harper & Brothers. He earned a lot of credibility there after *Native Son*'s success, and earlier that year he spent some of it on Nelson's behalf. He told his editor, Edward Aswell, that Nelson's unfinished book was going to be remarkable, so Aswell wrote to Nelson and asked for a copy of his manuscript. Nelson declined. He was wary of allowing an editor to read his work before it was finished, and didn't want to be rushed. He had written *Somebody in Boots* quickly, and believed it would have been much better if he had had more time.

Aswell persisted though. He wrote to Nelson again, and when Nelson turned him down a second time, Wright stepped in. Aswell is trustworthy, he told Nelson. "He is young, and he is new at the place. So far, he has been successful enough to bag three good writers, writers who can write and at the same time sell. If they take your stuff, they will push it. You can be assured of that."

Nelson relented then. He sent the first three hundred pages of his book to Aswell the month after Wright's visit, and mailed the same portion to Wright for his feedback. Then he went to North Park to spend some time with his sister before she died.

Bernice had been bedridden for months and had been keeping herself busy by translating books into braille. She continued working until she grew too weak, and then she received visitors. Gerson and Goldie stayed close to their daughter in the last weeks of her life, and so did her two children, her husband, Morris, and Nelson. When she died on August 9, 1940, she was well loved.

---

tute for Mortuary Research, and they sent rejection slips on institute letterhead. Jack Conroy claimed that he sent one to a young J.D. Salinger, and that Salinger wrote back to say he found the experience discomfiting.

The family buried Bernice in Memorial Park Cemetery three days later, and then they scattered. The force of Bernice's charisma had been the only thing binding the Abraham and Joffe families, and they drifted apart the moment she died. Morris began courting a new wife, remarried quickly, and began traveling widely for work—sometimes as much as ten months in a year.* Irene, Bernice's older sister, remained in New York and rarely visited Chicago. Gerson and Goldie stepped in to raise Bernice's children in Morris's absence, and Nelson receded further from the family and immersed himself in his writing.

The first draft of Nelson's novel was a gorgeous mess. There was dialogue that went on for pages, and thousands of words dedicated to describing the inner workings of a brothel. The style of interrogation employed by the Chicago police was reproduced in exacting detail, and characters who served no narrative purpose appeared just long enough to say evocative things. Children played in shadows and dreamed. Rain fell, and puddles refracted flickering neon lights.

The result was often beautiful, but it wasn't a book. The manuscript Nelson sent to Aswell and Wright had no plot and no real protagonist. It opens in an East St. Louis brothel, but then, after a few dozen pages, the action shifts to Chicago. A boxer named Pacek—better known as "Paycheck"—appears and commandeers the narrative for a hundred pages, but then the story returns to East St Louis. The book's only consistent elements are Nelson's perspective and the strength of his prose. They weren't enough.

Richard Wright sent Nelson feedback on his manuscript a few weeks after he received it. He lavished praise on the quality of its dialogue and settings, but took issue with its lack of sustained narrative. "I read page after page for the sheer poetry in them for the sheer way in which you make those folks talk and react to their environment," he wrote.

---

* Morris actually married the woman he had been engaged to when he met Bernice.

But the book's structure "puzzles me a little," Wright said. "I read 263 pages and I could not tell in what direction the story was moving." He argued that Nelson should develop Paycheck's character, and use him to weave the story's divergent narratives together. If you do that, your book will "flow without any breaks," he said, and you'll be able to "create a sense of sympathy, pity, and sorrow in the readers' mind for the whole lost crowd you depict." If you can pull that off, you'll have written something "utterly different than anything anybody is now writing, something new."

Edward Aswell agreed. He offered Nelson five hundred dollars for his unfinished novel—with provisions. He wanted Nelson to restructure the manuscript along the lines Wright suggested, give it a plot, move the entire narrative to Chicago, and rename some characters because they were too closely patterned on real people.

Aswell offered Nelson eight months to revise, and one hundred dollars in advance. Nelson agreed, and when the terms were settled, Aswell mailed him a check and a sarcastically encouraging note. "Nothing remains but to finish the book," he wrote. "It sounds easy doesn't it? I know, though, that it isn't."

Nelson embedded himself in his neighborhood after signing his contract and devoted himself to improving his novel. He turned his boxer into a proper protagonist and renamed him Bruno "Lefty Biceps" Bicek—also known as Lefty, also known as Bunny.* He moved all of the action to Chicago, and conjured a hermetically sealed version of the Triangle that's awash in shadow and testosterone, and thrumming with impotent violence. Then he populated it with a sprawling cast of characters who are so diverse and finely wrought they stand up to anything in Dickens or Dostoyevsky. Their names are Finger, Bibleback, Catfoot, Fireball, and Mama T., and Nelson got to know

---

* Johnny Paychek was the name of a real Polish fighter from Chicago, so Nelson had to change it. He was worried about getting beaten up, and Aswell was worried about being sued.

them so well, he could sketch the whole sweep of their lives in just a few sentences.

Fireball had "once pitched a shutout for St. John's over St. Bonifacius," Nelson wrote, "when he'd weighed a hundred and ninety-two pounds; calling him anything but Fireball now implied that he was no longer the man he had been that afternoon; it would be the same as asking him what was the matter with him. And there was nothing the matter with him—said Fireball. He was just taking off a little fat from around the waist was all. 'I'm on the whisky cure,' he would say bitterly, and drain a half pint without taking his lips from the bottle."

"I'm just temp'rar'ly stranded is all myself," Mama T. swears. "I've got friends, real friends. Boosters I bailed out, free-lance hustlers I paid their rent for—I got a friend a precinct captain I perjured myself for. I c'd go to him t'night . . . I just don't like to ask."

And an inmate proclaims, "Let them radios holler. Let them dice shakers shake. Let them boozers booze. I'm lettin' everythin' go."

Nelson worked on his revision for a year, then more. His deadline came, and went, and though he tried to maintain a steady pace, adversity and trauma kept interrupting his writing process. He was forced to register for the draft, and became preoccupied by the idea that he would be called up by the army before his novel was finished. He was laid off by the Writers' Project for four months, a close friend named Alexander Bergman killed himself, and then his father became ill.

After Bernice died, Gerson Abraham lost his will to live. He had a minor operation in the spring of 1941 and never recovered—*chose not to*, his grandson Robert always corrected. Pneumonia was the official cause of death when he passed, but Gerson's family said he was killed by a broken heart. He had lost his business, his property, his wife's love, his home, his son's respect, and a daughter. He had nothing to live for at the end, and death was almost a mercy.

Goldie and Nelson were both at Gerson's bedside when he died on August 24, 1941. She never shed a tear, and he rarely spoke about the events of that day afterward. They buried Gerson in the same cemetery as Bernice, and then Nelson went back to work. He submitted his manuscript to Harper & Brothers three weeks later.

Edward Aswell was stunned by the book Nelson sent him. "Everyone [at Harper's] who needed to read your novel has now done so, including myself," he wrote. "There is enthusiastic unanimity of opinion about it. It's a book of great integrity and unmistakable power. I myself am amazed at the skill you have shown in revising it."

He requested about a dozen minor changes to the novel—most concerned material that could be considered libelous, or indecent, and none required much work. Then he gave the book a worthy title. Nelson had been calling his manuscript *White Hope*, but when Aswell read it, he discovered a few lines of text buried in a dream sequence that suggest the entire arc of the book's narrative:*

> And the hunter knew where she hid, where she always hid; he passed and repassed, in an arc lamp's light, pretending to have no idea she was near. In order that the hunt might last till morning. Till the last arc lamp had faded and the last tavern had closed? Or because he knew, as she knew, that the night would be forever, the lamps would never fade, the taverns never close, morning would never come again; in order that, all night long and endlessly forever, he might be about to catch her at last.

Aswell insisted that the book's proper title was *Never Come Morning* after he read that passage, and he scheduled its release for April 1942. Richard Wright agreed to provide an introduction, and Nelson's

---

* Titles were never Nelson's strength. *White Hope* is not bad, but his other suggestions were cringeworthy. He wanted to call the book either *The Elephants' Graveyard* or *Below the Belt* for a long time. He also suggested *The Lost and the Lonely* and *He Shoulda Stood in Bed*.

expectations grew. He thought his book had the potential to become a best seller and make headlines the way *Native Son* had, and no one who had read his manuscript thought those goals were unrealistic.

But then the novel's prospects diminished drastically. Eleven days after Edward Aswell accepted *Never Come Morning* for publication, the Imperial Japanese Navy bombed the United States naval base at Pearl Harbor. Congress declared war the following day, and thousands of people rushed to enlist in the service—but not Nelson. He had been working on his book for six years, and though the war was certain to overshadow its release, he wanted to see it arrive in stores and sit on shelves.

Never Come Morning is the story of a neighborhood whose children survive by selling or risking their bodies, so it's fitting that the novel's opening scene is set inside an arena where a bloodthirsty and indifferent crowd is watching a lopsided boxing match. It begins:

> At the ten-second warning to the evening's first preliminary, a newspaperman on the apron of the ring stood up to get his slicker off. He had the right arm out and was pulling at the left while watching a Mexican featherweight in the corner above his head. At the bell he left the sleeve dangling: to see a Pole with an army haircut come out of the opposite corner straight into the Mexican's left hand. The army haircut went back on his heels, stopped dead, and glanced unbelievingly at the Mex; then kept coming in.

The Polish fighter is Casimir "Casey" Benkowski. He has a rag for a mouthpiece, and there's no bone left at the bridge of his nose because he had it removed. The Mexican fighter hits him solidly, and then lets a flurry of punches fly. Casey falls to the canvas, senseless. He twitches when the referee's count reaches six, and regains his senses at eight, but he doesn't rise because he accepted twenty dollars to throw the fight before entering the ring.

Casey is sore and broke when he wakes the next morning. He gambled with the money he earned in the ring, and lost it all. He's twenty-nine years old, he's been boxing since he was thirteen, and he knows of only two ways to get money: fighting and stealing. In his neighborhood, a man named Bonifacy Konstantine controls both trades, so Casey goes looking for him.

Konstantine is a barber, but he makes his living by running the Polish Triangle's petty crime. He offers protection to a brothel, fixes fights, runs a card game, and trusts no one. He's a paranoid, conniving man who works out of a cluttered and filthy shop and disdains all human company. When he's alone, he deals himself five hands of poker to kill time, and even then, he's plagued by the idea that someone's cheating him. "When the thunder kills a devil," he says cryptically, "then a devil kills a Jew."

Casey has to knock on the barber's door several times before he's allowed to enter. Once inside, he perches on a stool and begins pleading his case. I want another fight, he tells the barber. "All the time I'm perfectin' the old technique," he says, but the barber's disinterest is plain, so Casey switches tacks and begs for a loan. The barber wants nothing to do with Casey, though, so he cuts him off. "No more fight," he says. "No more borrow."

That interaction sets *Morning*'s plot in motion. Casey decides to steal a slot machine from a gambling joint outside the Triangle when he realizes the barber is finished with him, and he recruits Finger Idzikowski and Bruno "Lefty Biceps" Bicek—the novel's protagonist—as his accomplices.

Bruno is a fatherless seventeen-year-old who dresses in raggedy clothes distributed by relief workers. He can only imagine two potential futures for himself—pitching in the major leagues or boxing professionally—and the only measure of success he understands is the regard of his peers. He constantly scrutinizes their expressions and mannerisms for evidence of his standing, and he's haunted by the fear that he'll never be as tough as he imagines a man should be.

"Bruno Bicek from Potomac Street had his own cunning," Nelson wrote. "He'd argue all day, with anyone, about anything, in daylight, and always end up feeling he'd won, that he'd been right all along. He'd refute himself, in daylight, for the mere sake of argument.

"But at night, alone, he refuted no one, denied nothing. He saw himself close up and clearly then, too clear for any argument."

Casey can see Bruno for the meek creature he is, and understands recruiting him will cost no more than a few flattering words. He tells Bruno about his plan to steal the slot machine, and promises to get Bruno a paying fight at the City Garden afterward and make him the "president 'n treasurer" of their athletic club. Bruno, Casey, and Finger go through with the burglary, and as they drive away, Finger Idzikowski calms Bruno's nerves by encouraging him to picture his impending fame. "LEFTY BICEPS MATCHED WITH BILLY CONN!" he incants. "POLISH WHITE HOPE WINS TITLE! LOUIS DECLINES RETURN BOUT!"

The heist makes Bruno bold. He had never previously revealed any ambition outside the boxing ring or the baseball diamond, but when he realizes he isn't likely to be arrested for the robbery, he begins asserting himself in the neighborhood. He brags, swaggers, and delivers edicts to the other boys in his gang, and as a result he becomes a target for the Triangle's rougher characters.

Bruno has a girlfriend named Steffi Rostenkowski—a widow's daughter who lives above a pool hall. She and Bruno were born on the same block two months apart, and grew up sharing swings and praying in the same church. He trusts her enough to make a fool of himself for the price of one of her laughs, and she speaks to him tenderly and calls him Bunny. They see each other often, and a few weeks after the slot machine robbery, Bruno takes Steffi to a carnival, where they walk past a sideshow, see a parade, and drink. That night, they sneak into a shed hidden beneath the El tracks, where they have sex and then lay on a bedspring in postcoital repose and nod off to sleep.

Then Catfoot Nowogrodski enters. He asks Bruno to step aside so he can have a turn with Steffi, but Bruno refuses. Fireball Kodadek appears next. He pulled a knife on Bruno once, and they've been rivals since. Bruno refuses to let Fireball enter as well, but doing so makes him nervous and fearful.

Catfoot senses Bruno's reluctance, and reminds him that the slot machine robbery put him in a dangerous position: "any time the barber wants he can put a finger on you fer the syndicate," he says. Then Fireball taunts Bruno: "What's eatin' you, Left'—you in love?"

And Bruno folds. He steps aside and allows Catfoot and Fireball to enter. He knows they intend to rape Steffi and doesn't want to see it happen, so he leaves. When he steps outside the shack, he finds a group of neighborhood boys standing around. Ashamed that he failed to protect Steffi, Bruno pretends that he's an accomplice to the attack. "This one's on me, fellas," he says. Then he leaves the scene.

After wandering around the neighborhood, Bruno returns to the shack under the El tracks and finds a dozen boys waiting in line to assault Steffi. The sight sickens him, and he decides to conceal his shame with violence. He spots a Greek boy in the line, alone—an easy target—tells him to leave, and then insults him. "Beat it, Sheeny," he says, "this is a white man's party."

But the Greek doesn't move. He looks around instead, and replies, "Make half those gorillas stay out of it 'n I'll show you who the white man is."

The crowd forms a circle like a ring then. The Greek, moving casually, begins unbuttoning his coat. Bruno watches him with apprehension. Then he hears Steffi's voice. "Next!" she says. She can't fight off her attackers, so she has decided to mock them. She has already been raped a half dozen times, but she keeps calling, "Next! Next!" and laughing "a laugh like a single drawn-out sob, hard as a man in handcuffs laughs."

Bruno loses control of himself when he hears Steffi, and advances on the Greek while the boy's arms are trapped inside his sleeves. Bruno punches him square on the cheek, staggers him, and continues swinging until his opponent falls. He kicks the boy in the head then, and leaves his body beneath the El tracks a few feet from where Steffi is being attacked.

Bruno recedes into the Triangle after that. He becomes Casey's sidekick, and they rob, steal, and get caught. Bruno goes to jail eventually, but never stops dreaming of becoming a boxing champion and making amends to Steffi. Steffi winds up in Mama T.'s brothel and the barber's bed, but never stops hoping Bruno will rescue her.

The lyricism of *Morning*'s prose and the flow of its narrative are the first elements of the book that stand out. Nelson structured his sentences to match the cadence of his characters' idiomatic language, so the book moves with the feel of a well-written speech—conceived for the mind, but punctuated for the ear. He also suppressed his authorial voice, and used the physical spaces his characters travel through as extensions of their inner lives, so the book reads like the story of a single complex organism, not a drama with a sprawling cast of characters.

The depth and detail of the reporting that went into the book's composition are also remarkable. Nelson conducted research like a sociologist, and brought his story to life by inserting observations, overheard dialogue, and physical details he spent years gathering. The padding doesn't reach the ceiling on the walls of the cell the officers of the Potomac Street Station use when they plan to beat a suspect, Nelson reports. It ends at head level, and Louis Anderson reached up there and scratched his name and the date of his imprisonment into the paint with a fingernail on three separate occasions. The northern fork of the Chicago River is bound on either side by "great mounds of trash and garbage," Nelson explains, "and in the valleys between each mound sunflowers [crowd], slender and bent; their petals glinting, in the dull copper light, like petals of wetted metal." And confinement, he makes clear, warps both the jailer and the jailed. "The more humbly a man looked out at [Officer] Comisky," he wrote, "the worse Comisky wanted to treat him."

But the most compelling element of *Morning* is its novelty. The book could be described as a coming-of-age story, a treatise on urban poverty, a boxing novel, or a memoir about a place, but Nelson's curiosity ranges so widely that those designations obscure more than they reveal. The book makes no concessions to genre, and when it evokes clichés, it does so only to subvert them. Its locale suggests it will be a naturalistic novel, but its narrative voice is tender and personal instead of distant and coldly observed. The prostitutes in Mama T.'s brothel are self-assured and calculating. Bruno is a hard man who hungers for fame, but also a boy who longs "for the warmth and security of the womb"—and no one rescues the damsel in distress.

The book ends in an arena, just the way it began, but this time Bruno is fighting. He enters the ring wearing tennis shoes and a blue robe, and he faces a man named Honeyboy Tucker. The stakes are high for both fighters. Tucker is a former state champion who can't afford to lose another match, and Bruno needs the prize money at stake to buy Steffi's freedom.

"All I demand is a clean fight," the referee announces when the fighters meet. "Is that askin' too much?" he asks.

It is. Bruno and Tucker feel each other out for less than a round before they begin trading body blows. Tucker, the savvier fighter, retreats behind his gloves, then reappears and catches Bruno with an uppercut that sends one of his teeth flying in "an arc through the light into the blue-gray fog about the ring." Bruno begins swinging wildly then, and Tucker responds by thumbing his eye. They battle to the point of exhaustion, and then beyond, but Tucker is the more disciplined fighter, so he gains the upper hand eventually. He saved some of his strength, so when he feels Bruno weaken in the eighth round, he slams him with a right—and then does it again and again.

Bruno falls, swinging blindly on his way down. "That was all," Nelson wrote. "He knew it was all. Tucker could come and get him now. He had nothing left to throw and nothing left to try." But Tucker doesn't come. He thinks Bruno is unconscious, so he walks along the ropes and smiles at the newspapermen seated along the apron of the ring. Bruno rises while Tucker is busy collecting his praise, advances, and uses the last bit of strength in his body to strike Tucker from behind. His right fist connects with Tucker's jaw two minutes and forty-eight seconds into the eighth round. The better man falls forward until his chin catches on the second rope, and then he hangs there, "smiling vacantly."

Bruno is declared the winner, but the glory of his ignoble victory fades quickly. He leaves the ring thinking about Steffi and dreaming of all the victories he has yet to claim. He makes it all the way to the changing room in that hopeful state, but before he can remove his trunks, a plainclothes officer enters. Bruno crossed the barber before the fight, and afterward, two witnesses provided the police with evidence that Bruno is a murderer.

"Got you for the Greek, Lefthander," an officer says. He offers to take Bruno into custody without shackling him, but Bruno declines. He extends his wrists instead, and after the handcuffs have been secured, he says, with practiced nonchalance, "Knew I'd never get t' be twenty-one anyhow."

Never Come Morning struck Nelson's doubters like a well-executed hook—they never saw it coming, and after it found purchase, they never felt quite so sure of themselves again. James T. Farrell, who hadn't been on speaking terms with Nelson since 1935, wrote to say, "I consider Never Come Morning one of the most important American novels that I have read in many years." Bud Fallon stopped teasing Nelson, and critics heaped on praise.

The *Providence Journal* called *Morning* a "novel of deep social significance," and the Montgomery, Alabama, *Advertiser* said it was "[b]rutal, sordid, tragic . . . splendidly-written." The *Oakland Tribune* went even further: "It is not too much to say that Algren shows every promise of taking on Steinbeck's cudgel, of continuing the Hemingway tradition or performing the great deeds of a Zola or a Dickens."

The *New York Times* reviewed *Morning* twice. This is "an unusual book and a brilliant book," one writer claimed. The other went deeper. "Mr. Algren blends the staccato rhythms of his characters with his own sentences to create as harmonious a style as recent American fiction can show," he said. Behind his "air of complete objectivity there lurks a moralist, a writer of parables."

Malcolm Cowley even used *Morning* as evidence that a new "Chicago school" of fiction had emerged. He placed it next to *Native Son*, where Nelson thought it belonged, and James T. Farrell's *Studs Lonigan* trilogy. He said Nelson beat both authors on some accounts, and reached into the past to find an analogue for his literary sensibility. Nelson is "not by instinct a novelist," he said. "He is a poet of the Chicago slums, and he might well be [Carl] Sandburg's successor."

But then the critics moved on to newer releases, and a backlash to Nelson's book took shape in Chicago.

Nelson later said that he wrote *Morning* because he felt "that if we did not understand what was happening to men and women who shared all the horrors but none of the privileges of our civilization, then we did not know what was happening to ourselves." But the Polish Roman Catholic Union suspected he had a darker purpose. The group discussed the book at one of their meetings, decided they had been slandered, and started a letter-writing campaign that was promoted by the Polish press. They asked people to send complaints about the book to Harper's, and they began pressuring the Chicago Public Library to keep *Morning* off their shelves.

"I protest strongly against any further publishing of this book for it fosters nothing but racial enmity, religious intolerance and national disunity, and in trying times such as the present, should have no place in our libraries and homes," one letter said.

"It is contemptible in every respect," another said, "and can be suspected at aiming at but one thing: to discredit a nationality group."

"Herr Goebbels's devilishly cunning mind," a third letter claimed, "could not have published a more rotten propaganda volume to discredit and degrade the Polish people."

Aswell defended the book aggressively, and so did Nelson. He wrote pleading letters to his antagonists, insisting he was no bigot and asserting his goodwill, but conceding that the timing of the book's release was unfortunate. He had been working on *Morning* for years, he explained, and had no way of knowing Germany would invade Poland before he finished.

Neither Aswell's support nor Nelson's explanations did any good though. One of Nelson's correspondents hardened his stance as their dialogue continued, and became threatening. "You might care to know that probably my information regarding your person is somewhat deeper than you suspect," he wrote. Then the Chicago Public Library bowed to the union's demands. The library board held a meeting to discuss the book, and decided not to include it in their collection—it wasn't removed from the shelves, just never placed on them.

Nelson was broke and dispirited by July. When *Morning* was released, the Writers' Project fired him again because the book's publication counted as outside employment. He had been hoping that royalties would support him for a time, but they never materialized. The war suppressed the book's sales, and so did the Polish community's protest.

Bud Fallon heard about Nelson's plight, and wrote to offer a solution. He said Nelson could live with him for the summer and work as a welder's assistant in East St. Louis. It was a rare act of generosity on Fallon's part, and Nelson accepted and began packing.

Then *Morning*'s reception took another dramatic turn. A letter arrived at Nelson's apartment as he was preparing to leave Chicago, and the return address on the envelope said: Martha Gellhorn Hemingway, Finca Vigia, San Francisco De Paula, Cuba. Nelson opened it, and read: "I just want to tell you how terrific your book is, and it ought to be the best of the best sellers if books sold on a basis of their goodness and you ought to get one of the big prizes again if they give them rightly; and if you get none of these things it will be because people are dopes, which is just possible."

Gellhorn Hemingway was a war correspondent and, compared to Nelson, a veteran in the literary world. She had reported from Spain during the Civil War, and had four books to her credit. She was also married to Ernest Hemingway, and Nelson—who had admired Hemingway's work for years—must have swooned when he reached the end of her letter and read, "Ernest has been spreading your book around Cuba, and you have many devoted readers here."

Gellhorn Hemingway wrote a letter to Edward Aswell at Harper's as well, and sent him a promotional quote for the book that read, "*Never Come Morning* hasn't a dull or a useless sentence in it. Nelson Algren has done something wonderfully exciting to words, so that they look and sound new."

Aswell ordered a second printing of *Morning* on the basis of Gellhorn Hemingway's support, but by the time the book went to press, Nelson was living in East St. Louis, paying dues to the Boilermakers & Helpers, Local 363, and trying to master the acetylene torch.

"Do It the Hard Way"

(October 1942–July 16, 1943)

The military had a hard time finding soldiers at the beginning of the war. It drafted millions of people and gave them medical exams, and on the basis of those exams, millions had to be rejected—twenty percent had "mental disease," while ten percent had syphilis. Once it did find men, the military had a hard time keeping them. They often entered the service healthy, had sex on leave, and then developed ulcerated sores on their way back to the front lines. Before penicillin came into vogue, venereal disease was hell—the cure was arsenic, and men receiving treatment couldn't fight.

The army declared syphilis "military saboteur number one" and launched a major prevention campaign. Officers warned soldiers to avoid "victory girls" and "good-time Charlottes" when they were on leave. The Works Progress Administration created posters to raise awareness—SHE MAY LOOK CLEAN—BUT, one cautioned, while another advised, FOOL THE AXIS—USE PROPHYLAXIS—and major cities started initiatives designed to stop its spread. In Chicago, that job fell to the Health Department.

When Nelson returned to the city after working in East St. Louis for the summer, Jack Conroy told him that the newly formed Venereal Disease Control Project was hiring. Conroy had been laid off when the Writers' Project shut down a few weeks earlier, and afterward he became an investigator for the Health Department. Nelson applied for the same position, and he was hired as well.

Nelson and Conroy worked out of 56 West Hubbard Street, near the Chicago River. People visited their office to be tested for syphilis and gonorrhea, and if their tests came back positive, Nelson and Conroy asked for the names of their sexual partners, made a list of those names, and then tracked down every person on it and delivered the bad news. "You have been exposed to an infectious disease," they said.

Leads were often slim, so the job involved a lot of detective work. Sometimes, Nelson and Conroy had nothing to go on but a description and a favorite saloon, and it took them weeks to find their target. They visited boardinghouses and questioned desk clerks, stood around on street corners, interrogated bartenders, and then chased the tips they collected wherever they led.

Responses to their arrival varied. Some people pretended they weren't home; others ran, and a few became violent. A pimp came after Conroy once with a knife, and a woman swung a baseball bat at them. Many were unsurprised. "I was waitin' to see how she come out," a mechanic named Anton told Nelson with philosophical calm. Denial was common. "Not sick," one woman insisted. "When I feel weak, I go to doctor. Health Department not care when I on relief and baby sick, they not come then, why come now?"

Conroy hated the job, but Nelson loved it. "He was very sympathetic," Conroy remembered. He would sit and talk to people if they were interested, and wouldn't report them to the Health Department if they pleaded.

On occasion, pleasant news from the publishing world interrupted the monotony of infectious disease. The *New Republic* named *Never Come Morning* one of the fifteen best works of fiction published in 1942— along with books by Steinbeck and Faulkner—"Biceps," a selection from the novel, was adapted for the radio and included in the *Best American Short Stories* collection, and the Chicago Fiction Guild invited Nelson to deliver a speech at the Hamilton Hotel.

Then, in March, the magazine *The Writer* published an essay Nelson wrote. It had commissioned the piece six months earlier with the request that he write something about naturalistic fiction, and because it was a loosely defined assignment, he went beyond his mandate.

Nelson had been asking himself what purpose literature serves ever since *Boots* failed and proletarian writing faded. Why do people write? he asked. Why should they? Trying to answer those questions was one of the more enduring projects of his life, and for the next three decades he circled back to them periodically and updated his response—reiterating some points, adapting his ideas, and shifting the emphasis of his arguments. The essay he submitted to *The Writer* was the first draft of his answer. He called the piece "Do It the Hard Way," and in it he argues that literature is a social institution, not an academic or artistic one.

No tool at a writer's disposal—not symbolism, allusion, or motif—has any value outside the context of the broader world, Nelson said, and when authors use them in service of inconsequential ideas, their work is destined for irrelevance. "Their books—and we see them on the best seller lists every day—are artful dodges," he wrote, "*tours de force* which say nothing gracefully, or nothing lyrically, or nothing nostalgically, or—best of all—nothing mystically. But still: nothing. Like eating cotton candy—a mouthful of the stuff and wisp—nothing left but a sweetish taste and a clinging coat on the tongue."

Work that lasts grows out of experience, Nelson argued—but not necessarily the writer's own. He rejected the idea of writing in service of a political movement, and counseled authors to describe the world without making any concession for the way they would like things to be. "Feel" your way into a story, he wrote; don't "regard it from the sidelines by some formal outline." The trick is simply to be in touch with the world, Nelson said. "All the classics, read and re-read, can't help you catch the ring of truth as does the word heard first hand."

The literary vision Nelson describes in his essay is transgressive, but also profoundly democratic and optimistic. Writers are obliged to confront society with evidence of its shortcomings, he argues, but they can do so and still find a large audience. "There isn't a solid publisher going who won't take a book dealing with any strata of any society so long as it is a true book," he says. "The truth still holds that great rewards do, at last, come to the boldest; to those who permit neither avarice nor shame to modify what they truly feel and truly know."

Fatefully, Nelson believed it was possible for a writer to be famous, well paid, and uncompromising all at once.

In the spring, Amanda reentered Nelson's life. Russ Finch had recently been drafted and sent overseas, and when Nelson heard Amanda was living alone again, he visited her apartment. They had sex that day, and afterward they began seeing each other casually.

A few weeks after Nelson and Amanda reconnected, Nelson was jumped by two men who tore his coat and stole six dollars from him. The assault took place after midnight, but Nelson went to Amanda's apartment immediately to tell her about it. His hair was askew when he arrived, and his eyes were wild. The police had given him a card that guaranteed him admission to show-ups at the detective division when he reported the crime, and that meant he would be able to see who was arrested each week and hear the police question them. The possibilities excited him, and he wanted to tell Amanda about his good fortune immediately. She let him in that morning, and soon afterward she moved into his apartment.

Amanda was working as an administrator for a labor law firm at the time, and her days were long—twelve hours in a shift, sometimes more. She wasn't home much, but Nelson doted on her when she was. He made coffee, oatmeal, and poached eggs every morning, saw her to the door, and did the dishes before she returned. Amanda thought he was making a point—as if to say, "Now I can give you the life you wanted when we first met." "He had an awful lot of guilt in relation to me," she said.

The war dictated Chicago's rhythm that year. Gas, butter, coffee, beans, juice, sugar, and oil were all being rationed. Cars were puttering along at thirty-five miles per hour to extend the life of their tires, and people were being advised to eat lima beans because there wasn't enough meat to go around. But Nelson and Amanda floated above the strife in a lovers' bliss. They visited the racetrack and bet horses. They watched the police show-ups at 1121 South State Street and held hands while the chief detective questioned that week's batch of suspects. Amanda bought her clothes at Saks Fifth Avenue, and when Nelson received a royalty check from Harper's, he used the money to buy Amanda a honeydew melon—a rare luxury at the time.

The environment in Nelson's apartment had been free and easy since he returned from East St. Louis. He was working on a few short stories—one set in a Chicago vagabond hotel, one in a west Texas jail, another about a boxer—but he didn't have a big project in mind, so he let people drop by to play cards, scrounge a meal, or gossip. After Amanda moved in, though, Nelson began chiding his guests. Watch your language around her, he said. "She's a nice girl."

People soon stopped visiting, and when that happened, Nelson asked Amanda to move out so he could have the apartment to himself again. He didn't want to break up, but didn't communicate that well, and his request hurt her feelings.

Amanda didn't protest or start a fight though. Instead, she approached her boss and requested a transfer to the firm's San Francisco office. She bought a one-way train ticket when it was approved, and then she went home and told Nelson she was leaving.

Nelson tried to convince her to stay in Chicago, but couldn't. He asked if he could escort her to Union Station instead, but she refused, so they said their goodbyes in the West Evergreen Avenue apartment. He gave her a copy of Woody Guthrie's autobiography, *Bound for Glory*, as a parting gift, and then she walked through the front door and down the high front steps.

Six years and eleven months had passed since Nelson met Amanda, and though he knew they had no business being married, he had a hard time letting go of her. After she left, he rambled through the apartment and found a Kontowicz coffee-sugar ration book in the upper right-hand dresser drawer, along with a stack of recipes and a picture of Amanda at her high school graduation. He went to the track later, and bet on the horses she would have bet on, and then he wrote to her. "The fact of your being gone away left me feeling hollow and—I might as well admit it—a little afraid. Of what I don't know. Just like all of a sudden the world had gotten too big and too dark. . . .

"I still feel, at heart, that from where you're sitting, going to S.F. is a hundred to one chance that you'll eventually find more happiness than with me. By 100 to 1 I guess I meant 1 to 100. I mean the odds are all in your favor. . . . And yet it feels tough, very tough."

The months after Amanda left were a lonely and anxious time for Nelson. The war was turning Chicago into a city of widows and orphans, most of his friends were overseas or about to leave, and he suspected his draft number would be called soon. His fate was in the hands of generals whose armies were slaughtering their way across continents he had never visited, but there was nothing he could do but wait, and worry. He went to work and tried to write. He checked the mail for letters bearing government seals and scanned the papers for news from the front. YANK BOMBERS BATTER THREE JAP WARSHIPS, the *Tribune* announced. M'ARTHUR AIRFORCE POUNDS MUNDA, KAHILI, the paper gloated, and on July 15 it ran a margin-to-margin headline that read CAPTURE 12,000 IN SICILY!

The following day, Nelson's induction form arrived in the mail. It said he was going to be an army man.

The Anonymous Man

(July 17, 1943–November 26, 1945)

A very fit Nelson posing for Amanda at Camp Maxey in 1944.

Photo by Amanda Algren, courtesy of Rick Kinsinger

The army base at Fort Bragg, North Carolina, was organized chaos under open skies when Nelson arrived. Fog rolled between loblolly pines and single-story barracks in the mornings, and when buglers blasted reveille, one hundred thousand men wiped sleep from their eyes and stood at attention while American flags rose through the mist. During the day, the air was dense and clingy. Soldiers saluted in limp uniforms, and the snare roll of semiautomatic rifle fire buzzed in the background. Mortars exploded and infantrymen drifted toward sandy soil on parachutes made from the nylon of recycled stockings.

The army transformed Nelson into Private Abraham, serial number 36679611, gave him a cot, and assigned him to an artillery battalion where he became one small piece of a finely tuned machine.

Nelson's unit woke before dawn each day and did calisthenics. Then they boxed, marched through the scrub pine forest, rolled logs to build strength, and practiced shooting. They visited the rifle range, tucked the stocks of their M-1 carbines into the fleshy spot beneath their clavicles, and pulled their triggers—over and over—and they fired four-inch shells through the seven-foot barrels of their 105-millimeter howitzers and sent them flying for seven miles. Then, at night, they stood sentry beneath dark, insomniac skies.

Jack Conroy sent Nelson news from Chicago and the Fallonites when there was news to deliver, and Nelson reciprocated with the details of an infantryman's routines. "[T]hey play for keeps down here," he wrote. "I don't know yet whether it's killing or curing me— sometimes it feels like the one and sometimes like the other."

Martha Gellhorn Hemingway wrote to Nelson as well, and so did Geraldine Brooks from *Poetry* magazine. Nelson told them both there was nothing to tell—his life was repetition, the base was his world. "We put in so much time, with so little let-up that we don't get a chance to think or wonder about the war itself at all," he wrote. "I haven't seen a newspaper for a week and probably wouldn't bother reading it if I did."

Nelson did not consider himself a brave man, physically, but he became eager to get overseas after the army taught him to fight. The war was the defining event of his generation, so he wanted to see it firsthand, and as his training dragged on, his eagerness transformed into anxiety. The war seemed to be winding down, and he feared it would end before he shipped out. While he was stuck firing .30 bullets at paper targets in North Carolina, the Allies were bombing Berlin, and the Italian navy was dieseling toward Malta to surrender.

Nelson's anxiety continued to build until his unit received its orders in December, and then disappointment and confusion replaced it. They were being sent to the front, but he was going to Texas.

The army reassigned Nelson to the 758th Field Artillery Battalion and ordered him to report to Camp Maxey, a small military base on the Gulf Coastal Plain, just north of Paris, Texas, that had a Norman Rockwell feel. There was a movie theater on site, a barbershop, a whitewashed guest house overlooking a lake, and a faux German town emblazoned with swastikas where soldiers practiced sweeping streets and kicking down doors.

Nelson tried to leave Camp Maxey just after he arrived. He asked the army to send him to the front, but they denied his request. He tried again, and when they rejected him a second time, he changed tactics. He requested a transfer to a medical unit because medics were in high demand overseas, and when that request was denied, he began making a joke of his zeal. "Not that I'm feeling particularly sanguine these days," he wrote to a friend, "it's just that the endless tedium of doing right face and left face for six months could make anyone prefer to take his chances in action."

Nelson puzzled over the riddle of his denials. Three out of every four US soldiers were being sent overseas that year, but not him—not even when he volunteered; not even when he volunteered twice; not even when he offered to accept a less glamorous position. Eventually, he developed a theory: He thought he was being denied the chance to fight because he was Jewish. The man who ran Camp Maxey was a notorious anti-Semite named Buell Smith, and in the army, Nelson was Private Abraham, not Nelson Algren. He hadn't used his legal name in a decade, and when he convinced himself it was keeping him out of the war, he petitioned to have it changed.

A judge seated on the Circuit Court of Cook County granted his request on January 26, 1944, and afterward Nelson Algren Abraham became Nelson Algren—no middle initial. When the judge's order arrived in Texas, Nelson submitted it to the army so his personnel forms, uniform, and dog tags could be altered. They accepted the papers, but informed him the change could take time—maybe months.

While Nelson waited for the army to act, he became apathetic. He saluted poorly and stopped pressing his uniform or polishing his boots. He trotted casually behind his unit when they ran, and when they marched he slipped out of formation and returned to the barracks.

Don't bother with these routines, he told the men he bunked with. There's no point.

Nelson's sergeant was a stubborn man named Tadday who had a punitive mind. He took Nelson aside when he noticed his insubordination, and spoke about discipline. He yelled at Nelson when he realized talk wouldn't be enough, and then he threatened him. He assigned Nelson to Sunday detail for a month, told the mess hall staff to give him the nastiest job they had, and challenged him to a fistfight. Then he tried to have Nelson discharged.

"I have found this man to be a very poor soldier both in appearance and in the carrying out of orders," Tadday wrote in a report. "... [N]o amount of punishment or disciplinary action has any effect on him due to his sullen attitude." His effort failed though. A psychiatrist evaluated Nelson and determined there was nothing wrong with him. He suggested a transfer instead of a discharge, but his recommendation was rejected, just as Nelson's had been.

By March, Nelson was so desperate to get away from Tadday that he began begging for help. Once, he noticed a captain named Aptheker on base, approached him, saluted meekly, and asked for an audience.* He had never seen Aptheker before and had no reason to expect his request

---

* The Aptheker here is, serendipitously, Herbert Aptheker—the Marxist historian who wrote the seven-volume *Documentary History of the Negro People* (1951–1994). He is also the source for the claim that Colonel Buell Smith was an anti-Semite. Aptheker told the story of meeting Nelson to Robin D. G. Kelley many years later, and it was published in *The Journal of American History*. In that interview, Aptheker says, "The commanding officer over there was an anti-Semitic fanatic. And I'm Jewish."

would be granted, but he was pleasantly surprised by the response he received.

"I'm Nelson Algren," he said.

"Oh, that's wonderful," Aptheker replied.

Nelson was shocked. "You know my work?" he asked.

"Of course," Aptheker said. He was a historian, a reader, and a longtime member of the Communist Party. He invited Nelson to his quarters and told him to speak his mind.

"You've gotta get me out of this," Nelson said. "I'm going crazy, I'm going to blow my brains out, I can't remain in the artillery."

Aptheker demurred when Nelson pleaded, but later he approached a colonel named Parker and had Nelson transferred to the 460th Medical Collection Company. Parker, fortuitously, had also read *Never Come Morning*.

Amanda, who had recently moved to Los Angeles for work, boarded a train there in the summer and rode to Dallas, where she caught a bus that carried her across prairie grasslands until she reached Paris, Texas. She and Nelson had been corresponding regularly since their breakup, and they had developed a "really deep friendship" through their letters that was more satisfying than their romantic relationship had ever been.

Nelson wrote to Amanda about his frustrations with the army for months, and then, after his transfer, he told her he was going to be sent overseas. He said he would be supporting the troops who had just landed in Normandy, and asked her to visit before he left.

The army provided Nelson and Amanda with a small room on the second floor of the guest house by the lake. They moved in when she arrived, and for two days they pretended to be a couple again. She snapped pictures of him posing with his shirt off when they were on base, and took a shot of him strolling through Paris wearing his peaked private's cap when they went into town for dinner. They played Ping-Pong and they talked.

Nelson told Amanda that the army had kept him stateside because he was Jewish, but they would have to send him into the war zone now that he was a medic. He was excited about going overseas, Amanda said later, but also scared.

Nelson and Amanda went to bed together on the third night of their reunion as a way of saying goodbye. They lay down, and then Amanda reached for her diaphragm. Nelson balked. He was afraid he might die in the war, and he wanted to get her pregnant so that some piece of him was guaranteed to survive. Amanda refused, and then Nelson stalked the room with his head down until he exhausted himself, climbed into bed, and went to sleep.

Amanda left three days later, and Nelson escorted her part of the way home to make amends for his boorish behavior. They boarded a bus in Paris together, and rode to Dallas, where they parted sadly.

The 460th Medical Collection Company received its orders a few weeks after Amanda's departure. They were headed for the front on September 29, and Nelson was scheduled to leave with them. He climbed out of his bunk on the appointed morning and put on his uniform. He packed his duffel and headed for the train tracks just east of the base, where his unit had been told to assemble, but before he reached the station, someone pulled him aside.

You've been transferred, they said—you're not going.

Richard Wright called Nelson that same week. The two old friends hadn't been in touch since Nelson entered the army, and Wright wanted to catch up. He had avoided the draft since they last spoke, and had written a memoir called *Black Boy* that had become a best seller.

Nelson was glad to hear his friend's good news, but didn't have much to say for himself. He had no accomplishments to brag about, no stories to relay. He only had complaints, and he saved those for the letter he wrote after getting off the phone.

"I haven't hit the army with a bang; but there's been a mighty cracking sound when it hit me," Nelson told Wright. Until I joined the service, he said, "I didn't know there were so many ways of getting screwed. Needless to say—the Army does all the screwing."

Nelson and Wright had both been reluctant to enlist in the military, so Nelson felt compelled to explain why he was eager to get to Europe and disappointed to be stuck stateside. "I wanted the adventure of going across, of course; but I also wanted to share, as a writer, the big stuff of our times," he wrote. "I would have gladly stayed away from the big stuff, the real thing, had I had any choice. But since I've put in fifteen months I feel I ought, and have the right, to see it."

"I'd feel much better if I knew the reason" for the military's reluctance to send me overseas, he wrote. The army had changed Nelson's name to Private Algren by then, so he had dispensed with the idea that he was being held back because he was Jewish, and developed a new theory. "I've even gotten the notion that, somewhere along the line somebody a lot higher up wrote 'Subversive' in code" on my personnel form, he told Wright. "That's strictly a notion ... which I stumbled upon in my brooding over causes and effects in the army."

Nelson was guessing blindly, but he missed the mark by only a hair. His paperwork was stamped SPECIAL ASSIGNMENT, not "Subversive," and it wasn't in code—it was right at the top of the first page.*

The FBI had been keeping a file on Nelson since 1940, when his name was mentioned to the House Committee on Un-American Activities. They didn't add much to it at first, but the publication of *Never Come Morning* reinvigorated their interest. The Polish organization whose members sent letters to Edward Aswell at Harper's also contacted the FBI and accused Nelson of sedition, and the FBI had decided to investigate.

* It's not clear precisely why Nelson was held back from the front. The army never said it kept transferring him because he was a Communist, but that seems like the most likely explanation. Its scrutiny and the FBI's are well documented, and Nelson's army file is clearly marked SPECIAL ASSIGNMENT—even though he was given only menial tasks.

A special agent named John Bowker went to Nelson's apartment on West Evergreen Avenue in November 1943 and looked around. He asked the building's tenants what Nelson was like and where he had gone, and then, following a lead, he questioned one of Nelson's friends. He compiled a dossier when his investigation was complete, and because he knew Nelson had been drafted, he sent a copy of his findings to military intelligence, which, in turn, kept the FBI informed of Nelson's whereabouts.

According to Camp Maxey gossip, all of Nelson's mail was read—coming *and* going—because he was a Communist.

Nelson knew none of that, and never would. He was certain only that something was keeping him out of the war, and suspicion continued to plague him.

The army transferred Nelson to a medical company called the 125th Evacuation Hospital next. He moved into one of the base tents his new unit had erected on the sandy soil at the edge of Camp Maxey, and then he began training again. He bandaged fake wounds and carried soldiers around on stretchers. He helped collapse the unit's tents for practice, erected them again, and languished.

The evacuation hospital received its orders two months after Nelson was assigned to it. They were scheduled to board a train headed for the East Coast on November 27, and to proceed overseas from there.

Nelson prepared to leave on the morning of his departure. He packed his duffel and stripped his cot, but he didn't expect to make it off base. He had been through the same routine twice before, and had learned about wishful thinking.

Some of the men in Nelson's unit snuck into the barracks that afternoon and confirmed his suspicion. There were hundreds of duffel bags inside, organized into two piles—one composed of bags that had been stenciled for transport; one of bags that had no markings.

Nelson's bag was in the second pile, so the soldiers in his unit went looking for him. "You're not going," they said.

Nelson went into the orderly room then, saluted a sergeant, and asked if they could speak in private. The man agreed, and when they were alone, Nelson pressed his case. I know I'm not supposed to make it on the train, he said, but I want to see the war. "I don't want to get left behind, you know."

The sergeant pleaded ignorance while Nelson begged, but eventually he relented, and had Nelson's bag loaded onto the train.

Nelson filed onto a passenger car, shoulder to shoulder with a bunch of twenty-, twenty-one-, and twenty-two-year-old boys from Texas and Tennessee who were scared, boastful, and ignorant. The train rolled east until it reached Camp Kilmer, in New Jersey, and then Nelson's unit bunked down for a week and requested day passes so they could see New York City before they shipped out. "Looking forward to the next step in the game," Nelson wrote to Jack Conroy.

On December 8, the evacuation hospital traveled north to the New York Port of Embarkation, where its soldiers lined up on a pier. It was cold and raining. Wind blew in strong frigid gusts, and their ship—a luxury liner called the *Dominion Monarch* that had been modified to carry troops—loomed above them. Timid bay waves lapped against its hull, and Red Cross workers moved through the crowd, distributing coffee, donuts, and concerned farewells. It was dark by the time the *Monarch* was loaded, and darker still when it slipped away from its berth and began weaving its way through the tangle of boats in New York Harbor. When the troops woke in the morning, the American shore was already a memory.

The 417 soldiers in Nelson's unit disembarked from the *Dominion Monarch* when it docked on the southern shore of England after eleven days at sea, and began unloading their gear. That task consumed two days, and when it was complete, they moved into wooden barracks at Camp Penally, in Wales. They expected to move again soon, but instead they remained inactive for months.

The evacuation hospital returned to the English shore in March, boarded a ship called the *Llangibby Castle*, and crossed the English Chanel. SS *President Warfield* carried them up the Seine next, and closer, finally, to the front. The soldiers in Nelson's unit had trained for months and thought seriously about dying, but they were entirely unprepared to perform the duties they would be assigned in Europe. Ready to be heroes, they never suspected that their time in the field would be defined by monotony and tedium, not glory and daring.

When the unit reached the outskirts of Duclair, France, it moved into Camp Twenty Grand—a sprawl of square tents that had been erected on a muddy plain. It was bitterly cold, so they hacked away at the nearby forest and kept fires burning through the night to stay warm. "There was no war near there," Nelson said. They traveled east in freight cars next, and disembarked at Château-Regnault, where they dug pit latrines near the point where the Meuse River coils back on itself like a snake. Then they waited some more.

On April 3, they loaded into trucks and began driving. They passed through France, Belgium, and Holland, and then they entered Germany. They crossed the Rhine near Krefeld, and joined the battle of the Ruhr Pocket—a fight between three hundred thousand Allied soldiers and the four hundred thousand enfeebled Germans they had encircled. They reached the front lines late at night and decided to stop and pitch their tents. A sentry lit a bonfire to keep warm, and soon the Germans began to barrage them with artillery fire. "They were firing everything they could lay hands on," Nelson said later, "rocks, old bed springs, everything."

After operating under fire for a week, the unit loaded its patients and tents onto trucks and retreated to Mönchengladbach, fifteen miles behind the line. They moved again on May 1, and while they were in transit, Adolph Hitler raised a Walther PPK to his temple and pulled the trigger. The war in Europe was over, but the men in Nelson's unit had no idea. The news reached them several days later, and there was no celebration when it arrived because battles were still raging in the Pacific.

The unit occupied the St. Francis hospital next—a large, regal building in the countryside that looked like a gingerbread house. It was surrounded by manicured lawns, and it had thick Romanesque walls and narrow paired windows. Seventy nuns lived inside, and they had a bakery, steam cookers, and refrigerators at their disposal.

The members of Nelson's unit made themselves at home. They played volleyball, football, and softball on the hospital's lawns. They produced a daily newspaper called *The Gauzette*, and they slipped away at night to trade coffee and cigarettes for wine in nearby villages. They returned before the sun rose, and spent the small hours of the morning gambling—Nelson especially. He favored shooting dice with a man who insisted he was the only player allowed to roll.

"Don't worry," the man chided when someone tried to take a turn, "gotta golden arm."

The men in Nelson's unit had to rotate through the hospital in twelve-hour shifts when they weren't at play, though, so the time they spent at the St. Francis hospital was like vacationing in the circle of purgatory closest to hell. When they were at work, they bandaged lacerations that had begun to fester, watched diphtheria lesions spread across limbs, and listened to soldiers with pneumonia cough up hunks of phlegm. Two men on each shift did nothing but walk from bed to bed, carrying needles dripping with penicillin.

The unit's first patients were soldiers, but after the fighting stopped, prisoners and freed slave laborers began arriving. They were Russian, French, Belgian, and Dutch, and most were barely alive.

Once, Nelson helped care for a sixteen-year-old Russian boy. The Germans had forced him to work until his feet froze, and then they discarded him like trash. American soldiers discovered him in a barn, and by the time he arrived at the hospital, he weighed only forty-five pounds. There was a line of ulcerated sores running down his back, and the tip of a vertebra poked through the skin at the center of each one.

Nelson called him a "ghost." I "never hope to see another," he told a friend. "The terrible part of looking at him is that his breath still comes and goes—and you still have to reckon with the eyes—which are still living—and look out in a gaze of unrelieved horror from the skull."*

After forty-two days, the unit left the St. Francis hospital and drove to Bad Kreuznach. They camped on the shore of the Nahe River, and then they were ordered to prepare for deployment to the Pacific. They moved again, camping outside of Reims, France, and waited for further orders—first for days, then for weeks. Furloughs were granted, and soldiers took leave in Belgium and on the French Riviera.

Nelson was in Paris, staying at the Grand Hotel de Chicago, when the Japanese surrendered. The announcement arrived at 4 a.m., and the party it sparked lasted for four days. Soldiers poured into the streets, carrying English-language newspapers with headlines that read PEACE and JAPS QUIT, and then commandeered army vehicles and drove them in a slow, slithering conga line between the Red Cross club in the Hotel de Paris and the Place de l'Opéra—two miles in each direction. Men and women jumped on the trucks as they passed, carried flags through the streets, and yelled, and drank, and kissed.

The war was over, and Nelson had managed to experience all of its tedium without tasting a moment of glory. He returned to Reims when the party ended, and rejoined his unit. Then he boarded a third-class rail coach and headed for Marseille—his last stop, he hoped, before returning home.

Marseille was a ruin when Nelson arrived. The Germans had occupied the city for nearly two years, and they had been brutal stewards. In the Old Port district, walls jutted from piles of rubble like tombstones set at the heads of burial mounds, and cobblestones that had been ripped from the streets had collected into huge piles. Dozens of boats rested on their keels in the shallow water of the port, where the Germans sank them in a vain attempt to hold off the Allies, and the walls of

---

* Amazingly, this boy survived.

the cathedral overlooking the city—Notre-Dame de la Garde—were pocked with bullet holes.

The muddy hillside beneath the church had become a campground for GIs after the fighting ceased, and when Nelson reached Marseille, he joined them. His superiors ordered him to stay there until they could get him back to Chicago, but they couldn't say when that would happen or how. "I just had a cot and my belongings," Nelson said later, "and in the morning the Sargent [sic] would come and tell me what outfit I belonged to. . . . He'd say 'Now you're tank corps.' The next day he'd say, 'Now you're field artillery.' They tried everything to get us on that boat."

"The town was full, full of guys with arms," Nelson said. There were British troops, Americans, Canadians, and Senegalese, and because there were few military police to keep them in check, the black market thrived. Brothels operated twenty-four hours a day, poker games went all night, and soldiers were able to trade American cigarettes or oranges for sex or wine. The city was a wild and free place, and Nelson loved it. "Every morning I crept out of my little shelter-half, jumped on a truck without a pass, and spent the whole day living off the black-market," he explained. "I was responsible to nobody, or anything."

Nelson lived that way for three months, and later, when he thought back on the weeks he spent trading Eisenhower coats for Chianti and studying the wrecked ships rocking in the port, he recognized them as the "most isolated" but "least despairing" of his life. "I was the anony-mous man," he said. "I was finally myself. When I crept back into my camp" each night "with nothing to show for the long day's toil but half a bottle of cheap red wine, that, for me, was the happy time."

But eventually, Nelson began to long for home. "It seemed like it was time," he said. I had been drifting for years, "first riding the rails and then jumping around, then after that, jumping around with the Army from place to place." I was ready, he said, to stop moving and "do one thing the rest of my life and live in one place" and "write and simply not be preoccupied either with politics or with anything that wasn't pertinent to myself."

Part III

EVERY DAY IS D-DAY UNDER THE EL

You can't make an arsenal of a nation and yet expect its great cities to produce artists. It's in the nature of the overbraided brass to build walls about the minds of men—as it is in the nature of the arts to tear those dark walls down. Today, under the name of "security," the dark shades are being drawn.

—Chicago: City on the Make, *1951*

Exploring the Neon Wilderness

(November 27, 1945–February 20, 1947)

After returning from the war, Nelson often collected material for his stories by visiting Division Street. Photo by Art Shay, courtesy of the Art Shay Archive

The army delivered Nelson to Camp Grant, in Illinois, on a gloomy Tuesday in November, and moved him into a wooden barracks building. It was just above freezing, and snow was falling lightly.

The base was just a couple hundred wooden buildings set on a barren plain north and west of Chicago, and for four days, Nelson did nothing but mark time—something he had grown accustomed to in the service. Then, on his fifth day back in Illinois, he reported to the base's

separation center and accepted $160.60 and an honorable discharge
form that said: Private Nelson Algren spent two years four months and
seventeen days in the army. He earned two overseas service bars, an
American Campaign Medal, a European African Middle Eastern Theater Ribbon with one bronze battle star, and a good conduct medal.
He was a "literary writer" when he entered the service, and a "litter
bearer" when he left.

When Nelson reached Chicago later that day, he went looking for
a flower shop, and when he found one, he bought his mother a dozen
roses. Then he located a payphone and dialed Ravenswood 2405. He
let it ring for a while, but Goldie didn't answer.

Nelson wanted to hear a friendly voice, but there weren't many people left in Chicago for him to call. Amanda was living in California,
and most of his friends were gone. Some had chased opportunity east,
toward the publishing industry, while he was away; others had drifted
west toward Hollywood. Some died in the war, and a few let their radical pretensions die, bought tiny homes in Gary, Indiana, and spent
their time trying to earn enough money to make up for the years they
dedicated to the revolution.

Nelson tried a few more numbers, but they all rang in vain, so he
searched the directory until he found a listing for Margaret Butler,
Dorothy Farrell's widowed mother. He dialed, and Dorothy's voice
came through the line. She and Nelson hadn't seen each other in
years—not since 1939, possibly—but she was happy he called.

Come over, she said.

Nelson found Dorothy's building on a maple-lined street near the
University of Chicago, and when he rang her bell, she invited him
inside and told him to make himself at home. Her sister Virginia was
visiting as well, and the family apartment was large and comfortable.
There was food and liquor on hand, and Nelson spent the day talking
about the war, catching up on events in Chicago, and cracking jokes.
"He was one of the wittiest men I have ever known," Dorothy said.

Dorothy and Virginia asked Nelson to stay for dinner, and he accepted. He finally reached Goldie after he finished eating, said his goodbyes, and prepared to leave.

Do you want to take these flowers to your mother? Dorothy asked.

"No, the flowers are for you," Nelson lied.

Then he made his way to the single basement room at 2717 Lawrence Avenue where Goldie was living, greeted her, and settled in among the debris of their family's past—a framed newspaper dating back to the Civil War, a cuckoo clock, cotton doilies hanging from a hook on the wall, and all the dishes that had once filled the cupboards of their house on North Troy Street.

S pontaneous celebrations erupted all over Chicago when the Japanese Empire surrendered to the Allies in August of 1945. Two elderly women began marching through the streets, banging drums, and thousands of people fell in line behind them. Six young girls dressed as drum majorettes led a separate march through downtown, and a soldier standing on a rooftop at the corner of State and Randolph waved an American flag in each hand while crowds passed below him. Bonfires appeared at intersections, and a motorman drove an El train around the Loop, blowing his whistle the entire way.

Wild abandon ruled for a night, but days of somber reflection followed. This is "a day in which we should all express our eternal debt to those who laid down their lives or suffered wounds or torture that we might continue to be free," an Illinois senator said. "V-J Day means more than the end of hostilities," the governor proclaimed. "It means we are about to embark on a new era of peace and restoration." Sears, Roebuck ran an advertisement claiming that "[h]ope, thought, understanding and love" would safeguard America's future, and scores of people attended group prayers to reflect on the war and ask searching questions about the future of humankind.

It was an idealistic and heartening moment, but it passed quickly. Over the next few months, survival was reframed as victory and the reflective tone that defined the first days after the war was replaced with triumphalism —and paranoia. The *Tribune* published a picture of blanket-draped corpses above a caption that read: "German military detainees await hospitalization after mass suicide attempt," and its headlines became boastful. NAZI GENERAL DIES BEFORE U.S. FIRING SQUAD, they crowed, JAP PRINCE TO FACE TRIAL—and, ominously, RED MEDDLING IN U.S. AFFAIRS UNDER SCRUTINY.

"Love" and "understanding" seemed like quaint ideas by the time Nelson reached Chicago because, by then, mass consumption and status-seeking had supplanted them as guiding principles. "This 'Peace on Earth' Christmas give him the diamond ring he wants so much," advertisements counseled, and "Get Your Post-War Kitchen Now!" Plots of land on the outskirts of town were for sale, and so were prefabricated houses and "strobo-sonic" radios and phonographs. The Fidelity Loan Bank on Clark Street was selling the pawned jewelry it had bought during the war at "liquidation" prices.

The spoils of war were as available to Nelson as to any other veteran with an honorable discharge, but he did not indulge. That winter, he bought a radio, and a secondhand bicycle—but no diamonds, suits, or cars. He could have used his GI benefits to purchase a home on the edge of the city with no money down, but instead, he returned to his old neighborhood and looked for an apartment where he could work without distraction.

In January, he found a cold-water flat that suited him on the second floor of 1523 West Wabansia Avenue. Trash cans piled with refuse lined the sidewalk out front, and stray newspaper pages gathered in the gutters. There was no refrigerator, heat was provided by an oil stove, and the shower was down the hall, but the rent was only ten dollars a month, and the bedroom was large enough to double as an office. There were large windows in each room, and when he gazed through them he saw a street light, a peach tree growing through the sidewalk, a saloon called the Lucky Star that displayed a neon Schlitz sign in its window, and a yeast factory.

Nelson moved into the apartment when it became available. Then he began to reacquaint himself with the city. He watched the bar's windows, and the strangers passing them on the sidewalk. He could see well enough through the glass brick set in the bar's front walls to know when people were playing cards inside, and sometimes he joined them. He visited the YMCA to exercise and shower every day, dropped by his old haunts in the Triangle, and began attending police lineups again so he could transcribe the chief detective's interrogations.

"You're a jack roller," he wrote. "No I'm Mexican."

"Haven't worked the past year. . . . Just got out of the Bridewell Wednesday."

People were talking about recovery that winter. They said Chicago was destined to play a prominent role in the American Century, but the city didn't feel much changed to Nelson. The El still wobbled on uneven rails and sent sparks into the night. There was a housing shortage, and people were having a hard time finding jobs. Massive labor strikes were making headlines, and poverty remained endemic. The city's newest black residents were crowding into tenements on the South Side because redlining and housing covenants prevented them from moving to more affluent neighborhoods, and the suburban migration that mortgage brokers referred to as the American Dream was, Nelson knew, nothing more than white flight.

The only change Nelson could discern was the story Chicago had begun telling about itself. The city was defined by its industry when he was a child. It transformed into a gangster's town later, and then a battlefield for the class war. Now it was trying to remake itself as the backdrop to a domestic drama featuring men wearing gray flannel suits and chaste women in neatly pressed housedresses. They took their social cues from *Look*, *Leader*, *Pageant*, and *Bazaar*, and they believed that virtue and consumption were synonymous. There were Fords in their garages and the *Family Circle* magazine on their coffee tables.

That image seemed dangerously dishonest to Nelson, and the emphasis of his work shifted in response to it. He had been planning

to write a series of novels set in neighborhoods defined by their dominant ethnic group, but after he returned home from the war, he began
thinking in grander terms. Chicago, he realized, was a perfect synecdoche for the country—a place so in love with the idea of its virtue that it was willing to disavow, in the name of the common good,
anyone who failed to meet its narrow and exacting standards. It had
great symbolic value for that reason, and Nelson decided that using
his work to undermine that image would be more impactful than continuing to develop the naturalistic novels he outlined years earlier.

This project defined the next decade of Nelson's career. He used his
fictional writing to create a counternarrative by humanizing the people who had "failed before the radio commercials" and fallen short of
the "standards of every self-respecting magazine." And he addressed
the country's shortcomings directly in his nonfiction writing. Despite
what you've been told, he wrote, millions of Americans still "live out
their hand-to-mouth hours without friendship or love. They belong to
no particular street in no particular city. They pass from furnished
room to furnished room, and belong not even to their own time; not
even to themselves."

"Every day is D-Day under the El," he proclaimed.

And the lucky few who manage to climb the social ladder derive
little satisfaction from their reward. "Never has any people possessed
such a superfluity of physical luxuries companioned by such a dearth
of emotional necessities," he wrote. "In no other country is such great
wealth, acquired so purposefully, put to such small purpose. Never
has any people driven itself so resolutely toward such diverse goals, to
derive so little satisfaction from attainment of any."

Nelson didn't seek companionship when he returned to Chicago.
Instead, he worked on the collection of stories he had begun on Evergreen Avenue, pedaled around the city on his bike to collect material,
and waited for the world to knock on his door.

Amanda arrived first. She was living in Los Angeles at the time, and working as a secretary for the National Labor Relations Board. She was in a serious relationship with another man, but when Nelson returned to Chicago, she traveled east and moved into his apartment for a week. They shared a bed and referred to each other as husband and wife for the length of her stay, and when Martha Gellhorn dropped by the Wabansia Avenue flat, they greeted her as a couple.*

Nelson and Gellhorn had been in touch throughout the war. He wrote to her occasionally to let her know he was alive, and she encouraged him to get back to work when the service released him. "I'd like to see the short stories between hard covers," she said. He sent her a letter when the army returned him to the States, and she visited Chicago soon afterward and decided she wanted to meet him.

Nelson offered Gellhorn a tour of his neighborhood when she arrived. He brought her across the street to the Lucky Star tavern, and then guided her and Amanda south toward the Triangle. It was cold and raining, but they stayed out for hours. They visited a barbershop that was alive with the sound of fiddles and singing canaries, walked through quiet streets that reminded Gellhorn of European villages, and then passed a church society dance. Music seeping from the building stopped them, and they stood in the damp on the sidewalk and listened to it drift past.

Gellhorn left that night, and sent a letter of thanks soon afterward. "I love your Siberian country up there," she wrote, "your own country that is, not the melted chocolate ice cream with oil sauce which is Chicago." I am as glad to have seen it as "I was to have seen the island of Anguilla in the Caribbean, a small far off place as clean and perfect and untouched as the world must have been when it began."

"It seems to me you are as good as your writing," she said, "and this is a very serious statement. Something as rare as it is serious moreover."

---

* Gellhorn and Ernest Hemingway had divorced by this time, and she had reverted to her given name.

Nelson and Amanda resumed their tryst when Gellhorn left, but neither harbored any illusions about their future as a couple. He was committed to his work, and she, despite her sojourn on Wabansia Avenue, was serious about the other man. Their lives had always been moving along separate tracks, and after ten years of on-again, off-again romance, they finally made their peace with that fact and agreed to divorce.

Amanda stayed on at Nelson's apartment after the decision was made. They continued sleeping together, and one night when they were in bed, she asked if he would ever marry again. It was late, and he was barely awake. He mumbled something incoherent and drifted off, but after she returned to Los Angeles, he sent a proper response.

"It occurs to me that I'll probably stay single unless you get hooked up," he wrote. "Not necessarily, but, even with a divorce and legal freedom, I know I'll have to feel that you're taken care of, and reasonably happy in the process, before I'll be able to consider another plunge. If I ever do, I fancy it'll be just about when the yarn's all unraveled. Say, ten years from now. I would be very happy if you ever achieved, with someone else, what I somehow never truly provided: a place of your own."

Kenneth McCormick arrived next. He was a thirty-eight-year-old man from New Jersey with a long face and a lantern jaw. He wore sensible glasses and parted his hair to the right side. He looked like an English schoolmaster, but he was really the editor-in-chief at Doubleday and Company, the country's largest publisher.

McCormick had received a copy of *Never Come Morning* from a friend, read it, loved it, and written to Nelson to say so. They corresponded briefly, and when McCormick passed through Chicago in February, he visited Nelson and asked what he was working on.

Nelson said he was almost finished putting together a collection of stories, and that he had an idea for his third novel. He wanted to write an account of the war that took place after the armistice. His protagonist would be a soldier living off the black market in Marseille when the book began, and then the narrative would shift to Chicago and the book would catalog the soldier's struggle to readjust to civilian life and a changing world.

McCormick was interested in both books, and asked Nelson how much he wanted for them.

I want enough to live on for a year, Nelson said.

"What do you call enough to live on?" McCormick asked.

"Fifty dollars [a week]," Nelson said. It seemed like an impossible sum. The total, after a year's worth of payments, would be more than he had earned for his first two books and every magazine story he ever sold—combined, and then doubled.

But it was nothing to McCormick. "Well, how about sixty dollars for *two* years," he countered.

Nelson liked that idea very much, and he contacted Elizabeth Ingersoll, the literary agent he had recently hired, and asked her to see if Harper & Brothers could match McCormick's offer. She spoke to Edward Aswell a few days later and pressed him for a large advance, but he couldn't come up with it. He offered Nelson a bit more than half of what Doubleday had, and one year to write, not two. But he included a personal appeal as well, and the promise of his full attention. "I believe in you as a writer," he wrote, "and am willing to give you my time without limit—i.e. to help you in every way an editor can."

It was a persuasive entreaty, but Nelson had run out of money and time while writing his first two books, and didn't want to repeat that mistake. There was prestige in working with Aswell, but the extra year McCormick promised was worth more, so he signed with Doubleday.

The terms of Nelson's contract were finalized by late winter, and afterward he went to work revising and expanding his collection of stories. He did little else for the next five months.

Nelson had published eighteen stories since he began writing seriously in 1935, but he selected only seven of them for his collection—his five most recent pieces, and two of the earliest. He also chose an unpublished long short story called "Design for Departure" that he had spent months struggling with while writing *Never Come Morning*, a pair of stories derived from material he gathered while spending time with the Fallonites, and several unpublished pieces set in Chicago and the South.

Then he turned his attention to the war, and wrote three new stories that offered an alternative to the cliché about virtuous conquering heroes that was being pushed by the government and the press.

"That's the Way It's Always Been" is the account of a soldier serving in a medical unit in Europe run by a corps of unscrupulous officers and a spineless colonel who regularly proclaims his valor. "I get frightened sometimes," he says, "that the war might end before we really get in the thick of it."

"The Heroes" is the story of two army buddies serving in Germany. One is a "Paleface." The other is part Mexican and part Native American, but pretends to be full-blooded Osage when he wants to give his subordinates a hard time. They both drink heavily on base, sneak out at night, and rankle at military authority. "Our war was with the second lieutenants, the MPs, and the cooks," the Paleface says.

The best of the three is the story of a black soldier named Isaac Newton Bailey who has gone AWOL in Marseille. He lives with an Algerian woman, and spends his days hiding from the military police in her apartment. He leaves only when they run out of money or food and is forced to steal surplus, or buy goods at the PX that are easy to resell.

One night, Bailey goes out for supplies and sees some GIs mocking an elderly French drunk who's clowning for beer. Then he sees a second group harassing a prostitute, "giving her the come-on and then telling her to scram, bum, till, like an obedient dog that comes when called and runs when it's kicked at, the girl didn't know whether she was being accepted or rejected."

I'll "never feel homesick for Memphis again," Bailey thinks then. He doesn't love France, but that night, he realizes he isn't interested in returning home either. His race will restrict his potential in America, and after serving in the military, he's unwilling to pander or feign sub-servience. "He couldn't play an instrument," Nelson wrote, "he never clowned, and making berths for the Pullman Company had the same warm appeal for him as shining shoes."

Nelson finished assembling his collection in July, gave it the title *So Help Me*, and mailed it to New York City. McCormick accepted the manuscript, but rejected the title. The two men were at loggerheads until Nelson suggested calling his book *The Neon Wilderness*. McCormick agreed, enthusiastically, and Doubleday set the release date for January 1947.*

M ary Guggenheim arrived last. She knocked on Nelson's door a few days after he submitted his manuscript, and he invited her inside. They were acquaintances, but not quite friends.

Guggenheim was twenty-eight years old—clever, dark-haired, taut and poised the way dancers train themselves to be, and as much a creature of the world as Nelson was a hometown boy. She was born in Missouri, but spent a good part of her childhood in Switzerland. She returned to the Midwest as a teenager and began hanging around bars in East St. Louis, where she befriended Bud Fallon, Russell Finch, and Wallie Wharton.

She graduated from the University of Chicago when she was only eighteen, and she remained in the city to study dance. She moved to Los Angeles to study more, and then joined the Ballet Russe de Monte Carlo in New York City. She spoke French fluently, so when her dance company folded, the Office of War Information hired her as a trans-lator, and for the next several years she was in regular contact with

---

* This book's title, Nelson's name, and the title of each story, appeared in lower case letters when it was published—as in *the neon wilderness*. I would have repro-duced the collection's title and story titles here the way they appeared in the first edition, but Nelson later allowed it to be reprinted with standard capitalization, and I followed his lead to prevent confusion.

European intellectuals as they passed through the States. She knew the French poet André Breton, and a stateless author named Jean Malaquais, whom Nelson revered.*

Nelson and Guggenheim met when he was writing *Never Come Morning*, but they were never close. He was "such a solitary person," she said about him then. "I just barely noticed him." Nelson wrote to Guggenheim when he entered the service, though, and she wrote back. They corresponded for two years, so when she visited Chicago after the war, she went to see him.

Nelson spent two days squiring Guggenheim around. He guided her through his neighborhood, and brought her to Comiskey Park to watch the White Sox. It was the first summer after the war, and the city felt loose and liberated. He took her to the movies and the track. They bet on horses together, and when it was time for her to return home, he escorted her to Union Station.

Guggenheim's train pulled away without event, but before it traveled far, she had a realization. "It just hit me," she said, "just all of a sudden, that I was wildly in love with him."

Guggenheim wrote to Nelson when she reached New York, and for the next several months, they were in touch regularly. They didn't sleep together during her visit, but the letters they exchanged afterward are intimate and flirtatious. They traded pictures at her request, and she sent him sports columns clipped from New York papers. He sent baseball cards and bawdy jokes in return, and teased her for being close to the New York literary set.

"Did I ever tell you what the cornered mouse cried out, in his last moments, as the cat pounced on him? 'Lord!' the little fellow moaned, 'this pussy's killin' me.'"

---

* Nelson found a copy of Malaquais's second book, *War Diary*, in the library at Camp Maxey and stole it. He talked about it for years afterward, and claimed it was one of the few honest books written about World War II. (It discusses Malaquais's service in 1939 and '40—the very beginning of the war.)

"Give my regards to [Philip] Rahv," he wrote. "When I read his criticism I'm Rahvished."

By the fall, Nelson knew how his novel should begin. Its protagonist would be a veteran who makes his living dealing cards, and the book would be set in the Near Northwest Side. The lead character would be based on his army buddy—the one who never let anyone else touch the dice because he had a "golden arm"—and there would be a constellation of characters in orbit around him to give the book depth and add a tragic-comic touch. "I'd like to make it lighter, at least in spots," than my last novel, he told Amanda.

The project was ambitious, and demanding. Nelson haunted the watering holes in his neighborhood the way he had while researching *Never Come Morning*, but he also began visiting the Near North Side and West Madison Street—Chicago's skid row. There were nickel beer joints there, cage hotels where the walls of each room were sheets and the ceilings were chicken wire, and flophouses where people paid to sleep under tables. He made friends with strangers in derelict bars and all-night cafeterias, and then walked them back to their rooms and listened to their stories.

Then he went home and tried to turn his notes into identifiable characters and a sustained narrative. It wasn't an efficient process. He spent hours drafting scenes, and then tore them up and tried again. He wrote dialogue that didn't fit into his story, set it aside, and prayed he would find a use for it later. And when he ran low on ideas, he watched the column of steam rising from the yeast factory's chimney in the distance, clicked on his AM radio for distraction, or wrote to Mary Guggenheim to vent his frustrations.

"[I]f you think la vie ici is any less dull than la vie la, it aint," he told her. "I've even abandoned the police lineups: when you begin wishing they'd throw the whole damn lot of them into the bucket for 99 years so they'd quit bothering people it's time to rest for a while."

Guggenheim's response was light and teasing. She wrote to say that Jean Malaquais had been at her apartment for dinner—because she knew Nelson would be impressed—and needled him about his return to print. One of the stories he wrote for *The Neon Wilderness* appeared in *Harper's Bazaar*, and she assumed he would be embarrassed that his work had been published in a glossy magazine. But she was wrong. It had been years since Nelson thought of himself as a radical writer. He was aiming for mainstream recognition now, and the broadest audience he could attract without compromising his work.

"Far from being ashamed of being published in 'that rag,'" he told Guggenheim, "I've been waiting so long simply to be had, at the usual fee, in my little barren room above the traffic's roar, that I often wonder whether my agent is still procuring in earnest below: I still fear that she's a little choosey [sic] and doesn't solicit everybody with a buck to spend and an hour to kill. I keep hollering down: '*Anybody*, honey, *anybody*;' but she doesn't seem to hear."

Guggenheim flew to Chicago after she received that letter and spent seven days at the Wabansia Avenue flat. She was an elegant woman, and Nelson was proud to be seen with her. He planned their itinerary weeks in advance, and when she arrived, he brought her to Lawrence Avenue to meet Goldie. They went out to dinner and then dessert, and afterward they became lovers. "He was very gallant," she said.

When Guggenheim went home at the end of the week, she was determined to return to Chicago and pursue a relationship with Nelson—an ambition he did not encourage.

*T*he Neon Wilderness* was published with little fanfare in January. Doubleday printed only three thousand copies, and the book's release party was held in a tiny bookshop called Seven Stairs that attracted customers by keeping salami, coffee, and apples on hand.

Reviews were positive, but sparse. The *Tribune* praised Nelson for presenting his characters without the distortion of an ideological lens. "A writer of sociological slant would make specimens of them," their reviewer claimed. "A colorist would emphasize their depravity. . . . But

Algren sees them as they are, the product of their birth and environment, warped by 'a world they never made.'" The *Saturday Review* said "the staccato precision" of Nelson's "writing must be read, remembered, and admired." And the *Times* praised him for his empathy. He is "determined that we should . . . see, as he sees, the personal delinquency of his characters dissolve within the greater, more terrible delinquency of our synthetic society."

The muted response to the publication of *The Neon Wilderness* reflects the book's tone and sensibility. The collection contains twenty-four stories, and as a rule, they are quieter than Nelson's earlier work—funnier, more meditative. Some are just monologues. A few are character studies. Others are minor-key laments that only reveal themselves completely after repeated readings. The women in the book, in particular, are haunting characters.

In "Depend on Aunt Elly," the protagonist is arrested on a prostitution charge after sleeping with a soldier. Her name is Sissy, and she began picking up tricks after the defense contractor she worked for closed down. She had been planning to leave the business when she could afford to, but after her arrest, a judge sentences her to prison time and forecloses all of her other options. She earns a furlough by agreeing to make regular payments to the court that convicted her, and then she resumes picking up johns because she can't earn enough to fulfill her obligations any other way.

The arrangement is exploitative, and eventually she tries to run from her obligations to the court by marrying and leaving the town she had been living in. But the law tracks her down.

"Your best bet is to go back 'n do your time," her husband counsels. "We'll start all over when you get out."

"It'll be too late then, Baby," she replies. "You ain't got three good years left in you. 'N neither have I."

"It's too late awready," he concedes.

Another piece from the collection, "Is Your Name Joe?" is the story of an unnamed woman who unburdens herself to a stranger she calls

Specs. She married a man named Joe once, she explains, and he was a religious fanatic who punched her in the face. She began seeing another Joe afterward, and he "talked so smart I'd think whatever I could say'd be all wrong," she says. That Joe dropped her after a few months, and now she feels lost. "I hate t' see the spring 'n summer come so bad," she says. "I just don't seem so good as other people any more."

The Neon Wilderness's reception was underwhelming, but over time its renown and influence grew. Doubleday printed a second edition a year after its release, and many more followed. When Nelson became famous a short while later, people felt he had appeared out of nowhere. They sought out his early books to understand what he was trying to achieve, and as often as not, they found their answer in *The Neon Wilderness*. The skill of its prose seemed more pronounced with each passing year because the stories held up so well, and later generations celebrated it for documenting a portion of postwar America everyone else had ignored.

Algren can "suggest the whole contour of a human life in a few terse pages," the critic Maxwell Geismar wrote in 1958. This is the book that secured Algren's reputation as "one of the few literary originals of his time," Tom Carson wrote in 1986. So people kept buying. *The Neon Wilderness* has been through at least seven editions and twelve printings since its release. It sold more than a half million copies in paperback, and it remains in print today.

A Boy from the Provinces

(February 21–September 23, 1947)

Nelson boarded the El on a Friday evening and rode it toward the Loop—beneath Milwaukee Avenue, through the narrow tunnel under the Chicago River, and then south under State Street. He emerged at Monroe station and began walking east toward the Palmer House—a swank hotel where uniformed porters greeted soigné tourists beneath a gilded awning.

Nelson entered the Palmer House lobby and looked around. The floors were covered with thick carpet woven in intricate geometric designs. The walls were marble, and the ceiling was a mosaic of gold, alabaster, and mint-green tile. Eventually, he spotted the entrance to a cocktail lounge called Le Petit Café and sat at an empty table.

An hour earlier, he had been cooking himself dinner when his phone rang. He answered, heard a heavily accented voice he didn't recognize, and hung up. He did the same when it rang again. When he picked it up the third time, he hollered, "Wrong number!" He was angry by the fourth ring, but didn't yell into the mouthpiece because he heard an operator speaking.

"Please be patient and stay on the line for a moment," she said.

A woman's voice came through the earpiece then. She said she was visiting Chicago, and asked if he would like to meet. She was speaking broken English with a French accent, and he was about to decline when she mentioned Richard Wright and Mary Guggenheim.

"Where are you at?" he asked then. "I'll come down."

"Leetle café," she said. "Palmer House."

Nelson spotted the woman a few minutes after he entered the lounge. She was pale and trim, about his age. A white coat hung on her shoulders; a green scarf encircled her neck. Her dark hair was pulled up on top of her head, and she was walking in a loop between the café and the lobby—in and out of the bar's dim light and the warm glow cast by the chandeliers in the main room—and clutching a copy of *Partisan Review*.

Nelson watched the woman pace, and tried to decide whether or not to introduce himself. She had said her name was Simone de Beauvoir when they spoke on the phone, but that meant little to Nelson. He had read her name only once, in a letter from Mary Guggenheim. A well-regarded French philosopher visited my apartment, Guggenheim had said, and she has a fascinating relationship with Jean-Paul Sartre—they are collaborators, and partners, but both carry on affairs with other people as well.

Nelson made a joke of Guggenheim's enthusiasm when he replied, the way he usually did. "That Simone Boudoir sounds real chi-chi," he wrote, "and I'm sure J.-P. Sartre, whoever he may be, is real lucky. I bet she says, J-P honey, bite my little titties. And J-P, the hog, chews her clean tits off." But now that the woman in question was a few feet away, his attitude changed. She wasn't just an intellectual making a reputation for herself on the dinner party circuit in New York City, she was also a bundle of energy pacing the floor of a Chicago hotel like a predator.

Nelson finally decided to say hello, and then he invited Beauvoir to join him in the café and bought her a drink. They faced each other across a small table and tried to carry on a conversation, but it was no easy task.

The first problem was language. Nelson's French was limited to the slang he picked up after the armistice, and he spoke English with a

Chicago drawl that was almost indecipherable to Beauvoir. His sentences flowed with a rhythm like a twelve-bar blues, and he sprinkled them with idiomatic phrases that even native speakers found challenging. The lounge was quiet, and they were sitting close together, but she could only understand half of what he said.

But experience was a greater barrier. Beauvoir was a product of the Parisian bourgeoisie. She attended a convent school as a child, studied philosophy at the Sorbonne, and then taught at lycées for more than a decade before becoming a full-time writer. The French government was sponsoring her visit to America so that she could lecture on "the moral problems of the postwar writer," and over the last two weeks she had been to New York, Connecticut, Washington, DC, Virginia, New York again, then Ohio, and now Illinois. Nelson was the son of a semiliterate mechanic who went bankrupt. He attended a state college, spent five years drifting around the country looking for work after he graduated, and hadn't even been to downtown Chicago for months.

Nelson began talking about his time in Europe because he could think of nothing else they had in common. "I told her all about the war," he said later. "*All* about the war. Where I thought *she'd* been while I was fighting it I didn't stop to think." But eventually, he ran out of material and realized he should propose an activity that didn't require so much conversation.

We could go listen to music, he said, but then he undercut the suggestion by saying that most of the city's jazz clubs were dull. We can visit a burlesque if you want, or if you prefer I can take you to see some places you would probably never see otherwise.

Beauvoir accepted the last suggestion gratefully. The regal Palmer House Hotel seemed "monstrous" to her, and when she was in upstate New York, she had wondered, "Why did they build so many copies of the same house?" She was beginning to think America was a shallow and conformist country, so she was eager to see what Nelson could show her.

They left the hotel on foot, crossed the canal south of the Chicago

River, and then ventured down West Madison Street, past billiard halls, bars, and the Hotel Major, where rooms rented for three dollars a week. Signs extolling LIQUOR and PABST BLUE RIBBON bathed them in neon light as they walked, and Nelson talked about Chicago. He told Beauvoir about the bomb that went off at Haymarket Square in 1886, and the arrests and convictions that followed. Lately, he said, the city has been fixated on a serial killer named William Heirens, who murdered a woman with a knife and used her lipstick to write a note that said, *For heavens / Sake catch me / Before I kill more.*

I'm the only serious writer in this city, Nelson bragged, and I have been since Richard Wright left.

Nelson and Beauvoir visited a midnight mission and a cheap burlesque, and then entered a small club. They bought drinks and found seats near the back of the room, and then Nelson announced: Everyone here is sinister and dangerous. Beauvoir had developed a taste for his flavor of humor by then, so she shot back, "I think you're the only sinister thing around here."

The room thrummed with life. A few black musicians played with their backs to the rear wall, and couples moved in time with the beat. A woman with curly blond hair sat at the bar alone, screamed at antagonists no one else could see, drained her beer, and then hiked up her skirt and gamboled through the room. An old drunk woke up with his head flat on a table, grabbed the arm of a large woman dressed in rags, and pulled her toward the band. And then a man who waddled like a bird forced his way onto the dance floor and began jumping and prancing spastically.

He's here every day, Nelson explained, and he always does that.

The club reminded Beauvoir of Sammy's Bowery Follies in New York City, but there was something distinct about it. Wealthy socialites visited Sammy's for the cathartic thrill of drinking with the poor. Actors performed, and people cadged for drinks—but there were no socialites on West Madison Street. The club was a world all its own, and she was only welcome because Nelson was a regular.

"It's beautiful," Beauvoir said.

The comment surprised Nelson. "With us," he said, "beautiful and ugly, grotesque and tragic, and also good and evil—each has its place. America doesn't like to think these extremes can mingle."

If you like this place, he added, "I'm going to show you something even better."

They walked down the block and visited a saloon. The main room was almost empty when they arrived, but it filled after midnight when the temperature outside dropped. Some customers begged Nelson for money when they came in, or tried to sell him pencils. Others bellied up to the bar, bought beer from a woman with peroxide-blond hair, and paid her a dime so they could spend the night sleeping on a bench in the makeshift shelter on the building's second floor. Every one of them was filthy and rank—"so dirty," Beauvoir wrote later, "you'd think their very bones were gray."

Nelson motioned toward the woman behind the bar. "Everything I know about French literature is thanks to her," he said.

Beauvoir thought he was joking, but he wasn't.

Nelson asked the woman to join them for a glass of wine, and when she learned that Beauvoir was visiting from Paris, she began reeling off questions.

"How is [André] Malraux doing on his latest novel?" she asked. "Is there a second volume?

"And Sartre? Has he finished *Les Chemins de la liberté*?"

I was "stupefied," Beauvoir wrote later.

That woman runs the bar and the shelter at night, Nelson explained later, but she spends her days getting high and reading. She floats in and out of hospitals, and she's been to prison several times.

Beauvoir ordered a whiskey and swallowed it. Then she and Nelson left. It was around two in the morning and Beauvoir was tired, but she didn't want to return to the Palmer House, so she went to Nelson's apartment instead. They entered through the door that opened into the kitchen, but soon they were in the bedroom and their clothes were off.

She was upset by what she had seen that night, and they began making love "initially because he wanted to comfort me," she wrote, "then because it was passion."*

Beauvoir returned to her hotel the next day, delivered the lecture she was scheduled to give, and then met the two French government officials who were coordinating her visit for lunch. They brought her to a private club housed near the top of one of the skyscrapers in the Loop, and seated her so that she faced a set of windows that looked onto the Chicago River and the gleaming monoliths that stand guard along its banks.

A few minutes after they arrived, a baroness who was in the country to lecture on "French cheerfulness during the Resistance" joined their party and began reciting patriotic slogans. Beauvoir's minders listened respectfully, but she couldn't focus on anything being said because there was too much dissonance between the city Nelson had shown her the night before and the shining metropolis she was dining above—one felt real to her, the other seemed like a fraud.

Beauvoir's escorts had already scheduled the remainder of her day, but she couldn't stand the idea of wasting any more time. So she ran.

I have to visit a sick friend, she said when lunch ended. It was a lie.

She asked her escorts how to get to Nelson's apartment, but they forbade her to go alone. It's too dangerous, they said. We'll take you.

---

* Readers beware: My account of this night differs from all other accounts. Beauvoir wrote about it in *America Day by Day* and *After the War: Force of Circumstance, Vol. 1*, but neither of those accounts is accurate. She admits in her autobiography, for instance, that she conflated two trips to Chicago when she wrote about them in *America Day by Day*. Nelson was also interviewed about this visit, and he intentionally obscured several points. To create this account, I gathered every version I could find, checked them against the archival record—correspondence, interview material, and pictures taken on Madison Street during the period in question—and pared away all contradictory details. Deirdre Bair's biography of Beauvoir was also helpful.

They borrowed a government car—a dark, sleek thing—and sat her down in the back and began driving. The car threaded through the Loop, and then proceeded north and west. As it did, she gazed through the windows. She saw department stores at first, then train tracks, wooden shacks, rundown factories, and vacant lots.

Beauvoir jumped out of the car when she spotted Nelson's building and pounded on the door. The sound surprised him. He had been waiting for her to call, but wasn't expecting a visit. He grinned a big, toothy grin when he saw her, and chided her playfully for arriving in an expensive vehicle.

My neighbors will get the wrong idea, he said. They'll think I have money and start asking for loans.

They went inside then, and made love. When they finished, Nelson gave Beauvoir a tour of his neighborhood. They ogled pink and yellow pastries in a Polish bakery where no one spoke English, drank vodka in bars that had been speakeasies when Nelson was in high school, and teased each other. She called him Crocodile because he kept flashing his teeth when he smiled, and he called her a "crazy frog" for arriving at his apartment unannounced.

Beauvoir returned to the Loop that evening to have dinner with her minders. Lobster and martinis were served, and she thought: This is a facade. She called Nelson after her meal and said she couldn't see him again before she left. She was upset, and she refused to let go of the phone until someone removed the handset by force.

Beauvoir went to the train station, boarded her train, entered her cabin, closed the green curtain separating it from the corridor, and began reading *The Neon Wilderness*. She thought about Nelson and his apartment as the train rolled west, and as she did, his lifestyle took on metaphorical significance. "He seems to me," she wrote later, "one of the most striking examples of that great intellectual solitude in which American writers live today."

That night, she wrote Nelson a letter. "Before going to sleep I have to tell you I really liked the book very much, and I have thought I liked

you very much too—I think you felt it though we spoke so little—I am
not going to say thank you any more, because it does not mean much;
but you have to know I was happy, being with you." She said she would
try to visit Chicago before returning to Paris, but then hedged. It will
be even harder to say goodbye next time, she wrote.

After Beauvoir left, Nelson picked up a copy of *The New Yorker* that
had been sitting around his apartment. He began reading, and when he
reached page nineteen he found an article that taught him more about
the woman he'd just shared his bed with than she had revealed in two
days of stilted conversation. "Last week, we had a talk with Simone de
Beauvoir," it began, "the French novelist, playwright, and No. 2 Exis-
tentialist, just before she left town on a coast-to-coast lecture tour."

Beauvoir's letter arrived a day or two later, and Nelson responded
enthusiastically. I want to see you again too, he wrote. "Too bad for us
if another separation is going to be difficult."

The weeks following Beauvoir's visit were a heady time for Nelson.
He received a letter from the American Academy of Arts informing
him that he had been awarded a thousand dollars "in recognition
of his stories . . . in which . . . there is the dramatic sense of right
against wrong and everkindled hopefulness." Then he received a
package containing two of Carl Sandburg's books, and a letter from
their author expressing his admiration for *The Neon Wilderness*. Nelson hadn't been expecting either missive, and their combined effect
was bracing.

They were also hectic weeks. Ken McCormick visited Chicago to
read the first hundred pages of Nelson's novel. Jesse Blue, Bud Fallon, and a local actor named Ted Liss dropped by Nelson's apartment
repeatedly, and then Mary Guggenheim returned. She told Nelson she
was visiting him, but that was a lie. She had quit her job and given
up her apartment before leaving New York, and she was planning to
move into the Wabansia Avenue flat.

Nelson took time away from his novel to be with Guggenheim when she arrived. They slept together, and spent a weekend in Gary, Indiana, with Neal and Christine Rowland—friends from Rat Alley. It was a pleasant visit until Nelson realized Guggenheim was planning to move in with him. He withdrew from her then, and let her know she was going to have to find somewhere else to live. They barely spoke when they returned to Chicago, and she left soon afterward.

He didn't make a scene, she said. "He just let me go."

The memory of Beauvoir's visit and the letters she sent him from the road were the only constant in Nelson's life that spring. She wrote from California and then New York, and he responded in kind. He sent books to her Manhattan hotel, and when she received them, she asked him to visit before she returned to France. He said he couldn't leave because he had too much work to do, so she flew to Chicago instead.

Nelson and Beauvoir spent three days in his apartment, and then she convinced him to fly east with her. He had never been on an airplane.

They checked into a hotel called the Brevoort when they reached New York City, and then she visited the Pam Am ticket office and delayed her return to Paris by a week. She and Nelson had seventeen days together, and they spent most of them in seclusion.

They made love on the twin beds in their room, and then reclined, smoked, and talked. Beauvoir offered Nelson her impressions of American women and asked what he thought of her ideas. He asked her about the status of French women, and when he learned that France had only enfranchised women to vote two years earlier, he pressed her with questions. She was planning to write a long essay about the role of women in society, and its contours came into focus as they spoke. They agreed she should write a long article, or maybe a book, about "women's status throughout the world."*

Beauvoir led the way when she and Nelson emerged from their

---

* This project eventually became *The Second Sex*—the book that made Beauvoir an international figure.

room—to Harlem so that they could hear some jazz, and then through the Bowery and the Lower East Side. She had spent hours walking alone on her first visit, so she narrated as they explored. He listened intently when she spoke, and gawked at the city like a credulous child. He stared at brightly colored clothes when he spotted them drying on a line above a narrow street, a tattoo parlor, and a store selling "black butter" that was guaranteed to cure anyone with sore eyes.

I'm "only a boy from the provinces," he joked when she caught him looking wide-eyed—"a local youth," "a Chicago man."

Beauvoir had been warned about Nelson. Mary Guggenheim told her he could be moody and neurotic, and some New Yorkers claimed he was unstable. But over the course of the two weeks they spent at the Brevoort, she decided neither assessment was accurate.* "If he was sometimes blunt and rude, as people claimed," she wrote, "it was certainly only as a defense. For he possessed that rarest of all gifts, which I should call goodness if the word had not been so abused."

Nelson began falling in love with Beauvoir on that trip. She was beautiful to him, but also an intellectual and professional peer who managed to be both steeped in the European academic tradition and devoid of pretensions. It was as if she materialized from the ether to fill a need he wasn't aware of having, and he demonstrated his affection by presenting her with trinkets. He gave her a red fountain pen because they were both writers, and he bought her an ornately decorated silver ring.

When Beauvoir received the ring, she placed it on the middle finger of her left hand. It reached almost to her knuckle, and for the next several years she twirled it constantly. She was falling in love as well,

---

* Unfortunately, Guggenheim's assessment has become part of Nelson's legacy. She told several people he was "schizoid," and "scared to death of love"—and several of them repeated it. Tellingly, she minimized the fact that her assessment was formed after she tried to move herself into his apartment without asking. The perception among New York writers that Nelson was unstable is more understandable. Until Nelson's visit with Beauvoir, the longest stretch he spent in the city was in 1935—during the breakdown that followed his suicide attempt.

but even at her most infatuated, she understood that their relationship would be fraught. He was at the beginning of a project that would tie him to Chicago for years, and she had to tend to her editorial duties at *Les Temps modernes*, her writing, and her relationship with Sartre. She told Nelson at the Brevoort that she would never move to America, and though he claimed to accept that fact, she suspected he did not. "[H]e believed me," she wrote, "without at all understanding what I meant."

Beauvoir wanted to say goodbye in their hotel room when she left New York on May 17, but Nelson insisted on putting her in a taxi. She began sobbing when it drove away, but managed to compose herself before she reached Idlewild Airport in Queens. She boarded her plane without incident, but then she opened the copy of *Never Come Morning* Nelson had handed her that afternoon and found an inscription inside the front cover:

> *à Simone:*
> I send this book with you
> That it may pass
> Where you shall pass:
> Down the murmurous evening light
> Of storied streets
> In your own France
>
> Simone, I send this poem there, too,
> That part of me may go with you.

Beauvoir began sobbing again when she read it. Then she pulled herself together and wrote a letter. "I feel you with me," it said, "and where I shall pass you will pass, not the book only but all of you. I love you."

Nelson's life was a study in contrasts after he returned to Chicago that summer. He lived in one world by night, and another by day.

Evenings were for collecting material. Sometimes, he visited the Near

North Side and walked down Clark Street, or State Street, where the sidewalks became crowded after dark, and Brahmins and derelicts staggered shoulder to shoulder from nowhere to nowhere. There were bars along that stretch where people sat on upholstered furniture and sipped drinks beneath crimson lights, but they shared walls with cheap watering holes where glasses sweated on bare wood.

Nelson preferred the latter. They were lively places where men played cards and roulette behind locked doors, people danced beneath signs warning NO DANCING, and 26-girls stood behind small tables lined up along the walls.* Nelson enjoyed their company the most. They made good conversation and some were avid readers, so he chatted with them until customers interrupted, produced cash, and placed bets.

"Shooting sixes," the gamblers said when they approached, or "Going for sevens."

Then the 26-girl recorded their wager and handed over a cup containing ten dice. The customer tossed the dice thirteen times, and if their number turned up on twenty-six occasions, their wager multiplied.

Nelson visited the detective bureau to watch interrogations on other nights. He played poker in a back room lit by a single uncovered bulb once a week, but more often than not, he spent his evenings in a tiny apartment above the stretch of West Madison Street to which he had brought Beauvoir in February.

"Apartment" might be too big a word, actually. The space was just a pair of rooms with bare shelves, worn furniture, and three regular tenants. One was a man named Jack, whom Nelson had met before the war.† He was supposed to be hiding from the police because they were

---

* The game was invented in Chicago, and though it never became popular anywhere else, it was ubiquitous in the city for years. In 1941, the *Tribune* estimated that there were about five thousand 26-girls in the city. The job was popular because it paid better than anything else available to women—even factory work. The term *26-girl* is antiquated and sexist, obviously, but that was accepted nomenclature at the time.

† The name Jack *might* be a pseudonym—if it is, it's one of only two in this book. Nelson gave most of the people he met on skid row pseudonyms when he wrote about

looking for him in connection with a theft and a case of fraud, but he wasn't doing a very good job. He was a big, powerful guy, and he attracted people and attention effortlessly. The second was a woman who moved through the world as if there were a shroud covering her face. She and Jack were married, but the third roommate was her ex-husband and the father of her grown child. He was a drummer from Arkansas who played in Madison Street bars by night and drove a taxi by day, and he was a beast. He stood about six and a half feet tall and had an oversized head, a tragic face, and deathly pale skin.

Jack and his roommates were the core of a loosely defined group Nelson attached himself to that year, but there were others too. One was a pensive man named Bill Hackett who made his living dealing cards; another bought and sold lost dogs. Then there was Richard Majewski, a thief who had done a stretch in Cook County Jail in 1940 and was destined to return in '49. He looked up to Nelson and wanted to be a writer himself, but once he got on Nelson's bad side by claiming *Native Son* didn't deserve all the praise it received. Nelson laid into him for that, and Majewski backed off. "I consider myself properly squelched (or is it reprimanded?)," he wrote. You "made me read it again by making me doubt my own perceptiveness."

Paula Bays was another.* She was maybe twenty-seven years old and physically frail. Her skin was dull and gray and her long, straight hair was usually unwashed, but she had a forceful personality and a gift for storytelling that Nelson found beguiling. She had been supporting herself and her husband, John, by turning tricks since she left the Ohio farm she grew up on, but she desperately wanted to find another way to live.

---

them or spoke to interviewers. I have been able to discover many of their legal names, but in Jack's case, I could not. I could not even determine with certainty whether or not the name Jack is a pseudonym.

* Nelson gave Paula Bays the pseudonym Margo when he wrote about her later, and he gave Bill Hackett the pseudonym Acker. Every other biographical account of Nelson's life refers to them using those names.

There was usually a record spinning on the turntable in Jack's apartment, maybe a spare can of beans on the shelf, and Nelson— drinking the beers he brought with him, sitting quietly, observing.

Some of the people who visited the apartment worked in the bars below. A few were thieves. Others had no craft at all—lies, innuendo, myth-making and violence were their trades. They came to escape the elements, hide from the police, or sleep, and when they arrived, they plotted and fought with each other, while Nelson listened and watched. That's how I wrote my novel, he said later. I put myself in the middle of scenes "in which human beings were involved in conflict." Then I simply "recorded my own reactions and tried to catch the emotional ebb and flow and something of the fear and the terror and the dangers and the kind of life that multitudes of people had been forced into."

D ays were for writing. Nelson worked at a desk that he had placed in his bedroom, by a window overlooking the Lucky Star saloon. He kept his phone in a drawer with a blanket wrapped around it, drank whiskey and soda, and ignored his friends. "I even got rid of [Bud] Fallon," he told Amanda, "which was a triumph of skill, wit, daring, and finesse. Once in a while Jack [Conroy] calls up, but keeps his distance."

The novel advanced steadily that summer, but not quickly. Nelson had given his protagonist the name Frankie Machine by then and decided that he would die before the end of the book, but he couldn't decide why or how Frankie would meet his end—so he began rewriting his entire manuscript. "I'm reworking the first couple hundred pages on the assumption that, with that much clarified, I'll be better able to visualize the last hundred or two," he told McCormick.

Beauvoir was four thousand miles away, but when the sun was up, she was Nelson's primary human contact. He sent her long letters regularly, and she often sent two in return. Their initial meeting had been fueled by passion, but that summer, their relationship deepened and took on new dimensions through their correspondence.

Nelson sent Beauvoir character sketches based on the people he had been meeting on West Madison Street, and asked her opinion of the titles he was considering. I might call the book *Descent to the Edge of the Night*, he wrote, or *High Yellow and the Dealer*. *The Dead the Drunk and the Dying* might be better. She sent encouragement in return, and told him to work hard while they were apart. "Make it good," she said.*

Beauvoir wrote to Nelson about her work as well. She said she was going to put aside "the book about women" so she could write an account of her tour across America. She called it a "potboiler" when she started it, but after the first section was complete, she began to take the travelogue more seriously.† The greatest challenge presented by the project was the need to balance the relative merits of truth and tact. She wanted to mention Richard Wright in her book, but couldn't be honest about her impression of his character. He had a paternalistic attitude toward his wife, but she couldn't say that and remain his friend. Nelson was a bigger problem. She didn't want to expose their relationship, but couldn't write about Chicago without writing about him. "I have to find a way of saying the truth without saying it," she wrote.

They discussed literature, too, and encouraged each other to broaden their interests. Nelson sent Beauvoir copies of Faulkner's *Sanctuary*, Kuprin's *Yama*, and Gunnar Myrdal's *An American Dilemma*—a landmark study of American race relations that later influenced Beauvoir's writing. She sent him a copy of her second novel, *Le Sang des autres*,‡ even though he couldn't read it, and told him to buy Albert Camus's *The Stranger* and Sartre's *No Exit* because they had been translated into English.

But more than anything else, they wrote about love. Beauvoir's let-

---

* Any discussion of Nelson and Beauvoir's correspondence is necessarily stilted. Her letters have been made public, but his, which remain in the possession of Beauvoir's heir, have not been published.

† This book was published as *America Day by Day*.

‡ This book was later translated, and published as *Blood of Others*.

ters are filled with professions of longing. I looked at pictures of us and said tender, loving things, she said. "I can feel my love for you in my fingers when I write." She called him "my dearest husband," but she made it clear her loyalties were divided. She told him about traveling with Sartre, and said: "I could never give everything to you."

Nelson was not as circumspect. He said he hoped Beauvoir would stay in Chicago permanently when she visited next. He professed his love, too, and in July he said he wanted to marry her.

She turned him down, but did so gently, and afterward they negotiated an arrangement that accommodated each of their needs. They agreed to visit each other as often as possible, and to work furiously during their separations. When she was in Chicago, they would act like a married couple, and there would be no tears or drama when she left. Then he would visit Paris, and they would pick up where they left off. Monogamy was not required when they were apart.

Beauvoir was relieved when she and Nelson decided to continue their relationship, but she was struggling in other ways. Her life in Paris was unsatisfying and itinerant. She split her time between two different hotel rooms, she was drinking too much, and though she thought about her work constantly, she was barely writing. Some of her trouble could be attributed to missing Nelson, but Sartre deserved blame as well. When they were both in Paris, she was his adjunct—welcome to second his ideas, but rarely acknowledged as an important figure independent of him. She had tolerated that imbalance for years, but after she became involved with Nelson, the arrangement began to feel untenable.

She decided to get away from Paris to clear her head, and bought a ticket to Chicago. Then she told Nelson to expect her. They decided to keep her visit a secret so no one would intrude on their romance, and they began planning. He offered her a tour of the county jail and a trip to the beach, and she requested time at the stockyards and the Art Institute of Chicago.

I'll teach you some French, she said, and we'll drink whiskey, but most of all, "it is Nelson-seeing I want."

Beauvoir's trip began with a bad omen. Her flight was delayed, and then, after four days of waiting, the plane that was supposed to carry her across the Atlantic fell apart. It lifted off without incident, but then lurched sickeningly while in flight when an engine failed. The plane made an emergency landing for repairs, and when it made its second attempt to cross the ocean, a tire exploded during a refueling stop and caused another delay.

Beauvoir had requested that Nelson wait for her at his apartment because the airport was too impersonal, so he spent nearly a week looking for her through the window. He had a bottle of Southern Comfort on hand because she preferred it, and stacks of *Time* magazine and Chicago's daily papers because she asked him to collect research material for her travelogue.

Beauvoir was bruised and tired when she finally arrived, but she knew returning had been the right decision when she saw Nelson.

They drank, she rested, and then they saw the city. They visited the Near North Side so that she could meet some of the 26-girls Nelson had befriended. They attended police lineups and watched suspects take their place beneath glaring lights and announce, I live on "West Madison." They met up with Willard Motley to talk about his novel *Knock on Any Door*, ate dinner in a restaurant where mounted heads stared at them from the walls, and returned to the bars they drank in the night they met. They said hello to the bartender who studied French literature, toured the county jail, visited a psychiatric hospital, and drank Chianti in Little Italy.

But mostly, they stayed in the apartment Nelson had begun referring to as Rue Wabansia, ate rum cake, and acted out a fantasy. She read his manuscript, and the stack of American books he pushed on her— Carl Sandburg, Vachel Lindsay, and Edgar Lee Masters. He listened to her ideas about America, and told her to feel confident about her book because they were valid and insightful. The miles separating her from Paris provided the distance she needed to think about her work objectively, and she began to make plans for her book about women.

And they fell more deeply in love. They felt satisfied intellectually when they were together—but also physically and emotionally. It was a new experience for each of them. Beauvoir and Sartre had never had a passionate relationship, and Nelson and Amanda had always lived more like roommates than lovers. But Nelson and Beauvoir fell into each other's arms regularly, and danced across the chipped linoleum tiles on the kitchen floor. They made love on the buckled mattress whenever the notion struck them, and Beauvoir regularly caught Nelson staring at her with an uninhibited grin.

Nelson asked Beauvoir to remain in Chicago, again, and she turned him down, again, so they settled for fantasizing about traveling together in the spring. She flew back to Paris, and for the next eight months, they lived for the promise of the time they would spend together the following year, and worked tirelessly to earn their reward.

Exile?

(September 24, 1947–September 21, 1949)

Bill Hackett, one of the men who inspired the creation of Frankie Machine, the protagonist of The Man with the Golden Arm, dealing Nelson a four of diamonds. Photo by Art Shay, courtesy of the Art Shay Archive

Something about Jack and his friends perplexed Nelson. He knew how they earned their money, where they lived, and where they spent their time. He had taken notes about the physical condition of the hotels they stayed in, trained himself to follow the cadence of their speech, and made lists of the idioms they used—"whiz us" meant you should visit; "jump off" meant you should leave. But part of their lives remained enigmatic, and a few of their habits baffled him.

They carried cigar boxes under their arms when they went to the
bathroom, and moved at a pace that was about two clicks slower than
the straight world. They rarely drank beer, and never seemed to eat.
Once, Nelson offered to buy some food for Jack's apartment, and
a young woman accompanied him to the store. He headed for the
butcher shop, but she diverted them to a bakery and asked for chocolate rolls instead.

"Jesus, that's *dessert*," he said. "Don't you people eat?"

"Got a sweet tooth," she replied.

Then, one night, Nelson noticed Jack standing behind a curtain that
was being used to partition a room and pumping his arm—tightening
his bicep, then loosening it; tightening, then loosening. Nelson had
been drinking, so he stared at the curtain dumbly, wondering what he
was seeing, until someone explained: "Jack is having trouble."

Nelson pondered the meaning of that image for a long time before
he realized Jack had been trying to find a vein that would accept a
needle, and that morphine was the enigma at the center of his friends'
lives. They had been discreet about using in his presence at first, but
after he discovered their habit, they began visiting his apartment on
Wabansia Avenue when they were nearby and wanted to shoot up.[*]

Nelson wasn't interested in getting high himself, but he wasn't troubled by the fact that his friends did, because opiates had been commonplace for most of his life. Heroin had been sold over the counter until he
was five years old, and remained available as a treatment for diarrhea,
arthritis, and anxiety until he was a teenager. Dope developed a sinister reputation when it became associated with black jazz musicians
after the war, but it was still a niche product. The Chicago police had
just begun a citywide campaign to incarcerate users and dealers, but

---

[*] Nelson usually refers to morphine in his writing, but sometimes he says heroin,
or dope, when describing the narcotics his friends were using. It's likely they used
whatever they could get their hands on, and he seems to use the terms interchange-
ably. "Heroin is essentially the same as morphine," he said once.

they were averaging fewer than two arrests per day. The *Tribune* hadn't published anything about opiate addiction yet, and within the counterculture, casual use was still understood as a way to communicate a nonchalant attitude toward life.*

But Nelson's perspective soon changed. It wasn't long before he realized the drug was the organizing theme of his friends' lives, not a recreation, and that most of them had a fraught relationship to their addiction.

Jack was an advocate for his lifestyle. He was "on it," Nelson said, "but he was *for* it, too." The drummer from Arkansas dealt with his addiction the way a journeyman laborer might approach a pile of rubble—it was a challenge he faced with resignation and stoic resolve. But Jack's wife was a different case. The drug had consumed her personality and she moved through the world as if she were trapped inside a bank of fog. Bill Hackett, the card dealer, was trying to avoid that fate. He was troubled by his addiction, and was constantly devising schemes that would put him in a good position to get clean.

Paula Bays was also desperate to quit, and believed that doing so would allow her to restart her life. She had fallen in love with a charismatic stranger when she was a teenager, run off with him, and eloped. Afterward, he introduced her to morphine and put her to work as a prostitute. Her addiction was the shackle that kept her tied to her husband— not an escape, or a bid for coolness—and she was eager to break it.

Nelson felt protective of Bays, so he offered to help her kick her habit. He said she could use his apartment as a sanctuary and hide out until she got clean, and she accepted.†

---

* The first feature story the *Tribune* published about heroin addiction appeared on September 5, 1948—about a year after Nelson realized Jack and his friends were using. It had the amazing title SHADY LADIES: DOOMED BY DRUGS. About a month later, the paper ran a piece with the equally dramatic headline BREAK UP RING SELLING DOPE TO 'BE-BOP' CROWD.

† Nelson wrote a fictionalized version of these events in an article called "Previous Days," in which he refers to Bays as "Margo." The article misrepresents the tim-

Bays arrived on Wabansia Avenue in late October with morphine in her blood, but nothing to shoot when its effect wore off. She climbed into Nelson's bed and talked to him for a while, but when she felt the first queasy wave of withdrawal symptoms ripple through her body, she sent him away.

"I don't want you to see what I look like when I'm kicking," she said, but she was too weak to insist, so Nelson stayed. She fell asleep, and he watched her. It was midday, light from the street-facing windows filled the room, and she looked tiny and frail.

Bays had been using morphine for years, so her body was accustomed to receiving regular doses. Each time she injected opiates into her bloodstream, they attached themselves to the mu-receptors in her medulla oblongata and the synaptic membranes of the neurons responsible for transmitting pain signals. This made her feel numb and blissful, and caused her blood pressure to drop, her heart to slow, her breathing to become shallow, and her muscles to relax. But that process reversed itself when the opiates left her system. Her pores opened, and sweat seeped out of them and soaked the mattress. Her skin lost its color, and her muscles contracted. Her stomach tried to empty itself, and she began sobbing like a child who can feel something has gone horribly wrong inside their body, but lacks the vocabulary to explain the sensations.

Nelson realized he was out of his depth when Bays went temporarily blind. She is "either going to die or go mad," he thought, so he left the apartment and went to find her dealer.

Nelson reached West Madison Street around four in the morning. It was raining and the sidewalks were empty, but he noticed women soliciting work from doorways, so he approached one and mentioned Bays's name.

I'm a friend, he said, "and she needs help." The woman turned away. The next woman he spoke to ignored him as well, so he tried another, and another. Some pretended not to hear. Others fled.

---

ing of Bays's attempt to get clean, but is otherwise accurate. For a discussion of the article and the other evidence supporting the claim that Bays is "Margo," see the source notes.

There was a White Tower hamburger shop on the corner of West Madison and Aberdeen, and its lights were still on. Nelson went inside to escape the rain, found a seat facing a window, and sat down and stared into the night. He was looking for someone who looked like a dealer, but he had no idea what a dealer looked like.

Eventually, a short man walking with a limp entered the restaurant and sat at the counter. Nelson checked him out. The man was wearing glasses with thick lenses, and a cap tilted down so it would cast a shadow over his face. He looked off somehow, suspicious, so Nelson sat next to him and tried to get his attention by staring into the mirror behind the grill.

The man ordered coffee, and ignored Nelson studiously. He lifted his cup to take a sip, and just before it touched his lips, Nelson whispered: I'm a friend of Paula's, "and she needs help."

The man clacked the cup against his teeth. He kept his head down for a moment, maybe trying to decide whether he was in danger. Then he lifted his gaze toward the mirror, saw Nelson, and relaxed.

"She ought to know better than to send a square down here," he said. He was Bays's dealer.

Nelson brought the man back to Wabansia Avenue and let him in. They climbed the stairs, and when they reached the second floor, they heard Bays's voice. She was crying for help, and her pleas were just loud enough to escape into the hallway. When they opened the door, they found her lying on the floor in a puddle of sweat. She looked like warm death.

"What do you think you're doing?" the dealer scolded. He reached down to lift Bays, and the moment his skin made contact with hers, she regained some of the color in her cheeks and smiled faintly, anticipating the needle.

Nelson was still revising his manuscript when he watched Bays go through withdrawal, and afterward he realized that reimagining his

protagonist as an addict would solve most of his compositional problems. The perpetual need to find drugs would be an effective plot
device. The burden of maintaining a habit and the desire to break free
of it would add conflict to the story, and the danger associated with
prolonged use could explain Frankie Machine's death.

Nelson was reluctant to pursue the idea, though, because he was
running low on time, and researching morphine abuse would be labor-
intensive. Doubleday was scheduled to send its last advance check in a
few months, and Beauvoir was supposed to return to the States in the
spring. Nelson was planning to travel through the American South
and Latin America with her, and he wanted to send his manuscript to
Ken McCormick before they left.

There was risk involved as well. No American author had written
a novel about opiate addiction yet, and the subject was likely to turn
readers off. Censorship could also be a concern, so Nelson contacted
his agent, Elizabeth Ingersoll, and asked for her advice. "You think
that, uh—do you think it's too sensational?" he asked.

"No," she said. "Use it."

Nelson committed to the idea then, and began researching morphine addiction. He started visiting the weekly show-ups at the detective division again, and learned that users were sometimes arrested
for internal possession—having opiates in their bloodstream. Heroin
was selling for three dollars a hit that year, and the police believed a
line of track marks running along the length of a vein created enough
suspicion to justify detention. He visited the courts as well, and on
one occasion he had the good fortune to overhear a judge asking a boy
facing criminal charges how he spent his days. "Well," the boy said, "I
find myself a doorway to lean against, and I take a fix, and then I lean.
I just lean and dream."

But Nelson's friends were his best source of material. He asked one
of them why he got high, and the man said, "You gotta belong to somebody." And on another occasion, he attached himself to the drum-

mer from Arkansas and followed him through the city as he bounced between bars and cafés, looking for a dealer. The drummer's quest stretched on into the small hours of the morning, and eventually Nelson became tired and irritable. I want to go home, he said. "Well, you don't know what it's like to have a monkey on your back," the drummer snapped.*

Then someone agreed to inject himself while Nelson observed and took notes. "The morphine was heated in a little bottle with a match going underneath till it melted," Nelson wrote. "Then the hypo was pressed down into the cotton."

The man then tied a tourniquet around his arm just below the elbow, and started searching for a spot that was likely to accept a needle. His veins were thick with scar tissue, though, so it took a few tries. "I was on this arm for five years—this is where I started—I tapped that one out and went down here," the man explained. "Now I'm back on the original arm, tapping the very veins in search of joy, and finding, if lucky, an hour's surcease from pain."

"Up north he hit," Nelson wrote, "—the blood came up in the hypo, and then he was scratching his head furiously: that was a good wan whan owhan. A pink color came to the pasty skin, he looked the picture of good health."

Nelson soon realized that morphine addiction could add more to this book than he anticipated. The metaphoric language his friends used to describe their habits gave his book a surreal quality and diverted attention from the miserable conditions his characters live in. Addiction added emphasis to the divide between the novel's protagonist and mainstream society, but it also made him vulnerable in a way the violent children in *Never Come Morning* had not been.

Those were welcome developments—but they were complicated by

---

* This is a cliché now, but it didn't enter the lexicon until Nelson committed it to the page.

events outside Nelson's control. The country was undergoing a political transformation that year, and while Nelson was distracted by his
work, the culture took a conservative turn that made his new subject
both more poignant than anticipated, and more controversial.

The wave of relief that washed over the country after the armistice
had spent itself by then, and paranoia had replaced it. There was serious talk about guarding against left-wing ideas and "purging" "reds"
from positions of influence that year, and the word *loyalty* was being
redefined to mean submission to the status quo. Lists of suspected
Communists were being circulated in Hollywood, and Congress was
investigating the accused and broadcasting their interrogations.

The House Un-American Activities Committee (HUAC) ordered
hundreds of prominent figures from the film industry to appear before
them in Washington, DC, and newsreels reported on their hearings
breathlessly. "[T]he committee is seeking to determine if red party
members have reached the screen with subversive propaganda," they
announced.

Almost everyone who received a subpoena complied. Walt Disney
was one, and he played to the country's fears by claiming "reds" had
temporarily taken over his studio. Gary Cooper went the other way,
and made the threat of communism seem like a joke. "I could never
take any of this pinko mouthing very seriously, because I didn't feel it
was on the level," he told the committee.

But a handful of directors and screenwriters refused to cooperate.
They claimed that the First Amendment allowed them to associate
freely and believe anything they chose to believe. The House charged
each of them with contempt of Congress, and as a result they lost their
jobs. The group became known as the Hollywood Ten, and after fighting their contempt charges and losing, they were each sentenced to a
year in prison. They appealed their convictions and made bold statements about defending free speech, and for a while it was possible to
think of them as patriots standing up for the Bill of Rights.

Then it wasn't. In February 1948, the Communist Party of Czechoslovakia staged a coup and took control of that country's government. They turned it into a satellite state of the Soviet Union, like its neighbors, and thereafter, anyone with the audacity to argue that communism wasn't a threat to America was either a fool or a traitor.

Military spending rose sharply after the coup, and the hunt for Communist influence in society became a national preoccupation. A rabbi named Schultz wrote a series of columns urging the devout to "root the Russia-first network out of all faiths!" And the US Chamber of Commerce published a handbook entitled *A Program for Community Anti-Communist Action* that advised people to organize themselves into committees, make lists of suspected subversives, and ostracize them. "We should not tolerate teachers who poison the minds of the young with Communist propaganda," it warned. "Librarians are likewise not beyond public scrutiny."

Morphine abuse would have been a scandalous subject no matter how it was handled in that environment, but Nelson's treatment made it seem seditious. He wrote his protagonist, Frankie Machine, as a flawed but redeemable character who received his first dose of opiates from an army medic after being injured in the war. Frankie is a charming man, and philosophical about his circumstances—"I'm gettin' farther away from myself all the time," he says. His friends and associates are equally complex and articulate, and their confidence reads like an implicit critique of the status quo. They know they've "failed the billboards all down the line," but they aren't convinced they have anything to be ashamed of. "What I'd do for a quarter you'd do for a dime," one man tells a police captain, and a lay preacher announces, proudly, that he was defrocked for believing "we are all members of one another." That line is an allusion to Paul the Apostle's instruction that "we, though many, form one body, and each member belongs to all the others," but in 1948 it sounded like Marxist propaganda.

Nelson finished revising his manuscript in April, and sent it to Ken McCormick in New York with the title *Hustler's Heart*. He didn't think it was ready to be published, but he was no longer in a rush to finish because his money problems had been solved. The Newberry Library in Chicago had awarded him a $1,600 grant, and Avon had agreed to release a revised version of *Never Come Morning* as a pulp paperback. Nelson wasn't pleased that they cut forty thousand words from the text, but he was happy with the thousand dollars they advanced him.

Nelson spotted Beauvoir from his window. It was after midnight in the early morning hours of May 8, and she was walking down his alley, looking lost, so he went downstairs to greet her. She had been nervous about their reunion before leaving Paris, but her worries disappeared when he stepped into the street. At a glance, she could tell how excited he was to see her.

They spent their first morning in seclusion. They couldn't leave Chicago until they had procured their visas and received their inoculations, but they set those responsibilities aside and spent time catching up. They decided to keep a shared journal during their visit, and Nelson found a cheap notebook and made an entry: "Happened upon a strange creature, apparently of foreign extraction, running aimlessly down Wabansia—took her upstairs with intention of phoning police."

Nelson brought Beauvoir to West Madison Street to meet Jack and his roommates that afternoon, and they sat around eating barbecue chicken and listening to junkie ramble for two hours. They visited the wife of a thief who was in hiding from the police the following day, and then they began settling their affairs. ". . . bank, traveler's checks, laundries," Beauvoir wrote in their journal, "busy day—Fucking— and so on."

On their fifth morning together, they boarded a train bound for Cincinnati and rode it east and south—around the tip of Lake Michigan, and then across flat pastoral plains. They reached their destination the same day, found a diner, and gorged themselves while watching television—a first for both of them.

They boarded a steamboat the following night, and stayed up long enough to watch the shore recede and the paddle wheels on either side of the hull begin churning the Ohio River into a mist. They lounged on the deck and drank Scotch the next day, and every time their boat dropped anchor over the course of the following week, they went onshore just long enough to create a memory. Louisville was a sad warm rain on a Sunday morning. Kentucky was drunken farmers in a decrepit bar. Memphis was cotton bales wrapped in jute, and Natchez was a white man in a suit who explained that the local "Negroes led an extremely easy life."

They spent two days in New Orleans after their cruise ended, and then they boarded a plane bound for the Yucatán Peninsula. When they landed, they fell into the same rhythm they had adopted in New York the year before. She led and narrated, and he followed and stared credulously—first through Mérida's cobblestone streets, and then to the base of the pyramid at Chichen Itza, and the ruins of Uxmal. "Didn't even take time to have a cup of coffee" this morning, Nelson wrote in the journal, "our time was too limited for that."

They flew to Mexico City on June 12 and moved into the Hotel de Cortés on Avenida Hidalgo—a regal building clad in stone, and adorned by a crucifix—and each day afterward they ventured out to explore. They drank tequila in a dive bar, visited the Mayan ruins at Teotihuacán, and visited one of the city's great arenas. "Went out to the bull park to watch the local athletes do up a couple of steers," Nelson wrote to Jack Conroy. "Can't quite see the sport: you know who's going to win before the game begins. It's always a shutout for the bull."

The trip felt like the fulfillment of a promise to Nelson, proof that he and Beauvoir had a future. He had been entertaining doubts. They spent a few wonderful weeks together the year before, but after she returned to Paris, her affection seemed distant and abstract. He had begun to suspect the whole affair was a sort of fantasy, but he dropped his guard and lost himself in its promise when they began traveling together.

Beauvoir, on the other hand, was tense. She and Nelson had planned their vacation together and agreed to remain on the road for four months, but her situation changed just before she left Europe. Sartre had arranged for one of his lovers to stay with him in Paris for the duration of Beauvoir's absence, but that woman broke off their relationship days before she was supposed to arrive. Beauvoir didn't want to leave Sartre alone for so long, so she promised to cut her trip with Nelson in half. She didn't have the heart to put her choice into writing, though, so she told herself she would give Nelson the news in person.

But the proper moment never presented itself in Chicago. Then she couldn't tolerate the thought of upsetting Nelson while they were on the Mississippi, and the idea of spoiling their trip seemed obscene when they were lazing beneath a ceiling fan in New Orleans. The plane that carried them to the Yucatán was no place for a disappointment, and neither was their room in Mexico City—but eventually time forced her hand.

Nelson and Beauvoir boarded a bus headed east toward a city called Morelia one day. It was a four-hour trip, maybe more, and Beauvoir delivered her news while they were on the road. She had no choice. They had been traveling for almost two months and she had to leave for Europe soon.

I have to return to Paris in July, she said. She knew the news was devastating, but she delivered it casually, a fact that embarrassed her later.

"Oh, all right," Nelson replied flatly. He knew Sartre was the reason for the change in plans without being told.

Beauvoir was relieved. She believed his reaction was sincere, and later, that fact embarrassed her as well.

They checked into a hotel when they reached Morelia, and Nelson said he'd prefer to stay in their room by himself for the day. Beauvoir had already put their earlier conversation out of her mind, so she went out into the city alone. The weight she had been carrying for the last two months had lifted, so she strolled through the streets and the town square cheerfully.

They traveled fifty miles west the next day, and Nelson joined Beauvoir on a boat ride to a small island named Janitzio that was covered with white-walled houses with red roofs. They found an open-air market when they arrived, and saw fishermen casting nets into a lake. Beauvoir bought herself an embroidered blouse, and when they turned back toward the shore, she began making plans for the following day.

Nelson cut her off. I'm sick of Mexico and I'm sick of traveling, he said. He had been stewing over Beauvoir's announcement for two days, and disappointment had turned his mood dark. They crossed the water in silence, and when they reached land, he walked ahead of her and refused to answer when she called after him.

Beauvoir confronted Nelson in their hotel room. She still thought the news of her early departure was behind them. "What's the matter?" she asked. "Everything was going so well; why are you spoiling everything?"

Nelson stormed out instead of responding, and returned late the same evening. They reconciled without speaking about their fight, and the next day, they resumed their vacation as if nothing had happened. They visited a few more Mexican cities and made their way to the States together, but the connection Nelson felt at the beginning of their trip never returned. He stopped speaking to Beauvoir in the unguarded way he had before, and sometimes he fell silent for long stretches of time. "I began to pay for my cowardice," she wrote later, "and my thoughtlessness."

It was hot and humid in New York City when they arrived, and the time they spent there was disappointing and painful. They ate black raspberry ice cream in the East Village to cool off, and wandered about in silence. They shared meals because they felt obliged to, but they rarely had anything to discuss, and tension built between them.

One night, while they were having dinner at Tavern on the Green in

Manhattan, Beauvoir ran out of patience with Nelson's surly attitude. "I can leave tomorrow," she said brusquely.

Nelson responded noncommittally, but then let his guard drop. "I'm ready to marry you this very moment," he blurted out.

She finally understood what had gone wrong then, and how badly she had hurt him. "I realized," she wrote later, "I would never be able to harbor rancor in my heart against him for anything ever again; all the wrongs were on my side." She returned to Paris four days later, not knowing whether she would ever see Nelson again.

There was a letter from Ken McCormick waiting for Nelson when he returned to Chicago in July, and it contained mixed news. "I have read HUSTLER'S HEART with tremendous fascination and approval . . . ," it said. "I think the book marks a step forward technically but that in submerging yourself in the world of your characters you have lost some of the pace that the reader will require of you. . . . [T]here's a lot of tightening and drawing together to be done."

Nelson began revising his manuscript then, and completed a new draft in three months. When it arrived in New York, McCormick sent a telegram in response. I have finished reading your novel, it said, "and although I think there are many things you will want to do with it before we publish it it has the poetry of Faulkner and the doom of Gogol. It is really a great book." He flew to Chicago a few days later to discuss last-minute changes to the book, and afterward Nelson resumed revising, and gave a copy of his manuscript to his friends on West Madison Street so they could critique its authenticity. The last scene in the novel takes place in March 1949, and he was aiming to complete his manuscript around the same time.

Nelson was usually happiest when he was working the hardest, but not that year. He was in the middle of one of the most productive stretches of his career, but instead of being content, he felt isolated and lonely. His apartment felt like a cage, and he began to think he was a fool for falling in love with someone who lived on the other side of the Atlantic. He longed for companionship, and for a while he toyed with the idea of marrying a woman he met in Chicago. Their relationship was brief, and casual, but significant because of what it suggested about his emotional state.

"I won't have an affair with this girl, she doesn't really mean anything to me," Nelson wrote to Beauvoir. "But that doesn't change the fact that I still want what she represented to me for two or three months: a place of my own to live in, with a woman of my own and perhaps a child of my own. There's nothing extraordinary about wanting such things, in fact it's rather common, it's just that I've never felt like it before. Perhaps it's because I'm getting close to forty. It's different for you. You've got Sartre and a settled way of life, people, and a vital interest in ideas. You live in the heart of the world of French culture, and every day you draw satisfaction from your work and your life. Whereas Chicago is almost as far away as Uxmal. I lead a sterile existence centered exclusively on myself; and I'm not at all happy about it."

Nelson said he would visit Paris when his book was finished, as he had promised, but he made it clear the terms of their relationship had changed. "This girl helped me to see the truth about us more clearly," he wrote. "[L]ast year I would have been afraid of spoiling something by not being faithful to you. Now I know that was foolish, because no arms are warm when they're on the other side of the ocean; I know that life is too short and too cold for me to reject all warmth for so many months."

The sense of isolation that plagued Nelson that summer was a product of his relationship and work habits, but it was compounded by the country's political environment, which was making him feel vulnerable and besieged. While he and Beauvoir were on vacation, the House of Representatives passed a bill called the Internal Security Act, and by the time he returned home, the political left was in full retreat. The act required the Communist Party to divulge the names and addresses of its members, and the criminal penalties for violating its provisions included jail time, fines, and the loss of citizenship.

The Senate never voted on the act, but its passage in the House shifted the boundary of acceptable discourse and action.* A month after the House vote, a federal prosecutor in New York charged twelve members of the Communist Party with plotting to overthrow the government, and afterward it seemed everyone in the country either joined the hunt for "reds" or went into hiding. Soviet spies began defecting. People who had spent the Depression years marching to demand emergency relief burned old letters and avoided old friends, and activists betrayed their comrades.

Only a few political figures were willing to make common cause with the Left that year, and the biggest name among them was Henry A. Wallace. He was the Progressive Party's nominee for president, and his platform called for full voting rights for black citizens, the elimination of HUAC, and an end to the conflict between the United States and the Soviet Union that people had begun referring to as a Cold War. He was often barred from speaking in the South because his campaign staff was integrated, and when he did appear, people pelted him with rotten food. He refused to reject the endorsement of the Communist Party when they offered it, and people often called him a traitor.

Wallace's campaign was quixotic, but Nelson joined it anyway. He spoke at several Wallace campaign events in Illinois, and began signing his correspondence, "Yours for Wallace." Then he loaned his name to an

---

* A modified version of this bill received majority support in the House and Senate two years later, in 1950. President Truman vetoed it, saying that portions of the bill "move in the direction of suppressing opinion and belief. This would be a very dangerous course to take." He was overruled, and the Internal Security Act became law in September 1950.

open letter that offered support to the candidate, criticized the conformist environment in America, and made common cause with Soviet artists. "Our capitalists know the strength of culture," it said. "They want to
point out to us what we must and must not say in defense of their system."

Politics even found its way into Nelson's manuscript that year, though
subtly. His first novel had addressed its political moment directly, and the
effect was often jarring. His second was self-consciously antipolitical—
a coming-of-age story that was faithful to the perspective of its characters. Both books took extreme positions, but by the time Nelson began
the final draft of his third novel, he was talented enough to comment on
the political environment his work was created in without allowing his
opinions to invade the foreground of his narrative.

The book makes only one overt nod to the witch hunt under way in
Washington, and it's very sly. At one point, the novel's protagonist,
Frankie Machine, is incarcerated and sent to a prison with an exercise
yard that's laid out like a country garden. One day while he's watching
the yard, he sees four condemned men enter and begin doing calisthenics. The prison wall stands behind them, tall and imposing, and
above it two competing billboards are visible.

One says:

BUDINTZ COAL
One Price to All

The other says:

RUSHMOORE COAL
Fastest Delivery
Cheapest in Years

That's all. The signs appear in the text only once, and Frankie
doesn't comment on them, but the names they bear and the messages

they carry meant a great deal to Nelson and the radical writers he had associated with at the beginning of his career. Louis Budenz and Howard Rushmore were former Communists who had begun providing testimony to Congress, and naming names in the press.* Both had accepted money for betraying their former comrades, hence *One Price to All* and *Fastest Delivery—Cheapest in Years*.

Budenz was a member of the national committee of the Communist Party and the managing editor of the *Daily Worker* in the 1930s, but he transformed into a conservative in 1945. He entered academia, wrote anti-Communist books, sold information to the FBI, and testified at several trials and Congressional hearings. He received a small fortune for his revelations, and eventually distilled Red Scare paranoia to its purest rhetorical form by testifying, under oath, that nothing a Communist said could be trusted. The party trains its members to speak in "'Aesopian' language" designed "to protect the party in its activities before courts of law in America," he swore. Consequently, he implied, *yes* can mean *no* when a Communist is speaking, and an exculpatory statement might really be an admission of guilt.

Nelson knew Budenz well, but he knew Rushmore better. Rushmore had been an editor at both the original *Anvil* and the *Daily Worker*. He was the man Nelson wrote to when he needed information he could use to defend the Moscow show trials, and later he visited Nelson and Amanda in Chicago for a few days. He used their apartment to have sex, and afterward they discovered he had infested their room with bedbugs. He left the Communist Party in 1940, and later he wrote for a gossip magazine, sold information to the FBI, and told HUAC that the film stars Charlie Chaplin and Edward G. Robinson were either Communists or fellow travelers.

Nelson's novel reflected politics in more subtle and affecting ways as well. He had always tried to make sense of the world through

---

* The insertion of these names into the book was no accident. In early drafts of the novel, Nelson used different names and slogans on these billboards.

the process of writing, and that habit is most evident in a character named Bednar.

Bednar is a police captain with a preternatural talent for recollection. He can recall the name, pseudonym, and crimes of every person booked at the Saloon Street Station. He takes a hard look at everyone who appears before him, considers them briefly, and then judges them harshly. "For a quarter you'd steal the straw out of your mother's kennel," he says. "Tell the court that Belgian .22 was to pick your teeth with. Maybe they'll believe you. I don't."

The captain has been on the job for twenty years, and it has taken a toll on him. His mind has begun to drift, and he suspects he has been infected by the sins of the people who parade before him. He feels filled "with the guilt of others" when the novel begins, and as the story progresses, his condition worsens.

One night, the captain hears a defrocked priest proclaim, "I believe we are all members of one another," and afterward he feels compelled to walk into a cell of his own and "confess the thousand sins he had committed in his heart." He realizes he's "guilty of all the lusts he had ever condemned in others," and his faith slips. He wonders whether the men he has judged so harshly might really be "his own kind," and the implications of that thought terrify him: "if they were anything less than enemies he had betrayed himself a thousand fold," Nelson wrote.

The captain's moment of introspection doesn't last long. He can't face the prospect of atoning for his sins so—like Budenz, a man so warped he's willing to claim every person he betrays is confirming their guilt each time they proclaim their innocence—he projects the contempt he feels for himself back on the world. Punishment is always justified, he decides, because "every man was secretly against the law in his heart . . . and it was the heart that mattered. There were no men innocent of intent to transgress. If they were human—look out. What was needed he had learned long ago, was higher walls and stronger bars—there was no limit to what they were capable of."

Nelson finished revising in February 1949, and mailed his book to New York. Ken McCormick accepted the manuscript when it arrived, and then he and Nelson began their customary haggling over titles. Nelson suggested *The Long Nightmare*, *The Monkey's Kiss*, *Some Cats Swing Like That*, and *The Man with the Golden Arm*. McCormick only considered the last idea seriously, so it became the book's title.*

Nelson prepared to leave for Paris then. He left Chicago carrying enough baggage for a family, and made his way to New York City. He went to lower Manhattan on May 4, found Pier 92, crossed a gangplank, and boarded RMS *Mauretania*—a 772-foot ocean liner with a jet-black hull, a whitewashed deck, and two red steam funnels. The ship began its journey across the Atlantic the same day, and Nelson must have felt relieved when the American shore disappeared. Every mile of ocean he crossed was a mile separating him from his tiny apartment, a mile closer to Beauvoir, and a step toward the next chapter of his career.

Beauvoir was eager to make her reunion with Nelson memorable, so she put on the white coat she had been wearing the day they met, and went to Gare Saint-Lazare to wait for his train to arrive. She was standing on the platform when it pulled in and discharged its passengers, but she didn't see Nelson. She waited until the train seemed empty, and then returned to her apartment at 11, rue de la Bûcherie.

She slumped into a chair when she arrived, lit a cigarette, and told herself Nelson would be on the next train. She was still sitting there a half hour later, smoking and worrying, when she heard an American voice outside. She looked through her window and saw a man festooned

---

* Most of these are in keeping with Nelson's predilection for suggesting horrible titles, but some of his other ideas were even worse. He wanted to call his novel *Bedbugs Don't Bite Junkies* at one point, and he also suggested *The Weaker Sheep*, *The Monkey's Other Paw*, and *The Deadlockers*. No one has ever been good at everything.

with bags wander into the Café des Amis five stories below, then emerge and head for her door.

Nelson and Beauvoir enjoyed a sweet reunion in her apartment. He had seen her waiting on the platform, he explained, but he had checked so much luggage that she was gone by the time he collected it all. Then he opened his bags and presented her with a housecoat, chocolates, whiskey, and a stack of books.

Nelson had seen Paris only once, when he was on leave at the end of the war, so Beauvoir spent several days showing him the city. She was eager to make him happy after their sad parting in New York, so she kept checking his face for signs of displeasure, but she never saw any. "[H]is face was always radiant," she wrote later, and everything about Paris seemed to delight him—the crazy drivers, the van Goghs at the Galerie nationale du Jeu de Paume, and the architecture.

Beauvoir introduced Nelson to her friends after he acclimated, and soon he felt more at ease in Paris than he did in Chicago. He met Sartre and his secretary, Jean Cau, whose first novel was about to be released. He swapped army stories with the journalist Jacques-Laurent Bost, and charmed Bost's wife, Olga, with tales about West Madison Street. He listened to jazz at Club Saint-Germain, had dinner in a restaurant in the Eiffel Tower, and went to a party at the publisher Gallimard, where he was approached by several people interested in translating his novel. He and Beauvoir went out with Michelle Vian and the journalist Robert Scipion one night, visited every neighborhood street dance they could find, and didn't stop moving until seven the next morning.

Nelson worked, too, though not much. Gallimard had commissioned a French edition of *Never Come Morning*, and Nelson met with the book's translator, René Guyonnet, to help him work through its tangle of slang. He reviewed the page proofs for *The Man with the Golden Arm* as well, and tried to convince his editors at Gallimard to release French editions of Jack Conroy's books.

Nelson felt carefree in Paris with Beauvoir, but he could sense tension everywhere they went. The American government had just offered

France an infusion of cash as part of the Marshall Plan, and there was lively debate about whether the country should accept. They need the money, Nelson wrote to Carl Sandburg, but they don't like the terms being offered. "They know it is not out of kindness that any nation acts—there is always a bill, and the bill seems to be a willingness to accept the status of being an American colony and the attendant provision of supplying troops to back up the North Atlantic pact."

The country feels trapped between America and the Soviet Union, Nelson wrote, and it's so evenly divided it'll be stuck in limbo until its hand is forced. The French "seem to be looking about for someone to tell them whether they won or lost the last war," he wrote. "There doesn't seem to be anyone to tell them, and no way of finding out. So they go on welcoming the American tourist with open arms while at the same time despising him a bit for having so much after suffering so little."

Nelson was also disturbed by all the Americans he saw in Paris. He had no problem with the tourists, but he was disappointed to learn that the city was home to a large and growing expatriate population of actors, musicians, and writers. Nelson disdained them, as a group, for choosing to flee the United States when resistance was called for, and the more talented they were, the more he resented their presence in Paris. To his mind, Richard Wright was the worst of the group because his ideas were needed most back home.

Nelson and Wright hadn't spoken since Nelson was stationed at Camp Maxey, but Beauvoir had been keeping each man up to date on how the other was doing. Wright was living in a large apartment at 14, rue Monsieur le Prince with his wife, Ellen, their two daughters, and a maid who handled the cooking and cleaning. Beauvoir had been over to his home for dinner and had seen him around town. He always praised Nelson in her presence, and he was excited when she said Nelson was coming to Paris.

Nelson and Wright met only once during Nelson's trip, though, and their reunion did not go well. Wright assumed Nelson was moving to Paris, so he greeted him warmly and welcomed him to his new home.

Nelson recoiled. I'm only visiting, he said, and I'll never leave the States. "I'd be afraid to do that for fear of losing contact with my roots."

The comment hurt Wright deeply because it cut so close to the truth. He hadn't been able to complete a novel since *Native Son*, and he had barely written a thing since moving to Paris, so he responded defensively.

"Don't you realize that some of the greatest novels have been written in exile?" he said. "Look at Dostoevsky."

They were talking past each other. Wright left America because he and his family couldn't live there in peace. His wife, Ellen, was white, their children were biracial, and when he was home, he could feel the country's collective judgment like a weight pressing down on him. He had dreamed about moving to the countryside after making his fortune, but when he heard about a spate of lynchings in rural towns, he decided it was too dangerous. He and Ellen settled on the idea of moving to a liberal New England town instead, but the owners of the house they wanted to buy refused to sell to them. So they left for Europe.

Nelson knew none of that. When he looked at his old friend, he saw a man who had run from the most important political conflict of his generation, installed himself in a luxury apartment on the other side of the ocean, and begun spending his days sipping coffee with expatriates instead of putting his immense talent to use.

It makes a great difference, Nelson replied flatly, whether you've been exiled or exiled yourself.

He and Wright parted then, and never spoke again. It was a sad end to a sixteen-year friendship.

Nelson and Beauvoir decided it was time to leave Paris. His meeting with Wright upset him, and she was becoming increasingly uncomfortable in the city. The first volume of *The Second Sex* had just been published, and it caused a sensation. The book sold twenty thousand copies in its first week, and fans and detractors had begun seeking her out.

Some people approached her on the street and complimented her work, but others were enraged by the fact that she had criticized the church and written frankly about female sexuality. They sent threatening letters to her apartment, and once, while she and Nelson were making their way through a crowded street, a man began screaming, "You have no right to be here!"

Beauvoir and Nelson went on the road then, with no set plans. They flew to Rome first, and then visited Naples and Porto d'Ischia.

When they reached Tunis, a chauffeur named Hassine Ameur Djemail offered to drive them to an island called Djerba in a 1939 Citroen, and they accepted. When they arrived, they found an underground bar where the owner kept his beer—and his feet—cool by submerging them in a pool of water. They spent three days there; Nelson smoked a combination of hashish and tobacco the locals called "kif," and he and Beauvoir ate dinner with Djemail, smoked, and talked about Islam and America.

Algiers was next—then Fez, and Marrakesh. They stopped in Marseille so that Nelson could see the port he had looked down on while waiting to be sent home after the war, and they lost a bit of money in Monte Carlo. In Antibes, they visited friends of Beauvoir's, and Nelson got drunk and danced with a chair to make everyone laugh.

They returned to Paris in August, and for a month they lived the way they were always meant to—in the moment, and without undue pressure on either of them to be everything the other needed. They were happy to be together, and happy, too, because they were both ascendant. Beauvoir had just become one of the most famous writers in Europe, and Nelson was about to become one of the most renowned novelists in America. Several hundred thousand copies of Avon's edition of *Never Come Morning* had already been printed. *The Man with the Golden Arm* was about to be released, and *Harper's* magazine had just published an excerpt from it.

Nelson and Beauvoir parted at Orly Airport in mid-September with less drama than usual. He was eager to begin promoting his novel back in Chicago, and she was not apprehensive about saying goodbye because she felt certain they would see each other again. But then, suddenly, she was not. "He went through the door to customs," she wrote later. "[H]e disappeared; that in itself seemed so impossible that everything became possible, even or especially, that we might never meet again. I went back to Paris by taxi: the red lights on top of the pylons were all omens of some dreadful calamity."

"OK, Kid, You Beat Dostoyevsky"

(September 22, 1949–March 16, 1950)

Nelson and Eleanor Roosevelt sharing a laugh after the presentation of the first National Book Awards. Ralph L. Rusk, who received that year's award for nonfiction, is pictured to their left; William Carlos Williams, the recipient of that year's award for poetry, is pictured to their right. Roosevelt was a finalist for the nonfiction award. Photo by Bettmann/ Bettmann Collection/ Getty Images

When Nelson began signing copies of *The Man with the Golden Arm* in the Seven Stairs bookshop on September 22, the line of people waiting to see him stretched through the narrow main room, outside, down the steps, and along the sidewalk—and for the next three hours, it continued to replenish itself. Every time someone exited carrying a copy of the novel, another person took their place.

Customers lined up in pairs and waited patiently, and when they made it through the front door, they were confronted by a chaotic scene. The shop's owner, Stuart Brent, stood behind a counter and rang up sales, and newspaper photographers moved through the room, snapping pictures. Ken McCormick lugged books from the storeroom to the counter, and people clustered around a table where a barrel of beer and five large salamis had been set out. Jack Conroy mingled and told jokes in his basso baritone, and Nelson sat with his back to the rear wall, signing copies of his novel. He added lengthy inscriptions to every book that appeared in front of him, sometimes entire paragraphs, and when he made mistakes, he insisted that Brent provide a fresh copy.

Four hundred and fifty people filed through Seven Stairs that afternoon, and almost two hundred bought the novel. The event was mentioned in the local papers several times, and over the next two weeks, the shop sold eight hundred more copies.[*]

No one had expected the reception to be such a success—not Brent, not McCormick, and not Nelson. Early reviews of *The Man with the Golden Arm* were partly responsible for the turnout. The *Tribune*'s reviewer wrote, "I would crown him [Algren] the American Dostoevsky, were not such comparisons invidious and his place not assured." The book dips into melodrama occasionally, the *New York Times* said, but its shortcomings "are far outweighed, in so far as the writing is concerned, by Algren's acute ear for vernacular speech, his sure feeling for structure, and a smooth flow of prose which has nothing of the slick about it." And *Time* said, "Readers with queasy stomachs may shrink from an environment in which the unbelievably sordid has become a way of life. They will also come away with some of Algren's own tender concern for his wretched, confused and hopelessly degenerate cast of characters. In that, Writer Algren scores a true novelist's triumph."

But the timing of the book's release was also responsible for some

---

[*] In his book *The Seven Stairs*, Stuart Brent claimed that he sold a thousand copies of *Arm* that first night, but contemporaneous correspondence contradicts that claim.

of the excitement it created. For once, Nelson's tortured process produced a book that was perfectly suited to the moment it reached the market. *Golden Arm* felt timely because its protagonist was a struggling veteran, and the war had ended only four years earlier. It felt important because morphine addiction—a non-concern when Nelson added it to his manuscript—had recently become a major issue. And it felt exciting and subversive because the Red Scare had already homogenized much of American culture, but it dared to assert the humanity of addicts, prisoners, prostitutes, and thieves.

Captain Bednar is sitting behind a query room desk in the Saloon Street police station when *The Man with the Golden Arm* begins, feeling weary and "half drunken." He lays his head on his arms and slips into a reverie. "Yet it wasn't work that wearied him so," Nelson wrote, "and his sleep was harassed by more than a smoke-colored rain. The city had filled him with the guilt of others; he was numbed by his charge sheet's accusations."

Two minor hustlers are waiting when Bednar raises his head. One is a card dealer named Frankie "Machine" Macjinek. The other is a "loose bum" named Solly "Sparrow" Saltskin. Bednar knows both well.

"Ain't nothin' on *my* record but drunk 'n fightin'," Frankie offers without being asked. "All I do is deal, drink 'n fight."

The captain looks at Frankie closely—his faded army-issue wool pants, his broken nose, and his combat boots.

"What kind of discharge you get, Dealer?" he asks.

"The *right* kind," Frankie replies. "*And* the Purple Heart."

"Who do you fight with?" Bednar asks.

"My wife, that's all," Frankie says.

"Hell, that's no crime," Bednar allows.

Sparrow Saltskin is a more complicated problem. He's a pathetic creature—a peeping tom, a dog thief, a shoplifter, a clown—but he speaks with the authority of a respectable man, and his presumptuousness brings out the worst in people. Like a flea-ridden mongrel demanding affection, even gentle souls consider snapping a foot into his soft belly when he approaches.

The captain is no different. He has booked Sparrow so many times, he no longer finds him amusing, or even tolerable. He begins questioning Sparrow haphazardly, but their repartee quickly turns dark.

"I think you're a moron," the captain says. Then he addresses Frankie and Sparrow together. "You're both a couple of loose bums livin' off the weaker bums," he says, and orders an officer to lock them up.

As with the Russian novels Nelson most admired, the price of admission to *The Man with the Golden Arm* is high. The vernacular in its pages is thick and opaque at first, and the momentum created by the first scene slows drastically when Frankie and Sparrow reach their cell and Nelson begins describing their environment, and their friendship.

World War II has been won by the time the novel begins, and victory has transformed America into a wealthy, conformist, and status-obsessed country, Nelson explains—a place where "ownership and virtue are one," and the truest Americans receive their commandments from billboards and slick magazines. They drink "liquor that lends distinction" and "beer that gives that special glow of health," and as a result, they're able to "mount the broad stone stairways to success surely and swiftly and unaided by others."

But Frankie and Sparrow feel like foreigners in the world occupied by those "truer Americans." They can see it in the distance and feel the warm glow of its wealth, but they've been denied access to it. The portions of the city available to them, in contrast, have begun to feel like "some sort of open-roofed jail with walls for all men and laughter for very few." Like everyone else who has been written out of the narrative of the American Century, they "no longer felt they had been born in America. They felt they had merely emerged from the wrong side of the billboards."

Frankie and Sparrow live in the postwar world, but the Polish Triangle is their home, and older, simpler rules govern there. Little has

changed in the neighborhood since the armistice, and no one expects
much ever will. "For here," Nelson wrote, "God and the ward super
work hand in hand and neither moves without the other's assent.
God loans the super cunning and the super forwards a percentage of
the grift on Sunday mornings. The super puts in the fix for all right-
thinking hustlers and the Lord, in turn, puts in the fix for the super.
For the super's God is a hustler's God; and as wise, in his way, as the
God of the priests and the business men."

Disturbing that arrangement is the sin that landed Frankie and
Sparrow in jail. They work for a man named Zero Schwiefka—
Frankie deals cards for his backroom poker game, and Sparrow works
the door and steers players to the table—and the police picked them
up because Schwiefka declined to pay for protection that week.

Schwiefka corrects that error the day after Frankie and Sparrow
are arrested, and visits them in jail. He's an ugly, ill-kempt man, and
when he arrives, he stands outside their cell and rubs his "hamlike"
hands together and apologizes.

"Got here as soon as I could, Dealer," he tells Frankie. "You'll be
out in half an hour."

The Man with the Golden Arm feels like a traditional naturalistic novel
in its opening pages—a book created to highlight its characters' poverty and elicit sympathy for them. But when Frankie and Sparrow
return to their neighborhood and enter Antek Witwicki's Tug & Maul
Bar, the book's narrative focus tightens, and it becomes concerned
almost entirely with its characters' internal lives—their dreams and
fears, the dignity they imbue themselves with, their ethics, and the
existential worries that plague them.*

The Tug & Maul Bar is the neighborhood's living room, and it's there

---

* Malcolm Cowley made a similar point in a perceptive essay called "Personalism:
A New School of Fiction."

that Nelson introduces most of his characters. Drunkie John and his wife Molly Novotny appear first. They're sitting at the bar when Frankie and Sparrow first enter, and John is haranguing Molly for nothing—"The nuthouse is the best place for you," he says cryptically. Sometimes, he beats her. On other occasions, he humiliates her or kicks her out of their apartment to assert his authority, but on this afternoon, he settles for knocking over a shot of whisky and splashing it down the front of her dress.

"Have your own way then, have your own way," she says with practiced submissiveness.

John is a man near forty who hasn't worked in years. He lives off the money Molly earns serving drinks at Club Safari, but never shows her any gratitude. He's adrift in the world—just bobbing in the surf. "Some find themselves through joy," Nelson wrote, "some through suffering and some through toil. Johnny had till now tried nothing but whisky. A process which left him feeling like somebody new every day."

Molly is a woman in her early twenties, a "small girl with a heart-shaped face and eyes dark with exhaustion." She's generous, and had once been carefree, but she has learned resignation since marrying John. She takes his beatings and insults with a "sort of dull hopelessness" because she has no other options. She feels best about herself when caring for others, and it's her tenderness that traps her. "She's got too big a heart, that girl," Antek Witwicki says. "A guy can walk into her heart with army boots on."

Frankie and Sparrow leave the Tug & Maul when Molly runs out and John chases after her, but they return regularly and Nelson continues to use the bar to introduce his most important characters.

One is a blind man everyone calls Piggy-O. His sight first began to dim while he was watching a burlesque, and when he lost it altogether, he decided everyone still capable of seeing was allied against him. He coats his body with filth to keep the world at bay, but though people run when they catch a whiff of his stench, he never concedes that they have any reason to feel superior. "I got *my* kind of pride 'n you got yours," he says. "I'm proud of bein' how *I* am too."

Louie Fomorowski is another. He is an old-school hustler who knew some of Chicago's most famous gangsters back in his day. He is past fifty when the novel begins, but still dealing morphine and dressing like a player—amber-toed two-tone shoes, a green fedora, and polo shirts. He has outlived most of his contemporaries and managed to remain in business by adjusting his code of conduct to reflect the ethics of the postwar world. "My business is everybody's business," he says proudly, "—informin' is a racket like everythin' else."

Drunkie John, Molly Novotny, Blind Piggy, and Louie Fomorowski all play important roles in the novel's plot—and so do Antek Witwicki, Zero Schwiefka, Captain Bednar, and a beat cop named Kvorka—but Frankie, Sparrow, and Frankie's wife, Sophie, are the book's heart.

Frankie and Sophie grew up in the Triangle and spent their childhoods chasing "malt-hop trucks" to catch malt drippings in tin cans, and carrying the Easter lamb into St. Stephen's Church so Father Simon could bless it.* They have been sweethearts almost their entire lives, but Frankie has never taken Sophie's affection seriously, and his indifference "tortured" her. He was, Nelson wrote, "as careless of her love as if it were something he could pick up in any old can just by following a malt-hop truck."

So Sophie secured his devotion. She faked a pregnancy to pressure him into marrying her, and then faked a miscarriage after they exchanged vows. They have been husband and wife ever since, but even that isn't enough to keep him close. He went off to war, got injured by shrapnel, and came home as wild and indifferent to her as ever. On the night America dropped atomic bombs on Nagasaki and Hiroshima,

---

* This mention of malt-hop trucks is a reference to Nelson's childhood, and there are other references to his life scattered throughout the text. At one point Sparrow remembers collecting beer corks the way Nelson did as a child, and on another occasion a bit of graffiti mentions "Dr. Jesse Blue's Bay Rum." At the end of the book, a coroner named William Hackett—the name of one of the men Frankie Machine is modeled after—makes an inquest, and an officer named Otto Schaeffer—the name of one of the Fallonites—testifies.

Frankie got blind drunk and drove into a billboard on Ashland Avenue. Sophie was hurt in the accident, though not badly, but she has been pretending her legs are numb and useless ever since.

She knows Frankie will stay with her as long as she is unable to care for herself, so she calls the crash "[t]he blessed, cursed, wonderful-terrible God's-own-accident that had truly married them at last." They have been locked into an endless domestic battle ever since, and she finds her greatest pleasure in tormenting him. "What she could not gain through love she sought to possess by mockery," Nelson wrote. "He was too dear to her: into everything he did she must read some secret hatred of herself."

Sparrow's love for Frankie is more tender and familial. They met two years before Pearl Harbor, when Frankie found Sparrow huddled beneath newspapers in an alley. Frankie handed Sparrow a half dollar that night so he could afford to sleep inside, and Sparrow has loved and admired him since. He is the only person in the neighborhood who thinks Frankie is clever, tough, and important, and his devotion is often the only thing either can rely on.

Sparrow has been a creature of the alleys his entire life, but he's also a keen observer who occasionally plays the role of the nobleman's fool by speaking truth more plainly than anyone else. Once a woman asks plaintively, "Ain't nobody on *my* side?" And Sparrow answers, "You're all on your own from here on out. Ain't nobody on anybody's side no more. You're the oney one on your side 'n I'm the oney one on mine."

Frankie Machine, for his part, is a man with no real idea who he is or what he wants to become—if anything. He never finished grammar school, and for years, his ambitions were limited to bedding women, drinking, and gambling. But by the time the novel begins, he has realized there isn't much space left in the world for a man without profession, money, or class. He's proud of his talent for dealing cards and boasts that he's the "kid with the golden arm," but knows that doesn't count for much and has begun undermining himself just as often as he brags. "I never get nowhere," he says, "but I pay my own fare all the way."

The list of Frankie's wishes is long. He wants to leave Sophie so he can be with Molly Novotny. He wants to stop buying morphine from Louie Fomorowski and kick his addiction. He wants to become a drummer, join the musician's union, and "bang the tubs" for a bandleader like Gene Krupa, but he can't get out of his own way long enough to see any one of those goals all the way through—he begins an affair with Molly, but doesn't leave Sophie; he stops using morphine, but gets back on; he practices drumming on a pad he keeps in his room, but never tries to get a job playing professionally.

After Nelson introduces the novel's most important characters, he sets the plot in motion. Frankie ends up in the alley outside Zero Schwiefka's one night with Louie Fomorowski and Sparrow, and when they begin arguing, Louie mocks Frankie for being an addict. "You'll look me up ten thousand times to come," he says. "'N on yer knees to beg me to take your money too."

Until that moment, Sparrow has no idea Frankie is an addict, and Frankie can't stand the thought of losing his friend's admiration. He knows Louie is right as well, and can't stand the thought of that either. "I want people like you knocked on the head," he tells Louie. And when Louie laughs, Frankie snaps his neck and leaves his body in the alley.

Louie's death sets in motion the chain of events that determines the course of Frankie's life. The police begin to suspect that Frankie killed Louie almost immediately. Someone took the money Louie was holding when he died, and when Frankie begins to suspect Sparrow stole it, their relationship cools. They go shoplifting together, "just to do somethin'," and the police catch Frankie in the act and send him to jail for several months.

Frankie is a diminished man when he's released. Molly, whose love had been the most promising thing in his life, has left the neighborhood. Sophie has begun to lose her mind. He and Sparrow aren't talking, he's lost his touch with the cards, and he starts using morphine again. Once, he tells himself he's going to get a library card "the minute" he finishes the shot of liquor in his hand—but he can't even accomplish that much.

The police entrap Sparrow eventually, and after threatening him for weeks, they convince him to finger Frankie for Louie's murder. They get an arrest warrant for Frankie, and their pursuit moves the story along from that point forward, but the cat-and-mouse dynamic of their chase and his evasion never become the book's primary focus because there's no doubt who killed Louie—Sparrow knows, and so do Blind Piggy, Antek Witwicki, and everyone else in the neighborhood. There's no doubt as to what will become of Frankie Machine either. He's no survivor, but he is a dreamer, and the story remains compelling all the way through because he continues to believe he has a way out until his very last moments.

Frankie goes on the run to avoid the police, manages to find Molly, and then moves in with her. She finds purpose and contentment in nursing him off morphine, but then Drunkie John finds them, extorts them, and then calls the police and tells them where Frankie is hiding.

Frankie finally succumbs then. He leads the police on a chase, gets away, and hides in a cheap hotel room. He's alone, and he's been shot, and he's bleeding. "What am I waitin' for?" he asks himself. "For the ice in the blood to reach the heart? Or for the tread of heavy boots following a flashlight up the stairs?"

He takes a double strand of twine, secures it to the ceiling, and fashions a noose. "Have a good dream you're dancin', [Sophie]," he tells the empty room, and then he hangs himself.

Much ink was wasted discussing the "sordid" and "degenerate" nature of the characters in *The Man with the Golden Arm* when it was released. Frankie's morphine addiction seemed scandalous, though it plays a relatively minor role in the story, and so did Blind Piggy and a host of the characters Frankie meets in jail. But today, the book doesn't seem outré—it seems prescient.

When Nelson returned from the war, he began to fear that the end of hostilities in Europe and the Pacific was also the beginning of a struggle to shape the future. Other writers shared his concerns, of course. The most notable among them was George Orwell, who looked at the expansion of the central state in the Soviet Union and envisioned the dystopian world he described in *Nineteen Eighty-Four*—a place where government was all, thoughts were policed, and dissent was impossible.*

Nelson feared a different, but no less despairing future. Instead of looking to the government for guidance, he studied the class of people who had not benefited from the wartime recovery or the postwar economic boom. The thinness of the American Century's promise was evident in the quality of their lives, he believed, and he intuited that their fates foretold everyone else's. He looked at them and saw an atomized society where no one felt at home any longer, and masses of people cycled through prisons and jails—a place where irrelevance was both sin and punishment, and there was no need for a totalitarian government to stifle dissent because everyone was out only for themselves.

Everyone is "the only one on his own side," he wrote, and people are so divided by class and lacking in charity, that it's hard for someone down on their luck to "find five dollars in a city of four million people, most of them millionaires."

Incarceration is no longer the burden it was intended to be, he wrote, because "time off for good conduct means little to men with no place to go and nothing in particular to do when they get there." Prisons and jails, he reported, are not filled with dangerous people; they are packed with "men and youths who had never picked up any sort of craft—though most of them could learn anything requiring a mechanical turn with ease. It wasn't so much a lack of aptitude as simply the feeling that no work had any point to it."

And as cities had become wealthier, more complex, and more reg-

---

* *Nineteen Eighty-Four* and *The Man with the Golden Arm* were released three months apart—the first in June 1949, the second in September.

imented, people had begun to lose their identities and their sense of belonging. "You know who I am?" Frankie Machine asks. "You know who you are? You know who *anybody* is anymore?"

By the time Nelson began writing *Arm*, he had realized that the lives lived by people surviving at the margins of society provided a glimpse of the future. That insight was the reason Nelson focused so tightly on Frankie, Sparrow, and Sophie. A traditional naturalistic novel dwells on environment and studies its effect on characters. It tells its readers to pity these poor people, help them. But *The Man with the Golden Arm* reverses that dynamic so that its characters have to be acknowledged as individuals—no more or less capricious, vain, weak, lustful, and deluded than anyone else. It tells its readers, "Look at what's become of us, we need to help ourselves." Or, as the defrocked priest says, "we are all members of one another."

The excitement surrounding *Arm*'s release lasted through the holidays and into the New Year. It remained on local best-seller lists until mid-December, and then a subscription service called the Book Find Club selected it as its monthly reading for January 1950. Pocket Books paid twenty-five thousand dollars for the paperback rights—a record price at the time—and an abridged version of the novel appeared in the first issue of *Book Digest*.

Promoting the book kept Nelson busy for months. He cycled through the department stores in the Loop to sign display copies, and appeared on television and radio. He addressed a capacity crowd as the keynote speaker of the first *Sun-Times* book and author luncheon, accepted an award from *Time* magazine for writing the best novel of the year, and sat down with a writer from the *New York Times* for an interview. He speaks "a run-of-the-mill Chicagoese, an unpretentious colloquial," the reporter wrote later. "He looks like any guy—medium height, medium slim, medium sandy hair—and could be anything: a clerk, a sailor, a baker's boy, a soda jerk, an electrician, a bus driver. But not a writer."

Reviews of *Golden Arm* continued to appear as well, but the praise Nelson valued most came from peers. Kenneth Millar, a mystery writer who published using the pseudonym Ross Macdonald, wrote to say he had been reading *Arm* aloud to his wife and couldn't believe how good it was. "I think it's the strongest and deepest work of imagination that has been done in this country since the war," he wrote. And Robert Lowry, a novelist and reviewer from *Time* magazine, wrote to say, "I honest to God don't know how you did it. I mean the sustained invention, all in a pure, fresh-minted idiom. The turn of phrase on turn of phrase on turn of phrase, no two of them alike, all of them brand new and trembling. Brother it was wonderful."

Nelson knew Millar and Lowry and their letters flattered him, but the message that moved him most came from Ernest Hemingway— a man he had long admired but never met. Hemingway had been on record as a fan of Nelson's since he told a newspaper reporter that Faulkner was the best working writer in America and Nelson was the runner-up, but after reading *Arm*, he went even further.

> *Into a world of letters where we have the fading Faulkner and where that overgrown Lil Abner Thomas Wolfe casts a shorter shadow each day, Nelson Algren comes like a corvette or even a big destroyer when one of those things is what you need and need it badly and at once and for keeps. He has been around for a long time but only the pros knew about him. . . . Mr. Algren can hit with both hands and move around and he will kill you if you are not awfully careful.*

Hemingway's praise sounds hyperbolic and intended to maximize its effect on sales, but his regard was genuine and he repeated it privately. He told the critic Malcolm Cowley, "Algren is probably the best writer under 50, and name your own figure, writing today." And he wrote a note inside his personal copy of *Arm* that reads, "OK, kid, you beat Dostoyevsky. I'll never fight you in Chicago. Ever."

Nelson pressed Ken McCormick to use Hemingway's letter to promote the novel, but McCormick resisted. He said it would be best to wait until sales slowed. Then, when that happened, he said he was afraid the quote would offend Faulkner's fans, and Wolfe's, and do more harm than good. Nelson kept insisting, though, and eventually McCormick had someone at Doubleday create an advertisement built around Hemingway's letter and made plans to have it published in New York and Chicago papers. McCormick showed it to his peers at Random House and Harper & Brothers before he ran it though—Wolfe's publisher and Faulkner's publisher, respectively—and he shelved the advertisement when they asked him to.

"[P]lease don't consider that we're being derelict in our duty by not running an ad using this particular quote," McCormick pleaded.

Nelson let the issue drop, but he wasn't pleased. He kept Hemingway's letter, though, and hung it prominently in his apartment.

N elson was famous by early 1950, and entirely unprepared. He had no idea what to do with the money he was making, and hadn't even considered trading up for more acceptable friends. He felt indebted to the people he associated with on West Madison Street, so after his novel became a hit, he tried to repay them for the support they had shown him while he was writing, and their toleration of his endless questions.

He kept in touch with Richard Majewski, who was back in Cook County Jail, and he tried to help Paula Bays get sober again. He let her withdraw in his apartment for a second time, and then he paid for her and her husband, John, to travel to John's family's home in Monroe, Ohio.

"Nelson, I'd like to say again, thanks for everything, you were more than fine and I shant forget, not ever," John Bays wrote when they arrived. Paula is resting, he said, but she says to say hello. "She thinks there is no one quite like you. She says you possess a natural goodness of which you are quite unaware."

No one benefited from Nelson's largess more than Bill Hackett. Nelson had created Frankie Machine by combining the characteristics of several men, but Hackett was primary among them: some of Frankie's dialogue came from Hackett's mouth, they were physically similar, and they both shot dope and dealt cards. Nelson felt obligated to Hackett as a result, and when he was offered an opportunity to travel to Hollywood, he showed interest, and pushed to secure an invitation for his friend.

A man named Bob Roberts approached Nelson about turning *The Man with the Golden Arm* into a film when he was passing through Chicago.* He had already purchased the option to the book, and he owned a production company that had recently released a boxing movie called *Body and Soul* with John Garfield, a major star at the time. He said Garfield was interested in playing Frankie Machine, and asked if Nelson liked that idea.

Nelson thought Roberts was just talking. The Motion Picture Association of America enforced a production code that prohibited movies containing profanity, sex, or drug use from being screened in American theaters, so there was little chance *Arm* would ever be released.

Roberts said he was serious about the project, though, and offered to pay for Nelson to travel to California to discuss it.

Nelson was curious, so he agreed with one caveat. "I don't have any firsthand acquaintance with drugs," he told Roberts, "but I know a guy who has. He could be your technical adviser."

"Bring him out," Roberts said. Then he had a contract written up, and put Hackett's name on it, right along with Nelson's.

Nelson bought a pair of train tickets and told his friend the good news. Hackett was excited about the trip and the opportunity it would give him to get clean, but he very nearly missed it.

Nelson's phone rang the day before he was scheduled to leave Chicago, and when he picked it up, a man's voice came through the line.

"This is your brother," the voice said.

"Well, I don't have a brother," Nelson replied.

---

* Nelson gave Roberts the pseudonym Moxon when he discussed him in *Conversations with Nelson Algren*.

"Well, I'm talking *for* your brother," the man said.

Then Nelson realized what had happened. Hackett had been arrested, the police were holding him, and he had asked someone to call Nelson on his behalf. So, Nelson went to the station. The police there knew Hackett, and they didn't think much of him. One officer in particular couldn't stand him, and often picked him up for vagrancy.

Nelson approached that officer and asked about Hackett. "Well, that son of a bitch is no good," the officer said. "He's a junkie."

"No," Nelson corrected him, "he's John Garfield's technical adviser." He had the contract Roberts had given him in his pocket, and he produced it to make his point.

The officer was surprised. "You've got the wrong guy," he said.

"No," Nelson insisted, "he's going to take part in a play. You know, he might take the lead," he exaggerated for effect.

The police released Hackett. Nelson left with him, and the next day, they made their way to Dearborn Station to catch their train.

They must have made quite a scene when they arrived. The station was a red-brick building with marble floors and a large, sunlit atrium at its center. There were skylights cut into the ceiling, and a clock tower rose five stories above the roofline like a castle's spire.* They, in contrast, were an unmarried forty-year-old writer who lived in a cold-water flat behind an empty lot, a card dealer whose shirtsleeves concealed years' worth of track marks, and an entourage of about a dozen junkies.

The crowd from West Madison Street met Nelson and Hackett at the station to say their goodbyes. They were a random sort of family, bound by circumstance and shared experience instead of blood, but connected all the same, and their parting must have been bittersweet. The trip west was the start of something new for Nelson and Hackett, but an end for the people they were leaving behind. Nelson's head

---

* In *Conversations with Nelson Algren*, Nelson says they left from the LaSalle Street Station, but that's not accurate. The Super Chief—the train they boarded—only left from Dearborn.

was full of Hollywood dreams, and there was no reason to expect he would continue visiting Jack's apartment to listen to records. Hackett swore he was never coming back, so the group knew the farewells they exchanged were almost certainly final.

Nelson and Hackett moved into the Chateau Marmont when they reached Hollywood, and though they were only a couple thousand miles from home, they felt like visitors to an alien world. When I step onto my balcony, Nelson wrote to a friend, I see "a thousand merry-go-rounds going around and around and around way down below." In Los Angeles, he said, "everybody is a millionaire, nobody ever goes home, we all hate money and everything is love."

At first, Nelson and Hackett had nothing to do. John Garfield was in New York for work and not expected back for several days, so Nelson called Amanda and asked her to show him and Hackett the city. She agreed, and for several days she played chauffeur. She drove them to visit an acquaintance from Chicago who had moved west, to dinner with Sanora Babb, an old friend from the League of American Writers, and to Chasen's, where Nelson swooned when a twenty-five-year-old actress named Angela Lansbury sat at a table nearby.

The trip felt like a dream, and like a dream, its promise disappeared as suddenly as it had manifested itself. Nelson began negotiating with Bob Roberts after settling in, and their talks soured quickly. The problem was money. Roberts offered Nelson fifteen thousand dollars up front for the rights to *Arm*, but no cut of the film's profits if it earned any. Nelson thought he could do better, so he pushed for more, but Roberts had the advantage.* Nelson's agent hadn't accompanied him, and the representative she had arranged in Hollywood seemed to be looking out for Roberts's interests.

---

* That was the total—it breaks down to five thousand for the option to make the film, and ten thousand for the rights. That would come to about $150,000 today.

Tension built between Nelson and Roberts, and built. Nelson felt he was being treated like a child, or a fool. Roberts was eager to finish the deal and have Nelson begin working on a script, but he wasn't willing to increase his offer. Nelson said he was going to meet with other producers, and by the end of the first week, they were trading insults freely.

Roberts was in the middle of lecturing Nelson on his obligations one day when he switched tacks.

You're a good guy, he said. Here, have a bottle of whiskey. He shoved the bottle under Nelson's arm, and then the doorbell rang.

Roberts answered it. "Hey, Algren," he said, "here is a fan of yours, a *superior* fan."

The man who rang the bell entered the room and approached Nelson. "Am I speaking to Nelson Algren who writes books?" he asked.

You are, Nelson said. Then the man shoved a stack of summonses under Nelson's arm and left. Nelson had a bottle of liquor under one arm and the sheaf of papers under the other, and couldn't get at either without letting something drop.

Roberts began pacing to keep away from Nelson. "Why do you make me act like such a shit?" he asked.

"I *don't* know why," Nelson replied archly. "*Why* do I make you act like such a shit?" He followed Roberts around the room with his arms pinned against his torso, and then he set the whiskey bottle down and grabbed the summonses with his free arm. He had been served with an injunction that prevented him from offering the film rights to *Arm* to any other producer.

"I'd rather give the money to you than to the lawyers," Roberts added with a final condescending flourish.

The Chateau Marmont presented Nelson with a bill soon afterward. Roberts had promised to pay for Nelson's accommodations, but after legal proceedings began, he told the hotel he wasn't responsible for the rent.

Nelson paid the tab, and then he helped Hackett find a furnished room in Hollywood, and he moved into Amanda's apartment in Echo Park.

Nelson and Roberts settled their dispute within the week, and Nelson got what he had been demanding. He hired a Hollywood agent named George Willner to assist him, and the final terms guaranteed him fifteen thousand dollars up front and five percent of the film's profits. It was a victory of sorts, but also a disappointing end to the run of luck that had begun with *Arm*'s publication five months earlier.

Then good news arrived. Ken McCormick called to tell Nelson he was going to receive the National Book Award for fiction. *The Man with the Golden Arm* had been released after the deadline for submissions, but an exception was made. The award had recently been created by three publishing trade groups, and the organizers wanted to set the standard for winners as high as possible.

Nelson was forbidden from revealing the news, so he bought a ticket to New York and flew east alone.

The award ceremony was held in the ballroom of the Waldorf-Astoria Hotel on Park Avenue in Manhattan on March 16, 1950. There were more than a thousand people in attendance. The women wore gowns and the men wore tuxedos, and together they constituted the largest group of "critics, book editors, and famous authors ever gathered under one roof," the *Chicago Tribune* reported.

When the proceedings began, Clifton Fadiman took the stage. He was a writer who spoke with a broadcaster's honey-slick voice, so he was serving as the event's emcee. He welcomed everyone, and then he began bringing guests on stage. Eleanor Roosevelt, a US senator from Illinois named Paul Douglas, and the editor-in-chief of *Harper's* magazine each addressed the crowd, and then Fadiman returned and took control of the microphone.

William Carlos Williams has been awarded the prize for poetry, Fadiman said. Ralph L. Rusk has written the best nonfiction book of the year.

Nelson rose when he heard his name, and walked toward the stage wearing a tuxedo. He had never owned one before, and though it was cut well enough, he looked like a man wearing someone else's skin. He stepped to the microphone when he reached the stage and thanked Fadiman for his introduction, and for years afterward he wondered why he had. "I'm going around thanking the hanger-on for hanging on!" he joked.

Eleanor Roosevelt joined the three winners on stage after the ceremony concluded. She kissed Nelson, and flashbulbs began popping.

One image taken in that moment captures the scene, and Nelson's mood, nicely. In it, Williams is staring at the ceiling and Rusk is looking down toward the audience, but Nelson and Roosevelt are turned toward each other. A thousand people were watching them, but they look as relaxed as old friends sharing an inside joke. She's smiling so widely you can see her teeth, and he's holding the plaque Fadiman handed him with both hands, the way a father might display a newborn child.

"How Long Does This Sort of Thing Go On?"

(March 17, 1950–December 1951)

Nelson and his mother, Goldie Abraham, standing outside Nelson's house
in Gary, Indiana. Goldie is wearing an eight-hundred-dollar fur coat
Nelson purchased for her after he began earning royalties from The Man
with the Golden Arm. Photo by Amanda Algren, courtesy of Rick Kinsinger

Nelson returned to his flat on Wabansia Avenue after the book award ceremony, but not to his old life. He had been trying to live a solitary existence since returning from the war, so as to focus on his writing, but that was no longer possible. Work was available to Nelson in any volume he could handle for the first time in his career, and he felt compelled to take advantage of that fact. He taught a writing course at the University of Chicago that spring, while simultaneously writing a screenplay for the film adaptation of *The Man with the Golden Arm* with a collaborator named Paul Trivers. He began working on a long essay about Chicago's history for a slick magazine called *Holiday*, and reviewed books for the *Chicago Sun-Times* and the *New York Times Book Review*. Doubleday offered him money to revise *Somebody in Boots* for a paperback edition, and he accepted.

Nelson also met up regularly with a young, moonfaced photographer named Art Shay who had dropped by the apartment unannounced a few months earlier. Nelson had invited Shay in that day, and offered him a cup of tea. They talked, and soon they were touring the city's all-night cafés, police stations, and slums to collect images for a book of photos. They sent some to Ken McCormick, and he agreed to publish what they produced, with an introduction by Nelson.

Lovers, old and new, also required attention. Nelson and Amanda had rekindled their long-fraught romance in Hollywood, and begun discussing marriage and parenthood. If they got back together and had a daughter, they decided, they would name her Madeleine. He and Beauvoir were also corresponding, and he was seeing two other women as well. One was a librarian named Mari Sabusawa; Paula Bays was the other. Her sojourn in Ohio didn't last long, so she was back in Chicago. Her marriage was disintegrating and her husband, John, had become physically abusive, so she ran to Nelson for protection and companionship when she could.

But nothing weighed on Nelson's mind more heavily than the country's political climate, and the chilling effect it was having on artistic expression and political dissent. Senator Joseph McCarthy had recently forced his way into the headlines by declaring, "Today we are engaged in a final, all-out battle between communistic atheism and Christianity. The modern champions of communism have selected this as the time. And, ladies and gentlemen, the chips are down—they are truly down."

McCarthy was an ugly man and a hard drinker whose words ran together in a manner that suggested folksy humility, if you were inclined to be generous, or an inebriate's slur, if you weren't. He was speaking to a group of women in West Virginia, and before the end of his tirade, he announced that he possessed a list of subversives who were both employed by the government and trying to undermine it. "While I cannot take the time to name all the men in the State Department who have been named as members of the Communist Party and members of a spy ring," he said, "I have here in my hand a list of 205."

McCarthy's rhetoric was baseless and paranoid, and it struck fear into dissidents and patriots alike. Suddenly, everything was fair game—the ethics that govern political discourse, the presumption of innocence, the Bill of Rights.

The Hollywood Ten learned that lesson when the Supreme Court upheld two of their convictions that spring, and denied a request to rehear the others. The Ten had no more legal options, so they prepared to surrender themselves to the authorities and made a short film to raise awareness about their case. It was a low-budget affair. The ten men headed for prison pose with their families during the opening scenes while a voiceover provides the highlights of their careers. When the next shot comes into focus, they're seated together behind a long table, smoking anxiously, looking weary and defeated.

We refused to testify before the House Un-American Activities Committee to protect your rights as well as ours, they say. The country's future will only be secure if people like us, and like you, resist. "We are aware of a developing nightmare of fear in our land, in which increasing numbers of citizens are being forced to swear, 'I am not this.' 'I am not that.' 'I don't belong to anything.' 'I don't believe in anything.' 'I don't criticize anything.'" The pressure to conform will become general now, they prophesied, and the result will be devastating. "Thought control entering the university campuses . . . labor leaders being framed . . . lawyers sent to prison for defending their clients."

Their predictions sounded dystopian and fantastic when they were delivered, but they soon began coming true. Two months later, an anti-

Communist group called Counterattack published the names of more than one hundred public figures who were, they claimed, allied with the Communist Party. They included no evidence to support their accusations, but by then none was needed.

The vehicle for their denunciations was a pamphlet called *Red Channels* that sold for a dollar a copy. Its cover was dominated by the image of a microphone resting comfortably in the palm of a bright red hand, and the introductory text inside had an apocalyptic flair. The "Red Fascists and their sympathizers" have infiltrated our media, it said, and we have to fight back. "The hour is not too late for those in the patriotic and intelligent majority to immediately undertake a suitable counter-attack. No time is to be lost," it warned. The names of the accused appeared next—page after page of them, organized alphabetically for easy reference.

The Hollywood studios had been maintaining an informal "blacklist" for at least three years, but *Red Channels* expanded it dramatically. It also lowered the evidentiary bar for making accusations, and as a result, dozens more names were added over the course of the next few years.

Nelson wasn't named publicly, but friends and associates from every phase of his career were. Richard Wright had been added to the list a year earlier, along with a poet named Edwin Rolfe, whom Nelson had known since his days as a proletarian writer. The writers Millen Brand and Ted Ward—more friends from the thirties—were listed in *Red Channels*, and so was John Garfield, the star who was supposed to play Frankie Machine on the big screen. And before the end of the year, every other person involved with the film adaptation of *Arm* made the blacklist alongside Garfield—Paul Trivers, the screenwriter; Bob Roberts, the producer; and George Willner, the agent who represented Nelson in Hollywood.

Nelson could have avoided the controversy surrounding his friends and tried to safeguard his career, but instead he made common cause with them. He created a support committee for the Hollywood Ten, and sponsored a fundraiser to help pay for their legal appeal. He appeared on stage with Jack Conroy and a blacklisted actress named Gale Sondergaard at the event, and managed to bring in about five hundred dollars.* Then he signed his name to an open letter condemning censorship, and helped pay for it to be published in the *New York Times*. "American artists are being judged, convicted and fired solely on the charges of professional informers," the letter warned. "American writers have been forced to choose jail rather than betrayal of their beliefs."

Nelson took those actions as a matter of principle, but he had no illusions about their effectiveness. He met with some lawyers to discuss the Hollywood Ten case after the fundraiser, and then relayed the lawyer's opinion to Edwin Rolfe. "It looks like a year in the pokey apiece, from out this way, hope I'm wrong," he wrote. He didn't think there was a chance of defeating McCarthy or the forces aligned with him, but he hoped it would be possible to outlast them. "How long does this sort of thing go on?" he asked Rolfe sarcastically.

B eauvoir was afraid to leave Paris when it was time for her to visit Nelson that year. The Korean People's Army crossed the 38th parallel and entered South Korea two days after she received her travel visa, starting a war. American armed forces entered the conflict almost immediately, and it seemed as though World War III was about to begin. She thought the Soviet Army was likely to invade France while she was in America and bar her from returning, but Sartre convinced her to go. The Russians don't have enough atomic bombs to start another war, he said, and the Americans don't have enough soldiers. They won't fight each other for a few more years. "Go."

So Beauvoir did, but not without trepidation. "I hope the war will

---

* That would be about five thousand dollars today.

stay local in Korea, I hope my plane will not crash, I hope your heart is nearly as stupid and faithful as mine," she wrote to Nelson. "I hope I'll find my way to your arms again." Then she boarded her plane and, after a short stop in New York City, arrived in Chicago.

The trip wasn't worth the anxiety that preceded it. Nelson and Beauvoir had been drifting apart since their trip to Latin America, and when they met in Chicago, Nelson greeted her with the news that he was no longer in love with her. "But," he said, "we'll have a nice summer together all the same."

It didn't begin that way. Nelson brought Beauvoir to the racetrack that day, and spent the afternoon talking to friends and ignoring her. She drank heavily to kill time, and wondered why she was in America. That question became even more pressing when they returned to Chicago. She felt trapped inside Nelson's apartment, so she went out alone, but the world outside his walls was even less hospitable. Every time someone recognized her accent, they became antagonistic. "Why are you all Communists in France?" a hairdresser demanded. Nothing like that had ever happened to her in America before.

Nelson and Beauvoir began to enjoy each other after they left the city, though. Before she left Paris, he had told her that he was going to rent a cottage for them to spend the summer in, but, flush with cash, he spent seventy-five hundred dollars to buy one in Gary, Indiana, instead.

It was a two-bedroom house at 6228 Forrest Avenue* in the Miller Beach neighborhood, but it felt like an outpost at the edge of civilization. It was the last structure on a road that dead-ended at a park, and it had been built on a long, thin plot of land that was surrounded by tall bushes. There was a yard in front, and a lawn and a bit of wooded land out back that sloped toward a lagoon. Gray squirrels ran along the ground. Birds perched in the trees, and muskrats lived in burrows along the edge of the water.

Nelson and Beauvoir moved into separate bedrooms when they

* The name of this street has since been changed to Forest Avenue.

arrived—a nice metaphor for the distance that had grown between them, but a misleading one. Their relationship had transitioned into something less than the grand romance they once believed it was destined to become, but there was still more than friendship between them.

They spent their mornings working in their separate rooms, or reading. Sometimes, Beauvoir sprayed herself with insect repellent, lay on the lawn, and read Carl Sandburg's *Lincoln* or Fitzgerald's *The Crack-Up* while mosquitoes buzzed around her. They pushed a white rowboat into the lagoon behind the house around noon each day, crossed the water, climbed the sand dunes on the other side, and then descended toward Lake Michigan. The sand burned their feet, and they cooled them by walking into the lake until their heads rested just above the waterline. Neither of them could swim well, so they rooted themselves in place at the far edge of caution and allowed the waves rolling past them to rock their bodies gently. They walked back toward shore when they caught a chill, and lay down and baked in the sun.

They returned to the house for dinner, but sometimes they went back to the beach after dark, walked along the shore, and talked "idly," Beauvoir wrote later, "about the beginning of the world or about its end." Stars lit their path, as did the moon, and fire. The largest steel mill in the country loomed on the horizon, two miles west, and flames leapt from its smokestacks while they pondered the apocalypse.

But tension was present even in the summer's most carefree moments. The radio was reporting that the war was bound to spread, and Nelson was on guard against intimacy with Beauvoir. He retreated behind a facade of indifference whenever he felt them getting too comfortable, and once he went into Chicago alone and didn't return for days.

Beauvoir was no more considerate. She asked Nelson if a friend of hers could visit them, and he agreed without knowing what he was agreeing to. The woman Beauvoir invited was an old lover, and they embraced and began kissing when she arrived. The woman expected to sleep with Beauvoir in the cabin, but Nelson couldn't tolerate that idea, so he rented a room for her in a house about a block away.

The last month of Beauvoir's visit was stilted and disappointing. She went to Chicago with her friend, and when she returned to Gary, Nelson announced that he was thinking about remarrying Amanda. "So be it," Beauvoir thought. Then she walked to the edge of the lagoon, threw herself on the grass, and cried. They said little to each other for the remainder of Beauvoir's visit and never discussed their breakup, but the following year, each of them wrote to the other about how they felt at the end.

"Because I gave you so little, I found [sic] quite fair that you chose to evict me from your heart," Beauvoir wrote. "But thinking it is fair did not prevent it to be hard."

And Nelson replied by saying he still loved Beauvoir, but knew they could never be together again. "One can still have the same feelings for someone and still not allow them to rule and disturb one's life," he wrote. "To love a woman who does not belong to you, who puts other things and other people before you, without there ever being any question of your taking first place, is something that just isn't acceptable. I don't regret a single one of the moments we have had together. But now I want a different kind of life."

Nelson and Beauvoir returned to Chicago on the final day of her trip and visited the track again. Nelson wagered all the cash in his wallet, lost every cent, and had to borrow money from a friend to pay for a cab ride to the airport. Beauvoir would visit Chicago one final time the following year, but by then they were only friends.

Nelson spent the fall and the winter nesting in his new home in Gary. He installed an oversized mailbox at the end of the driveway and painted the word ALGREN on its side in block letters. He retrieved his typewriter, his books, his records, and a picture of Amanda from his apartment in

Chicago, and he paid friends from the city to paint his house, patch the roof, and work in the yard. Then he got a squat cat that waddled instead of walking, and named it Bubu de Montparnasse in honor of the pimp in a French novel.*

Then Nelson opened his doors. Age had imbued him with the desire to act like a patriarch, but he had no wife and no children, so he lured friends to his little estate with the promise of hospitality. He kept beer on hand, and food. Marijuana grew wild in a field near his house, and he harvested it regularly, sat on his porch sorting seeds and stems into a colander, and then threw the smokable bits in a bowl he kept on his coffee table.

Lovers arrived first. Amanda visited the month after Beauvoir left, and spent three weeks living the domestic life she had been dreaming of since she met Nelson fifteen years earlier. They talked about decorating the cabin together, and then they attended a party thrown by old friends from their Rat Alley days. Music played and people drank, but Nelson just sat and watched Amanda. She was smoking Dunhills, which she held with a thin cigarette holder, and laughing in all the right places. She had been a coy and mysterious character when they met, but ten years in California had transformed her, and Nelson was struck by how confident she had become. He was "wide-eyed," someone said. A few days later, he raised the possibility of remarrying.

Amanda returned to California without either of them committing, and then Paula Bays replaced her. Nelson and Bays had been seeing each other regularly since her marriage started to fray, and their bond was growing stronger. She was still using morphine and working as a prostitute, but she had made several serious attempts to stop using and

---

* The novel in question was written by Charles-Louis Philippe, and its protagonists were a pimp and a prostitute. Nelson thought the female character's name was Bubu de Montparnasse, but he was wrong. He later learned that he had given his female cat a pimp's name, but he saw the humor in that and decided not to change it.

he believed she wanted to go straight. They kept late hours when they were together, and sometimes they stayed up through the night, sipping whiskey and trading stories in low, sleepy voices.

Friends visited too. Jack Conroy rode the train south when he needed a break from family life. Art Shay drove down when he and Nelson had business. Neal and Christine Rowland, who had been living in Gary since the end of the war, dropped by regularly. Dave Peltz, an old friend from the Writers' Project, moved into a house down the road with his family, and started visiting Nelson every Sunday so they could watch boxing on TV. Carl Sandburg stopped by when he was in town, and a progressive Chicago lawyer named Len Despres spent weekends there with his wife, Marian, when he could.

Then word of Nelson's hospitality spread more widely, and misfits and dissidents began dropping by in search of shelter and support. Bud Fallon, who had been in Florida for the past year or so, moved north when he heard Nelson had bought a house, and he lived there until he found a job. He had mellowed some, and eventually a racetrack hired him as a mutuel clerk. Jesse Blue, the toughest character among the old Fallonites, also came to stay with Nelson, but he was just as wild as ever. He had recently married a much younger woman to "save" her from her abusive father, and he had been taking advantage of her himself ever since. Everyone called the woman Shotsy, and she worked as a prostitute three weeks out of every month so that Blue didn't have to get a job.

James Blake, a writer Nelson met the year before, also stayed at the Forrest Avenue house several times. He was a Scottish man who moved to Chicago as a child. He attended Northwestern University for a while, but left before graduation so he could play piano professionally. He spent a few years accompanying the spoken-word artist Lord Buckley, and the jazz musicians Stuff Smith and Anita O'Day, but then his career took a dark turn. Benzedrine and marijuana began to play an outsized role in his life, and his job prospects dimmed. He pounded out-of-tune pianos in saloons and strip clubs for a while, and then he graduated to burglary, breaking and entering, robbery— and prison.

Blake was thirty, but seemed much older. He was missing some teeth, and his face was bloated and mottled, so he looked like a jack- o'-lantern when he smiled. He spoke a pidgin that combined slang from Chicago slums and Southern chain gangs, but there was a gifted and intelligent man beneath that ragged facade. He played piano well when he wasn't high, and he was a talented writer. He was perennially struggling with a novel, and sometimes dabbled in short fiction, but his natural medium was the epistle. He corresponded widely when- ever he was incarcerated, and the letters he produced were beautiful, confessional, funny, and salacious.

I just left prison, he wrote to Nelson, and when I walked away, "I did not, for a fact, know whether I had been cast out of Heaven or Hell . . . but when I crossed the bridge over the river and the road took a sharp turn, I was in the world I had not been able to see from behind the fences. I took a deep breath and said to myself, ready or not motherfuckers, here I come, and felt exhilaration on top of the apprehension."

I had a black lover in prison once, he wrote. "Our arrangement was an eminently workable one. We were aware that the powerful attrac- tion we felt was because we were bizarre to one another, and we were also aware that hate was just as much present as love in our relation- ship. That was a really swinging affair, no nonsense at all. Not a hell of a lot of conversation, but then there wasn't much time for it either."

Nelson felt protective of Blake, and looked after him despite the odds. He allowed Blake to live with him at least twice, and sent him money, clothes, books, a typewriter, and a radio during his various incarcerations. Once, he even mailed Blake an envelope filled with cash so that he could pay off a guard and escape from a Florida chain gang. But most importantly, he championed Blake's work. He had Blake's let- ters published in *Les Temps modernes*, connected him with an agent and a publisher, and helped him revise a collection of correspondence that Doubleday eventually published as *The Joint* in 1971.*

The fall of 1950 rolled into the winter, and Nelson nestled behind the thick walls of his cabin while the lagoon behind his house froze and snow covered his lawn in a blanket of sacral white. Then winter melted into spring, and he began to wonder what had happened to all the work he'd lined up after he returned from California.

Most of it had disappeared. The film adaptation of *The Man with the Golden Arm* was dead. Bob Roberts had fled the country after being blacklisted, and no one expected him to return. John Garfield was hiding out in New York and unable to work. The House Un-American Activities Committee was investigating him, and he died of a heart attack before they finished. He was only thirty-nine years old.

The photo book Nelson and Art Shay collaborated on had also fallen through. They applied for a Guggenheim grant to fund the project, but their application was denied. Shay submitted some of the photos they collected to *Life* magazine and thought they were going to be published, but they were pulled at the last minute, and afterward Doubleday shelved the book.†

---

* Blake's career was perennially derailed by his incarcerations, but he broke into the publishing world in the 1970s when the *Paris Review* published some of his letters and a piece of his fiction. *The Joint* was released the same year, and was praised effusively. Blake was poised to become a star, but then he developed cancer and died before he completed a second book.

† This book's fate has always been hazy. Nelson and Ken McCormick discussed it regularly in their letters, but then they stopped, and there is no mention in the surviving letters of why the book was shelved. The failure of the *Life* article seems like a likely cause, but even that's shaky. Art Shay always claimed that *Life* unexpectedly sent him out to obtain a photo release from a woman who appeared in one of his pictures, and that he expected the story to run after he got it. "I got the release, but meanwhile *Life* used its essay space that week for a story on a Mexican prison with marriage privileges," he told me. His account has been printed as fact repeatedly, but it's at least

The *Holiday* essay was the only new project Nelson had left, so he invested all of his time and energy in it. He had been commissioned to write a history of Chicago, but the parameters of the assignment were loose, so he used the space he had been promised to advance some of the ideas he had been developing since he returned from the war.

The account of Chicago's history that Nelson wrote that year begins when the Pottawattamie tribe controlled the area. "To the east were the moving waters as far as eye could follow. To the west a sea of grass as far as wind might reach," he wrote. The area was peaceful, by Nelson's account, until Europeans arrived, constructed a fort, and began laying down roads. The white men encircled themselves with walls, and drank, and raged, while the Pottawattomies mourned beside the river. "And heard, in the uproar in the hotel, the first sounds of a city that was to live by night after the wilderness had passed. A city that was to roll boulevards down out of pig-wallows and roll its dark river uphill."

The essay toggles fluidly between perspectives, time periods, and styles from that point forward, and presents the city's history in a series of anecdotes. One man listed his vocation as "generous sport" in the first city directory, Nelson reports. An alderman named Hinky Dink Kenna, one of Chicago's most famous, traded meals for votes without shame. A robber named Dwight L. Moody used to prowl the streets wearing a black clerical collar, and before he robbed anyone, he always asked, "Are you a Christian?" Jane Addams and the do-gooders who follow her lead "go doggedly forward" year after year, Nelson says, but the game is rigged against them and always will be.

Chicago is all of these people, Nelson says. It was founded by men who "slept till noon and scolded the Indians for being lazy," and it has been populated by grifters, thieves, and reformers who never had a chance ever since. It's a hustler's city and always will be, never mind

---

partly false. *Life* ran no such story. It did run an article called "Mexican Prisons Allow Conjugal Visits in Jail," but it was published on October 27, 1941—about eight years before Nelson and Shay met.

the fact that our leaders have begun wearing "the colorless gray of self-made executive types playing the percentages from the inside."

The essay reads like an indictment, but then the narrative shifts and Nelson begins to argue that the conflict between the grand ambitions of Chicago's residents and their sinful natures is the thing that defines the city. The frisson created when those impulses clash, he says, is the thing that drives the city—its imperfections are its greatest virtue, not a flaw.

You can spend your entire life in a single neighborhood here and still be forgotten the week after you leave, he writes. "Yet once you've come to be part of this particular patch, you'll never love another. Like loving a woman with a broken nose, you may find lovelier lovelies. But never a lovely so real."*

The tension in the essay feels resolved, but then Nelson brings the timeline to the present day and advances his argument further. Some of the finest poets, singers, sculptors, and painters the country ever produced came from Chicago, he wrote, but that won't be the case for much longer because everything that made this city great is being denied. Our history is being whitewashed, and everyone is under pressure to conform.

"[W]e stand on the rim of a cultural Sahara," he wrote.

"You can live in a natural home," he warned, "with pictures on the walls, or you can live in a fort; but it's a lead-pipe cinch you can't live in both. You can't make an arsenal of a nation and yet expect its great cities to produce artists. It's in the nature of the overbraided brass to

---

* The title of the book you're holding comes from this passage. I chose it because the sentiment it expresses—that our imperfections are often the wellspring of our virtues—is beautiful, and it nicely describes the tension between Algren's flaws and his immense talent. The use of the term *lovely* gave me pause, however. Referring to a woman as "a lovely" was tame misogyny by 1951 standards, but today it would be considered offensive. I decided to entitle this book *Never a Lovely So Real* despite that concern for two reasons: firstly, and most personally, because I was introduced to Algren's work when my mother quoted this line to me; and secondly, because it seemed there was some justice involved in using the line to describe its creator, and referring to Algren as "a lovely."

build walls about the minds of men—as it is in the nature of the arts to tear those dark walls down. Today, under the name of 'security,' the dark shades are being drawn."

Nelson's editors at *Holiday* were not expecting the story he submitted. They pushed him to insert himself into the text to soften its tone, and write a disclaimer they could print ahead of the main essay. He added a section of memoir to make his account more personal, as they requested, and agreed to write a short preamble—but he never backed away from the political portions of the text.

So the editors at *Holiday* did so for him.

Nelson submitted his manuscript ahead of deadline and it was accepted for publication, but the magazine's staff altered it before laying it out for print. They cut the text by half, and removed all of the political content without consulting Nelson. He was furious when he received a copy of the magazine, and accused his editor of "seriously handicapped" judgment. He attributed the conflict to a lack of professionalism at the time, but later he would see *Holiday*'s censorship in a more malicious light.

Ken McCormick, luckily, was bolder than *Holiday*'s editors. He read the complete essay in manuscript form, and decided to publish it in its entirety. Doubleday released the essay as a slim hardcover called *Chicago: City on the Make* in October 1951, but very few people noticed.* The first print run was only five thousand copies, and virtually nothing was spent promoting it. Nelson was only invited to two signings, and reviews were sparse and—for the first time in his career—starkly divided.

The *Saturday Review* claimed, "It is necessary to go back to the 'Chicago Poems' of Carl Sandburg . . . to find a book about the city

---

*   Though he referred to it as an article or an essay while he was composing it, Nelson later described *Chicago: City on the Make* as a prose poem, and that is generally what it is underststood to be.

comparable to Algren's." The literary editor of the *Chicago Daily News* was quoted saying it was a "work of genius and absolutely the greatest piece of writing contemporary Chicago has produced," but his paper ran a savage critique that called for "Ra(n)t Control" and said Nelson's "poetic license" should be revoked. *The Nation* said the prose was "kaleidoscopic and somewhat adolescent," and the *New Republic* called it "an embarrassment."

The book survived its reception, though, and like *The Neon Wilderness*, its renown grew over time. A second edition was released in 1961, and then others in '68, '83, and 2001, and somewhere along the line, it entered the Midwestern canon as the Third Coast's answer to E. B. White's *Here Is New York*. People buy copies when they move to Chicago now, so that they can quote its most famous lines while drinking in dimly lit bars. Local reporters flip through its pages when they need to add color to their stories, and portions of the text appear online regularly.

Chicago is "an October sort of city even in spring," they read. You'll know the city "by nights when the yellow salamanders of the El bend all the one way and the cold rain runs with the red-lit rain. By the way the city's million wires are burdened only by the lightest snow; and the old year yet lighter upon them. When chairs are stacked and glasses are turned and arc-lamps are all dimmed." In Chicago, "our villains have hearts of gold and all our heroes are slightly tainted."

City on the Make was a bold declaration when it was written. I intend to challenge authority with my writing, Nelson was saying—expose hypocrisy, and "tear" down the "dark walls" that are being constructed around "the minds of men." But it's remembered now for its metaphors, poetic phrasing, and descriptions of Chicago. It has survived the cultural moment that it was written to challenge and outlasted the people it attacks, and it has managed, over the course of several decades, to permanently alter the way people think about, and write about, its subject. No one could ever ask more from a piece of literature.

Nonconformity

(January 1952–October 2, 1953)

Paula Bays couldn't tolerate her circumstances any longer. She was living in an SRO hotel with her husband, John, and supporting them both by turning tricks. Morphine still dictated the rhythm of her days, and because her habit made her a less-than-responsible parent, her daughter, Constance, was living with relatives in Ohio. She had been married for eleven years and miserable for just as long, but starting over still seemed possible because she wasn't even thirty yet—so she ran.

Bays went to Nelson's house in Gary near the end of March, and he welcomed her and said she could live with him for as long as she needed. It was a cold, bleak spring, and so they kept the house's thick walls between themselves and the world, and for the next several weeks, they rarely left home. When Paula's absence became pronounced, John Bays spread word that he intended to kill Nelson, but he never did try.

Nelson and Bays had never spent much time alone, and they were surprised to discover they had a natural, unforced comity. When they were hungry, they ate, and when they were tired, they slept. They had sex when they felt the urge, and never argued. They could talk for hours, or sip whiskey silently while gazing through the living-room windows and playing records—jazz, or maybe Bessie Smith, one of Nelson's favorites, singing, *Gimme a reefer and a gang o' gin / Slay me, 'cause I'm in my sin.* Other times, Bays pulled a book off a shelf, sat on the couch, and read while Nelson worked. Occasionally, they smoked the marijuana Nelson harvested from the field near his house and giggled like children.

They were falling in love, but passion wasn't the thing Bays needed most. She was looking for stability—a straight marriage, a legitimate job, custody of her daughter—and knew Nelson couldn't provide it.

Nelson said he wanted a quiet life and a family, but his actions betrayed him. *City on the Make* had been relegated to discount tables, where it was selling for nineteen cents a copy, but he showed little interest in bringing in money. He was spending his time writing an essay about the Red Scare that he wasn't being paid to compose, and taking ever-greater political risks. He had recently joined an antiwar group in Gary, endorsed a gay public defender named Pearl Hart who was campaigning to become a Chicago alderman, and taken on a leadership role in the campaign to free Julius and Ethel Rosenberg, a married couple who had been convicted of conspiracy to commit espionage for the Soviet Union and sentenced to death. Most people considered them traitors, but Nelson believed they were scapegoats.

"I would like to state that this whole business is straight out of Cotton Mather," he told a crowd gathered to raise funds for the Rosenbergs' legal appeal."* It's "as though, as a nation, our conscience is so troubled that we hope to gain peace of mind by offering the blood of the innocent. It is nothing less than medieval."

Those weren't the actions of a man ready to settle into domestic life, so Bays decided to leave. She and Nelson had a mutual friend named Caesar Tabet, and she thought he would be in a better position to help her. He was wealthy, stable, respected—an insurance executive and small-time landlord, but also an orphan who grew up in poverty and regularly extended himself for people in need.

---

* Cotton Mather was a Puritan minister and a prominent supporter of the Salem witch trials.

Bays returned to Chicago to see Tabet, but her husband, John, got
to her first. He punched her in the face when he found her, and black-
ened her eye. Then he pounded her body until her ribs fractured, and
forced her into a taxi. When it stopped, he threw open the door and
shoved her with enough force to send her sprawling on the sidewalk.

Bays escaped, went to a hospital, and then called Nelson and Tabet.
They both came to her aid, but only Tabet was in a position to do
much. He offered to pay for Bays to enter a recovery program in Kentucky, and Nelson encouraged her to accept. "You hang on to me,"
he said, "you're hanging on to a straw. You hang on to Caesar, you're
hanging on to a rock." It was the right thing to do, but later he would
wonder how his life would have been different if he had clung to Bays
more tightly in that moment.

Bays took Nelson's advice. She entered treatment for the third time
that spring, or maybe it was the fourth, and when she returned to Chicago, Tabet found her a job and an apartment. She regained custody
of her daughter about a year later, and never used morphine again.

Nelson stopped seeing the other women he had been dating after Bays
left, and spent weeks alone in his little house at the edge of the woods.
The war in Korea was on his mind, as were Senator Joseph McCarthy,
the House Un-American Activities Committee, the FBI, and his old
friends—the many who held fast to their ideals and lost their careers
and freedom as a result, and the few, like Budenz and Rushmore, who
betrayed them for lucre.

It was a paranoid time, and dangerous. Most Americans believed
the Communist Party was controlling their media and trying to subvert the government. The Cook County state's attorney was blaming
the flood of morphine washing over Chicago on a Communist plot to
"destroy" American youth. Republicans were accusing Democrats
of treason, and federal agencies were testing the limits of the powers

granted to them by the Internal Security Act.* The State Department was denying passports to suspected Communists. The Subversive Activities Control Board was investigating left-wing organizations and individuals to determine whether they should be forced to register as Communist agents. And the Justice Department was compiling a list of people they intended to detain in the event of a national emergency to prevent them from engaging in "acts of espionage or of sabotage."

Caution was called for, but Nelson exhibited none. He appeared at the Hamilton Hotel in June to address a crowd gathered in support of the Rosenbergs, and spent his writing time polishing his Red Scare essay. He had been invited to speak during a writers' workshop at the University of Missouri, in Columbia, in the third week of June and intended to read it publicly for the first time there.

Nelson arrived at the workshop in time to meet with young writers and review manuscripts for a few days, and then, near the end of the conference, he stepped on stage carrying a stack of papers, turned to face his audience, and began to read.

"The struggle to write with profundity of emotion," he said, "and at the same time to live like a millionaire so exhausted Scott Fitzgerald that he was at last brought down to the point where he could no longer be both a good writer and a decent person. 'So I would cease to be a person,' he planned, 'kind, just or generous. I would be one with the beady-eyed men who say, 'Business is business,' or 'You should have thought of that before you got into this trouble,' or 'I'm sorry, but that just isn't my department.'"

The emotional requirements of his craft diminished Fitzgerald, Nelson said, so he hid from the world and decided that "the natural state of the sentient adult is one of qualified unhappiness.'"

* This act is often referred to as the McCarran Act or the McCarran Internal Security Act.

Mark Twain suffered a similar fate, Nelson said. He became a caricature of himself, and knew it. Once, late in his career, he turned to
a friend after delivering a lecture, and said, "I am demeaning myself. I
am becoming a buffoon. I cannot endure it any longer."

Authorship has always required sacrifice, Nelson said—that's
what Fitzgerald's life teaches us, and Twain's—but the cost of honest
expression has never been higher than it is today. "For the writer's
lot, like the policeman's," he said, "is not a happy one. A hardy life,
as the poet says, with a boot as quick as a fiver. But it isn't till now, in
the American Century, as we have so recklessly dubbed it, that tribal
pressures toward conformity have been brought to bear so ruthlessly
upon men and women seeking to work creatively."

The audience was half-receptive, Nelson said later. The year before,
he had given a speech warning against the tendency to deify law
enforcement agencies, and been booed off the stage. The students gathered to listen to him at Missouri were not as antagonistic, but they must
have become increasingly uneasy as his critique became more explicit.

Nelson spent fifteen minutes on stage, thirty—more—and his comments developed an elliptical, poetic quality. He sounded, for a while,
like a soloist who has lost himself in improvisation. He called American
prosperity a myth, and spoke about loyalty tests, Senator McCarthy,
the war economy, and the false promise of consumerism. If your life is
defined by "no passions and small cares," he said, it's not worth living.
"[A] whole houseful of gadgets do not of necessity add up to happiness."

But Nelson collected the strands of his argument near the end of
his time on stage, and bound them into a forceful plea for the establishment of a new trend in American literature. Opposition is a writer's proper role in society, he argued. It's the writer's job to defend
the weak and the maligned, no matter the cost. "We have too many
denouncers of the denounced," he said. We need to stand with the
accused—"guilty or not guilty, with the accused."

It is not "the writer's patriotic duty to subserve the private political
purpose of members of the U.S. Congress. . . . His loyalty is to his own

lights, and to his own lights alone. His only duty is to that woman, however red her legal guilt, who asked the judge in open court, 'Ain't nobody on my side?'"

The speech sounded like a call to arms as it neared its conclusion, but Nelson ended with a sober thought befitting 1952's ethos of noble defeat. Chekhov said it best, Nelson told the audience. He understood that writers owe their allegiance to the truth, and that truth serves no political faction. "'We paint life as it is,' he wrote, 'and beyond that, even if you lashed us with whips, we could not go. We have no politics, and we do not believe in revolution. We have no God and we do not believe in ghosts. And personally I have no fear of death or blindness.'"

Nelson was sitting on a lawn chair near the lagoon behind his house, wearing checked trousers, threadbare canvas shoes, and a gray sweatshirt, when Van Allen Bradley arrived in early September. Steel-framed glasses were perched on his nose and his hair, thinning slightly by then, was tousled.

Bradley was the literary editor of the *Chicago Daily News*, and he was visiting to collect material for a profile. He was a clean-cut man who wore conservative suits and wrote tomes about book collecting, but he had daring literary taste. He admired Nelson's work so much that he publicly contradicted his paper's assessment of *Chicago: City on the Make* by declaring it "a work of genius."

Nelson led Bradley inside the house and introduced him to Amanda, who was in Gary for a three-week visit. The kitchen table was set with plates of cold chicken, cheese, ham, and vegetables, and the three of them sat down and ate while Nelson and Amanda reminisced. Nelson talked about his time on the road during the Great Depression, and writing his first novel. Amanda told the story of their wedding, and teased Nelson for showing up at City Hall without a ring. Then Bradley got Nelson talking about *Never Come Morning*, the war, his rise to fame, and the little house he bought on the dunes with his "Hollywood money—that fine Hollywood gold."

It was a pleasant late-summer afternoon spent in good company, but Bradley must have picked up on how lonely Nelson was feeling that year, because the profile he wrote later was infused with melancholy. The man it describes is both a success who has reached the peak of his chosen field despite incredible odds, and a sad character. Algren is a man of "average height who looks more like a factory hand" than a successful author, Bradley wrote. He was "anything but impressive" when he shuffled toward me.

Nelson had delayed thinking about marriage and children for years so he could dedicate himself to his writing, and afterward he invested all his hopes for the future in Beauvoir. When he realized she would never leave Paris, he tried to find someone who could take her place, but failed, and now he was alone—a forty-three-year-old man living on a dead-end road with a thousand books and two rangy cats.

Amanda was the only woman left in Nelson's life, so he decided to ask her to marry him a second time. Love didn't factor in the decision much, and romance played no part in their courtship. They knew each other too well for that. They discussed marriage while Amanda was in Gary, and when she returned to California, Nelson sent her a sarcastic letter of proposal.

"When am *I* going to ask *you*?" he wrote. "Of all the silly nerve, with me waiting for *you* to ask *me*! Leap year, silly. *1952*. And I'm not getting any younger."

Amanda accepted, and they started to plan. Nelson suggested she begin shipping her books, and aim to arrive in Gary before Christmas. Amanda said she wanted to sell her car and fly east, and Nelson promised to buy her a new one when she arrived. They decided to marry at City Hall, again, and then honeymoon in Paris and spend six months traveling through Europe. Beauvoir, who was dating an actor named Claude Lanzmann at the time, said she was eager for them to visit.

Amanda packed and cleaned out her apartment, and Nelson applied for a new passport and placed a deposit on an outside cabin on SS *Liberté*. He had been joking about playing Russian roulette since Eisenhower was elected president, and he was eager to get overseas. "[I]t strikes me we're kind of smart to get out of the country," he told Amanda. "By the time we get back we'll at least be part of the way toward 1956."

The details of Amanda's move were settled a few weeks after she accepted Nelson's proposal, but by then, he had already realized that remarrying was a mistake. He kept thinking about Paula Bays, and how content and relaxed he had been when they were together earlier that year. He realized he was happier with Bays than with any other woman in his life, and that she was the woman he should be marrying, but he didn't dare propose. She would have said yes, and he couldn't tolerate the thought of disappointing Amanda. Their lives had been linked for seventeen years, and he still felt guilty for not providing her with the lifestyle she expected when they first married, so he went forward with the engagement.

Amanda flew into O'Hare Airport in December, carrying a few bags and a cat in a carrier. She expected to be married by spring, well acquainted with the best Parisian cafés by summer, and pregnant before she returned to America. She visited Kaiser Hospital before leaving California to ask about giving birth, and a doctor there told her she wasn't too old.

Nelson was waiting at the airport with Neal and Christine Rowland when Amanda's plane landed. They had given him a lift because he didn't drive, and after the four old friends exchanged greetings, they made their way to the Rowlands' car and loaded Amanda's bags and cat in the back.

Neal Rowland pulled into traffic and began driving south and east. Gary was only fifty miles away, but everyone was miserable long before they arrived. It was cold outside and the car had no heater, so soon everyone was shivering, and stiff from being crammed together.

"You wanna get a drink?" someone asked, to break the tension.

The question was posed to the group, but Nelson responded as if it had been directed at him. No, he snapped, I don't have any money.

Rowland pulled over anyway. Amanda handed Nelson some cash when the car stopped outside a liquor store, and he went inside and bought a bottle. He was surly when he returned; everyone could tell.

Rowland continued south, and tried to make conversation. "How long you staying, Amanda?" he asked. "Are you here for a vacation?"

Amanda was stunned by the question. She had presumed the Rowlands knew she was moving to Gary, and couldn't think of any reason why Nelson hadn't told them. It seemed like a dark omen, and she began to question the logic of walking away from her life in California.

The atmosphere in the car was tense for the remainder of the trip. Rowland entered Gary, and then turned onto Forrest Avenue and drove to the end of the block.

Amanda stepped out of the car when it lurched to a stop, and looked around. The ground had been covered with brightly colored leaves when she visited three months earlier, and birds had serenaded her from the branches of the trees in the backyard. The air blowing off the lake and over the dunes had still been warm when it reached the chairs on the side porch. But now the grass was dead, the birds had flown south, and the air was so cold it stung bare skin.

The Rowlands pulled away, and Nelson and Amanda went inside. Fortunately, the house felt as familiar to Amanda as the car ride had been foreboding. She noticed furniture she had selected when they moved to Rat Alley, a framed picture of herself, and the simple comforts she had associated with him over the course of their long romance: shelves overflowing with books, a typewriter, manuscripts stacked in irregular pillars, a record player, and piles of vinyl.

Amanda readjusted her expectations over the next several weeks and overcame her initial disappointment. She and Nelson relaxed into each other's company, and eventually found equilibrium. Their relationship wasn't what she had expected, but it provided what she needed. He bought her a new Chevrolet Deluxe as he had promised, she didn't have to work, and Nelson didn't object when she began sleeping in the second bedroom. She had always been happiest alone, and there was no reason for them to share a bed. They had sex once that winter, twice at the most.

In some ways, the arrangement was better than Amanda had expected. She and Nelson lived more like roommates than lovers, so they had no reason to argue or maintain pretenses. She had known him since she was a married man's shy mistress and he was a frail boy who lacked the nerve to speak at his own book release party. He was the only close friend she had ever had, and preserving that relationship seemed like reason enough to marry. She began to think about what life would be like when they got old, and decided it would be ideal because she was never bored when he was around.

The remainder of December passed languorously, and New Year came and went. Then suddenly, the pace of their lives quickened. They hurried to prepare for their wedding and their trip across the Atlantic, and then Nelson was sidelined by work.

The speech he delivered in Missouri the summer before had become a small sensation. He read it a second time at Indiana University in July, and afterward a literary magazine called *California Quarterly* printed it in full. Van Allen Bradley was impressed by it, and decided to print an excerpt in the *Chicago Daily News* under the title GREAT WRITING BOGGED DOWN IN FEAR, SAYS NOVELIST ALGREN. He expected a torrent of criticism in response, but none arrived, even though the article contained the line "Never has any people been so outwardly confident that God is on its side while being so inwardly terrified lest He be not." Instead, a reader ordered a hundred copies so he could send them out as Christmas greetings, *The Nation* reprinted the article, and progressive clergy members read it to their congregations.

Bradley wanted to release Nelson's speech as a short book with the help of a local publisher, and he wrote to Ken McCormick to ask for permission. McCormick declined. He decided Doubleday should publish the speech instead, and offered Nelson fifteen hundred dollars to revise it for release as a slim hardcover.

Nelson accepted the assignment in early January and began writing. He had to finish before SS *Liberté* sailed on March 24, so he worked frantically, separating the speech into chapters, focusing each section, eliminating some of the repetition in the original, and expanding the scope of his sources to draw from the ideas of people as varied as Judge Learned Hand, John Quincy Adams, F. Scott Fitzgerald, Leo Durocher, Georges Carpentier, and Herbert U. Nelson—the leader of a trade group that lobbied for the interests of the real estate industry.

Nelson made steady progress through January and February, but he was anxious while he worked. About a week after he began writing, the State Department notified him that his passport application had been delayed for further investigation. They provided no specific reason, so he assumed the worst. He continued writing at a pace that would allow him to complete the book before he was scheduled to sail for Paris, but he told his friends the government wasn't going to allow him to leave the country.

The passport division confirmed Nelson's fears when they sent a second letter in the first week of March. "I regret to inform you," it said, "that after careful consideration of your application for passport facilities the Department of State is obliged to disapprove your application tentatively on the ground that the granting of such a passport facilities is precluded under the provisions of Section 51.135 of Title 22 of the code of Federal Regulation."*

A funereal atmosphere descended on the house then, and Nelson's mood turned dark. It "ruined him," Amanda said later. He became paranoid and began to think of himself as a captive, sealed inside a trap whose exit was guarded by several sentries—the State Department, his

---

* That law prohibited "[p]ersons, regardless of the formal state of their affiliation with the Communist Party, who engage in activities which support the communist movement" from receiving passports.

writing, his relationship, his home. The ability to travel took on outsized importance in his mind, and he began to fantasize about walking away from everything and starting fresh.

Nelson and his friends made a grim sort of game out of trying to guess the justification for the passport denial. James Blake was convinced Nelson's work for the Rosenbergs was the cause—"I wish you would stay out of those loaded issues," he wrote. "It's the wrong battle at the wrong time. I love you for it, and for all that you are, but you must try for detachment." Kenneth Millar thought the portion of Nelson's speech that ran in *The Nation* was responsible, and Nelson feared that the evidence against him might go back two decades.

"[W]hatever I'm accused of I'm guilty," he told Millar. "So what's the use. You're damned if you do and you're damned if you don't. I could go there [DC] and perjure myself by saying I was secretly pro-Franco in the thirties and name names. Or I could go there and defy the powers that be. . . . Either way, I'm not going to see my friends in Paris soon again.

"Everybody in the world, it seems, is innocent of something."

Blake, Millar, and Nelson were each partly correct, but none of them suspected the most direct cause of Nelson's trouble was Louis Budenz—one of the men Nelson mocked in *The Man with the Golden Arm*. "BUDINTZ COAL," he wrote. "*One Price to All*." Apparently, Budenz didn't appreciate the slight.

An FBI agent visited Budenz on April 4, 1950—nineteen days after Nelson received the National Book Award—and asked him to elaborate on a comment he made earlier that year. Budenz had claimed to know the identities of four hundred "concealed Communists" operating within the United States, and the agent wanted to know who they were.

During the interview, Budenz said he couldn't remember making that statement, but claimed it was essentially accurate and offered the agent a few names. It wasn't the first time he had spoken to the FBI, but it was the first time he mentioned Nelson. "I knew Algren well in Chicago," he said. And it was "reported" to me that he was a "loyal member of the Communist Party."

The FBI already had a file on Nelson. They had opened an investigation into his political connections in 1940, but their interest was never acute. They tracked him when he was in the army, but lost his scent after the war. A confidential informant brought his advocacy for the Hollywood Ten to their attention years later, but after investigating that lead, the Chicago office closed his file.

The bureau's attitude changed once Budenz's claims circulated, though. When J. Edgar Hoover heard about them, he personally requested that Nelson be investigated. "You are instructed to reopen this case and bring the activities of the subject up to date," he ordered in January 1951.

Agents began circling Nelson. They collected his clippings to track the progress of his career and his political activity, and interviewed sources who knew him when he was working with the League of American Writers. Confidential informants in Chicago reported on what he was saying when he spoke in defense of the Rosenbergs, and informants in Gary kept an eye on his house. Gary's postmaster logged Nelson's mail at the FBI's request, and when he forwarded them a list of Nelson's correspondents, agents investigated every one of them.

When an agent had no other way of finding Nelson, they called Goldie. Once, believing that the agent she was speaking to was a friend of Nelson's, she bragged about her son's accomplishments at length. And on December 18, 1952, she picked up the phone and said, He'll be over for dinner at 6 p.m.

The intensity of the bureau's scrutiny increased when Nelson applied for a passport. Soon afterward, an agent named William J. Davis walked down Forrest Avenue and peered at Nelson's house, and a man who identified himself as "Agent Z" called the bureau while drunk and claimed Nelson was a Communist in the thirties. When he called a second time, agents arranged to meet him in Chicago, at the corner of State and Van Buren, and tried to wring more damaging information out of him. Then the city editor of the Gary *Post-Tribune* informed on Nelson, and so did the man living next door at 6216 Forrest Avenue. A neighbor across the street began providing regular updates on Nelson's whereabouts, and the bureau used the provisions of the Internal Security Act to add Nelson's name to the list of people eligible for "apprehension or detention" during national emergencies.

Then the second man Nelson insulted in *The Man with the Golden Arm* informed on him. Howard Rushmore was Senator Joseph McCarthy's research director when an FBI agent named Angelo Robbe sat down with him in the spring of 1953. They were supposed to be speaking about a different investigation, but Rushmore offered Nelson's name spontaneously. He claimed to have heard that Nelson had recently denied being a Communist, and said he could prove that was false. Then he showed Robbe a letter dated July 30, 1937. Nelson was the author, and the subject was the Moscow show trials. The content was relatively benign, but the third paragraph contained a damning sentence. It began "Politically, speaking as a party member . . ."*

That was all the justification the FBI needed to continue its surveillance and begin laying the groundwork for legal charges. They could go after Nelson for failing to register as a Communist agent if they chose, suggest his name to the House Un-American Activities Committee, or just wait for him to appeal his passport denial. If he denied being a

---

* The information provided here—and in every other instance where material contained in Nelson's FBI file is mentioned—is drawn from a version of that file requested through the Freedom of Information Act on September 23, 2013, and supplied by the National Archives two months later. Most of the information contained in it has never been made public. In the 1980s, a newspaper reporter named Jan Herman and Nelson's first biographer, Bettina Drew, each requested Nelson's FBI file and received approximately four hundred heavily redacted pages in response. Others have since requested Nelson's file and received approximately the same number of pages. The version I was provided with, however, is 886 pages long and very, very lightly redacted.

Communist under oath at any point, they could prosecute him for perjury or defrauding the government.

Amanda opened the door to her new Chevrolet Deluxe on March 16, 1953, slid behind the wheel, and turned over the engine. Nelson sat beside her. She peered over the car's steel dashboard and down the hood toward the bug-eye headlights, and then pulled out of the driveway, turned onto Forrest Avenue, turned left on Lake at the end of the block, and then merged onto the highway and headed north.

Amanda parked in the Loop, and then she and Nelson walked to Randolph Street and entered City Hall—an imposing granite building fronted, on that side, by a colonnade of nine Corinthian columns. They met Paula Bays and Caesar Tabet, and then the four of them entered the Marriage and Civil Union Court.

Nelson and Amanda waited for their turn before the judge with something less than giddy anticipation. The stress of Nelson's passport denial had driven them apart, and though they were still living under the same roof, they were barely speaking. He was marrying her because, many years ago, she had cared for him when no one else had—and, as she later admitted, she was marrying him because she was tired of living alone.

The judge called them, and they stepped forward. Bays and Tabet moved with them, and lingered nearby to serve as witnesses. The judge recited the vows, and paused.

"I do," Nelson said. "I do," Amanda said. Then they considered each other for a tense moment. Tradition demanded that Nelson kiss Amanda, but instead he turned his head and kissed Bays.

Amanda responded casually. "My turn this time," she said. Then she looked up and kissed Nelson. The taste of Bays's mouth was still on his lips.

Tabet took everyone to dinner after the ceremony, and they ate and drank. It should have been a joyful occasion, but it wasn't. Nelson made sure of that. He spent the meal staring at Bays with "wonder" in his eyes, and Amanda barely spoke. She wanted to leave when she finished eating, but he wanted to stay, so she drove home alone and went to sleep by herself in her single bed near the back of the house.

A few days later, Nelson wrote to Beauvoir and told her he had made a horrible mistake. He said he had fallen in love with someone after proposing to Amanda, and that he had not had the courage to admit his error and break off the engagement. He said the fault was all his, but he didn't know how to fix the situation. He wrote again the following month, and by then he had begun to see his personal misfortune as a reflection of the world's troubles. When the war in Korea ends, he told Beauvoir, I will slip into a deep depression. It will last for ten or twelve years, and when I come out of it, another war will begin.

Nelson dedicated himself to his essay that spring, shunning everything else. He worked by night and slept by day, and when Amanda woke each morning, she found his manuscript waiting for her—covered with corrections and deletions. She retyped portions of the text each day, and on the rare occasion she eliminated an adjective, or changed a comma to a semicolon to conform to the rules of grammar, he noticed and reversed the change the following evening. The book was that important to him.

Nelson had conceived of the essay after the Hollywood Ten convictions and thought of it as an act of protest, but as he revised, he inserted more personal and confessional elements—a declaration of his ideals, a perceptive critique of American culture, an implicit admission that writing left him feeling isolated and lonely, and the clearest explanation he would ever provide for dedicating his career to documenting the lives of people not normally considered worthy literary subjects.

The book begins with a satirical account of Nelson's negotiations with Bob Roberts in Hollywood. The scene is written as a comedy, but Nelson draws a lesson from it. My trouble, he says, is just a small example of the challenges every artist faces when they try to make a living in a society whose first concern is capital. Roberts had a genuine desire to "do a creative job of work," Nelson wrote, and it "pulled him hard. But the demands of the bank financing that impulse pulled him the other way, and harder."

The scene with Roberts is brief, and when it ends, the book's tone becomes more serious. Nelson describes the emotional toll of honest expression using the same examples he used in his speech the summer before, and warns that the "tribal pressure" to conform has been increasing.

However, he says, no matter how high the cost of resistance becomes, the cost of conforming will always be higher. The people demanding obedience have plans for the country that make no allowance for minority rights or democratic processes, and their logic is dangerous and seductive. Dozens of journalists have already accepted it, and they're busy now, "hawking the alarm on every newsstand that only by napalm and thunder-jet may the American way of life be saved. That no man may now call himself loyal who will not pledge allegiance to the commander of the closest American Legion Post and to that mob-mindedness for which he stands. That by placing economic boycotts on dissenters we thereby ensure the liberties of conformists."

Authors unwilling to challenge authority with their work are no less complicit, Nelson argues. Consider Frank Yerby, who said recently, "I try to give pleasure to the reading public. The novelist has no right to impose his views on race and religion and politics upon his reader."* Or take the example of James T. Farrell, a novelist who has documented the lives of poor people in a score of novels without ever identifying with them personally. Both men feel so comfortable in mainstream society, Nelson says, and approach their work so cautiously, that they will never create anything lasting.

---

* Nelson was especially offended by Yerby's obsequiousness because they had history. Yerby was then one of the best-selling writers in America—known for his romance novels—but he was a radical in his youth. Nelson and Jack Conroy published Yerby's first short story in the *New Anvil*.

Contrast them with Fitzgerald, Nelson says, whose "art tri-umphed" because he was willing to destroy himself in the process of creating it, or Dostoevsky, who drew vitality from "degradation," and you'll understand that authorship is an essentially antisocial endeavor. "If you belong to things as they are," Nelson wrote, "you won't hold up anybody in the alley no matter how hungry you may get. And you won't write anything that anyone will read a second time either."

Then Nelson places his body of work within the context of his ideas about writing and the period he was working in. We were promised prosperity and fulfillment after the war, he says, but we received "spiritual desolation" instead. Now we're a country of people who own nothing we want in our hearts, and possess only those things we've been taught to desire. We've drifted so far from shore, even our rebels have no idea where to direct their anger. They want "to be of real use to the world," but fear being used by it even more—so they drink their days away, or spend them shooting dope. They want to live, but don't know how. "That's the trap," Nelson says, that's the "American disease."

Near the end of the book, Nelson grows defensive. When he began writing, authors willing to write about the poor and the marginalized were celebrated. Their names were John Dos Passos, John Steinbeck, and James Agee—Richard Wright, and then Nelson Algren. But the American literary scene changed after the war, and criticism developed a more patrician character. The number of acceptable subjects had diminished since, the value placed on social context had declined, and artful, symbol-laden books seemed to receive consistently high praise, no matter their relevance.

Nelson's work had begun to seem anachronistic in that context—a throwback to a time before suburbs and gray flannel suits—and critics had begun sniping at him and referring to his characters as freaks.*

---

* Worse yet, some thought he was just a pulp writer. A million people owned a paperback version of *Never Come Morning* sporting cover art that featured three muscle-bound men and a woman clutching her blouse to keep it from falling open.

Nelson addresses those critics in the final section of his book, indirectly, by revisiting the ideas he introduced in its first section. Any author who wants to write honestly about America, he argues, must be willing to risk their career, shake off their sense of superiority, lose their neatly hewn ideas about literature and morality, and engage honestly with people living at the fringes of society.

The well-being of a country's least powerful people is the only true measure of its moral character, he argues. Even though America has grown wealthy, people still live in slums and sleep behind billboards. "It is there that the people of Dickens and Dostoevsky are still torn by the paradox of their own humanity; yet endure the ancestral problems of the heart in conflict with itself," Nelson says. "And it is there the young man or woman seeking to report the American century seriously must seek, if it is the truth he seeks."

Nelson completed his manuscript near the end of June and mailed it to Ken McCormick, and while he waited to receive Doubleday's verdict, he receded from the world. He felt emotionally exhausted as a result of his work, but also by the political climate and his personal life. Julius and Ethel Rosenberg had just been executed, and he had recently appealed his passport denial and been rejected a second time.

Nelson felt beset upon, and he responded by acting recklessly. Jesse Blue, his wife, Trixie, Bud Fallon, and James Blake all visited Nelson and Amanda that summer, and while they were there, Nelson woke late and wrote little. He joined whoever was living in the house at the time on the side porch in the afternoons to get high, and for weeks he did nothing but drink, smoke, and gamble.

Nelson had been careful with the money he made from writing *The Man with the Golden Arm*. He bought government bonds with some of it, and instructed Doubleday to release the remainder slowly so that he wouldn't feel pressure to produce a new novel too quickly. They had been sending him $250 a month for years, and he still had about three thousand dollars on account—then he didn't.* While Nelson was waiting to hear what Ken McCormick thought of his book, he requested a thousand dollars from Doubleday, and then he did it again, and again.

The longer Nelson waited for Doubleday to respond to his submission, the more careless he became. He gambled constantly, and he once brought a thousand dollars to a card game and left with nothing. Amanda was already awake by the time he returned home, and she knew something was wrong the moment he entered because he looked green and sickly.

"Guess what happened?" he asked. His voice was a mix of fear and mischief. I lost it all, he said.

Doubleday's response to Nelson's manuscript arrived in August in the form of a young editor named Timothy Seldes. He was a character out of the old school of American publishing—he dressed well, spoke the King's English, and had a nearly religious faith in literature.

Seldes's instructions were to shape Nelson's manuscript so that it would appeal to a broader audience, and he wielded a scalpel while pursuing that goal where others might have swung a hatchet. He moved into the house on Forrest Avenue, and he and Nelson spent long days together, tightening the text, sharpening the arguments, and polishing the prose.

They finished editing after a week, and decided to call the book *A Walk on the Wild Side.* Then, before Seldes boarded a plane to carry the manuscript back to New York, Nelson got him high. They were both feeling giddy and proud of their work, and after the drugs they consumed took their effect, they sat around for hours, trying to remember how to pronounce the word *quotidian.*

Q-tidian, they said. Qoootidian.

Quotttidian.

Otidian.

Quetidian.

---

* That is about twenty-seven thousand dollars in today's money.

Nelson had to endure more waiting after Seldes left, and doubt began plaguing him again. Some days, he felt sure his book would be released soon. On other occasions, he doubted it would ever see print. It was the most honest, revealing, and dangerous thing he had ever written, so sometimes he wasn't sure he even wanted it to be published.

Nelson had a friend named Maxwell Geismar who was a well-respected literary critic, and when his manuscript was nearly complete, he sent a copy to Geismar for feedback. "I am so depressed at the present political situation in this country," Geismar replied, "that I think the only reaction must be one of rage and violence: fireworks of revolt; and for that reason I got real pleasure that at least you had done this as it should be done; and this will be one of the first books they will burn: congratulations."

In the end, it wasn't necessary to burn the book. Doubleday finally responded to Nelson's submission in September and said they didn't intend to publish the book. They never explained why, except to say that Nelson's career would be damaged if the book was released.

Nelson was devastated. Doubleday's decision seemed like confirmation that dissent was no longer tolerated in America, and by the following month, he was convinced there was no reason to continue writing because the publishing industry would never support him again.*

An old friend named Millen Brand wrote Nelson an innocuous letter that month—just a hello, really—and Nelson responded with a diatribe. "I'll tell you what I think is this: that you can't be a good writer in the States any more," Nelson wrote. "Not you nor I nor anyone. Because to be a good one you have to have a country where you can be poor and still eat, and still make your living standards secondary to your writing. Thoreau himself couldn't do that in the States today, I don't believe."

---

* This book was never published in Nelson's lifetime, but excerpts appeared in *The Nation*, and Seven Stories Press released it as *Nonconformity: Writing on Writing* in 1996. It hasn't received much attention since, but it deserves to. The ideas it presents about the purpose of literature remain as relevant now as they were then. Nelson later recycled the title *A Walk on the Wild Side*, using it for his fourth novel.

"Riding Day-Coaches
to Nowhere"

(October 3, 1953–September 1955)

Nelson opened a copy of *Somebody in Boots* in late 1953 and flipped to
the third page, where the story begins. "Why Stub McKay turned
out such a devil he himself hardly knew; he himself did not understand
what had embittered him," he read—and then he pressed the tip of a
pen to the page and dragged it across the surface.

Doubleday was paying Nelson to trim the book for a paperback
edition, so his mandate was light revision, but he couldn't constrain
himself. The novel's prose embarrassed him, so he removed extrane-
ous adjectives, phrases, and then whole sentences. He filled the book's
margins with notes scribbled in red, blue, and brown ink, and then
he crossed out entire pages. He smoked Lucky Strike cigarettes while
he worked, and when he had a fresh idea, he ran a sheet of paper into
his typewriter, tapped out a paragraph or two, scissored out the lines
he composed, and pasted them into the book where he thought they
should appear.

Nelson worked that way for weeks before he finally admitted he
was writing a new novel, realized he should create a proper manuscript, and picked up a stray piece of paper. There was an advertisement for a record on the front—a company called Freedom Discs was
selling LPs containing the Senate testimony of a journalist named

William Mendel, who accused Joseph McCarthy of leading a "witch hunt" while he was under oath—but the back of the page was blank, so Nelson wound it around his typewriter's platen and began to write his seventh book.*

He typed "Angel's Trade" at the top of the page, hit return several times, and began describing a rundown restaurant in Texas. "[T]he last of the sun threw an unreal light on Puerta's decaying walls," he wrote, and then he resigned himself, reluctantly, to the fact that the book would take at least a year to write. He wouldn't have even started the project if he had had a choice.

Nelson had sold his first four books before writing them, but his luck had been failing him since. Doubleday never released the photo book he assembled with Art Shay. It bought *Chicago: City on the Make* after it was already complete, and declined to publish his book-length essay. He had begun writing a haunting, closely observed novel based loosely on Paula Bays's life the summer before, but when he asked Doubleday for an advance to complete it, they refused. Instead, they offered to pay him one hundred dollars a week for a revision of *Boots*—payments to stop after a year.†

Nelson accepted the contract because he had no other options, and he made it seem tolerable by telling himself it was a means to an end, but when he decided *Boots* needed a complete rewrite, he began to despair. He felt trapped, and for several months he couldn't decide whether to complete the book or walk away from his obligations.

---

*   This figure includes Nelson's book-length essay, even though it was not published in his lifetime.

†   Details are hazy here. Nelson says, in his correspondence, that Doubleday would only fund a new novel after he handed in a revision of *Somebody in Boots*, but he never made it clear whether he sent them a portion of his unfinished novel. It's possible they didn't want to see it. They had already paid him fifteen hundred to revise *Somebody in Boots* three years earlier—and received nothing for their money. Nelson never delivered because he thought the book was beyond saving. He forgot about the contract for years, but Ken McCormick didn't.

Sometimes, Nelson worked frantically, and productively, on the rewrite of *Boots* for days. The novel was challenging because it required him to write about the past—something he had never done—but he adapted. He added surreal elements to the novel, and gave it a darkly comic feel to leaven its often-brutal content. He turned the story into a parable about the futility of pursuing the American Dream, and he changed the style of his prose to give his sentences a meditative rhythm that made his narrative less reliant on the accretion of reported detail than his other books had been.

But there were other times when the project so disgusted Nelson that he flirted with the idea of running away from his life entirely. He asked Amanda for a divorce, and when she refused to grant him one, he started riding the train into Chicago and disappearing for days. Sometimes, he stayed in the basement of a mansion on Lake Shore Drive where he and a man named Jack Potter hosted a weekly poker game.* He often acted as the game's dealer, and found that he could earn as much in a night at the table as Doubleday was paying him for a week of writing. It was a case of life imitating art, and occasionally he considered abandoning his craft and becoming a professional card player.

On other days, Nelson sequestered himself in his room and fantasized. He told Beauvoir that he would leave for Paris with nothing but a typewriter if he could get a passport, and live like a pauper while he wrote something important. He nurtured that dream for months, tweaking it slightly each time his mind returned to it, so that sometimes he pictured himself living in a house on stilts in Port au Prince, Haiti, and on other occasions, he dreamed about the cobblestone streets in Marseille.

---

*   The mansion was owned by the heiress Ellen Borden Stevenson, the ex-wife of Adlai Stevenson—a former governor of Illinois, and the Democratic Party's nominee for president in 1952. She was also a patron of the arts who tried to turn her family mansion into an arts center and private club. *Poetry* magazine was operating out of the building at the same time Nelson and his friend Jack Potter were running their poker game. Later, Nelson and Borden Stevenson reportedly had an affair.

But eventually, Nelson made peace with his circumstances and decided to finish his novel so he would have the funds he needed to complete the book he wanted to write—the one about Paula Bays's life. It was the first time he had agreed to write something he didn't believe in, and he judged himself harshly for it.

Everyone in my generation has fallen short of their ideals, he told his friend Max Geismar in April, and I'm no better. "I think that the writers of the twenties were sounder of heart; they took scars but they stayed." The writers who got their start in the thirties are a different sort, though, Nelson said. They "came in on themselves: gave up, quit cold, snitched, reneged, begged off, sold out and copped out, denied all and ran." Jack Conroy, Millen Brand, Leonard Ehrlich, Richard Wright, and Meridel Le Sueur all wrote good books, Nelson said. "But when the thirties were done, they were done."

It was a harsh assessment, and it ignored how the Red Scare had side-lined his generation of writers, but there was truth in it. Conroy was editing an encyclopedia. Millen Brand was working in publishing. Ehrlich hadn't finished a book since *God's Angry Man* in 1932. Wright had just published an embarrassing potboiler because he was desperate for money, and Le Sueur was waiting tables and struggling to manage that much—the FBI was tracking her as well, and agents visited every diner that hired her, informed them she was a Communist, and got her fired.

Kenneth Fearing, Nelson continued, was "the truest poet, for my money, of the decade," but he began repeating himself. "Now he's hacking, Ben Appel is hacking. I'm hacking too. Nobody stayed."*

Nelson preferred to focus solely on his writing when he was working on a major project—digging in like a mole, he called it—but

---

* Benjamin Appel was a friend of Nelson's and the author of several early proletar-ian novels Nelson respected—*Brain Guy* and *The Power House* among them—but he had recently begun writing for pulp publishers.

that was no longer an option. Although he had asked Amanda for a divorce and offered her significant alimony, she was refusing to leave the house on Forrest Avenue. He resented her for that and found he couldn't work when she was around, so he found ways to put distance between them.

The beach was Nelson's first refuge. When the weather permitted, he gathered up his portable typewriter and his manuscript and carried them to the dunes. Then he found a quiet place to sit, and, with the sand beneath him and the white thrum of water lapping the lake's shore in the background, he worked until the light failed and he was forced to go home. But eventually, Nelson decided the dunes were too close to home, so he made plans to visit the American South—the setting of his novel.

Nelson packed a bag in July and boarded a Delta Air Lines flight bound for Brownsville, Texas. When the plane landed, he headed west and went looking for the Sinclair station he operated in the summer of 1932. His writing career began with the letters he wrote after fleeing the station, so the visit was both a means of collecting material for his novel and a pilgrimage back in time to a period of his life when writing was pure—but it was a failure on both accounts.

The station had been run down when Nelson and Luther Luther discovered it on their way to the border twenty years earlier, but it had disappeared entirely in the years since. The garage was gone, and the gas tanks were dry. The wild boars that scavenged under their floorboards had moved on or been killed, and there was no sign of the creek where he had collected drinking water. The land had been leveled and a field of cotton had been planted, and now there was nothing to see but neat lines of brittle plants hoisting their white blossoms toward the sky.

Nelson surveyed the area in dismay, and then returned to Brownsville, defeated and directionless. He sulked for a while, and then he caught a bus across the Mexican border and entered Matamoros.

The center of the city was full of tourists heading for the bull ring, oo Nelson avoided it and wandered until he found a marketplace. He bought a wood carving of Don Quixote, paid a barber three pesos to cut his hair, and entered a saloon called Jess's Place.

He ordered a beer without asking the price, and when a bottle appeared in front of him, he pulled a handful of change from his pocket and extended it toward the bartender.

The man plucked a half dollar from Nelson's palm and left him to his thoughts.

There's little chance they were pleasant. The First National Bank had just closed Nelson's account because it had been overdrawn too many times. Doubleday was about to send its last advance check, and Nelson was so desperate to get overseas that he was considering perjury. If he couldn't get a passport by any other means, he planned to sign a sworn statement asserting he had never been a Communist and pray that the State Department lacked the evidence to prove he was lying.

Nelson ordered a second beer when his bottle was empty, and extended his hand again. There was a half dollar in it, a quarter, and a nickel. This time, the bartender removed a quarter.

When Nelson's second bottle was empty, he ordered a third beer. This time the bartender removed the nickel.

Nelson was amused. "Is beer a half dollar or a quarter?" he asked.

"It is only a nickel, Senor," the bartender replied.

"Why did you take a half dollar and a quarter then instead?"

"Because it is all one," the bartender said, "a quarter or a half dollar, Senor. That is why I only took a nickel."

Nelson returned to Brownsville that night feeling homesick. He wanted to return to Gary, but couldn't tolerate the idea of living with Amanda, so he resolved to stay on the move until his book was complete. He knew being on the road so long would turn his life into a blur of buses, trains, and cheap hotels—months, as he later described them, of "riding day-coaches to nowhere"—but he didn't believe he had any choice.

Nelson began his journey the next day, and from the beginning, it seemed ill fated. He traveled to New Orleans first, got sick, and spent two days lying in bed with a fever and staring at a crack in the wall of his hotel room. Then he flew to Chicago, and moved in with Jack Conroy and his family for three weeks.* He returned to Gary then because he was running low on money, but nightmares plagued him while he was at home, so he left after a few days. He returned to New Orleans and spent the weekend with a writer named Tom Sancton, and then he moved on again—a bag, his manuscript, and his typewriter in tow.

Nelson's last stop of the year was East St. Louis. He reached the city just before Christmas, moved in with his friend Jesse Blue, and accompanied him to a bar for a holiday party. He spotted an empty seat near two acquaintances when he entered, and claimed it. He was at the end of a long, regrettable, and tiring year, so he began drinking—and didn't stop for hours. He and the men he was sitting with consumed three gallons of egg nog, and then poured a layer of Budweiser on top of it. They ate steak, ham, and eggs to keep their strength up, and then they began sloshing scotch over ice, and continued pouring until four in the morning.

Nelson had known Jesse Blue for almost fifteen years by then, but they had never been close. He had used Blue's life—and Bud Fallon's— to inform the characters in *Never Come Morning*, but he had always maintained a distance between himself, Blue, Fallon, and their old gang. He didn't drink the way they did, and while they embraced wild abandon, he found sanctuary in his work. He avoided them diligently after the war, but he felt drawn to Blue now that his life was collapsing. His days were defined by worry and regret, but Blue and his friends

---

* Nelson was planning to live with the Conroys through the fall, but tragedy ended his stay prematurely. Just after he moved in, Conroy's son Tom swallowed a handful of sleeping pills and died. The family decided to bury Tom in Moberly, Missouri, so Nelson had to move on.

seemed to have neither. They made no plans for the future and placed no faith in respectability or careerism, and that made them seem free, unencumbered, alive.

Nelson had to return to Gary after the party because he had nowhere else to go, and when he got there, he would have to finish writing a book he didn't want to write just to secure the privilege of writing one he did want to write—but if he returned to the bar the following week, he believed, he would find his companions where he had left them, feeling just as content.

"I can't tell you how right it it [sic] seems to me to live—even for an evening—among men and women off the legit," Nelson wrote to Max Geismar after the party. "What true, solid people pimps and whores can be—I'm serious. So much more natural, right and sound than business people. I sat the whole evening opposite five women, ranging in age from 25 to 38 and in income from a hundred a week to four and five hundred. Of two I know little—but of the other three I can honestly say they are happily married and that I don't know three business-man's wives who are. All three of these women have been with the same men for years—one for twenty-two. Between them and their husbands is honest to god love.

"And I'll tell you what else. Everyone of those women, and their men too, sat there for hours just having themselves one hell of a time. I mean they were enjoying their lives all the way."

The Super Chief, a luxury train, pulled into Union Station in Los Angeles on Wednesday, January 26, 1955, and when it stopped, Nelson stepped out of one of its red-trimmed cars. He was planning to slip away and find a taxi before anyone recognized him, but he failed.*

---

* Nelson gave an interview, usually cited as fact, in which he claimed a different timeline of events: "I came into town on a Sunday," he said, but contemporaneous correspondence shows he was off by a few days.

An employee of the Jaffe Agency spotted Nelson when he exited the train, and soon they were driving west together through the California afternoon, into the sunset. They parked at an Art Deco hotel called the Beverly Carlton a few minutes later, and Nelson checked into the room that had been reserved for him. Inside, he found a neatly made bed, cups bearing seals that promised they were germ-free, and windows that looked down on a pretzel-shaped pool and a fountain spraying pink water.

Nelson was in town for work, but even a few days earlier, he had had no idea that this would be the case. The week before, an agent from the Jaffe Agency had reached out to ask if Nelson would be interested in working on a screenplay for *The Man with the Golden Arm*. The query was a surprise. The last Nelson had heard, Bob Roberts owned the rights to make a film from the book, and there was no chance of it being produced in America because of the motion picture production code. But the Jaffe Agency said a director named Otto Preminger had purchased the film rights and was willing to pay Nelson a thousand dollars a week to work on the script.

Nelson's phone rang the morning after he checked into the Beverly Carlton, and someone on the other end of the line said, "Mr. Preminger is coming by in his car. Would you mind being outside so he doesn't have to get out of the car or park the car. Be on the curb."

Nelson didn't move. He waited in his room instead, and didn't leave until the concierge called to say someone was asking for him. Then he went downstairs to meet the man who wanted to put Frankie Machine in a movie.

Nelson and Preminger greeted each other in the lobby, and then got into a red Cadillac. Preminger was a veteran of more than twenty films and a powerful figure in the industry, but Nelson had never heard of him and his first impression was not good. He was wearing a bespoke suit, spoke with a thick eastern European accent that sounded affected, and he seemed imperious and condescending.

Preminger pulled into traffic, began driving toward Hollywood, and tried to make small talk. There was a newspaper on the seat next to him, and its headline said a wealthy stock manipulator and convicted draft dodger named Serge Rubenstein had been strangled. Preminger tossed the paper to Nelson. "Old friend," he said, indicating Rubenstein. "Terrible man." Then he mentioned *The Man with the Golden Arm*—the book, not the film he was planning to make. "How come you know such terrible people you write about?" he asked Nelson.

Few questions could have offended Nelson more. He had written his book out of compassion, and only after getting to know and care about the people his characters were patterned after. Their names were Bill Hackett, Paula Bays, and Richard Majewski, and each of them were less venal than Serge Rubenstein.

The red Cadillac stopped at the Columbia Pictures lot on Gower Street after about fifteen minutes, and by then Nelson had made two decisions. He distrusted Preminger, but he would try to work with him anyway because he needed the money and wanted to protect his book.

Preminger gave Nelson a tour of his offices when they arrived, and Nelson bristled as Preminger badgered his staff and issued orders. At one point, a man walked into a room smoking a pipe, and Preminger told him to extinguish it. The man obediently tapped the smoldering tobacco out on his coat, but Preminger sent him out of the room anyway. "Now you *and* pipe *oudt!*" he hollered.

Nelson returned to his hotel that evening intending to work on his film treatment, but before he made any headway, he began receiving unsettling information.

Someone from Preminger's office contacted Nelson to say that his salary had been reduced from $1,000 a week to $750. Then, in a separate call, they said it had been reduced further to $500, and told him to go back to Chicago if he didn't like it. Later, an agent from the Jaffe Agency asked Nelson if he was "politically clear" to work in Hollywood, and said Preminger had purchased the rights to *Golden Arm* from Bob Roberts a year earlier, but kept his acquisition a secret.

Then Nelson began collecting rumors. He heard that Roberts made money on the sale of the film rights, but didn't intend to pay Nelson the portion he was entitled to.* The transfer obviated the clause in the contract that guaranteed Nelson a percentage of the film's profits, and Preminger made his job offer under false pretenses. He was hoping to keep Nelson from filing a lawsuit challenging his ownership of the film rights by putting him on the payroll. More troubling still, Preminger was planning to have the film in theaters before the end of the year, no matter what. That was a serious problem because a director named Jack Kirkland had been developing a stage version of *Golden Arm* that was scheduled to open around the same time, and the film was likely to destroy the play's chances of earning money. If that happened, Nelson would be left in the cold. He was guaranteed almost half of the profit from the Kirkland production, but nothing from the movie.

Nelson was supposed to deliver a film treatment to Preminger a few days later, but he no longer wanted anything to do with the man, so he went for a walk instead of working. While he was out, he passed a movie theater playing B films, and noticed a poster out front featuring a woman wearing a leopard skin and a caption that read, WHITE GODDESS NOT GO THAT PART OF FOREST. He bought a ticket, went inside, watched the movie, and then returned to the Beverly Carlton and tapped out a twelve-page film treatment.

Preminger parked his red Cadillac outside the Beverly Carlton on Sunday, January 30, and began honking the horn. Nelson was in the middle of typing a letter to Jack Conroy when he realized he was being summoned, and chose to complete it before rising. The letter said Hollywood lures people in by promising them a ride on the Super Chief and thirty-five dollars "a day just to stand around looking willing."

"And while you're standing around they stand in line with their

---

*   The sale price of the rights was never firmly established, but Preminger once said he paid $100,000 for it. If that's accurate, Roberts made $85,000 on the sale—meaning he owed Nelson $42,500. Or, a little less than $400,000 in today's dollars.

big greased dicks—when you bend over for the pennies is when they get you."

Nelson grabbed the treatment, got in the Cadillac, and accepted a ride to Preminger's house in Malibu. When they arrived, Nelson handed over his work.

"So little pages," Preminger said. Then he began reading. He stopped when he reached the part of the script where Nelson had Frankie Machine say, "White Goddess not go that part of forest."

Preminger set the papers down and looked at Nelson. This is not a story I will pay for, he said. Then he called the Jaffe Agency, and said, "Mr. Algren and I have agreed that he doesn't care to do the sort of script I want."

Nelson moved into a dive on Hollywood Boulevard called the Hotel Vermillion the next day. His room had a view of a parking garage, and a red neon sign that burned through the night. It said:

G
O
O
D

B
O
O
Z
E

The Jaffe Agency assigned a young agent named Clancy Sigal to Nelson, and they spent February trying to dredge up work. They moved from studio to studio and packed their days with meetings, but their time together soon developed a cruel monotony. Everyone they spoke to swore they loved—just loved—Nelson's books. They respected him as an artist—they really did. But the only work they had available at the moment was beneath him—rewriting, fixing dialogue, gangster flicks, and cheap romances.

"Trouble is that, though I need the dough," Nelson wrote to Amanda, "I don't have the heart for their kind of assignments. In fact I don't know what I'm doing here at all. Never felt so lost and fish-out-of-waterish in my life. Would sure like to get out."

The Jaffe Agency informed Nelson that Preminger wanted to compensate him for his travel expenses, but Nelson was not inclined to accept. He was so wary of the man, by then, that he feared taking the money would put him in a precarious position if he decided to go to court to sue for control of his film rights, so he turned down Preminger's offer and memorialized their rift with a letter. I heard you were planning to reimburse me for my expenses, it said. "Though your thoughtfulness is appreciated, I must in turn advise you that this money was spent for no purpose to which you are member. Thank you all the same."

Nelson's trip to Hollywood was a waste of time and money, with one exception: a tender reunion with Bill Hackett. Nelson had heard that Hackett had become a sign painter, so after he stopped looking for work, he left his name, his number, and a message, at the office of the local painter's union.

Hackett called Nelson early in the morning about a week later, and they arranged to meet the same afternoon. When Hackett arrived at the Vermillion, he looked like a new man. He was wearing a sweater and a little white hat, and his skin looked healthy and his eyes were clear. He had been off heroin for years, and his wife, who had joined him in California, was clean as well.

Nelson stayed with the Hacketts that weekend in their new home in a subdivision called La Mirada. Their neighborhood was a maze of identical houses sitting on gently undulating land, but somehow they fit in. They had a lawn, a car, and a pair of TVs, and they were happy.

Hackett's "one big worry," Nelson told Amanda, "is that he is only working 7 hours a day."

The weekend Nelson spent with the Hacketts lifted his spirits, but his friends' contentment also put his own troubles in stark relief. He decided it was time to end his marriage—with or without Amanda's consent. "Coming back to Gary is just something I can't do," he wrote from California. He said he would get his own apartment in Chicago when he returned, file for divorce, get another poker game going, finish his novel, and then leave America. "I'll sign the 'I'm not-and-have-never-been' [a Communist] clause" on the passport application, he said, and get as far away as I can. "If I don't make France I'll make Havana and if I don't make Havana I'll make the slammer."

When Nelson returned to Chicago, he rented a single room in an apartment building not far from where he had lived while writing *Never Come Morning*, and then he settled down to finish writing his novel.

The book was almost complete by then, and bore only a faint resemblance to *Somebody in Boots*. Nelson's new protagonist was a boy named Dove Linkhorn, the last in a long line of Scottish Linkhorns who had been talked out of their ancestral lands by "unremembered" kings, came to America with nothing, and several generations later, had nothing still.

The Linkhorns were "fierce craving boys," Nelson wrote, and they knew only two things for certain. "Weaker men, full of worldly follies" always beat them, and no matter how low they fell in the world, their whiteness would ensure they always had people to look down on. "Slaveless yeomen," Nelson wrote, "—yet they had seen how the great land-owner, the moment he got a few black hands in, put up his feet on his fine white porch and let the world go hang. So the Linkhorns braced their own narrow backs against their own clapboard shacks, pulled up the jug and let it hang too."

Dove's father is a "pore lonesome wife-left-feller" named Fitz Linkhorn, and his brother is an unemployed drunk named Byron who put-ters around the family's shack performing "useless" tasks. The two of them fight endlessly, and Dove has no feeling for either.

Fitz is an old-school street preacher who mounts the steps of the local courthouse each night carrying a bottle of "Kill-Devil" and announces the approach of the end of days. "Un-*utter*-uble sorrows is in store for all," he proclaims. "Invasion by an army! A army of lepers! Two hundred million of flame-throwen cavalry! A river of blood and burnen flesh a hundred mile long!"

His audience is always the same. Farmers gone broke. Drifters. Drinkers. Men just cagey enough to know that egging the preacher on will earn them a swig of his liquor—and Byron, who taunts and mocks his father. "O God who scorns the shoeless—forget our daily bread but hasteth thy vengeance!" he cries into the night. "Hasteth!"

Dove is ignorant and adrift. He's sixteen but not in school, unemployed, illiterate, and on his own because neither his father nor his brother provide for him. He can be cagey, though, and eventually he finds work at a café and gas station on the edge of town that's run by a woman named Teresina Vidavarri. He starts off changing tires, sweeping the floors, and making coffee, but when he earns Vidavarri's trust, she takes him under her wing and begins teaching him how to read.

They grow close, and make love—something Vidavarri enjoys, but then regrets. She fires him afterward and refuses to see him again, and her rejection devastates Dove. He decides to run away, but before he goes, he stops by Vidavarri's café and rapes her. Then he boards a train on its way out of town—a motherless child, an illiterate boy from a town of only seven hundred souls, a guilty fool who hurt the only person who ever showed him kindness.

Nelson's five most recent books can be read as constituent pieces of a single literary project—each volume building on the one that preceded it. *Never Come Morning* asserts that no person can be defined solely by the economic and cultural constraints brought to bear on them. *The Neon Wilderness* is a chronicle of men and women struggling to orient themselves within a world that seems to grow colder and less forgiving by the day. *The Man with the Golden Arm* champions those same people, makes a bold claim for their humanity and individuality, and prophesies that every indignity they suffer will be visited upon the rest of society in due time. *Chicago: City on the Make* places the books preceding it in a historical and political context, and *Nonconformity* argues for their artistic relevance and articulates the ideas that guided their creation.

But the novel Nelson completed in the spring of 1955 is different. Its tone is bitter and cynical, and it's more concerned with its protagonist's environment than his inner life, and for those reasons, the book doesn't cohere the way its antecedents do. Instead of a deeply reported account of individuals wrestling with guilt and existential doubts, it's a picaresque tale about a comically naïve boy with no personality to speak of.

Once Dove leaves home, he wanders until he reaches New Orleans. He's an empty vessel, and as he moves through the world, Nelson uses his innocent gaze to present America as a cruel, hypocritical, and immoral place. Dove is constantly falling in with unsavory characters, and because he's so guileless, people regularly offer him unsolicited advice and opinions. Each of their edicts is dark and amoral, and their pronouncements give voice to the fatalistic turn Nelson's mind had taken in the six years since he completed *The Man with the Golden Arm.*

"Everybody got to eat," someone says, "everybody got to die."

"You know what the best kick of all is, Red?" another asks. "It's when you put a gun on grownups and watch them go all to pieces and blubber right before your eyes. That's the *best.*"

"Never play cards with a man called Doc," an inmate advises Dove at one point. "Never eat at a place called Mom's. Never sleep with a woman whose troubles are worse than your own. Never let anybody talk you into shaking another man's jolt. And never cop another man's plea. I've tried 'em all and I know. They don't work."

Dove spends a good deal of time in search of employment, and usually offers his labor for free. "It's just the boys who were willing to work just for the experience got to be the millionaires!" he says. But despite his eagerness to be exploited, Dove has a hard time finding a job that suits. He sells coffee, scams people by selling fake beauty certificates, manufactures condoms, and works as a salesman for Watkins products—but none of those positions lasts long.

Dove becomes a success only when he hires on as a performer at a sex show run by a pimp named Finnerty. He begins going by the name "Big Stingaree," and when it's time to perform each day, he enters a room and finds a woman waiting for him. The prostitutes in Finnerty's employ take turns working with Dove, and each, when it's her time to perform, pretends to be a virgin and tries, and fails, to fight him off to preserve her chastity. This scene—enacted again, and again—contains both elements of the social critique at the book's core.

Dove's success makes a mockery of the meritocratic ideal because he failed to earn a living legitimately and makes more as a sex worker than he ever imagined. "Couldn't read my name were it wrote a foot high on the side of a barn," he announces once, "but I make more in a single day than some educated fools earn in a month."

And Nelson uses the scene to puncture the sense of superiority he imagines readers will bring to the text. Dove, though he makes a spectacle of himself each night, is not the freak in the story. The only debased characters in the book are the people who pay to watch his act through peepholes—men who had "been sheltered all their lives" and "gave no sign of knowing that the country was in the very depths of an economic disaster." Each of them believes he's witnessing a rape, not a performance, but leaves feeling smug and superior. My deepest suspicions have been confirmed, one thinks; "a man was a two-legged animal and a woman a four-legged one, nothing more."

Each of these men, Nelson wrote, is more despicable at his best than Dove is at his worst because they have used their privilege to seal themselves off from humanity. They "wanted to know of life—'What's the answer?' Without pausing once to wonder what was the question."

Eventually, Dove falls in love and leaves Finnerty's. It seems, for a short while, that his story might end well—but then it takes another dark turn. Dove's girlfriend has a jealous former lover, and eventually, that man beats Dove so savagely that he loses his sight. After he goes blind, Dove returns to Texas and goes looking for Teresina Vidavarri. He hopes she'll forgive him, but the story ends before he makes it to her door to ask.

When Nelson completed his manuscript in June 1955, he gave it the title he had intended to use on the political essay he completed two years earlier: *A Walk on the Wild Side.* Then he sent a copy to Ken McCormick, packed up the little apartment he had been renting, and traveled to Missoula, Montana, where he had lined up work as an instructor at a writers' workshop.

The position was not demanding, and he was looking forward to relaxing, but first he had to settle the question of his marriage. Amanda was still refusing to divorce, and Nelson was out of patience. She said she thought they could still be happy together, eventually, and he thought she was delusional. "For Christ's sake let's get this misery done and over . . . ," he wrote just after he arrived in Missoula. "I'm utterly dead sick of running here and there trying to find some place I can work in again, some place I can live in again. . . . I never before heard of a man giving all his time and energy simply trying to be unmarried to a woman he doesn't want to be married to. But that's how it is all the same."

Nelson apologized for writing so harshly the next day, but remained insistent they divorce. "I don't do myself any good by belting you," he wrote. "In fact it makes me a little sick. But how the hell else can I save myself if I don't keep pushing to get us apart?" He offered to give Amanda enough money to buy a house, when he had it, and wished her well. "I think there is still a chance for you to have a life that will, with time, make this one you have seem like a nightmare that's done."

Amanda agreed to divorce then, and Nelson hired a lawyer to file the required papers. She countersued, and it looked like they would finally be through with each other by the end of the year.

Nelson was finally able to calm down then. He was only teaching two days a week, and when he wasn't meeting with students, he swam in the college gym, worked out on a speed bag, and wrote. Amanda sent him a portion of the novel he had begun writing about Paula Bays, and he began making headway on his next novel.

But soon after Nelson's marital troubles were resolved, distressing news began to arrive. The newspapers were reporting that Otto Preminger had signed Frank Sinatra to play the lead role in his adaptation of *The Man with the Golden Arm*, and every lawyer Nelson consulted said they could find no legal means of stopping the production. Nelson did have a good legal case against Bob Roberts, he learned, but Roberts was overseas and not expected to return. The film was scheduled to be released around the end of the year, and Jack Kirkland had delayed his stage adaptation so they wouldn't coincide.

Then an officer with the local police department tracked Nelson down and presented him with a subpoena from the House Un-American Activities Committee (HUAC). Francis E. Walter, the committee's chairman, wanted Nelson to appear before Congress and testify under oath about his political connections.*

Nelson pleaded with the officer, and said he couldn't afford to go to DC, but the officer was unmoved. "These are the papers," he said. "You either go to Washington or I'll take you."

"Do you know what for?" Nelson asked.

"No, you just go there," the officer said.

---

* The fact that Nelson received this subpoena has never been widely reported, mostly because he tried to hide it. He spoke about it on the record only once, in an interview with two student journalists writing for a college magazine that doesn't have an archive and hasn't been digitized. His correspondence from this period contains several mentions of a subpoena, but without the corroborating interview, there was no way of knowing it came from HUAC.

Nelson accepted the subpoena and promised to report to the capital, but then he reached out to Doubleday instead, and asked them to have their lawyers contact the Committee on his behalf. It wasn't a call he wanted to make. Ken McCormick had just read *A Walk on the Wild Side*, and Doubleday's editorial board was in the process of deciding whether to publish the book.

"They Don't Exactly Give Me Any Medals for Caution"

(October 1955–May 20, 1956)

By the time Nelson rented a dimly lit walk-up in Manhattan's West Village in October, he had been on the move for nearly two years. He had traveled more than fourteen thousand miles and slept in at least fourteen different rooms since he began writing *A Walk on the Wild Side*—but the book was finally complete. He had delivered a revised version of the manuscript to Doubleday just before he reached the city, and for the first time in a very long time, he had nothing to do but wait for Ken McCormick to call.

A few days after Nelson moved into his apartment, two aspiring writers visited to interview him for the *Paris Review*. Their names were Alston Anderson and Terry Southern, and they were both in their early thirties, struggling to get their work into print, and in awe of Nelson.[*] "He strikes one as a man who feels and means just what he says," they

---

[*] Southern later became famous for writing *The Magic Christian*, and screenplays for movies such as *Dr. Strangelove* and *Easy Rider*. But Anderson is an obscure figure. He published a widely praised collection of stories called *Lover Man* in 1959, and a novel called *All God's Children* in 1965, but then he faded into obscurity and died a pauper in 2008. Nelson remained in touch with both men after this interview, and assisted their careers.

soon wrote. "To talk with Algren is to have a conversation brought very quickly to that rarefied level where values are actually declared."

Nelson, Anderson, and Southern left the door to Nelson's apartment open when they began speaking, and the space soon filled with strangers. The Village was a warren of cafés, jazz clubs, and studios occupied by young artists and writers at the time, and Nelson was a hero within its confines—so when people heard he was granting an interview, they found his building, climbed the stairs, let themselves into his apartment, and sat down.

Anderson and Southern began by asking Nelson about getting *The Man with the Golden Arm* published, but then their questions became more general. They invited Nelson to discuss his writing process, his thoughts on style, his forthcoming book, his next project, and his contemporaries.

"Nothing was easier" than getting *Arm* published, Nelson said, "because I got paid before I wrote it."

I write in drafts, he explained. "I've always figured the only way I could finish a book and get a plot was just to keep making it longer and longer until something happens," and I've never tried to cultivate any style. "The only thing I've consciously tried to do was put myself in a position to hear the people I wanted to hear talk talk."

The novel I just finished, Nelson said, is a "reader's book."

"Mechanically and, I think, technically, it's done more carefully, and probably reads better than other books," he said, but I didn't want to write it. "I've got a book about Chicago on the West Side—I did a hundred pages in a year, and I still figure I need three years on it—but I was under contract for [*A Walk on the Wild Side*], so it took precedence. . . . now I'm going back to the one I want to do."*

"Do you have a feeling of camaraderie, or solidarity, with any contemporary writers?" Anderson and Southern asked, and Nelson said he didn't.

---

* This is the book Nelson was writing about Paula Bays's life.

"No, I couldn't say so," he replied. "I don't know many writers."

"How do you avoid it?" They wanted to know.

"Well, I dunno, but I do have the feeling that other writers can't help you with writing," Nelson said. "I've gone to writers' conferences and writers' sessions and writers' clinics, and the more I see of them, the more I'm sure it's the wrong direction. It isn't the place where you learn to write. I've always felt strongly that a writer shouldn't be engaged with other writers, or with people who make books, or even with people who read them. I think the farther away you get from the literary traffic, the closer you are to sources. I mean, a writer doesn't really *live*, he observes."

Nelson was unguarded, almost confessional, for the entire interview—with one exception. Eventually, Anderson and Southern asked Nelson about his politics, and when they did, he responded tersely. He was still shaken by the subpoena he received from HUAC, and seemed unwilling to take any risks.

"Do you vote? Locally, there around Gary?" they asked.

"No. No, I don't," Nelson said.

"Still you do frequently get involved in these issues, like the Rosenbergs, and so on," they said.

"Yes, that's true," Nelson said.

"What do your publishers think of that?" they asked.

"Well," Nelson said sarcastically, "they don't exactly give me any medals for caution."

Nelson heard from Doubleday near the end of October, arranged to have lunch with Timothy Seldes, and arrived for his meeting on the appointed day feeling confident. He was sure *A Walk on the Wild Side* was going to be a best seller, and had already begun mentally allocating the money he was going to make on it. He would save some to support himself while he finished his next novel, give a chunk to Amanda as alimony, and use the remainder on lawyers—one to sue Preminger, one to fight the State Department over its passport denial, and one to handle his divorce.

Seldes ordered a martini when he arrived for lunch, and Nelson felt doubt sneaking up on him. Seldes was not normally a drinker, never mind a day drinker, and his request seemed like a dark omen.*

Seldes emptied his glass and ordered a second, and Nelson became worried, and anxious. He had been telling his friends that he was lucky to be signed with Doubleday because they were so supportive, and he had taken it for granted that they would publish his novel, but now it seemed Seldes was about to announce they would not.

Nelson didn't reveal his doubts. Instead, he kept calm, and waited. There was too much at stake for him to act rashly. His financial future was in question, but also his liberty. Doubleday's lawyers had been in touch with HUAC on his behalf, and there was no way to know what they would do if his relationship with the publisher became strained, or ended.

Seldes emptied his second glass, ordered a third martini, and found his courage. We're not going to publish your book, he announced. There's too much sex in it, and it'll be banned if we release it.

At the time, it was illegal to publish explicit descriptions of sex, and Doubleday had just gone through a protracted legal battle over Edmund Wilson's *Memoirs of Hecate County*—a less salacious book than *A Walk on the Wild Side*. They published it in 1946, and four months later, the Society for the Suppression of Vice sued them, and won. The book was pulled from storefronts and the New York Public Library, and afterward Doubleday spent years in court trying to get it back on the shelves. They lost two appeals, then argued their case before the Supreme Court—and lost again.

We don't want another legal fight on our hands, Seldes explained without any joy. He was just a messenger, and a reluctant one. His

---

* It's true that Nelson and Seldes once got high, but that was out of character for Seldes—so out of character, in fact, that he talked about it for decades afterward.

superiors had decided to reject Nelson's book, but none of them had had the nerve to deliver the news.

Nelson was too stunned to say much, so Seldes kept talking. Besides, he said, you were supposed to be revising your first novel, not writing a new one. We didn't order this book, so we won't publish it.

When Seldes finished speaking, Nelson said: I'll stand by my book. Then he left the restaurant.

Nelson gave his agent a copy of his manuscript the next day and told her to sell it—he didn't care to whom—and then he prepared to leave New York. He was reluctant to go back on the road after traveling for so long, but his desire to escape the world of editors, lawyers, agents, and publishers was more powerful.

Nelson's first stop was Baltimore. He traveled there by bus, went looking for Jesse Blue and his wife, Trixie, and found them living in a row house in a poor neighborhood. They were the guests of a couple named Blackie and Norma, and when Nelson arrived he was welcomed in as well and allowed to stay.[*]

The environment in the house was not what Nelson had been expecting. He had found sanctuary with Jesse Blue in East St. Louis the year before, when he spent a day partying with men and women living "off the legit" who seemed happier, more carefree, and more content than he was in the world of deadlines, budgets, and mortgages. He had been looking for more of the same when he traveled to Baltimore, but instead he was exposed to a darker, more squalid, and violent part of Blue's life.

Blackie, the patriarch of the house, was a wild character. He had earned his living as a pimp and petty criminal for decades, but had recently turned fifty and decided to try his hand at a more respectable profession. He was working as a car salesman when Nelson arrived,

---

[*] In the letter this account is based on, Jesse Blue is identified as "Whitey." "Blackie" is almost certainly a pseudonym, but this man's legal name has been lost to history.

and was trying to act the way he imagined "taxpayers" acted, but he wasn't doing either well. He can "live only in terms of battle, challenge, skirmish and war," Nelson told his friend Max Geismar.

Blackie beat and threatened his wife regularly, lied fluidly, and made a spectacle of himself as a matter of course. Sometimes, he stood on the sidewalk wearing hot pink pants and waited for someone to mock him so he had an excuse to fight, and he cut in and out of lanes at high speed when he drove a car. People often shot him disapproving looks, and when they did, Norma leaned out the passenger side window and yelled, "Get on your side, motherfucker."

Dogs growled when Blackie approached, and he kicked one under a moving car and killed it a few days after Nelson arrived in Baltimore. That caught the attention of the police, and they dragged Blackie out of bed and into the street before dawn the next day. There were four of them, but Blackie didn't back down. He was ready to fight, and would have, if Nelson and Blue hadn't begged him to submit.

"Blackie," Jesse Blue said afterward, "it's just such fluke pinches as that will get you and maybe me into the pen."

"It's too late to get scared," Blackie said.

"It's not too late for *me*," Blue said. "I *am* scared."

After the police left, Nelson, Blue, Trixie, Blackie, and Norma loaded into two cars and drove west—through Maryland, Pennsylvania, Ohio, and Indiana, then into Illinois and on to East St. Louis.

The city was seething when they arrived. A six-year-old boy named Bobby Greenlease had been kidnapped and murdered by a man with Mafia connections the month before, and three people had been killed since. The police were trolling all the seediest bars in search of the usual suspects, and that included Blue and Blackie.

So, Nelson and Blue went back on the road, alone this time, and raced south and east with no destination in mind. They drove through Kentucky and Tennessee, and then entered Arkansas, where they spent a night in a hotel that boasted a sign warning: "You think you can go back to town and pick up a woman and bring her back here in a cab and stay all night with you but you're only fooling yourself. It's been tried. This is a *moral* hotel."

Then they continued on, through Louisiana, Mississippi, and Alabama, and finally into Florida, where they saw Seminoles piloting jon boats through the swamp.

When they reached the eastern shore and spotted a development called Playland Estates, they stopped driving. Nelson found an unoccupied house and paid to rent it through Christmas. It had a lawn, and out back, there was a swimming pond with a white sand beach. It was near the ocean, so the air was warm and the blue sky was endless, but most importantly, as far as Nelson was concerned, it had no phone line and no more than a handful of people knew he was there. Ken McCormick had tried to call Nelson twice—first in Baltimore, then in East St. Louis—but Nelson had refused to speak to him both times. He told his agent he was done talking to McCormick, and was done talking about his book.

For the next six weeks, Nelson did nothing—or very close to it. He and Jesse Blue spent their mornings reading the daily papers and drinking coffee in silence. Then, in the afternoons, Nelson swam in the pond out back. He tried to work on his novel after dark, but more often than not, he was too depressed to focus.

Farrar, Straus & Cudahy purchased *A Walk on the Wild Side* only weeks after Doubleday passed on it, and afterward the firm's owners sent Nelson letters filled with praise. "I really do think this is the best you have ever done," Sheila Cudahy said. "It is a hell of a novel," Roger Straus agreed, adding, "and I am so glad we are going to be publishing it."

But Nelson was too preoccupied by his troubles to be heartened by their enthusiasm. Doubleday was claiming he owed them eight thousand dollars—everything they had advanced him for the novel, and everything they had paid for the two books they chose not to publish— and then there was Preminger. The Motion Picture Association of America had declined to grant the film version of *The Man with the*

Golden Arm its seal of approval, but Preminger had decided to release it anyway. The film was about to premiere in Chicago, and as a result, Jack Kirkland's theatrical production was indefinitely postponed.

Preminger's film "has me breathing in short, sharp pants," Nelson told a friend. "I'm also having trouble with small red mists, which keep floating across the typewriter keys. In all seriousness, it's hard to work feeling so victimized. I don't know another word for it. And who wants to be a victim?"

Nelson left Jesse Blue at the house in Playland Estates three days before Christmas, traveled to Miami, and rented a hotel room. Then he went for a walk, spotted a movie theater, and sat through a Walt Disney documentary called *The African Lion*. The next day, he went to the port of Miami, paid forty-two dollars for a ticket on SS *Florida*, boarded, and began sailing toward Cuba—the farthest point from American shores he could reach without a passport.

The ship arrived in Havana on Christmas Eve, and Nelson stepped on shore and spent the day wandering. The capital, which was still under the control of Fulgencio Batista, was thick with casinos, bars, and prostitutes, and it reminded Nelson of Marseille after the war—wild and free.

When the sun set, Nelson found a phone directory, looked up the number for Ernest Hemingway's house, and dialed. Hemingway got on the line and said he was sick, but told Nelson to come for a visit anyway.

So Nelson hired a car and rode for twelve miles until he reached the long driveway that led to La Finca Vigía—a large white mansion with a colonnaded entrance.

Hemingway was lying in bed, wearing a white baseball cap and rimless glasses, when Nelson entered his room. He had a short beard of white whiskers that made him look like Santa Claus, an aged professor, or some combination of the two. He had survived a plane crash the year before—and then another. He injured his head the first time, and injured it more seriously the second, along with his back, his shoulder, a kidney, and his liver. Newspapers reported that he had died in the crash, and it's possible he might have preferred it if he had. He was badly burned in a brush fire a few months after the second plane crash, and his face, arms, and torso had all been singed. His hair caught fire, too, and for a while, he was bald.

There was a sheet draped over Hemingway's torso when he greeted Nelson, but his abdomen was so distended that its swelling was obvious nevertheless. He wasn't supposed to be drinking, but there was a glass of whiskey within reach of his bed, and he told Nelson he was allowed a certain number of shots each hour.

Nelson and Hemingway had never met, but each man admired the other. Hemingway had loved and promoted both *Never Come Morning* and *The Man with the Golden Arm*, and Nelson had been looking to Hemingway's work for inspiration for most of his career. He respected the man's prose, but also saw him as a kindred spirit—a writer whose work made no accommodation to literary critics or trends.

"Sorry to see you down," Nelson said when he found his words.

"I'm not down," Hemingway replied curtly.

Nelson accepted a glass of whiskey, and realized he wasn't going to be receiving any learned counsel that evening. Hemingway was not feeling loquacious. He had been consuming a shot of liquor every hour all day long, and there was a pain throbbing behind his eyes that had been lingering for months.

Nelson had a second drink, and then he tried to fill the silence. He remembered the film he had seen two days earlier, and began telling Hemingway about Africa. When a lioness needs to feed her cubs, she'll knock an impala down and then kill it, he said. Cheetahs are the fastest things on four legs, and they chase down their prey to exhaust them.

Telling the story excited Nelson, and he began waving his glass to simulate the grace and athleticism of the animals he was describing. Impalas leap such great distances when they reach top speed, he explained, it looks like they're flying.

Hemingway listened, patient and bemused, and allowed his guest to ramble.

Eventually, Nelson took a breath and looked around the room. Behind him, high on a wall, hung the stuffed head of a water buffalo Hemingway had killed in Africa.

Nelson boarded the *Florida* alone on Christmas Day, and began making his way home. He stepped onto American soil the next morning, was back in Chicago by the afternoon, and reached Gary before midnight. He had agreed to let Amanda live in the house on Forrest Avenue by herself until their divorce was finalized, but when he showed up on the doorstep, broke and exhausted, she allowed him inside.

For the next two weeks, Nelson and Amanda lived together but barely spoke. She went to work each day for a company installing sewer lines, and he reviewed the page proofs for his novel. Farrar, Straus & Cudahy was also concerned about the book's content, and so he spent his time removing all the overt references to sex or genitalia from the text to avoid the condemnation of censors.

At 5 a.m. on January 16, 1956, Nelson entered Amanda's room and stood at the foot of her bed. Dave Peltz, their neighbor, lingered nearby to provide moral support. Later that day, Nelson and Amanda were due in court to finalize their divorce, but he was having second thoughts.

"Look," he said, "let's forget about the whole thing."

Amanda didn't even get up. "I think it's a little late for that now," she said.

Nelson moved into Chicago after divorcing Amanda so that she could have the house to herself, and he rented a single room without a bathroom at 1817 West Division Street. Then he began plotting his escape from America. He wanted to leave when he received his first royalty check from *A Walk on the Wild Side*, so he reapplied for a passport with a letter of support from his literary agent—and the State Department turned him down again.

Nelson moved again two months later, and began residing, rent-free, in an apartment owned by his friend Caesar Tabet. Then he hired a lawyer and appealed his latest passport denial. It was his fourth try, or maybe his fifth, and this time, he signed his name to the statement the State Department had been demanding he make since his first application in 1953. "I wish to affirm and take oath that I am not at present a member of the Communist Party," he wrote, "nor have been a member of that party in the past."

A Walk on the Wild Side

(May 21, 1956–August 31, 1956)

On Monday, May 21, Nelson entered the University Club of Chicago, wearing a dark suit and a polka-dotted tie, and joined a luncheon that had been organized to celebrate the release of his novel. He found a seat waiting for him next to his publisher, Roger Straus, and for the next couple hours, he and Straus held court—shaking hands, posing for pictures, and offering perfunctory smiles. There was a cake sitting in front of him that had been carved in the shape of a hardcover book and decorated to look like a copy of *A Walk on the Wild Side*, and the room was full of well-wishers and hangers-on.

The event had been billed as a celebration of the "birth" of Nelson's fourth novel, but the room was thrumming with gossip instead of congratulation. Preminger's film—a movie Nelson saw once, and dismissed as inauthentic—was one topic of conversation. The quarter-million-dollar lawsuit Nelson had recently filed against the man was another, and Simone de Beauvoir's latest novel, *The Mandarins*, was the third. It had been released in English that week, with a drawing on its cover that resembled Nelson, it was dedicated to him, and it credited a character patterned after him with giving Beauvoir's fictional counterpart her first "complete orgasm."

When the lunch ended, Nelson and Straus moved on to Kroch's &

Brentano's bookstore, where Nelson signed copies of his novel until his hand cramped, and then they attended a cocktail party. The following day, he signed books at an event that had been promoted with the promise that attendees could "see him! meet him!" and for the remainder of the week he maintained that frenetic pace—two radio appearances, two TV appearances, a speech at the *Sun-Times* book and author luncheon, and a party organized by Jack Conroy and Studs Terkel.

None of Nelson's earlier books had been promoted so well, and the effort that went into the release of *A Walk on the Wild Side* paid off. It appeared on the *Tribune*'s best-seller list at number six after a week of sales, and then it moved up to number three. It entered the *New York Times* best-seller list next, stayed there for fifteen weeks, and remained a top seller on the West Coast and in the Midwest through the summer.

But the novel's commercial success did nothing for Nelson's state of mind—he was distraught, and promoting the book felt like a grim ceremony. He had begun obsessing over Preminger's film and the way his story had been taken from him, and he was offended that Beauvoir had revealed so much about their time together. He felt betrayed by her, and when a reporter asked him to comment on her book, he said, "I think Madame de Beauvoir has invaded her own privacy."

Nelson was also distressed by the reviews *A Walk on the Wild Side* had received. Despite its strong sales, it was getting mixed notices— some enthusiastic, some tepid, and a few nasty.

The book had a solid core of fans, some of whom saw it as an innovation that built on Nelson's earlier novels and suggested a new direction for his writing. Maxwell Geismar called it "an ironical parody of the American success story" in *The Nation*, and lauded its prose. James T. Farrell called it "the product of a distinguished American writer" in the *New Republic*, and a reviewer for the *Saturday Review* declared, "The Chicago School of Realism has a new headmaster who frames his materials in back-country balladry and earthy lyricism."

"The point Algren sought to make," a review in the *Tribune* said, "was that lost people who have suffered, 'little' people often are the biggest human beings. He has made the point with crushing impact."

As a rule, though, the novel's detractors were more influential. Alfred Kazin, writing in the *New York Times*, accused Nelson of "puerile sentimentality," and said, "I don't think his book has anything real about it whatever." Orville Prescott, also writing in the *Times*, called the book's characters "human monsters" and said the story was nothing more than "a series of offenses against decency." What Algren wants to say, Norman Podhoretz wrote in *The New Yorker*, "is that we live in a society whose bums and tramps are better men than the preachers and the politicians and the otherwise respectables." In *The Reporter*, Leslie Fiedler declared that Algren was "a museum piece—the last of the proletarian writers."

Nelson's work had always courted controversy. He was first censored in 1935 when the *Windsor Quarterly*—at the insistence of their college sponsor—printed blank pages in their magazine where one of his stories was supposed to appear. The Chicago Public Library had refused to purchase copies of *Never Come Morning*, and *Holiday* magazine removed all of the political content from his essay on Chicago. But the literary community had reliably supported Nelson. Reviewers were rarely critical of his work, and never questioned his motivation for writing about "bums and tramps," because they identified his fiction, as he did, with a long tradition of American writers who used outsiders as a means of commenting on society's imperfections. That tendency included Nelson's contemporaries, like Wright and John Steinbeck, but also writers from earlier generations such as Stephen Crane, Upton Sinclair, and Walt Whitman, who wrote, *I feel I am of them—I belong to those convicts and prostitutes myself, / And henceforth I will not deny them—for how can I deny myself?*

The terms of debate within the literary world had shifted dramatically in the years since Nelson's last novel was published. Just as painters were moving away from realism and toward abstract expressionism, writers were abandoning "social novels" in favor of technique-driven works that placed more emphasis on metaphor, irony, and paradox than on research, compassion, or story. A book's social relevance no longer mattered to many reviewers, and the quality of Nelson's work that had earned him the greatest praise for the first twenty-one years of his career was suddenly a liability.*

After a week of promoting *A Walk on the Wild Side* in Chicago, Nelson visited his home in Gary, packed a bag, labeled it "Paris," and then flew to New York and moved into a fourth-floor walk-up in the West Village. The apartment had two large bedrooms and a sundeck, and it rose above the neighboring buildings so that when Nelson looked through his windows toward downtown at night, he saw "lights like candle-lamps burning all about."

A few days after he moved in, Nelson walked to the Cherry Lane Theater on Commerce Street to attend the inaugural theatrical performance of *The Man with the Golden Arm*. Jack Kirkland had been planning to open his play on Broadway, but he lost most of his funding when Preminger's film reached theaters, and afterward the Cherry Lane was the best venue he could find.

Nelson was in the audience and watching intently when Robert Loggia took the stage to make his debut as Frankie Machine on opening night. Kirkland's production of the play was a low-budget affair, scheduled for a

---

* Nelson commented on this trend regularly, beginning with the interview he gave to the *Paris Review*. "I got a glimpse into the uses of a certain kind of criticism this past summer at a writers' conference," he said then, "—into how the avocation of assessing the failures of better men can be turned into a comfortable livelihood, providing you can back it up with a PhD." This tendency is associated with the New Criticism, a movement of academics whose aims are described in *A Glossary of Literary Terms* as follows: In evaluating a piece of writing, "they eschew reference to the biography and temperament of the author, to the social conditions at the time of its production, or to its psychological and moral effects on the reader; they also tend to minimize recourse to the place of the work in the history of literary forms and subject matter." For a more in-depth (critical) assessment of this phenomenon, and the accompanying rise in the prominence of creative writing programs, see Eric Bennett's *Workshops of Empire*.

short run and never well attended, but it was faithful to the original story and Nelson found it deeply affecting. He saw the show at least five times, and on each occasion, he scrutinized the performers on stage and compared their version of their characters to the image in his mind.

Nelson spent six weeks in New York, seeing friends, attending cocktail parties, appearing on the radio to promote his novel, and visiting clubs to hear jazz—but then he had to face the inevitable. He had flown east primarily to reckon with his finances, and on July 18, he, his lawyer, and his agents gathered in Roger Straus's office near Union Square Park to discuss the matter.

The news Nelson received that day was worse than he had imagined. *A Walk on the Wild Side* was on best-seller lists in at least three cities at the time, the Associated Press had just selected Nelson as their author of the week, and a paperback publisher that had already sold a half million copies of *The Neon Wilderness* was preparing a new edition—but despite all his success, Nelson was in debt and unlikely to break even anytime soon.

Much of Nelson's trouble—and later, his regret—could be traced to a single miscalculation. He had been offered $32,500 for the paperback rights to *A Walk on the Wild Side* before it was published, but turned it down because his agent told him to hold out for more.* Then Alfred Kazin's review appeared in the *New York Times,* the initial offer was withdrawn, and the highest offer that came in afterward was only ten thousand dollars—of which Nelson was entitled to half. Roger Straus had been working with Nelson's agents to raise money to make up for the shortfall, and they had had some success, but not enough. They received an offer to reprint *Somebody in Boots* as a paperback, and Ballantine Books also offered Nelson twenty-five hundred dollars for unpublished material they could release as a pocket book—but that was all.†

---

*   That would be about four hundred thousand dollars today.

†   Avon Books eventually released this edition of *Somebody in Boots* as *The Jungle*— but Nelson had little to do with it. Someone at Avon marked up the text and Nelson

Nelson had access to a little more than eleven thousand dollars when all was said and done, but he owed far more than that. He had promised Amanda seven thousand in their divorce agreement. Doubleday was demanding more than eight thousand as repayment of their advances, and he owed money to a Chicago lawyer who represented him during his divorce, the lawyer he was paying to represent him for his passport appeal, and the lawyer he hired to sue Preminger, whom he had agreed to pay whether or not she ever secured a settlement; her fee, already large, would eventually come close to eight thousand.

Nelson's financial troubles had many causes. His agent's bad advice contributed, as did Bob Roberts' treachery and the three thousand dollars Nelson lost playing cards after his first passport application was denied. The nasty reviews *A Walk on the Wild Side* received damaged his confidence, and the FBI's scrutiny was beginning to cause him to act irrationally—but Nelson blamed only himself and his sentimental attachment to Amanda.

When he realized how desperate his financial situation was that summer, Nelson wrote a confessional letter to his friend Max Geismar that attributed all of his troubles to a failure of will. He said that he had been working for the last two years just to make enough money to support himself while he wrote the novel he wanted to be writing, but that all of that time had been wasted.

> *When I began* that *one I was just beginning to write—I had the place to write it, the emotion for it, and the people about whom to write it. I have a bad, bad pang, at the moment of writing this for not holding on to that place, the emotion and the people. All I had to do was to be willing to live lonely—the way I prefer—for a couple years. I didn't.*
>
> *Up to that time I did everything right—blindly, but in some way*

---

approved the changes, but that was all. He tried to pull out of the deal at the last minute, but couldn't. He never accepted Ballantine's offer.

*becoming somebody. Only one little thing, very deep, was wrong—
and that was the shadow of guilt toward the girl [Amanda] I got
married to a long time ago, and who wanted to try again. I tried
every way of getting out of letting this happen—but I never quite cut
the knot. I never said 'No.' I let it happen. . . .*

*Now I'm down, and kicking. What I'm kicking about is that, in
my hands, was the luckiest chance ever given an American writer—
I mean that without exaggeration, for this reason: I made myself a
voice for those who are counted out, and I did this because of compassion and not for what was in it. All I had to do was keep my nose
clean. I didn't. My devotion was to the outcasts, that was the real
thing—the girl [Amanda] was just a kind of obligation I thought I
was supposed to fulfill.*

After his meeting with Farrar, Straus & Cudahy, Nelson requested
seven thousand dollars from his publisher—everything available to
him, at the time—and made his way to Washington, DC. Someone
had put him in contact with a lawyer there who claimed to have access
to the FBI's files. The man in question said he could enter the bureau's
offices, access any dossier in the building, and remove all the incrimi-
nating content inside.

It was a ridiculous story, but Nelson was desperate enough to
believe it. His passport application had just been denied again, and
the passport division had scheduled an interview for his appeal
where he was expected to discuss his past connections to the Communist Party under oath. He was fearful of imprisonment, so he met
with the lawyer and gave him fifteen hundred dollars—and it seems
they never spoke again.

A few days later, Jesse Blue left Baltimore, went looking for Nelson,
and found him wandering the streets in a fugue—barely able to speak,
and too depressed to care for himself. Blue called Amanda and told
her that Nelson was sick and needed help, but Amanda did nothing.

Somehow, Nelson made it to back to Gary by himself, and showed up on Forrest Avenue. His arrival surprised Amanda, and so did his state of mind. He was crying and pleading with her. He asked her to allow him in, and said he had nowhere else to go.

She agreed, and then he gave her all the money he had left, along with an IOU for the portion of her alimony he had given to the attorney in DC.

By summer, there was general agreement that Nelson was losing his mind. He spent his time pacing and chain-smoking while muttering to himself. He lay in bed for hours each day, trying to quiet his mind so he could rest, but rarely managed to. When he did drift off, it never lasted long. As soon as he fell into a deep sleep, he woke screaming—"Nooooo! Nooooo!"

Dave Peltz, Nelson's friend and neighbor, made a point of visiting regularly to check on Nelson, and once he arrived just after Nelson woke from a nightmare. He entered the house, and in place of a greeting, Nelson said, "Dave, man oh man, are you fucking in trouble but I gotta tell you."

"What happened?" Peltz asked.

I had a dream, Nelson said, "that you were laying right here on this fucking living room floor face down with a hole in your back . . ."

"It's your dream, Nelson," Peltz said. It has nothing to do with me.

The comment struck Nelson like a revelation, and he jumped out of his chair and lit a cigarette. "Wooooo," he grunted. "Wooooo."

"What the fuck?" he demanded nonsensically. "Who shot me in the back? And why am I bleeding?"

Amanda observed Nelson's deterioration closely. She watched him fall apart one piece at a time, and the farther he receded from the world, the more helpless she felt. She told herself for weeks that he would recover on his own, but on the night of August 18, she realized she would have to intervene. Nelson stayed up all night that night, and before dawn he was willing to admit there was something wrong. He was distrustful of doctors and drugs and claimed that he had never even taken aspirin, but by then he hadn't slept a full night in more than a month, and he was willing to try anything. "Help me," he pleaded with Amanda. "Help me."

She just looked at him. "I didn't know what to do," she said later.

The next morning, Amanda called Neal Rowland and Dave Peltz. They came to the house and found Nelson in a shocking state. He had become preoccupied by an internal dialogue, and didn't seem to hear them when they spoke to him. After some time, though, he acknowledged Peltz and Rowland and agreed to see a doctor.

The four of them piled into Peltz's 1954 Oldsmobile sedan and began driving north—out of Gary, and then through Chicago. After about an hour and a half, the car pulled into the driveway of the North Shore Health Resort in Winnetka, Illinois, and everyone got out. They approached the building—a large four-story with a peaked roof that was surrounded by manicured lawns—climbed the front steps together, and passed through the ivy-framed main entrance.

But then Nelson recoiled. When he saw the resort's waiting room, he realized his friends had brought him to an institution, not a doctor's office, and began screaming—"Noooo! Noooo!" The facility couldn't treat Nelson unless he signed himself in, so he backed away from the register on the front desk and kept away from the staff.

Amanda watched him squirm, and felt helpless. Rowland just stood there. But Peltz was out of patience, and he snapped. "Let's go home already, then," he said. "Don't blow my day. Sign it, or don't."

Nelson considered his options then, decided he couldn't face the prospect of returning home, walked to the desk, picked up a pen, touched it to the register, and wrote: E.

Then he set the pen down and paced the room while his friends watched and waited. Eventually, he returned to the desk, picked up the pen, and added a letter to the register so that it said: E A.

Then he set the pen down, paced, returned to the desk, and added two more letters so the register said: E AL R.

He paced the room some more, then returned—paced, and returned—until finally the register said: NELSON ALGREN.

Two large men dressed in white entered the room the moment Nelson scribbled the last letter of his name. One of them grabbed his left arm. The other grabbed the right. They lifted him, and then turned toward the far wall of the lobby and began dragging him toward a door that had just opened.

Nelson started to cry then. He looked at Amanda and said, between sobs, I don't want to. Then he turned toward Peltz, and begged.

"Dave," Nelson pleaded, and then "Daaaaave." The men in white continued dragging him, and the farther they carried him, the more pathetic and belabored his cries became. *Daaaaaaaave*, he wailed. *Daaaaaaaaaaaaaaaaave*.

"I felt like hell," Peltz said later, "like I betrayed him."

Nelson stayed at the clinic for twelve days, and then climbed out of a window, descended a fire-escape ladder, and ran away. *A Walk on the Wild Side* was still on the best-seller list in Chicago at the time, but he had no money, so he hitchhiked into the city and called Dave Peltz for a ride to Gary. When he returned home, he discovered that Amanda had moved out and the house was empty.

Nelson's stay in Winnetka had little therapeutic value and did nothing for his depression. He was diagnosed with "anxiety" while he was there, and a doctor determined that he had a "passive aggressive personality," but he received no medications or therapies. The doctor who had been assigned to treat him was at a conference when Nelson arrived, and while he was away, the staff gave Nelson baths and left him alone in his room until, one day, they discovered that he had disappeared.

And yet, admission to the clinic may have been the most fortuitous

event of Nelson's life. Earlier that year, he had scheduled an interview as part of his passport appeal, and he had been planning to make
statements under oath that would have constituted perjury. The date
for that interview fell during the period he was at Winnetka, though,
so his lawyer requested an indefinite postponement. The State Department agreed, and then informed the FBI of Nelson's whereabouts.

The bureau decided to use the delay caused by Nelson's institution-
alization to their advantage and began reviewing the evidence they
had against him—but when they did so, they found it lacking.

The most damning document in the bureau's possession was the
letter Howard Rushmore had provided them with—the one in which
Nelson calls himself a member of the Party "in good standing"—so
they invested time into attempting to verify it. They requested samples
of Nelson's handwriting from Caesar Tabet, Roger Straus, the secretary of the Division Street YMCA, the head of the Harper & Brothers
contracts department, the police department in Alpine, Texas, and
the registrar of the University of Illinois. Most everyone complied, but
none of the samples they provided matched the signature on the Rushmore letter precisely.

The FBI also found they had problems with their witnesses. They
contacted Louis Budenz and asked if he was prepared to testify
against Nelson in court, but he said he was too ill to do so. Things that
were clear in my memory in 1950, he told them, no longer are. Howard
Rushmore's testimony had also become problematic. He had recently
suffered his own breakdown and become fodder for the tabloids, so
the FBI believed he was too tarnished to serve as a witness.

Consequently, at the end of their review of Nelson's file, the FBI
determined they had neither hard evidence nor compelling testimony that could be used against him in court—so they placed his
case on hold.

Nelson stopped contacting his lawyer when he left the clinic, and
his passport appeal was eventually dropped as a result of inactivity.
The lawyers Doubleday assigned to have Nelson's HUAC subpoena

quashed had succeeded by then, so by the time Nelson returned home, all of his legal entanglements were either resolved or dormant.

The FBI continued to track Nelson for the next thirteen years, and during that time they talked regularly with his landlords, neighbors, and employers, but they never prepared charges against him again. It's likely he would have faced prison time if he had attended his interview and perjured himself, but he remained a free man because he never did.

It's also possible to think of Nelson's admission to the clinic as the most tragic event of his life—not the most fortuitous—and for the same reasons.

The FBI's scrutiny had a profound effect on Nelson, but few people ever suspected their involvement. The bureau never gave Nelson the opportunity to become a martyr, so when his career began to falter and his mood turned dark and paranoid, it seemed he was the sole author of his own decline. People extended him little sympathy, and later, when it became possible to resurrect the careers of artists who had suffered during the Red Scare, his name was rarely mentioned.

No one passed judgment on Nelson more harshly than he did on himself, and that may be the most tragic result of the FBI's scrutiny. He never knew how many of his friends and professional contacts the bureau had spoken to, or how closely they were watching him, so when publishers began distancing themselves from him, he assumed his work simply wasn't wanted or wasn't good enough. He blamed himself for the resulting anxiety and depression, and when he discovered he couldn't concentrate well enough to write the way he once had, he attributed his trouble to personal weakness—when, in fact, the truth was far more complicated.

A Lightless Cave off
a Loveless Hall

(September 1, 1956–February 1959)

Nelson went outside a bit before noon on New Year's Eve and walked through his backyard toward the lagoon behind his house. It was cold, but not freezing, and the sky was cloudy.

When he reached the embankment at the edge of his property, he descended toward the water line. There was a sheet of ice covering the lagoon, and Nelson stepped onto it, continued walking, and crossed to the far shore. He climbed the bank on the other side, passed through a stand of trees, stepped into the street, and walked down the block toward a general store called Pignotti's, where he bought milk and bread.

Then he retraced his steps, groceries in hand. He walked down the street, between the trees, and back onto the sheet of ice covering the lagoon, but this time, he didn't take the most direct route. He looked down at the ice as he walked, and noticed the surface was slick where the late-morning sun had begun melting it. There were puddles here and there, and he approached one and gazed into it—a portal between the gray sky and the frigid water beneath.

By then, it had been months since Nelson had been able to focus well enough to write, and he had begun to question whether he even wanted to. There didn't seem to be much point. He had returned from the war armed with limitless faith in the power of the written word and dreams of literary greatness, but both had faded since. He had written five books in that time, and seen four of them published, but there was no money in his bank account and no one waiting for him at home, and he no longer believed his writing had changed the world, or ever could.

Melancholy tinged with regret had been Nelson's resting state for months, but as he stood at the edge of that puddle and looked down into the frigid water, he felt light-headed, carefree—an odd sensation, given recent events.

For the first time in seventeen years, Nelson had no publisher. Roger Straus had been pressing him to sell the film rights to *A Walk on The Wild Side* to a businessman named Lebworth who had never produced a movie. Nelson found the idea repellent and said he intended to focus on writing his next novel and wait for a better offer, but Straus objected. He was tired of hearing about Nelson's financial problems, and said he would only release an advance for a new novel if Nelson accepted Lebworth's money. So Nelson ended their relationship. "I feel I may be able to climb out of the financial pit where I now so restlessly abide," he wrote near the end of the year, "were FS & C to give me a release."

Nelson considered the abyss beneath his feet. Then he moved the toe of one of his shoes closer to the puddle—"playing around," he called it later—and leaned forward. He was still for a moment, and so was the world. It was just him, the indifferent sky above, the bare trees lining the shore, and the container of milk slowly warming in his bag—and then the ice collapsed beneath his feet and the lagoon swallowed him whole.

Nelson sank, flailed, and then bobbed to the surface and gasped. He grabbed the edge of the sheet of ice and tried to pull himself onto it, but it wouldn't support his weight, and he slipped back into the water. He tried again and slipped again, and then he started screaming.

Cold water enveloped Nelson's body while he waited for help, and his blood vessels reacted by narrowing to preserve the temperature of his heart and brain. He began to feel weak, his breathing slowed, and he became drowsy—but he kept screaming.

Three brothers who shared the last name Larson were working on the roof of a house about five hundred feet away when a child approached them and said someone was calling for help. The brothers hadn't noticed anything, but once they knew to listen, they could make out Nelson's wails. They looked around for their source, but saw nothing, so they descended from the roof and looked again. They still saw nothing, so they piled into a truck, drove to the concrete bridge that crosses the lagoon at Lake Street, and stopped in the middle.

Finally, they saw Nelson. He was about two blocks away, so they drove toward him, parked at the edge of the lagoon, assessed the ice, and decided it was too weak to cross.

The Larsons tossed a rope toward Nelson, and when it landed within his reach, he grabbed it. They tugged on it, but it slipped through his numb fingers and slithered toward the shore. They tossed it again, and again, but the result was the same each time.

Nelson could barely keep himself above water by then. His hands were mitts, so the Larsons told him to wrap the rope around his arm. They tossed it again, and he did as they said, but when he was finished, he realized his fingers were so numb he couldn't tie a knot, so he wrapped the rope around himself again, and again, and again.

The Larsons tugged the line, and this time they pulled Nelson out of the water and onto the ice. He was dead weight, soaking and miserable, and they dragged his body all the way to shore.

The Larsons drove Nelson home. He was humiliated, and cold. He walked to his front door wearing his wet clothes, and then he stripped. He pulled off his shirt, his shoes, his pants, and his underwear, and left them in a pile outside. Then he crossed his living room naked, climbed into his bed, and burrowed under the blankets.

Dave Peltz knew something was wrong the moment he turned into Nelson's driveway. The pile of clothes on the stoop had frozen in place, and when Peltz saw it, he thought, "The damn fool, the miserable mother, he committed suicide."

Peltz tried the doorknob, but it was locked—to keep him out, he figured—so he found another way in and entered Nelson's bedroom, where he found him in bed, shivering.

"What the fuck's the matter with you?" Peltz said.

"Boy, did I have a fucking experience," Nelson minimized.

"What the fuck's the matter with you?" Peltz insisted. "What did you do?"

I need coffee, Nelson said. So Peltz went into the kitchen and made some and brought it back. "Tell me the truth, Nelson," he said. "Don't fuck around. Tell me the truth. Tell me if you tried."

Nelson accepted the cup and replied honestly. "I don't know if I did. I don't know if I didn't. I honest to God can't tell you, but I know something wanted me to and something didn't want me to."

Peltz suspected the plunge was more intentional than that. Nelson said he felt euphoric right before he crashed through the ice, and Peltz thought that detail was significant. "You see," he reflected later, "he was light-headed because he knew maybe the whole thing would be over soon . . . he felt a sense of being liberated."

Nelson put on a brave face after he plunged into the lagoon. That night, he attended a New Year's Eve party, recounted the story, and made it seem like a joke—but in truth, the accident had a profound effect on him, and over the course of the following months, he made significant changes to his life that, in retrospect, seem like a reaction to his near-drowning and the events that precipitated it.

The first thing Nelson did was fire his agent. He had been dissatisfied with Ingersoll & Brennan since his first trip to Hollywood, in 1950, when he found himself negotiating the sale of the film rights to *The Man with the Golden Arm* without assistance. But he felt loyal to them because they took him on after he returned from the war, and he kept working with them until March 1957, when he traveled to New York City and hired the McIntosh & Otis agency.

Next, Nelson dropped his lawsuit against Otto Preminger and sold the film rights to *A Walk on the Wild Side* to Marion Lebworth—the same man whose offer he had rejected a few months earlier. He had been adamantly opposed to entrusting Lebworth with his intellectual property at the end of 1956, but by the spring of 1957, he was willing to accept Lebworth's money. He was more interested, by then, in stabilizing his life and paying down his debts than he was in securing his literary future, so on June 1, he signed the same contract Lebworth had offered the year before, and accepted a check for twenty-five thousand dollars.

Then Nelson abandoned his book. A week after he fell into the lagoon, he told a gossip columnist that his next novel was called *Entrapment* and that it was half-finished—but a few months later, he set the book aside.* That decision was in keeping with his other choices that year, but it's likely Paula Bays played a role in it as well. She and Nelson had remained on good terms after she entered rehab in 1953, and he had continued to believe they might be together again—but that dream died abruptly when Bays married a pipe fitter in the summer of 1957. Her new husband didn't know she had once been an addict and prostitute, and after their wedding, she made a clean break with her past. She called Nelson to invite him to the ceremony, but he declined, and they never spoke again.

The tenor of Nelson's writing, speeches, and comments to the press also changed dramatically that year. As a public figure, he had been earnest almost to a fault for the first twenty years of his career, but after his

---

* Though the novel Nelson began writing about Bays was never completed, a portion of it made its way into Nelson's archive. It sat there unread for years, but eventually Seven Stories Press resurrected it and published an excerpt in *Entrapment and Other Writings* (2009). It's picaresque, but gorgeous and *sui generis*. You should read it.

plunge into the lagoon, his pronouncements became cynical, detached, and self-pitying. That summer, he told a group of college students that "most writers of the new school are on the side of the winners. Nobody seems to want to defend the accused." And soon afterward, he began calling himself a journalist, referring to himself as a loser, and claiming that he was planning to pawn his National Book Award.

Despite the fact that he needed money desperately, Nelson couldn't make himself cash the check Lebworth had given him. He kept it on his person for weeks, and regularly caressed and fiddled with it. Sometimes, he removed it from his wallet while he ate, rested it on the table, and gazed at his name on the PAY TO THE ORDER OF line and the numbers following the dollar sign. Nelson announced he was finally ready to go to the bank sometime that summer while Dave Peltz and Jesse Blue were at the house on Forrest Avenue. The check was dog-eared by then, and covered with coffee stains and butter marks, but the writing on it was still legible, so Nelson, Peltz, and Blue went downtown, and entered the Gary National Bank.

Peltz did the talking when they got inside. He asked the manager to verify that the check was still good, and when the issuing bank confirmed that it was, Nelson became abashed. He still harbored doubts about selling his film rights to Lebworth—not least because the contract didn't promise him any share of the profit if a film were ever made from the book—but by then, he had gone too far to turn back. He told the teller he wanted the money in cash, and then he handed Dave Peltz a paper bag and left the building. The teller began placing stacks of bills into the bag, and while she did so, Nelson stood on the sidewalk with his nose pressed to the bank's plate-glass window like a dog.

When Peltz exited carrying the bag, Nelson accepted it. Then he and Jesse Blue rode the South Shore Line to Chicago and went to the Pullman Bank on West 115th Street. Nelson was worried his money could be seized if the IRS audited him or one of the lawyers to whom he was indebted sued him, so he rented a safety deposit box and placed the cash inside. Then he gave Blue one of the two keys the bank provided, and said, If something happens to me, make sure my mother gets this money.

Nelson had been cautious with his windfalls in the past, but not that year. For the first time since 1933, he wasn't writing a book or planning to, so he allowed Lebworth's money to trickle through his fingers at a steady rate. He used some to pay down his debts, and some to buy an unremarkable racehorse named Jellious Widow.* He purchased an apartment building in Chicago and then resold it at a loss when he realized he didn't want to be a landlord, and he lost a bit at the track, and a bit playing poker.

N elson's depression dragged on for more than a year, and as it did, disturbing stories about his behavior circulated. Someone said they spotted Nelson walking around Chicago, sweating and glancing furtively over his shoulder. A friend reported that they rode the train to Gary for a visit, and found him hiding in the bushes because he was scared to step into the lights on the platform. And Amanda claimed that he dropped by her house when he learned she was returning to California, searched her shelves to make sure she didn't have any of his books, and left without saying a proper goodbye.

For months at a stretch, Nelson did, and wrote, very little, but then, seemingly out of nowhere, *Sports Illustrated* asked him to cover the 1958 Kentucky Derby. It was the first prestigious magazine assignment to come his way since 1950, so he accepted. It was an honor just to be asked. William Faulkner had been commissioned for the same assignment three years earlier, and another Pulitzer Prize winner named J. P. Marquand got the job after him.

---

* The horse is often referred to as Jealous Widow, but in racetrack programs the name was spelled Jellious Widow.

Nelson arrived a week before the race at the house *Sports Illustrated* had rented for the occasion, and brought Jesse Blue with him. An editor named Whitney Tower welcomed them and handed them keys and press passes. When Blue received his, he said, "This may be one of the nicest things that has ever happened to me."

Tower saw little of Nelson or Blue afterward. They spent their mornings trackside, watching the horses and jockeys warm up. Blue napped in the afternoons while Nelson wrote, and at night they explored the local bar scene.

On May 3, a three-year-old colt named Tim Tam won the Derby, and Nelson stayed up late polishing his story. The assignment had enlivened him, and after being out of print for so long, it seemed he was eager to impress. He boarded a plane the next morning with his manuscript, and then personally delivered it to the offices of *Sports Illustrated*.

The text Nelson submitted that day was distinct from everything he had written before. The story, though putatively nonfiction, features a protagonist named Nelson Algren who is more sarcastic, droll, and bumbling than the real Nelson Algren. Much of what happens in the story is either fictitious or greatly exaggerated, and the subject—the Derby—is less important than the narrator's character and impressions.

"The first thing I did, of course, was to head for the Mint Julep concession," Nelson wrote, "where they are billed $1.35 a throw, and I was given a shot of gin to which something snagged from a lawnmower had been added. I could have gotten the same effect from two sticks of Wrigley's Juicy Fruit." Later in the story, Nelson claimed that a railing collapsed beneath his weight. "Whether the grandstand holds up until Derby Day or not is out of human hands," he says. "It's strictly up to the ants."

And the horse Nelson describes most lovingly was not the winner, but the twelfth-place finisher—a colt famous for lagging behind the pack, then breaking late. "Nothing comes easy to Silky Sullivan...," he wrote. "He has to make you feel the way you feel when you see the Happy New Year wino on the curb with snow in his hair and a bottle of Mogen David in his hand, beaming up at the promise of the New Year's first big bells—then looks down at the bottle broken on the curb and sees one missing from his hand. He gives you that outcast, nobody-loves-me-moment just long enough—then he starts his run, and who, that has ever run from behind the field, can be against a horse like that?"

Prose like that would become familiar to readers a decade later when authors began writing in a style eventually called New Journalism. "[I]n a different age of magazine writing," Whitney Tower said later, "it might have been a prizewinner." But the article was out of synch with what readers expected at the time, so *Sports Illustrated* killed it, it was never published, and Nelson added another indignity to the long list he had begun assembling in his mind a few years earlier.[*]

Ten days after Nelson filed his Kentucky Derby story, one of the three lawyers he hired in 1955 sued him for four thousand dollars. Nelson probably had enough cash remaining to settle the debt, but instead he sold his house and moved into a tiny apartment at 920 North Noble Street in Chicago.[†]

Nelson's new building faced St. Boniface Church—a touchstone of his writing—but his rooms were dank, cramped, and stunk of gas fumes and roach spray. This place, he told Max Geismar, is a "lightless cave off a loveless hall."

Nelson moved again in February 1959, and this time he chose a railroad flat on the third floor of 1958 West Evergreen Avenue—less than a block from the apartment he lived in when he wrote *Never Come Morning*. He was hoping the move would get him back in touch with

---

[*]   Sadly, only portions of this story survive. A piece of it is in Nelson's archive at Ohio State University, and a small portion not held by the archive appeared in a remembrance Whitney Tower wrote for *Sports Illustrated* in 1986.

[†]   Details here are hazy. It seems Nelson sold the house to a friend who was also a lawyer, and continued to have occasional access to it through the summer of 1961.

his roots, but he realized when he arrived that that wasn't possible—either he had changed too much or the city had; he was never sure which. I don't feel that I'm "coming back to anything," he told Geismar. "The Chicago I knew, the neighborhood I knew, is either gone or I'm not with it. I see the same neon signs I used to see but I don't see them the same. I just look, and that's it."

Part IV

WANDER YEARS

I was critical of him [Wright] for going, but he had to go.
He was happier [in Paris]. . . . I don't know, really,
if you'd call it running—I don't know. I don't feel I'd
want to judge a guy who goes to France or Mexico. I'm
not so confident that by staying here I'm doing the smart
thing at all. . . . Help yourself to the bourbon there.

—*Nelson Algren in an interview with Michael Edelstein
and Robert Lamb on April 4, 1962*

"No, No Novel"

(February 1959–July 1961)

Nelson at his work space inside his third-floor apartment
at 1958 West Evergreen Avenue.

Chicago History Museum, ICHi-068771; Stephen Deutch, photographer

I took three strong men only a bit more than two hours to move Nelson out of 920 North Noble Street and into his new apartment at 1958 West Evergreen. He didn't own much anymore—books and records, a typewriter, a metal bread box full of letters from Simone de Beauvoir, cardboard boxes stuffed with loose manuscript pages, and a large writing desk the movers managed to wedge so tightly into the hallway, it took them thirty minutes to get it unmoored.

When they were finished, the apartment was a mess, and Nelson began the long process of settling in. He bought a ladder, and used it to install a light fixture in the kitchen and to paint over his bedroom windows. He placed his desk in the front room so he could look toward Wicker Park while he worked, and he set a pair of rubber plants on it so they could catch the midday light. Then he arranged to have someone bypass his gas and electrical meters so he could avoid the cost of utilities, and hung pictures—one of Gerson changing a tire, and others of Beauvoir, Paula Bays, his high school basketball team, Dostoyevsky, Hemingway, and Joan Baez.

Then Nelson reordered his career. Once, he had been a zealot who placed his faith in literature above concern for money or status, but no more. Now he was a proud apostate who expected to be compensated for his labor. "No, no novel," he soon told a friend. "I'd as soon attempt that as I would to open a pizza joint on Chicago's Westside without getting protection first. My only chance of getting out of hock is to quit writing. You think that's too far-fetched but it's exactly how it has worked out. And anyhow, who for? I used to think it was for some vague assemblage called 'readers.' I used to think it was for some people named [Malcolm] Cowley and [Jean-Paul] Sartre and such too. But all that it turns out it is for is for" the lawyers who end up taking all the money.

Not writing a novel sounds like a ridiculous way for a renowned novelist to earn a living, but it worked out well for Nelson. The publishing industry had changed dramatically since Nelson last worked regularly, and with his agent's help, he took advantage of those changes.

Nelson's agent's name was Candida Donadio, and thanks to her, he was soon earning more from being a writer than he ever had by writing seriously. Over the course of the next few years, she found foreign publishers for Nelson's books, arranged for him to be paid handsomely to edit a collection of stories entitled *Nelson Algren's Own Book of Lonesome Monsters*, and had *Never Come Morning, The Neon Wilderness*, and *Chicago: City on the Make* reissued in new editions that generated more excitement than their initial releases. Pulp paperbacks—books that sold for as little as a quarter and paid authors pennies per copy—were being replaced by high-quality trade paperbacks by then, so Nelson's reissues sometimes went for several times their original price.*

Glossy magazines had also begun multiplying, and competing for writers by inflating their rates. They were called *The Dude, Gent, Coq, Rogue, Nugget, Cavalier*, and *Playboy*, and they were willing to pay Nelson more for an essay or a review than he had been advanced to write each of his first three books.† He wrote for all of them over the course of the next few years, and enjoyed both the money they paid him and the chance to boast that he never read the publications his work appeared in.

University writing programs were proliferating as well, and offering generous sums to authors willing to teach seminars and deliver speeches. Nelson could earn almost a year's rent by spending an afternoon on stage, and from that point forward, he accepted almost every offer he received and tried to put on a good show. When I appeared at the University of Washington, he told a friend, I "sucked and smiled and wheedled and lapped and meached and dandled and fondled and whinnied and altogether played it so winning and coy that I may get invited back next year."

---

* This point can't be overstated. The peak of Nelson's career—roughly, 1942–1956—coincided with the peak of the pulp paperback market, which meant that, early on, the sale of his books brought in a fraction of what they would have if they had been released later. He was paid well when his hardcovers sold, but almost nothing on his paperbacks. Nelson may have received only one thousand dollars for the first paperback edition of *Never Come Morning*, for instance, even though it sold a million copies. He received (by my rough estimate) about fifteen thousand dollars for the paperback edition of *A Walk on the Wild Side*, even though more than 1.2 million copies were printed. *The Neon Wilderness* sold at least 500,000 copies, and at least 120,000 copies of *The Jungle* (the edited version of *Somebody in Boots*) were printed, but it seems Nelson recieved only a few thousand dollars from the sale of these books.
† This is true both in absolute terms and when adjustments are made for inflation.

"A man who won't demean himself for a dollar," he added sarcastically, "is a phoney is my thinking, and I couldn't live with myself if I tried to keep my self-respect when opportunities to get rich . . . are so abundant."

Nelson also made a critical assessment of his social life and rearranged it. He stopped writing or speaking to Maxwell Geismar because every time he sent Geismar a lengthy missive, he received a postcard in return. He stopped speaking to the photographer Art Shay because he thought Shay had been using their friendship to advance his own career, and when he heard that Jack Conroy had made a disparaging remark about him during a speech, he stopped speaking to Conroy as well. Then he made new friends, and established a new routine for his days. He began visiting the Luxor Steam Baths on North Avenue every morning, and eating lunch at Louis Szathmary's Bakery restaurant on the Near North Side. He visited the YMCA to swim in the afternoons, and spent several nights a week at Jazz Ltd., where he became close to the manager, Ruth Reinhardt. And on Sundays, he visited his mother, Goldie, who was still living in the basement apartment on Lawrence Avenue that she had begun renting during the war. Their relationship had settled into an uneasy truce by then, and though they were never close, Nelson was a dutiful son. He had been paying her rent for years, and she cooked soup for him when he stopped by to express her gratitude.

Once the details of Nelson's personal life were settled, he began cultivating a public persona. His politics and his writing had once made him a social liability, but that was no longer true. Since Nelson last lived in Chicago, Joseph McCarthy had been sidelined by the Senate and then drank himself to death. Howard Rushmore had murdered his wife in the back seat of a taxi, and then shot himself in the head with the same .32 Colt he used on her. Louis Budenz had parted with his publisher and begun receding from public life, and blacklisted writers and actors were working again in Hollywood.

The Red Scare was over, or close to it, so Chicago's tastemakers welcomed Nelson home, and soon he was a mainstay on the cultural scene. His name began appearing in the *Tribune*'s gossip column, and he was on television and the radio more than ever before. Celebrities and well-known writers passing through town began feeling obliged to pay their respects to him, and before long, his hospitality was legend. Typically, he offered visitors guided tours of the remnants of skid row, and brought them to a North Clark Street bar frequented by hard-drinking members of the Menominee tribe. He challenged his guests to arm-wrestling matches, drank them under the table, and brought them to the Cook County Jail so they could touch the electric chair.

Nelson never forgot he was being embraced by people who spent years shunning him, though, and when he was in public, he adopted an arch, comic persona that suggested his disdain for Chicago's fair-weather regard. He regularly appeared at formal events dressed in a torn and threadbare sport coat, made jokes about the self-importance of his hosts, and pretended to be greatly flattered when people professed to admire his work. He wasn't above raising his voice in polite company, and he often wore a tie that lit up when he pushed a button concealed in his pocket.

Sometimes, people were offended by Nelson's act, and an interviewer once accused him of affecting a pose. "Your stance," he said, "is that of a clown and you are in absolute control as you do it."

"Well," Nelson replied, "I can't just stand there. I have to react. . . . And my way of reacting is by mockery. And if I mock myself, I assume that people around don't take themselves any more seriously than I do."

The State Department informed Nelson in the summer of 1959 that his passport application had been approved, after years of denials and at least half a dozen appeals. It provided no explanation for its decision.

Nelson was elated, and wrote to Beauvoir immediately to ask about the possibility of visiting Paris. They had been corresponding irregularly since *The Mandarins* was published. He wrote to her once in 1957, once in '58, and then once at the beginning of '59. He sounded nostalgic about the early days of their relationship in those letters, but also morose and depressed. His mood improved drastically after his passport application was approved, though, and Beauvoir thought he seemed excited about life—and her—again, and she in turn became excited by the prospect of seeing him.

Come, visit, she said. I live alone now. "So you could even be my guest, since my place is wide enough and you could have a little room of your own. Well, we'll see. What is really important is your coming." We can travel in my car, and I'll cook our meals, and "in our oldish way we'll be wonderfully happy together."

Beauvoir had been feeling politically isolated in France, and old and lethargic. She had aged out of the Paris literary scene, and had begun working at home, alone, instead of in the cafés, where she wrote her early books. She spent much of her time caring for Sartre, whose health was deteriorating, and she was losing intimates rapidly. Claude Lanzmann, her lover, was seeing another woman, and Boris Vian, her good friend, had just died of a heart attack. But the thought of seeing Nelson again enlivened her, and she arranged her schedule to accommodate a lengthy sojourn in her apartment, and weeks of traveling.

Nelson and Beauvoir were in touch several times to plan his visit, and in their correspondence they spoke intimately for the first time in years. She confessed that she thought their reunion might be awkward, and that she was worried he would no longer find her attractive. And he responded with tender reassurances and tokens of his affection—a leaf he had pressed between the pages of a book, cartoons snipped from the newspaper, and a box of books at Christmas.

Beauvoir was relieved by Nelson's enthusiasm at first, but then doubt crept up on her. The outlines of the trip were settled by the end of the year, but he wasn't supposed to arrive until March

1960, and while she waited, she became increasingly anxious about seeing him.

Nelson arrived at Beauvoir's apartment at 11 bis, rue Victor Schoelcher in mid-March and unpacked. She was in Cuba with Sartre and not due to return for more than a week, so he made himself at home. He placed his typewriter on her desk along with a stack of yellow paper, went out to buy imported American food, and spent days writing and listening to the records he brought—Charlie Parker, Mahalia Jackson, Big Bill Broonzy, and Bessie Smith.

It was a good time for Nelson, and he felt free and easy while he waited for Beauvoir. A musical version of *A Walk on the Wild Side* had been staged in St. Louis just before he left America, and he had arrived in London in time for a party celebrating the release of a new edition of *The Man with the Golden Arm*. He visited Ireland afterward and spent two days with the poet Brendan Behan, and when he reached Paris, he reconnected with friends and other expatriates living in the city and began writing the series of essays that eventually became his next book, *Who Lost an American?*

Beauvoir returned home on March 20, still nervous about seeing Nelson. She felt anxious when she rang the doorbell to her apartment, then more anxious when there was no answer. She rang it again, harder, and the door opened.

"You?" Nelson asked with surprise. He had been told her flight was arriving the following day, and he wasn't prepared to greet her.

They looked at each other then, for the first time in nine years. He had replaced his glasses with contacts, so his eyes were bare, but aside from that, she thought he hadn't aged since their last summer together in Gary. And she looked, to him, the same as she had when he first spotted her in the lobby of the Palmer House, pacing in her white coat with a copy of the *Partisan Review* in her hand.

After their reunion, Nelson and Beauvoir became lovers again and fell into their old habits. He called her Frenchy and she called him Crocodile. He told bawdy jokes to provoke her, and she grinned and wagged her finger in response—the one still encircled by the silver ring he gave her. Then she began leading him through the city on long walks—past her old apartment at rue de la Bûcherie, a flea market they visited in '49, and the Musée de l'Homme.

They traded stories for days. She told him about the trip she had just taken to Cuba, her time with Che Guevara, and the crowds that began following her after Fidel Castro announced that she and Sartre were friends of the Cuban revolution. And he told her about how much Chicago and America had changed. He said that their old apartment on Wabansia Avenue had been demolished, and a highway overpass and some apartment buildings had been built on the lot where they fell in love. The witch hunts directed by Congress have ended, he explained, but the cultural consensus that has followed them is no less stifling. "The arrogance of the respectable he found more intolerable than ever," she wrote later.

In the evenings, they went out to theaters where they listened to flamenco and sipped sangria, a bar where they drank akvavit from bottles sheathed in ice, a Senegalese restaurant where they tasted pineapple flambé, an arena where they watched a boxing exhibition, and a pleasure boat that carried them down the Seine.

At first, each of them pretended the other was the same person they had fallen in love with twelve years earlier—but slowly, each began to understand how much the other had changed.

Nelson saw Beauvoir more clearly with time. She was still trim and elegant, her hair was still dark, and her face had the same serious-but-not-severe expression when it was at rest. But there was something sad and lonesome about her that he had never noticed before. She had become a much more famous figure, but also a more private one. Her circle of friends was smaller, and she spent most of her time traveling, at home alone, or caring for Sartre. She was preoccupied with death because her friend Albert Camus had just been killed in a car crash, and instead of a grand feminist treatise, her major writing project was the third volume of her autobiography—*Force of Circumstance, I.*

Beauvoir also began to see Nelson more clearly with time, and the changes she noticed distressed her. The years that had passed since they were last together had not been as kind to him as they had been to her. His hair, which he ran his fingers through compulsively, was thinning. He was still wearing clothes she recognized from a decade earlier, but he had put on weight, so now his shirts strained across his belly. His eyes had lost their glint, and his mind had taken a bitter, obsessive turn.

Nelson had been a collector of other people's stories when he and Beauvoir were first close. He spoke in metaphor and parable, and his conversation overflowed with literary references, overheard dialogue, and apocryphal tales. He was a gifted storyteller who kept his own counsel on all serious matters, rarely spoke about himself, and never betrayed his weaknesses. But by the spring of 1960, he had become obsessed with the story of his own descent. After the elation of his reunion with Beauvoir passed, he began waking up angry and remaining angry for hours afterward. He played records to soothe himself, and incanted the names of the people and institutions that had taken advantage of him, and expounded on their misdeeds. The list was the same each day—Bob Roberts, Otto Preminger, the State Department, his lawyers, Ken McCormick, and Roger Straus.

"Once I used to live in America," he said, "now I live on American occupied territory." My country has become the status-obsessed, conformist place I feared it would become after the war, and "I've been eaten alive, made a sucker of, betrayed."

Beauvoir also felt like a stranger in her own country, so she could relate to Nelson's distress. "He had been promised one world and then found himself in quite a different one," she wrote later, "a world directly opposed to all his convictions and all his hopes." But being sympathetic to Nelson's troubles was not the same as being interested in hearing a fresh accounting of them each day. She listened to his complaints patiently for weeks, out of respect for their shared history, but eventually, she began making excuses to get away from the apartment so she could return to the work she had been neglecting since he arrived.

N elson left France in May without Beauvoir and flew to Mallorca, Spain, to attend a writers' conference that had been convened to establish a literary prize called the Prix Formentor. Then he went to Barcelona and explored the rooftops of the Barrio Chino, which were covered with shacks occupied by people who couldn't afford to live anywhere else.

Madrid was Nelson's next stop, and when he arrived, he visited the US embassy. The State Department had only granted him a temporary passport, and it had already expired. The embassy didn't have the authority to give Nelson an extension, so it cabled Washington, DC, for guidance, but Nelson didn't wait in Madrid long enough for their response to arrive.

Beauvoir joined Nelson in Madrid after a few days. They spent their first evening together drinking with a group of young intellectuals who opposed the rule of Francisco Franco—the general who had been ruling Spain since their civil war—and then they began to wander. They went to Seville, where employees from the US Consulate stopped Nelson in the lobby of their hotel and questioned him about his passport renewal. Then they continued on to Triana, where they visited a dance hall hung with paper wreaths and listened to a flamenco singer's lament.

They got a car in Malaga and drove to Torremolinos where white-washed buildings with tile roofs climbed the hills at the edge of town. Then they drifted farther—to Almeria, where Nelson took pictures of a troglodytic village that had been built into the cliffs outside the city, then Granada, and finally the Alhambra.

N elson and Beauvoir returned to Paris at the end of May so that Nelson could prepare for his trip home, but when they arrived, he learned that his passport extension had been granted. He had been trying to escape America for almost a decade and couldn't face the idea of returning earlier than necessary, so he decided to remain in Europe through the summer. Beauvoir said he could stay with her, but made no promises about how often they would see each other.

The next few months, the last Beauvoir and Nelson spent together, were a sad coda to their long romance. She was more influential than ever, and her greatest challenge was dividing her time between her personal, political, and literary obligations—articles, books, protesting France's occupation of Algeria, and Sartre. Nelson was marginalized and directionless—a fifty-one-year-old man living in self-imposed exile. He spent his days alone for the most part, contriving excuses to see Beauvoir and writing magazine articles about his time in Europe that he used as opportunities to mock himself. "I can assure you that, at one time, I was well read," he wrote. "But that was before I consciously set forth on a course of knowing less and less, especially about literature."

In July, Nelson and Beauvoir left Paris and set off on a second vacation—to Marseille, where they discussed the Cuban revolution; to Istanbul, where they drank coffee in an outdoor café; and then on to Athens, a fishing port called Heraklion, and Crete.

They returned to Paris in August, and then it was finally time for them to say goodbye. Beauvoir was scheduled to fly to Brazil and then Cuba, and Nelson was planning to return to America while she was gone.

Beauvoir felt content when they parted. "Not a single shadow of disagreement had troubled our five months together," she wrote later. She didn't feel "nostalgia." She felt his visit had "completed" their relationship.

But Nelson's emotions were more complicated—tinged by regret, longing, and lonesomeness. Once, he told Beauvoir that he had taken a long walk by himself and ended up near her old apartment without intending to—"As if my body hadn't given up the past," he said.

"Was it so much better, the past?" She asked.

"When I was forty," he said, "I didn't realize I was forty; everything was beginning!"

After she left, he lingered at her apartment alone for several weeks, writing, and once drinking so heavily, her friends had to carry him home and put him in bed. When it was time for him to return to America, he cleaned her apartment and placed a small pile of cash where she would see it to compensate her for some of the time he lived there.

When Beauvoir returned from her trip, she found a stack of mail with Nelson's name on it, a few magazines, and a candy bar he forgot to throw away, but nothing else—no note, no books, no love poem. A friend of hers had visited the apartment while it was empty and pocketed the cash Nelson left, so not even that small token remained to remind her of their summer together. They never saw each other again.

Nelson arrived in Chicago in mid-September to attend a book signing at the Marshall Field & Company department store. The event had been organized to promote the release of a new edition of *The Neon Wilderness*, and when it ended, Nelson secluded himself inside his apartment so he could focus on the collection of travel essays he had begun writing in Paris. For the next ten months, he did little else.

The travelogue Nelson produced in that time was released in May 1963 as *Who Lost an American?*, and it is distinct from everything he had published in the past. Like the essay he wrote for *Sports Illustrated* in 1958, it's comic, and satirical, and blends fact and fiction—but unlike that earlier work, it is also bitter, vengeful, self-pitying, and wildly uneven.

The book begins with a fictional account of Nelson being evicted from his home after failing to pay his legal bills, and fleeing from the sheriff who served him papers. "Excusing myself," he wrote, "I rolled my stamp collection into my G.I. blanket, mounted my British lightweight bicycle made in Dusseldorf and, with the cry of 'Sink the Bismarck!' broke through the cordon and sped swiftly down the Indiana Turnpike till I came to a tollway."

The story shifts to New York City, where Nelson attends a literary party filled with fictionalized stand-ins for all the people who, he felt, had wronged him. Roger Straus makes an appearance as "Trustworthy Ex-Naval-Eye Roger Blueblade," and Farrar, Straus & Cudahy becomes "Blueblade, Suckingwise, Scalpel & Tourniquet, Trustworthy Publishers." Ken McCormick appears as "Kenwood McCowardly" of "Doubledeal & Wunshot." The literary critic Alfred Kazin transforms into "Alfred Paperfish, Leading Footnote King." Elizabeth Ingersoll, Nelson's former agent, becomes a lush named "Ginny Ginstruck." Norman Mailer is "Norman Manlifellow," author of *Look, Ma, My Fly Is Open*, and James Baldwin makes an appearance as "Giovanni Johnson," an offensive caricature of a gay man who prances instead of walking, and speaks with a lisp.* The chapter ends with Mailer pinching Baldwin's ass and then running from the party into Central Park. Nelson then boards a ship and sails for Europe alone.

Who Lost an American? follows Nelson across the ocean, and when it does, the writing improves dramatically. The book was dedicated to Simone de Beauvoir when it was published, and the portions of the text Nelson spends discussing her career and their common friends are among the best.

Juliette Gréco, a singer I met in 1949, Nelson wrote, was "a woman who had been made by times in which there had been no hours to spare to pretension." Marcel Mouloudji "emerged from the kind of winter that war makes upon children, one when the only heat in Paris was that of the

---

* Most of these references make sense in the context of Nelson's life, but Mailer and Baldwin require explanation. Mailer made it into the book because he insulted Nelson in *Advertisements for Myself*. Baldwin is a more complicated story. Nelson gave Baldwin's first book one of its first good reviews, and he later visited Baldwin—bearing a signed copy of *Chicago: City on the Make*—and tried to befriend him. The visit ended badly. Baldwin accused Nelson of trading on Richard Wright's name, and they ended up shouting at each other. Though by no means a virulent homophobe, Nelson was, unfortunately, not above trading in homophobic stereotypes as a means of insulting Baldwin. To complicate things further, Nelson later said Baldwin was one of the best writers of his generation, and quoted him frequently.

café." Jean-Paul Sartre was "dangerous because of his total commitment to the nature of man and his opposition to formal assaults, from left or right, upon the nature of man." Beauvoir was ridiculed for her political positions in 1949, Nelson wrote, but by 1960, "[s]he had broken through the defenses of the bourgeoisie, of the church, the businessmen, the right-wing defenders of Napoleonic glory, and the hired press. She was, at once, the most hated and the most loved woman in France. It had become plain: she *meant* it."

The book's narrative progresses in the same order as Nelson's travels, and as it does, it continues to toggle between passages of earnest commentary, and mawkish and self-pitying sections that muddle their effect. After having suffered so much for honest writing, it seems Nelson had developed a compositional tic—after penning a line of insightful prose, he felt compelled to undercut himself immediately. "Any challenge to laws made by people on top, in the interest of people below, is literature," he wrote on one page. Then, four paragraphs later, he announced, "I am no better informed on Spanish literature than on American, my entire library consisting of the works of Max Shulman."*

The last four chapters of the book are set in Chicago and contain a brief history of the city that begins with Nelson's childhood and advances to the present day—a time when Hugh Hefner dominates headlines and the city has become "a middleman in business-blues who has one daiquiri before dinner and the filet better be just as he ordered it or somebody is going to catch hell." There are bright spots in these chapters as well—moments of insight and thoughtful critique— but the book's cynical tone overshadows them. And as a result, it's difficult, when you compare the book to Nelson's earlier work, to feel anything other than the sentiment that so obviously dominated his thoughts while he wrote it: disappointment.

Who Lost an American? is interesting for several reasons. It cleanly divides Nelson's career into phases—the first, defined by earnestness

---

* Shulman was a humorist who wrote for television, as well as novels and short stories.

and an evangelical zeal for truth telling; and the second, in which he called himself a journalist and insisted the written word was powerless in the American Century. It was born out of a desire to experiment, and the conviction that fiction writing had become too restricted by the biases of professional critics to allow for experimentation. And it anticipates many of the stylistic changes that would soon become commonplace in nonfiction writing: the sarcastic tone, the mesh of fact and fiction, and the exaggerated incompetence of the narrator.

But that's not the same as saying it's a good book, and when it was released, not a single reviewer claimed it was. Nelson is a great writer, the *Tribune* said, "But it doesn't necessarily follow that everything he writes will be great." The *Times* said the same: "It would be fine to discover him working once again on people whom he could feel in his blood and within an action that might carry his special melody." Most insightfully, a reviewer for *The Reporter* wrote: "[Caught] between his own past, in which a deep identification with the social outcast and the working class was all but inseparable from his sense of literary vocation, and the present, in which money seems to brutalize equally those who have too much and those who have too little, Algren seems to have lost all sense of what useful literary tasks might remain open to him."

Nelson visited his mother, Goldie, in July 1961, just before he completed his manuscript.* She was living in a nursing home at the time, and had been for the past four months. Her doctors had been expecting her to die since the beginning of the year, and though she had outlasted their best predictions, it was clear she wouldn't continue doing so for much longer.

Nelson sat down when he arrived, lit a cigarette, and looked at his

---

* Macmillan, the book's publisher, requested changes to the manuscript, so it wasn't finalized until June 1962, but Nelson's correspondence shows he considered it complete in early August 1961.

mother. They had never had a good feeling for each other. She was all rules, modest ambition, and respectability, and he was late nights, big ideas, and irreverence. But no matter their differences, they were still mother and son, and at the end, each was all the other had left. Nelson's sister Irene had died the year before while he was in Europe.

"Give me one," Goldie said, meaning a cigarette.

"No, you don't want to smoke, Ma, do you?" Nelson asked. Goldie had smoked one cigarette in her life, maybe two.

"Well," she said, "I have to do *something.*"

They sat there together for a while, smoking, and attendants from the rest home gathered nearby to watch. They had barely seen Goldie move in weeks. Then there was a murmur in the room, maybe something moving through the pipes in the walls, and Goldie looked at Nelson and said, "Voices are coming up from below."

"But she said it in this rhythm, with a certain rhythm to it that surprised me very much," Nelson said later. "I was surprised that she should put her last strength into trying to make a poem."

Goldie died the next day.

A Character Named
Nelson Algren

(August 1961–June 1964)

Nelson playing poker in 1962. Chicago History Museum, ICHi-019379;
Stephen Deutch, photographer

S omeone was cheating. Nelson was certain of it. It was a Friday
night in the middle of June 1962, and he was seated at a table with
his old friends Dave Peltz and Studs Terkel, an acquaintance named
Francis Moretti, and someone he knew only by the nom de guerre
Big Injun. There was a pile of cash between them, and each man was
clutching a fistful of playing cards.

Nelson had been hosting a weekly poker game in the back room of his apartment since he returned to Chicago. A real estate and insurance agent named Ted Kozlowski played regularly, and so did Peltz, Terkel, a local television director named Billy Friedkin, and a handful of other men.* The pots for each hand were often large, and Nelson took a cut of each one because he hosted the game and often dealt. The percentage he collected usually guaranteed him a profit, but lately he had been losing money.

Nelson scrutinized the players. He watched their facial expressions and kept track of how they bet and when they folded, and before morning, he was convinced Big Injun and Moretti were the cheaters. Injun was Moretti's bodyguard, so they always arrived and left together, and that night, at least, their play seemed synchronized—when one of them lost a hand, he usually lost to the other so that, collectively, they took in the majority of the money being wagered.

The game dragged on past midnight and into Saturday—4 a.m., 5 a.m., and then through dawn. The players rose from their chairs around six or seven in the morning and settled up. Peltz and Studs each gave Moretti a check to cover their losses. Then everyone left.

Dave Peltz reached his house in Gary around 8 a.m., tired and eager to get to sleep, but his phone rang before he could lie down.

It was Nelson. "Dave," he said, "stop payment on that fuckin' check."

"Why?" Peltz asked.

"Because Francis and Big Injun were playing out of each other's pocket." I'm going to tell Studs to cancel his check too, Nelson said. "I'm tired of that shit and I think they've been playing out of each other's pocket and that's why they've been taking down all the fucking money."

Peltz hadn't noticed anything suspicious, but he went along with Nelson and cancelled the check—a dangerous move. Moretti was a loan

---

* Friedkin later became famous as the director of *The French Connection*, *The Exorcist*, and *To Live and Die in L.A.* (among others), but at the time he was working for television station WGN.

shark with a reputation for toughness—not a man to be toyed with. His brother was a former Chicago police officer who had been convicted of murder after drunkenly shooting three unarmed men in a parking lot—killing two of them, and wounding the third. Moretti had been supporting the whole family since, so he couldn't afford to let Nelson malign him, or allow Peltz and Terkel to walk away from their debts. He paid Big Injun to ensure that such things never happened, and it was understood he would get his money one way or another.

Nelson stayed close to home after he called Peltz, and whenever he heard someone banging on the downstairs door, he stepped into the hall carrying a baseball bat. He spoke to Moretti on the phone and said they should get together and talk about their dispute, but not right away.

I'm leaving town, Nelson said. Let's meet in October.

Moretti threatened Nelson with torture, and when Nelson dared him to try, Moretti threatened Peltz too.

About two weeks after the poker game, Peltz was asleep on his living room couch in the middle of the night when a cement block crashed through the window near his head. Then he heard another crash, and rushed into the bedroom to check on his wife. There, he saw a second cement block resting on the floor, surrounded by a spray of shattered glass. He ran outside and looked into the dark, but all he heard was the sound of Big Injun's feet slapping the pavement as he ran away.

Maybe half an hour later, the phone rang. Peltz answered and heard Moretti's voice. "Pay up, you cocksucker, or get killed," he said. Then he hung up.

Peltz drove into Chicago that Sunday and parked outside the Russian and Turkish Baths on Division Street. He had been in touch with Moretti after receiving that threatening phone call and arranged to meet him. Moretti pulled up in a Lincoln Continental, parked across the street, opened the trunk, and removed two baseball bats. Holding one in each hand, he called to Peltz. "Are you alone?"

"Yeah, I'm alone," Peltz said.

Moretti threw the bats back in his trunk and crossed the street. He handed Peltz the cancelled check, and then they went inside the baths and gave each other *platzas*. When they were finished and their clothes were back on, Peltz gave Moretti the money he owed him, and Moretti insisted he never cheated.

The problem with you and Nelson is that you "don't understand the game," he said. "You don't understand mathematics. You don't understand percentages. You don't understand averages." Then he lamented the end of Nelson's poker night. "I had a good, sweet thing there," he said. "Maybe I won too much. Maybe I should have given a little bit back, especially to Nelson." If I had, "he'd have kept the game alive."

"OK," Peltz said. "I'm ready to go home."

"You ain't going home," Moretti said.

"Where am I going?" Peltz asked.

"You're going with me, and we're going to spend this $250. We're going to drink this fucking money up, every dime."

And they did. They spent the remainder of the day drifting from one bar to the next, bonding, and talking about what a horrible poker player Nelson was. Nelson would have been offended if he heard them, but by then, he was on a freighter bobbing across the Pacific Ocean.[*]

The *Malaysia Mail* pulled away from its dock in the port of Seattle in late June and made a sound like "its rusty heart would break," Nelson told a friend. Once it was floating free, it powered north through Elliott Bay, then west through the Strait of Juan de Fuca, and into the open ocean. It entered a bank of fog near the Aleutian Islands that obliter-

---

[*] Keen-eyed readers might recognize that these events resemble a scene in Saul Bellow's novel *Humboldt's Gift*—there's a reason for that. Dave Peltz was a friend of Bellow's, and after he met with Moretti, he described the experience in a letter to Bellow. Later, Bellow wrote a fictionalized version of the events into *Humboldt's Gift*. In the book, Peltz is a character named George Swiebel and Moretti is Rinaldo Cantabile. For a discussion of the conflict Bellow's appropriation created with Peltz, see James Atlas's *Bellow: A Biography*.

ated the skyline for days, and before it emerged, the sounds emanating from the hull had become less worrisome—more a "low grieving" moan than a death rattle, Nelson said.

The *Mail* was a tramp steamer that operated on no fixed schedule and made no accommodations for comfort. There was a common mess hall, small cabins, and a laundry room where everyone washed their own clothes. The crew was experienced, gruff, and taciturn. Some had no home on land in any country, no family, and no reason to ever stop sailing. There were only two passengers on board. One was a Chinese woman heading for Hong Kong to visit relatives. Nelson was the other.

The *Malaysia Mail* was expected to drop anchor in South Korea first, but not before it spent a week on the open ocean. Nelson peered at the endless horizon during those first days, played cards with the crew, read, and tapped the keys of his typewriter.

There was a stack of books, magazines, and journals in Nelson's cabin, and Ernest Hemingway was either the author or the subject of nearly every one of them. He had killed himself the year before, and critics had been steadily turning out critical reappraisals of his career ever since. Many of the same men who attacked *A Walk on the Wild Side* were trying to diminish Hemingway's influence, and Nelson was greatly offended by their efforts. Their true purpose, he believed, was to reframe American literature as an essentially academic pursuit—more concerned with structure, symbolism, and style than what he sometimes called "the things of the earth."

Nelson also saw opportunity in Hemingway's death—but unlike most critics, he wanted to assert the importance of Hemingway's work. He was planning to spend his time on the *Malaysia Mail* writing a long essay that claimed Hemingway deserved a place in the canon, and that added nuance to the common perception that he was just an alpha male—a man on the cover of *Look* magazine, one hand resting on the body of the leopard he had just shot, the other on his rifle. That's not Hemingway at all, Nelson soon wrote. In truth, he was a "broken" man who had seen more loss of life than anyone should have to, and in his writing, "the whole buried burden of American guilt, the self-destructiveness of a people who felt their lives were being lived by somebody else, found expression."

Nelson had tried to do something similar for Richard Wright, though on a smaller scale. Wright died a few months before Hemingway, and afterward Nelson wrote a touching remembrance that made a claim for the enduring importance of his work. Wright "came to Chicago because there was no other place for him to go," Nelson wrote. "He came as a stranger, lived as a stranger, and he left without looking back. . . . Yet his impact on Chicago has been more enduring than that of any merchant prince, Mayor, or newspaper owner. For his impact was upon the city's conscience; and therefore upon the conscience of humanity.

"His voice," Nelson wrote, "opened a wedge for the inarticulate of the world, both black and white."

Nelson continued to reference Wright and Hemingway as examples of what a writer should be for the remainder of his career, and though he never said so directly, his defense of their work was a defense of his own as well. He had begun to worry about his legacy, and he knew that asserting the importance of writing that speaks for the "inarticulate of the world" and gives expression to "the whole buried burden of American guilt" was one way of arguing for the importance of his own books.

Nelson hoped the forced seclusion of life at sea would motivate him to work on his Hemingway essay, but that wasn't the primary reason he booked passage on the *Malaysia Mail*. Mostly, he did so just because he could. He had no long-term writing projects tying him to Chicago, and the only woman he was seeing at the time was a twenty-five-year-old named Madeleine Gobeil, who lived in Canada. He no longer had to care for Goldie, either, and so traveling was becoming a regular part of his life. In the nine months since his mother died, he had been to Michigan, Washington, Florida, and New York, and at some point after that last trip, he decided to visit Asia, "simply," he said, because he "didn't have any experience in going."

The *Malaysia Mail* dropped anchor for the first time in the Choryang-dong port in Busan, South Korea, and Nelson went onshore and wandered the streets near the waterfront. The smell of kimchi permeated the town, he noticed, but America's influence could be felt everywhere. It was common to see people wearing hand-me-down army fatigues, and all the street vendors pretended they were selling branded products—they put handmade soap in used Palmolive wrappers, every candy was called Baby Ruth, and cigarette stubs came in wrinkled Chesterfield packs.

Nelson followed a member of the ship's crew through Kowloon when they reached Hong Kong, and watched him buy transistors that he planned to resell at a profit on the black market. In Bombay, Nelson explored the city until he found the Kamathipura district, where young prostitutes solicited johns from behind the bars of street-facing cages. He began interviewing them, and continued to do so until the ship returned to the sea and sailed for Singapore.

The *Malaysia Mail* docked in Calcutta in September, and by then, Nelson had become preoccupied with the ship and its crew. He had been fascinated by them at first, but after more than two months of forced intimacy, their attitude toward the people they traded with had begun to disgust him. Every time the ship docked, he said later, the crew was inundated by peddlers and prostitutes, and over time, they had begun to believe they were virtuous simply because they had money to spend.

Once, Nelson explained, the *Malaysia Mail* was greeted by a madam piloting a small boat loaded with women when it pulled into a port in the Philippines. "When a ship doesn't dock here for a month," she said, "we have to sell our clothes."

"Their lives depend on the crew," Nelson said, "so the crew is too used to having it their own way. . . . I think this is why I say the ship represents in a way what is wrong with the United States because in our dealings with a lot of the smaller countries they can't say no. Underneath that is a lot of resentment toward Americans."

The *Malaysia Mail* made a second stop in Singapore after it left the Philippines, and then headed back toward the American coast. Nelson had been at sea for more than three months by then, and he was sick of the crew, but he still faced the last leg of the trip—two weeks of nothing but "unrelieved" tedium.

The ship reached the port of Los Angeles in late September, and soon afterward Nelson returned to Chicago with an unfinished essay and a stack of notes from his travels. There was no one waiting to greet him when he got home, and nothing but a stack of newspapers leaning against his apartment door to show he had been gone. He looked at his wall calendar when he entered his apartment, and noticed it hadn't been changed since February.

Nelson worked on his Hemingway essay through the fall and winter. He told an interviewer for the *Chicago Daily News*, "Creative writing is dead. There is no one today to replace Faulkner and Hemingway, not even James Baldwin or Joseph Heller." And then he went east in the spring of 1963 to promote the publication of *Who Lost an American?*, visit friends, and sit down with a writer named Harold Edward Francis Donohue.

Donohue went by H.E.F., or just "Shag," and he was thirty-nine years old and married with three children. His dark hair was receding, like Nelson's, and he wore thick-framed glasses and a thin mustache. He had been raised in New Jersey, but later spent about a decade in Chicago, working and going to college, and while he was there, he fell in love with Nelson's work. He was a freelance journalist, a short-story writer, and the author of an as-yet-unpublished novel called *The Higher Animals*—but his major project that spring was interviewing Nelson.

Donohue first stumbled on the idea of meeting with Nelson in early 1962, when the film version of *A Walk on the Wild Side* reached theaters. The lead roles were being played by major stars—Jane Fonda, Barbara Stanwyck, and Laurence Harvey—but the film's promotional materials made no mention of the fact that it was based on one of Nelson's novels, and Donohue heard that Nelson had disavowed the film and didn't stand to benefit from it financially.

If that's true, it would make a good article, Donohue thought, so he reached out to Nelson through Candida Donadio—his agent, as well as Nelson's—and she put them in touch.

Nelson agreed to tell Donohue about his experiences with Hollywood, but when they met for their first interview, they ended up talking for two straight days. They agreed to remain in touch afterward, and eventually Donadio suggested that they turn their discussions into a book, and she sold the idea to the publisher Hill & Wang.

By the time Nelson visited New York in the spring of 1963, he and Donohue had already met ten times and corresponded extensively. They spoke in Donohue's den, with a tape recorder running, three more times before Nelson returned to Chicago, and afterward, there was nothing left to do but transcribe, edit, and arrange their material.

The product of their collaboration was released the following year as *Conversations with Nelson Algren*. It was later reprinted as a paperback by Berkley Medallion, and then again by the University of Chicago Press. Over the past several decades, nearly seventy thousand copies have been printed and it has become the primary source for most of the biographical writing about Nelson.[*] Donohue claims, in an afterword to the first edition, that the book is so comprehensive, it should have been released

---

[*] Donohue provided this estimate. He claimed the book's initial run was fifteen hundred, and that the Berkley Medallion edition was sixty thousand copies. The University of Chicago edition brings the total close to seventy thousand.

with the subtitle *Notes toward a Biography*. But that claim is misleading because, in truth, the book contains quite a bit of fiction.

When Nelson began meeting with Donohue, he recognized their interviews as another opportunity to shape his legacy, so when he told the story of his life and career, he distorted his history to create a character that resembles the one he had begun writing into his nonfiction—a wilder, coarser, less disciplined, and more callous version of the real Nelson Algren.

"My mother had a candy store," Nelson began truthfully. My father "was a machinist. He worked at the screw works." Then Nelson explained that, though most people believed he was Polish, he was really a Swede, and that his father's father had been the first member of the family to emigrate from Europe.

Then Nelson told Donohue the story of Isaac. He explained that his grandfather had been born in Stockholm, converted to Judaism, traveled through America, and spent time in Jerusalem—and as he did, he placed the greatest emphasis on the wildness of Isaac's character, the sincerity of his faith, and the depth of the depression he fell into when he lost it. "He decided to take the Old Testament at its literal truth," Nelson said—no one was "orthodox enough for him." But eventually, his God failed, and he told his family, "There is no truth, there is no religion, no truth. It is all nothing."

The arc of Isaac's life, by Nelson's account, strongly resembles the arc of his own—a point he hints at repeatedly. "I've always felt much closer to . . . this grandfather" than I did to my father, he said. When I became interested in socialism, he said, "I was repeating my grandfather's life in a way." To make their connection clearer still, Nelson altered the timing of Isaac's death. "I was in high school" when my parents "got word" that he died, Nelson claimed. When in fact, Isaac passed away at least a decade before Nelson was born.*

---

* Nelson's claims about Isaac's death have always been reported as fact, and because it is difficult to verify (or disprove) events that happened almost a cen-

Nelson's decision to link his own story so closely to his grand-father's has tantalizing implications. It suggests that Nelson saw his political convictions and faith in literature as almost religious experiences, that their loss was a kind of death, and that he felt so abashed by the earnestness of his early years that he was most comfortable speaking about them in parable, using his grandfather as a stand-in.

The remainder of the biographical material Nelson provided reinforces those impressions, because when Nelson began telling the story of his own life, he minimized his intellect, his courage, his ambition, and his stature. By his account, he had always been an archetype of early-twentieth-century working-class masculinity —a solitary creature who rarely applied himself and therefore couldn't be disappointed by the recent trajectory of his career.

"I flunked everything in high school," Nelson claimed. "It took me five years before I could get out." He discussed his time on the road after college, and becoming a writer, without mentioning the John Reed Club, and he denied being a former member of the Communist Party. He did admit to being involved with the Communist movement, but dated his activity to the start of the Spanish Civil War—several years after he was first involved.

I goofed off all the time when I was in the army, Nelson claimed. "At first I was certainly content to stay stateside," he said, without

---

tury ago, I should acknowledge that I may be mistaken. That said, it seems unlikely. A census taker recorded in 1880 that Isaac was 60 years old that summer—meaning he was born around 1820, and he would have been about 103 years old when Nelson entered high school. Additionally, Jette Abraham began listing herself as a widow on the census in 1900—nine years before Nelson was born—and continued doing so for the remainder of her life. There's also the fact that Nelson was named for his grandfather—Isaac was born Nils Ahlgren—and by tradition, Jewish families name their children in honor of deceased relatives, *not* living ones.

mentioning his requests to be sent overseas, or the disappointment he experienced when they were denied.

About the McCarthy period, Nelson said only, "I didn't really do much." He didn't mention slighting Louis Budenz and Howard Rushmore in *The Man with the Golden Arm*, raising money for the Hollywood Ten, the political essay Doubleday refused to publish, or the subpoena he received from the House Un-American Activities Committee. He couldn't deny the work he did for the Rosenberg Committee, because it had been widely reported, but he minimized his contributions by saying, "All I did was lose my passport."

Many writers would have seen a book-length interview as a forum for self-aggrandizement, but Nelson did not. Instead, he referred to himself as a "loser" and insisted that he was not a novelist. "I consider myself a free-lance journalist," he said.*

Collectively, Nelson's fabrications, elisions, and diminishments obscure some of the greatest disappointments of his life: the failure of the political movement to which he dedicated himself in his twenties, the fact that he never saw combat in the war, his victimization during the Red Scare, the foreshortening of his career and his inability to regain his former renown, and, most poignantly, the fact that his relationship with Simone de Beauvoir never became what he wanted it to be.

The volume of Beauvoir's autobiography that covers the postwar period had been published by the time Nelson and Donohue concluded their interviews, and in it, she discusses her relationship with Nelson in great detail. In that book, she presents Nelson as a charming, intelligent, and loving man—but also vulnerable, and hurt by her ambiva-

---

* There has long been some question about whether these fabrications can be attributed to transcription error, or confusion on Donohue's part. That question can now be answered. Hill & Wang was eventually purchased by Farrar, Straus & Giroux, and they later transferred Hill & Wang's archives to the New York Public Library. A review of those records shows that Nelson read and approved Donohue's entire manuscript before publication.

lence toward him. Nelson felt the book was an even greater violation of his trust than *The Mandarins* had been, and from that point forward, he downplayed Beauvoir's importance in his life in every forum available, insulted her writing, demeaned her, and consequently, made himself seem shallow and sexist.

Our relationship "assumed the secondary status of the female in relation to the male," Nelson told Donohue. Beauvoir, he claimed, "is a rather puritanical woman. She understood that in the relationship between a man and a woman the man is the dominant factor specifically."*

The most engaging sections of *Conversations with Nelson Algren* are the portions dedicated to Nelson's ideas about politics and literature. In them, he comes across as an independent, irreverent, and rebellious thinker—if sometimes offensive by the standards of later generations.

Nelson championed the civil rights movement in the South as "the only movement that goes against the trend toward the right . . . the only movement that sustains the old American radical tradition, sustains the original idea of the country." But he dismissed the Nation of Islam and Malcolm X because they were offering, to his mind, a conservative version of resistance—"No jazz, no joy, and no juice, no smoking, no drinking, no gambling," he said. "It's a horror."

Nelson accused America of being an "Imperialist son-of-a-bitch" as well, proclaimed himself an atheist, said he reserved the right to be a Communist one day and an anarchist the next, and endorsed interracial marriage. If I had my way, he said, "I'd mix things up as much as possible—I mean racially." But he also betrayed some homophobia.

---

* The irony here, of course, is that one of the first things that attracted Beauvoir to Nelson was the fact that he treated her like an equal at a point when Sartre and his cohort did not.

When pressed by Donohue, he said, "I prefer masculinity in writing, simply because it's stronger. And I like a country to be masculine. It's a weakening thing. I'm not talking about morality. I'm talking about the kind of thinking that goes with homosexuality—it is a very inferior kind of thinking because it's a very cold way of thinking."

Nelson also provided Donohue with a provocative definition of American literature that broke with his earlier attempts to define the institution. Though still focused on advocating for society's outcasts, he claimed that literature is not the sole purview of authors—it is any defiant utterance or act meant to challenge the powerful.

American literature, Nelson said, "is the woman in the courtroom who, finding herself undefended on a charge, asked, 'Isn't anybody on my side?'" It's also "the fifteen-year-old who, after he had stabbed somebody, said, 'Put me in the electric chair—my mother can watch me burn.'" And it's the "thirty-five-year-old Negro who told me recently, 'The only times I ever felt human is when I've been in jail.' The other times he's been on guard, on guard day and night."*

"I think American literature consists of these people," Nelson said. "It doesn't consist of the, of the contrivers of literature who, after a certain number of years on campus, are entitled to grow a beard to look like Hemingway although they opposed Hemingway all the time he was alive."

*C*onversations with Nelson Algren was published in October 1964, and with its release, Nelson acquired a public persona that was both misleading and enduring. For the remainder of his life, and for decades afterward, he was the man he presented himself to be in that book—a

---

*   During this period, Nelson wrote two other definitions of literature that echo this idea. In the first, written in 1961, he argues: "I submit that literature is made upon any occasion that a challenge is put to the legal apparatus by conscience in touch with humanity." The second, written around the same time, reads: "Any challenge to laws made by people on top, in the interest of people below, is literature."

shallower, tougher, more careless, more misogynistic, less ideological, and less intellectual person than he had ever truly been.

The book received spare, but positive reviews. A writer for the *New York Times* called it an "extraordinary book." The *Chicago Daily News* said it was a "totally delightful, irreverent, mad, sensible, acid, hilarious talkathon." The *Tribune* proclaimed it "a remarkably lively document, less ordered and selective yet enormously more revealing than a formal biography or an essay in critical evaluation."

Nelson appreciated the attention the book received, but as always, he cared most about the judgments of other writers. Of all the notes generated by the book's release, he saved only one: a letter Candida Donadio had received from one of her youngest clients and forwarded to Nelson. That writer's name was Thomas Pynchon, and his letter reads: "I know he [Nelson] is behind a great deal of what I do. . . . I only wish I had not read the book right at this time because it raises certain inescapable truths about writing, being a writer in America, that I've been trying to avoid, like knowing the number of bars on a jail cell for one thing, the whole business of reconstruction, contrivance, as against naturalism in its American, its best sense."

Sea Diary

(July 1964–January 1965)

"Boys," Bruce Jay Friedman told his three sons, "a Great Writer is coming to stay with us." It was July 1964, and Friedman and his family were vacationing in the Fair Harbor section of New York's Fire Island—a tiny hamlet on a thin peninsula sandwiched between the Great South Bay and the Atlantic Ocean. Friedman's second novel, *A Mother's Kisses*, had just become a best seller, and he had decided to celebrate by renting a vacation house large enough to accommodate his family, a housekeeper named Mrs. Sullivan, and Nelson.

Nelson and Friedman didn't know each other well. Nelson had spotted a copy of Friedman's first novel, *Stern*, on his agent's desk a couple years earlier, picked it up, read it, and liked it so much that he wrote a glowing review in *The Nation*. He claimed Friedman's work was more interesting than Philip Roth's, Saul Bellow's, or Bernard Malamud's, and later he included one of Friedman's stories in the collection *Nelson Algren's Own Book of Lonesome Monsters*. He and Friedman became friends afterward, but mostly through correspondence.

Friedman's oldest son, Josh, was eight years old at the time, and his father's announcement intrigued him. "I wondered what a Great Writer would look like," he said later, "how he might talk and dress, and how old you had to be to become such a person. It seemed like a statue was coming, some figure upon a horse."

The man who arrived on Fire Island that summer was nothing like Josh imagined. He was a fifty-five-year-old Midwesterner who wore clothes that had been softened by years of use, and who arrived by ferry, carrying a suitcase in one hand and a typewriter case in the other. He walked with a pigeon-toed shuffle, and his laugh was an uninhibited cackle, but in later years Josh always remembered him as a great man nonetheless.

Nelson only stayed with the Friedmans for a week, but his visit was the source of several enduring anecdotes. Mostly, the family was struck by how unabashedly himself Nelson was—a man who was at once fatherly, pugnacious, and wise.

Every morning that week, Nelson got up before dawn and began writing. He broke away from his work when the family woke, and before long, he was sitting with Mrs. Sullivan—a middle-aged Irish woman with gray hair and a thick brogue. The family saw her as the help, but Nelson spent hours with her each day, listening to her stories, telling his own, and flirting shamelessly.

The house the Friedmans rented was less than a block from the beach, and it was hot that summer, so everyone spent time by the water. The family liked to lounge on the sand or play volleyball in the afternoons, and Nelson often sat outside and watched them. And occasionally, he walked along the shore by himself while they played, and listened to the waves.

Once, Nelson climbed a sand dune to get a better view of the ocean. He was standing there peacefully, looking at the water, when a man emerged from a nearby house and began yelling. That's my land, he said—get off. So Nelson left and went to find Friedman—a big, muscular guy at the time—and then he returned to the sand dune and turned toward the yelling man's house. Nelson called the man outside, and then did his own yelling. "Where I stand is where I live," he said.

Nelson played patriarch at the Friedmans' house. When he saw the family's three sons playing near the stove, he took them aside and told them to turn the handles of the pots so they weren't sticking out. That way you won't knock anything off and burn yourself, he said. He and Friedman drank at night and discussed their careers, and Friedman later remembered their conversations for their singularity. Most writers, he said, want to talk about women and money—but not Nelson. He was only interested in literature, and when he spoke about his own books and his stature, he was very self-effacing. His work was "iconic," Friedman said, but if "you listened to him you'd have no idea that he was Nelson Algren."

And whenever Nelson felt the need, he spoke his mind. One night, Friedman threw a large party—a "Gatsby-like" affair with "lots of drinking and bad behavior," he said. Nelson flitted about, chatting and telling stories until he noticed Friedman and his wife, Ginger, arguing. They were yelling at each other, and Friedman became so upset that he cut his hand with a bread knife by mistake. Until then, Nelson had had the impression their marriage was a happy one, and when he saw Friedman bleeding, he shook his head, turned away, and said, loudly enough to be heard, "Why do people destroy themselves?"

"That lingers, you know," Friedman said later. "I remember that moment."

The Friedmans packed up their things at the end of the week and returned home, but Nelson liked being on Fire Island so much he decided to stay, and moved eleven miles down the peninsula to Davis Park—an even smaller hamlet where nothing was more than a block from the sand.

Nelson's new summer home was a four-bedroom house that had been rented by six young women for the season. His roommates worked on the mainland from Monday to Friday each week, then swept in for two days each weekend, so for the most part, Nelson was alone. There was no phone in the house, no radio, no television. "Conditions for writing here are so ideal," Nelson joked in a letter to a friend, "I see no chance of getting anything done at all."

There was a complication though. There was no electricity at that end of the peninsula yet, but no one had informed Nelson before he agreed to move. If they had, he never would have rented his room. He had a long essay to write for a magazine called *Sky*, but his typewriter was electric.*

Nelson was reduced to writing in longhand, a form no magazine would accept, so at first he barely worked. He explored the area instead, and discovered a bar called the Casino a short distance from his house. It had a large dining room, a deck built on the beach that faced the Atlantic, and a big, rumbling generator. It was the only place in the area with electric lights, so he began hanging around there at night. He had nothing better to do.

A few days after Nelson arrived in Davis Park, a young man named Donald DeLillo approached Nelson's house and asked to see him.

DeLillo was not usually so bold. He was twenty-seven years old at the time, and shy—a product of the Bronx, and working class. He had been a copywriter for the advertising firm Ogilvy & Mather for the past several years, but recently quit because he was sick of working. He wanted to be a novelist, not an adman, but he had published only one story—a piece called "The River Jordan" that appeared in a college magazine called *Epoch*—and he had no connection to the literary world. He didn't know any agents, or publishers, and none of his friends were aspiring writers.

DeLillo was sharing a house with ten other people that summer, and though he was supposed to be writing, he wasn't. He had been drinking at the Casino instead, and one night while he was there, he noticed a man who looked familiar. "It was odd," he said later. I knew his face, but couldn't place him.

---

* This magazine folded before its first issue was scheduled to appear late in 1964.

Maybe the next day, maybe the day after, DeLillo heard someone say that Nelson Algren was staying in the area. He realized then that the familiar face he spotted at the bar was Nelson's. I should have "recognized him immediately," he thought. Then he summoned his nerve and went to find the famous author who had just become his neighbor.

Soon, Nelson and DeLillo were sitting outside Nelson's house, watching the surf and talking about writing and life.

Nelson told DeLillo about his typewriter problem, and the next time DeLillo visited, he brought along his manual upright. Nelson accepted the loan gratefully, and for the remainder of the summer, he alternated between writing the essay *Sky* had commissioned—a travel piece about Butte, Montana—and visiting with DeLillo on the front porch, where they watched people emerge from the water.

On those afternoons, DeLillo told Nelson that he wanted to become a writer, and Nelson rehashed all his usual stories. He told DeLillo about Bob Roberts, Otto Preminger, and Simone de Beauvoir, and though they were tired old tales by then, they seemed fresh and exciting to DeLillo. He could hear bitterness in Nelson's voice, but not too much, and later, the feeling he associated most with those afternoons, he said, was "longing."

Nelson had been given a chance to make a comeback that year. He had just signed a three-book deal with G.P. Putnam's Sons that guaranteed him almost eleven thousand dollars for the book-length essay about Ernest Hemingway that he had begun on the *Malaysia Mail*—a significant amount for a collection of stories—and another eleven thousand if he wrote a fifth novel.* But he was apprehensive about committing to a serious project, and increasingly interested in exerting his influence on the arts in other ways.

Over the past several years, nurturing young talent had become a

---

* That would be about eighty thousand dollars today.

significant part of Nelson's life. He was still trying to help James Blake publish his prison letters, and he had been helping Alston Anderson and Terry Southern with favorable reviews, connections, and recommendations since they interviewed him for the *Paris Review* in 1955. He was trying to help a friend from East St. Louis named Joan Kadesh get her start as a writer, and he had befriended a young director named Philip Kaufman and appeared in his first film, *Goldstein*. Nelson "was the voice of a prophet," Kaufman said later. "[E]verything he wrote about, everything he talked about was true, I think." Nelson had also given Joseph Heller's *Catch-22* its first rave review, and when the book failed to catch on, he reached out to Heller, met him for lunch, and began a letter-writing and word-of-mouth campaign to promote the book.

Working-class writers had a special place in Nelson's heart. The year before, he had hired on as an instructor at the Bread Loaf Writers Workshop in Middlebury, Vermont. It was the kind of job he had been relying on for income since returning to Chicago, but not one he felt at home performing—he didn't fit in among the instructors, and felt most of the students were sheltered and out of touch with the world.

One young man caught his eye that year, though: a twenty-three-year-old pipe fitter from New Hampshire named Russell Banks.

Banks, like DeLillo, wanted to be a writer but didn't know anything about the literary world. He didn't even know what a writers' workshop was, and had only registered because he saw an advertisement promising that Nelson would be teaching.

When Banks arrived, he sat down with Nelson to discuss the manuscript he had submitted when he applied to Bread Loaf.

Nelson began leafing through Banks's book, and then stopped and said, "This is a good paragraph, kid." Then he turned about forty more pages, and said the same thing. He turned some more pages, and said, "There's some nice dialog in here, now all you gotta do is write the rest of it at the same level as those two paragraphs and that bit of dialog and you've got a good novel."

He didn't do a line edit the way some instructors might, Banks said later, but "he did the thing every young writer needs." He took the book seriously, and didn't condescend by pretending it was better than it was. "It was like a laying on of the hands for me."

When Nelson was done flipping through Banks's novel, he said, "I see you've got some wheels, kid. I'd like to get out of here. This place is driving me nuts, and I've only been here a day. Let's go to the town for some beers." Banks agreed, and after a few drinks, Nelson suggested they drive to Vermont and visit his friend Paul Goodman, who had recently made a splash with a book called *Growing Up Absurd*. Goodman was another one of Banks's heroes at the time, so he agreed to that suggestion as well.

Nelson and Banks spent two days at Goodman's house, and when they returned to Bread Loaf, Nelson was fired for absconding with a student. He and Banks hung around the conference for a while longer, and then they drove to Banks's home in New Hampshire and spent two more days drinking, trading stories, and talking about writing. "It was the beginning of a deep education for me, and a crucial crossing over for me from being this isolated adolescent as a writer to becoming an adult writer," Banks said later.

Nelson and Banks began corresponding after the week they spent together—and after Nelson met DeLillo on Fire Island, he tried to play a similar role in DeLillo's life.

Nelson introduced DeLillo to Candida Donadio that year, and asked her to read some of DeLillo's stories and consider representing him. He and DeLillo began corresponding afterward, and when Nelson returned to New York City the following year, he invited DeLillo to visit the apartment of another young working-class writer named Robert Gover.

Gover's first book, *One Hundred Dollar Misunderstanding*, had been a best seller a few years earlier, and he had used its proceeds to buy an apartment on the tenth floor of a luxury building on the West Side of Manhattan. He had invited Nelson to live with him for a week, and they had been staying up late together, drinking martinis and talking about the literary world.* DeLillo visited Nelson at Gover's apartment, and afterward Nelson gave him feedback on some of his stories and his first novel, *Americana*. He didn't pull any punches with his criticism, DeLillo said later, and his forthrightness was appreciated.

Nelson retuned to Chicago at the end of the summer of 1964 with the story he owed *Sky* magazine in hand, and a book to write. Putnam wanted the Hemingway essay by January.

Nelson had begun writing about Hemingway just after the man shot himself in July 1961, and had been doing so intermittently ever since. He didn't have enough material for a book yet, though, so he decided to pad his critical writing on Hemingway with travel essays he had written about his trip on the *Malaysia Mail* two years earlier.† The book created by that mash-up conforms to the pattern Nelson established with *Who Lost an American?* It has a solid core of well-reasoned, articulate critique, a shell of comic writing, and a series of suggestions that readers shouldn't take it, or its author, seriously.

"An essay on Ernest Hemingway was a labor to which I felt compelled," Nelson began. "Everyone else was acting so compulsively I had

---

* In keeping with his habit of coarsening his image, Nelson lied about his time at Gover's. In a letter to a friend, Nelson claimed that he read an unpublished novel of Gover's during his visit, and savaged it so cruelly that Gover went pale with fury. "The guy's eyes," Nelson wrote, "when he took his baby back, were ice-green." That letter has been used in the past to make Nelson seem like a nasty and uncharitable man, but no one ever verified it. When I spoke to Gover on November 10, 2013, and read the letter to him, he was shocked. He said nothing like the events Nelson described took place. We "enjoyed each other," Gover said, "had some nice meals, some nice conversations." Three years later, Gover saw Nelson at a writers' conference and they had dinner several times, once with James Dickey (the author of *Deliverance*).

† Nelson told Robert Gover that he merged the Hemingway book with his travel essays so that he could write the cost of his trip off as a business expense on his taxes. I'm not sure how seriously to take that comment, but it seems plausible given his state of mind at the time.

to do something compulsive too or I wouldn't get invited to any more parties." That sarcastic statement is juxtaposed with a serious critique of the current emphasis of literary criticism, which is then followed by a statement intended to undercut its effect. I wrote this book, Nelson says, because I thought it would be "a fresh contribution to write the same old thing at sea. I would be the inventor of the very first essay on Hemingway smelling of salt!"

Nelson writes beautifully about Hemingway and his work, saying he "had felt his life fluttered like a pocket-handkerchief by the wind of death. In the watches of the night he had heard retreat beaten. Out of dreams like Dostoyevsky's, endured in nights wherein he had lost his life yet had not died. Hemingway forged an ancestral wisdom in terms usable by modern man: that he who gains his life shall lose it and he who loses it shall save it; into a prose magically woven between sleep and waking."

But as the narrative progresses, Nelson introduces travelogues and memoirs that hopelessly muddle the book's feel and purpose. Soon after the passage about Hemingway's "ancestral wisdom," Nelson begins reminiscing about a county fair performer he saw as a child—a scene that transitions into a series of interviews with the caged prostitutes of Kamathipura, and then into a fictionalized account of an argument Nelson once had with James Baldwin. Another lengthy passage about Hemingway appears next, but when it concludes, Nelson begins writing about the Bay of Bengal, and a fight he had with a member of the *Malaysia Mail*'s crew.

Nelson completed his book in early 1965, and it was published as *Notes on a Sea Diary: Hemingway All the Way* in August of the same year.

Most of its reviewers, predictably, were harsh. The book has "brilliant bursts" that are "so honest and incisive that one finally finds it offensive" to find them buried "here with all the coyness," a reviewer for the *Tribune* said. This book's "arch, arbitrary" tone is the only thing binding it together, a reviewer for the *Times* wrote, and even Van Allen Bradley—the *Chicago Daily News* editor who called Nelson brilliant in 1951, profiled him, and published a portion of Nelson's anti-McCarthy speech—trashed the book. I take a "back seat to nobody as a card-carrying member of the Algren Fan Club," he wrote—but "the question remains: Why did Mr. Algren write this appalling book?"

In an earlier phase of his career, reviews like those would have destroyed Nelson, but by all accounts, they didn't bother him in 1965. He never expected the book to be well reviewed, and it seems he may have even designed it that way. Nelson's draft of the Hemingway essay could have been expanded to fulfill the book contract he had with Putnam, so he had no compelling reason to add the travelogue material— except, possibly, to ensure that no one took the book seriously.*

---

* The Putnam contract called for a book about Hemingway—not a travelogue—of approximately forty thousand words. The published book was approximately twice that length.

"On the Ho Chi Minh Trail"

(February 1965–August 1969)

Nelson submitted this image to the passport division of the State Department in 1968, and it, in turn, sent the image to the FBI, which reproduced it and placed copies in Nelson's file. By that point, the FBI had been surveilling Nelson for more than a quarter of a century.

Betty Ann Bendyk arrived in Chicago by train in February 1965 with a bag in hand and no apartment to return to in Manhattan, where she had been living until the day before. She was a forty-year-old woman with a Hollywood smile, big, innocent eyes, and the ability to find humor in any situation. She laughed often, and when she did, it was hard for anyone within earshot to retain their composure. There was real joy in it.

Despite her relative youth, Betty had already been many things—a wife at nineteen and then a widow at twenty, a student at the Community Theater in Milwaukee, a stage actress in New York, a minor television star, an educator, and an office worker. Now she was about to take on a new role in Chicago: wife of famous novelist.*

Betty had read *A Walk on the Wild Side* in 1964 and fallen in love with it. Everything about the book seemed remarkable, she said later—"the images, everything"—so she wrote Nelson a fan letter. He replied, and when he visited New York City that summer, he invited her out for a drink. She agreed, and enjoyed herself so much she decided to see him the next night as well, and the next.

They went on maybe five dates that week, and before Nelson returned to Chicago, he proposed marriage. Betty declined, but he wasn't hurt when she did. They were walking to her apartment on Lexington Avenue at the time, and he said: Visit me anyway, I'll show you the electric chair in the Cook County Jail.

Betty was originally from Milwaukee, and in February 1965, she decided to visit her parents. When she learned she would be changing trains in Chicago, she told Nelson. He met her at Union Station—just "to hear her laugh again," he told Don DeLillo—and before she continued her trip north, he suggested marriage a second time.

Betty was surprised by Nelson's persistence, and smitten, so she said yes. It was a "whirlwind romance," she said later. "I thought that was terrific."

Nelson's proposal wouldn't have flattered Betty so much if she had known him better. Suggesting marriage had become habit for him since he returned to Chicago. He did so playfully, flirtatiously, whenever he felt a connection to a woman—romantic, or not—and he had raised the issue with at least a half dozen people in recent years: a painter named Lily Harmon, whom he dated briefly;

---

* Betty appeared on several early television shows, including *The Goldbergs*, *The Edge of Night*, and *Mr. District Attorney*. Her name is sometimes misspelled "Bendyke."

a woman he met in London before visiting Beauvoir in 1960; the Canadian student he had been seeing; Bruce Jay Friedman's house-keeper, Mrs. Sullivan; his agent; and others.

Betty didn't know that, though, so she took his proposal seriously and proceeded with confidence and purpose after she accepted. She told her parents she was engaged when she arrived at their house, and then she returned to Manhattan and quit her job. She began planning her wedding then, cleared out her apartment, and bought a one-way ticket on a Chicago-bound train.

Nelson and Betty were married at St. Pauls United Church of Christ in Lincoln Park on February 27, 1965—about two weeks after they were engaged. An Episcopal minister named James Garrard Jones—a former Freedom Rider, and a chaplain at Chicago's Bridewell Jail—performed the rites, and the church's pews were full. Betty's extended family had all traveled from Milwaukee for the ceremony, and they shared the pews with a few of Nelson's friends.

After the wedding, there was a dinner, and before it ended, Nelson had begun chafing at the civilizing conventions of married life. He seemed uncomfortable wearing a suit, and he was glum and unenthusiastic throughout the meal. At one point, he dripped gravy on his necktie, and when Betty tried to clean it for him, he recoiled. He pulled the tie away defiantly, picked up a salt shaker, seasoned the stain, and then added more gravy to it.

The winter of 1965 was bleak in Chicago—cold, windy, gray, and freezing through March. Betty didn't know anyone in the city and had nowhere to be, so for weeks at a stretch, she and Nelson were rarely more than a few yards apart. Forced intimacy soon taught her much about her new husband and his lifestyle—most of it surprising to her.

The apartment was Betty's first shock. Nelson had been living on the third floor of 1958 West Evergreen Avenue for six years by then, and over time, he had transformed the space into a physical extension of his psyche. One room was full of boxing gear, jump ropes, and a used bicycle. Another was reserved for his work. There were stacks of books everywhere, even in the bathroom, and a complete collection of *Police Chief*—a magazine Nelson subscribed to so that he could "keep an eye on the opposition." His collages, drawings, framed bits of writing, and mementos, covered the walls all the way to the ceiling.

The apartment was clean and well maintained, Betty said later, but incredibly busy. "It was like living in his studio," inside his "atelier."

Betty was also surprised by Nelson's writing habits. He told her that he would never write another "big" book, but even when he took on minor projects like a review for *Harper's*, the *Herald Tribune*, or *Ramparts*, he immersed himself in them. He moved about in a daze when he was working, and sat down at the typewriter whenever a clear idea formed in his mind—early morning, noon, evening, or at 3 a.m. Sometimes, he wrote for hours; other times, he tapped the keys of his typewriter for only a few minutes, and then got up and paced and thought. He slept little, and ate whenever he felt hungry—sometimes while standing, and often while working.

Nelson's financial situation was also a shock. Like many people, Betty had assumed Nelson was wealthy. He was famous, after all. He had published eight books, his work had been the basis for two major films, and he regularly appeared on television and the radio to discuss literature, his relationship with Simone de Beauvoir, or his opposition to the death penalty. But as Betty soon learned, Nelson's high profile didn't translate directly into income. He had earned about fourteen thousand dollars the year before—a respectable sum—but had spent most of it on meals, travel, and gambling, and he had to work hard to maintain his lifestyle.*

Betty was surprised by Nelson's attitude toward her as well. He had been charming and chivalrous during their short courtship, but after they married, he became ambivalent about her. They began sleeping

---

* That was about three times the country's median family income in 1964, or about a hundred thousand dollars in today's dollars.

in separate rooms almost immediately, and never shared meals. She cooked and ate alone around dinnertime, and then placed her leftovers in the fridge so he could grab them in the middle of the night when he got up to write. She could never predict how he would respond to her presence either. He barely noticed her when he was writing, but when he wasn't busy, they sat and talked for hours and he went out of his way to make her laugh. "I loved his humor," Betty said. "He was just terribly funny."

The marriage seemed destined for a short run, but Betty and Nelson each made accommodations to extend its life. He bought her a car—a red Rambler—and let her remove the paint from their apartment windows so that sunlight would bathe their flat during the day. When she said she wanted a cat, he agreed, and in the same spirit of generosity, she allowed him to name it Stokely in honor of the civil rights leader Stokely Carmichael. She found a job doing office work for Time Life in Chicago so they would have one steady income, and he made an effort to bring in more money as well.

Nelson had been deliberating over whether to part with his manuscripts and correspondence for years, and when he married Betty, he decided it was finally time to sell them. He began negotiating with a professor named Matthew Bruccoli from the University of Ohio, and by July they had reached an agreement. In exchange for twenty thousand dollars, Nelson would give the university his entire archive— with the exception of Beauvoir's love letters.*

The following month, Nelson made an even greater compromise: He got a job. He had been turning down offers to become an instructor at the Iowa Writers Workshop for some time, but when Paul Engle, the workshop's director, extended his offer again that summer, Nelson accepted—with one condition. He told Engle the university would have to hire Betty as well, and Engle agreed.

———

* That would be about $150,000 today.

Betty rented a large, open flat on the top floor of 1730½ Muscatine Avenue in Iowa City and had their things shipped from Chicago. She and Nelson drove to Iowa together in their red Rambler and settled into their new home. Their apartment was only thirty minutes from campus on foot, and the street out front was lined with trees. Betty loved it, but Nelson couldn't stand the quiet, missed the city, and immediately regretted accepting his job.

Nelson did not think it was possible to teach people how to write, and consequently, he thought creative writing programs were a hustle. He believed that good writing was derived from life experience, and he doubted that anyone who went straight from college to graduate school would ever write a book worth "rereading." That conviction was derived from his own experience and the experiences of peers like Wright and Conroy, and he had been espousing it for years—in private, in writing, and in public whenever college English departments invited him to speak.

The administration at the writer's workshop must have been aware of Nelson's views, but hired him despite his antagonism toward their program. Maybe they doubted the sincerity of his convictions, or thought he would change his mind when he met their students. Whatever the case, they quickly realized how mistaken they were.

When the semester began, Nelson was not on campus. He wasn't even in the state. Philip Kaufman had offered him a part in a film called *Fearless Frank*, so he was in Chicago, acting. He returned to Iowa the following week without making any excuse for his absence, and when the administration asked him to speak at a faculty banquet, he delivered a jeremiad against the Vietnam War instead of talking about literature.

Nelson's attitude in class was no less dismissive. There are conventions that dictate the way writing workshops are taught, and he abided by none of them. Students expect that their stories will be read and discussed in class, but Nelson saw no point to that. He didn't think most of his students wrote well enough to warrant consideration, so instead, he circulated stories written by Terry Southern and Joseph Heller. He believed only one of his students was gifted—a woman named Hualing Nieh—and he used class time to praise her writing and compare it favorably to everyone else's.* He often arrived in class carrying a stack of magazines, newspapers, and book reviews, and encouraged his students to help themselves. He told them that they would need to read if they wanted to be writers, and they would need to experience the world outside of the academy.

Drop out, he told them. Get a job. Go to Vietnam. Go to South America. Go anywhere but here.

Nelson began the semester with eighty students in his lecture course, but within weeks, that number had decreased by half, and when his classes got smaller, he made them shorter as well. He often arrived late, read something by Hemingway or Southern, relayed one of his well-worn anecdotes, and then dismissed class and went to the student union.

Students soon realized it was best to approach Nelson outside of the classroom. He hated teaching but loved people and conversation, so when young writers handed him their work in public places, or at his home, he often held forth until they excused themselves and slipped away. Sometimes, he invited his students to the bar after cutting his class short, talked to them more earnestly than he ever did on campus, and then paid for everyone's drinks.

It was in casual meetings like those, where people spoke freely, that Nelson got to know his students and confirmed, he wrote later, the dismal opinion he had always had of writing programs. "The longer I hang on here the longer I stay out of Vietnam," one student told Nelson.

"It's a respectable way of dropping out," another said. "There isn't

---

*   Nelson was right about Nieh. She has written more than thirty books to date— poetry, essays, and novels—and founded the International Writing Program, also based in Iowa. She later married Paul Engle, and changed her name to Hualing Nieh Engle.

anything I really *want* to do—but hanging on here makes it look to my folks like I do."

Nelson soon found ways to fill the time he wasn't spending in the classroom. He became friends with, and began hanging around, a writer named Kurt Vonnegut Jr., whose fifth novel, *God Bless You, Mr. Rosewater,* had just been released, and whose sixth, *Slaughterhouse-Five*, would soon make him famous. He wrote a lengthy anti-Vietnam speech, reviewed books, and gambled heavily.

Iowa City had an active poker scene. There were two big games at the time, and many of the university's students and some of its professors played in them. One was held at the lodge of the Loyal Order of the Moose. The other was in the basement of a shoe salesman named Gilroy—a man in his mid-twenties who was already bald as a cue ball. He charged three dollars a head for a seat at the table, and in exchange, players were welcome to stay through the night and into the next day. His wife, very pregnant that winter and spring, supplied sandwiches throughout.

Gilroy's basement was Nelson's game. He would arrive on Thursday nights with a thermos full of coffee laced with brandy and strip to his undershirt. He had quit smoking cigarettes by then, but he still enjoyed a cigar occasionally, and when he sat down at Gilroy's table, he would light one, place it between his teeth, hunch his broad shoulders forward to cast a shadow over his cards, and take a drink. Then, all night long and into the next day, he rambled, cajoled, and played more recklessly than anyone else—and enjoyed himself more.

The regular crowd at Gilroy's was eccentric. There was a poet named James Thede who sported a handlebar mustache, wore a green three-piece suit, and carried a briefcase that contained nothing but a bottle of Irish whiskey. There was a tough whom everyone called the Cincinnati Kid who arrived each week with a "moll" who never spoke. There was also a writer named Pablo, who claimed to be Anaïs Nin's godson, and another poet named Micky Hagen. The biggest loser each week was a local everyone called John the Barber. He usually went broke quickly, and then spent hours sitting at Nelson's elbow, studying his play. Donald Justice, a poet and professor, played most weeks as well—and so did a young man named Burns Ellison, who had been attending the writers' workshop, on and off, for years and had returned to the Midwest specifically to register for Nelson's class.*

Nelson had been glum since he arrived in Iowa because he regretted marrying Betty and resented his job—but he came alive in Gilroy's basement. He started talking as soon as the cards were dealt, and didn't stop until the table cleared. He relayed intricate stories while other players calculated percentages, told bad jokes, and placed wagers without looking at his cards.

Once, during a game of lowball where the worst hand wins, Nelson raised the stakes with a pair of kings showing. He raised again, and when someone called, he said, sarcastically, "You gotta be kidding. You say the game is *lowball*! No, don't tell me that."—and flipped over two more kings.

The game lasted all night that week, and through midday on Friday. It stopped at 6 p.m., and by that time, Nelson had lost twelve hundred dollars—about three months' wages for the average American family that year.

It went on like that through the winter and into the spring of 1966, and by the end of Nelson's term at Iowa, rumors of his exploits and crushing losses had proliferated. Some people said he gambled away every cent of his salary. Others said he lost half of what he made. Betty, who would know, claimed the total was five thousand dollars. But no one ever said Nelson seemed upset by his losses.

---

* This account is based largely on an essay Burns Ellison wrote after Nelson's death. It was published by the *Iowa Review* in 1988, and it's called "The First Annual Nelson Algren Memorial Poker Game." It's a tender, loving, and well-written piece.

Nelson had gambled that heavily only once before—in 1953, after his passport application was denied. He lost his savings then and felt sick because he knew he had damaged his chances of finishing the novel he had begun writing about Paula Bays. But by 1966, he had stopped making plans for the future, and he was happier for it. He told everyone he was a freelance journalist, not a novelist, and that money comes and money goes.

Nelson and Betty drove back to Chicago together when the workshop's semester ended in June, and when they arrived at the flat on West Evergreen Avenue, Betty asked for a divorce. Nelson acted surprised, but she didn't believe he really was. They had slept in separate bedrooms in Iowa and barely seen each other, and she suspected he had gambled irresponsibly to force her hand. "He was giving me leverage," she said, and he didn't object to the divorce.

Nelson and Betty had barely known each other when they married, and they barely knew each other still, so parting amicably wasn't difficult. Nelson spent the summer with a friend in Belleville, Illinois, and Betty stayed in the apartment. She drove to New York that fall with Stokely, and afterward she and Nelson became what they always should have been—friends.* For the next ten years, they met up for dinner and sometimes spent the night together whenever they were in the same city, and in between visits, she wrote him long letters, addressing them "Father Confessor and Listener to My Woes."

After Betty left, Nelson's major preoccupation was Vietnam. America had been involved in the conflict between North Vietnam and South

---

* They divorced officially on January 30, 1968—about a year and a half after Betty moved back to New York. Nelson arranged everything, even witnesses, and Betty later said that he had a friend fabricate details about their relationship because there was no such thing as a no-fault divorce at the time. Betty claimed, in an interview, that someone testified during the divorce proceedings that Nelson was physically abusive. But, Betty said, the claim was false.

Vietnam for a decade by then, but for the majority of that time, the military's commitment was minimal. That changed in early 1965, when President Johnson assigned thirty-five hundred marines to protect US Air Force bases in South Vietnam, and before the end of the year, more than two hundred thousand US troops were stationed in the country.

Nelson first delivered a speech opposing American involvement in the war when he arrived at the writers' workshop in 1965, and he did so many more times in the months afterward. In an average year, he lectured on college campuses, perhaps, ten times—but that year, he made many more stops. Being on staff at the Iowa Writers' Workshop had raised his profile, and in the spring of 1966, he appeared on fourteen campuses. He went back on the road that fall, and again in the spring of 1967, and by the end of his speaking tour, he had delivered his speech maybe twenty times. He called it "Going on the Ho Chi Minh Trail."

There was a problem though. When colleges invited Nelson to speak, they expected him to discuss literature, not the war, and so he was often forced to find creative ways to justify delivering the speech he wanted to deliver.

Once, at the Carolina Symposium in Chapel Hill, North Carolina, Nelson stepped on stage and said, "I'm scheduled to examine the relationship, sometimes strained, between myths and mores. Well I feel obliged to whatever heroes or heroesses, as the case may be, who inserted that 'sometimes strained' as I feel there is a strain between our myths and our minds and it is rather ominous."

Then, having nodded in the direction of the topic he had been assigned, he edged toward the subject of Vietnam. He linked the word *strain*, very tenuously, to *restraint*, and then, a few lines later, he demanded: I wonder whether calling for an additional four hundred million dollars to "widen the war in order to bring to us all the wondrous works of peace" was an example of restraint. "Or perhaps it was in perpetuating a myth that we are in Vietnam at the request of the Vietnamese people."

Then he was off and running. As a result of the war, Nelson said, "I think that between ourselves and the Great Society there now stands a great weight of dead souls and I think that the more we pile up the heavier the reckoning that the generation to come will have to pay." And for the next hour, Nelson continued to prosecute his case. This conflict, he argued, is "basically a cowardly war being fought in a cowardly fashion" and its true purpose has nothing to do with spreading democracy. When you have a defense industry as large as America's, he said, "you have to have an enemy."*

The Vietnam War had broad public support when Nelson began his speaking tour in 1965, but less than half the country approved of the way America was handling the conflict in 1966. Antiwar protests were growing larger steadily, but counterintuitively, Nelson felt progressively *more* isolated and powerless as the antiwar movement grew, not less. He spoke at Southern Methodist University in Dallas that May, and afterward, he wrote a disheartened letter to Don DeLillo. I've been announcing that "we are now in World War III" for over a year now, he said, but "I don't have any illusions any longer that I'm doing something socially useful by talking against the war. I just go for the check and fly home."

Nelson's isolation was a function of his age, and a changing culture. His politics were at least as far left as the younger generation that was out in the streets, but there was no place for him in a movement whose watchwords were "Don't trust anyone over thirty." He was a fifty-eight-year-old man who favored hanging around racetracks and poker rooms. His first three books were published before the average college student had been born, and he made frequent reference to Solly Levitt—a

---

* In the past, this speech has always been described as a comic routine. That's because Nelson—in keeping with his tendency to present himself as a bumbling and cynical character at this point in his life—told friends he clowned around on stage and spent his time talking about Batman. That description held up for years because there was no record of the speech itself, but a transcript recently turned up in the archives of the University of North Carolina at Chapel Hill, and they reveal that it was, in fact, a very serious address. (It *does* contain a joke about Batman, but that's hardly the focus.)

boxer whose career peaked in 1948. There weren't many people left in the world who remembered him from his time in the Communist movement, and when he finished speaking, as often as not, he got the impression that no one in attendance had been listening. His audiences didn't ask about the war when it was time for questions. Instead, they asked, "What did you think of Sinatra in the movie?"

Nelson felt even more isolated among his own generation of radicals because there were so few left. Richard Wright was dead, and no one had heard from Abe Aaron in more than twenty years. Jack Conroy, whom Nelson wasn't speaking to, had retired and returned to Moberly, Missouri, and everyone else had either joined him in obscurity or switched sides. John Dos Passos, one of the most important left-wing writers of the thirties, had become a conservative and a Richard Nixon supporter. John Steinbeck had recently traveled to Vietnam and sent back dispatches praising the war effort. Even Frank Meyer— the Communist Party functionary who scolded Nelson for lacking discipline in 1940—had become a contributor to the *National Review* and a close friend of William F. Buckley's.

One exception was Kay Boyle—a contemporary of Hemingway's, and part of the Paris café scene before the war. Her first book had been published by Black Sun Press in 1929, and she had written more than two dozen since. She had been a foreign correspondent for *The New Yorker* for several years while living in Europe, but she was blacklisted when she returned to the United States in the 1950s, and afterward, she became an activist as well as a writer.

Nelson and Boyle didn't meet until the mid-sixties, when she read one of his books and wrote to him, but after that first contact, they became close friends. She lived in the Bay Area and he was in Chicago, but for the remainder of Nelson's life, they leaned on each other for support. They traded books, collaborated on a campaign to end the death penalty, complained about the war and the American government, and griped about the indignities of aging.

Boyle wrote to Nelson after having surgery in 1968, looking for sympathy, and he provided it. "I've had a bad operation," she said, "and I'm furious with life. I was relieved of about half of my anatomy, and it shows, and I am hideous, and I am going to become a recluse." Nelson sent a bouquet of flowers in response, and tried to cheer her up by making a joke of his own recent weight gain. "Tough about losing a hunk of your anatomy," he wrote, "but, as I've *attached* a quarter to mine, nothing has really been lost. It's just on me instead of you. How about that? Thinking that this fine flabby flesh I've gained really belongs to you makes me feel better about everything."

Nelson wrote to Boyle about his worries as well. After the chaos of the Tet Offensive in Vietnam and the assassinations of Martin Luther King Jr. and Robert F. Kennedy, he said that he was also thinking of becoming a recluse. "I have in mind," he joked, "a cave in Upper Tibet, where I'll stay stoned on fermented yak-milk the year round. You may come see me on moonless nights—you'll know you have the right cave by the sound of dentures clacking, stertorous breathing and an occasional senile giggle in the dark."

Then, more seriously, he said, "Actually . . . I don't know what to do about this fucking country." I'd like to get away, he said, maybe move to Cuba, but I can't. "How can I be Cuban even though I would rather—much rather—be? I can't be a Yugoslav or nothing. I'm stuck with these Forspacious Skies and Beautiful Swift Swords."

After campaigning against the war for three years, Nelson asked *The Atlantic* magazine to sponsor his application for a press credential so he could see it for himself. Then he booked passage on a freighter that left San Francisco on November 14, 1968, and sailed to Japan. He spent a week in Yokohama and Tokyo, and then continued on to Vietnam, where he knew no one and had no connections to draw on.

When Nelson reached Saigon, he moved into a room at the Hotel Embassy—about half a block from the Presidential Palace. But then he was at a loss. He couldn't leave the city safely because he hadn't yet been able to secure a press credential, so instead he spent weeks exploring his surroundings on foot and by jitney. "This is a mean, sick city," he wrote to a friend. "Poverty, pimpery, parades, Col. Ky, thousands of cowboys on Hondas with nothing to do all day and night but race the streets. And the American GI's who want to go home. And the people wishing the hell they *would* go home. The Americans are definitely not liked here."

After living near the heart of Saigon for a month, Nelson moved into the Hotel Victoria at 937 Tran Hung-Dao Street in Cholon—a Chinese neighborhood that had been heavily bombed by the US military earlier that year. His room had a desk large enough for a typewriter, a plastic crucifix on the bedroom wall, a Buddhist shrine in the kitchen, and not much else.

There was only one other American in the hotel—a soldier gone AWOL who was living with a Vietnamese woman—and Nelson had no way to communicate well with anyone else. He sold two stories around the time he moved—one about his ocean passage, and one about Japan—to a magazine called *The Critic*, but there was no easy way for them to get a check to him, or for him to cash one, so he was soon broke.

Nelson finally received his press credential at the end of February, and afterward he made a series of forays outside the city. He rode forty miles to the east in a jeep driven by a war correspondent named Don Hirst, and observed a military trial. He flew over the jungle in a plane that was dropping pamphlets as part of a psychological operations program, but never went up a second time because the first plane was shot twice before it landed and he was afraid of dying in a crash. He spent several days interviewing soldiers who were running an amnesty program for Communist fighters called Chieu Hoi—which translates as "open arms"—but by then his interest in the war was fading and he was eager to return home.

On March 28, 1969, Nelson turned sixty in Cholon, and by then, he was spending more time trying to earn money in the informal economy than he was writing.

Soon after he arrived in Vietnam, Nelson realized that most people bought their food, liquor, clothes, and electronics on the black market, and after a few months, he devised a scheme to take advantage of the situation. The exchange rate was his angle. If he could get American cash into the country, he could use it to buy Vietnamese piastres on the black market at rates that far exceeded the official exchange rate. Then, because he was American and had a military-issued ID, he could purchase military payment certificates with the piastres, and these in turn could be used to buy products at the post exchange (PX) at reduced prices—tripling or quadrupling his money with each transaction.

Nelson put his plan into action around his birthday, and for a while, it worked well. He had friends send him cash wrapped in carbon paper through the mail—then exchanged it twice, bought consumer goods that he stored in his room, and went into the streets near his hotel to spread the word about his wares. Soon, he had a store of goods and maybe a thousand dollars in cash, maybe more. But his luck didn't last. He was an aging American living in a Chinese neighborhood of a Vietnamese city during one of the most violent periods of one of the most violent conflicts of the twentieth century. He couldn't have possibly been more out of place or vulnerable, and there was never any chance of him emerging unscathed.

At some point in April, Nelson entered into a negotiation with two local men. The three of them had a disagreement, maybe over a price, and Nelson's trading partners decided to settle it with violence. They hit him in the face hard enough to break his dentures, and then they took his merchandise and bankroll, leaving him with nothing.

A few days later, Nelson booked passage on a ship sailing for Hong Kong on May 2 and told a friend he was "counting the days till I get out of this pit." He had maybe forty pages of notes to show for his five months in the country, but nothing much written. "I'd like to get it into some coherent shape and send it to *Atlantic*," he said. "But I'll never get it coherent in *this* chaos, I'm sure."

———

Nelson took his time returning home. He stopped in Hong Kong, Taipei, Kobe, Yokohama, Ngoya, San Francisco, and then Los Angeles. He reached Chicago in early August—ten months after he left town—and began going through the notes he took in Saigon. "[I]t simmers down to very little. . . . ," he told a friend. "You never realize how little you have, or how close you came, till after you've left a place. But I sure as hell ain't going back."

Helen Corbett was one of the first people to notice Nelson's return. She was his landlady, and when she realized he was finally home, she called the Chicago field office of the FBI and let them know.

Sometime after Nelson and Betty married, the bureau had learned that Nelson had been speaking against the war, and it decided to reopen his file. Eventually, it determined that he was a "key" organizer of the antiwar movement, and gathered his new passport photo from the State Department, informed the Iowa City sheriff's office that Nelson was moving to town, and asked the administration at the Writers' Workshop for his information. Then it called Helen Corbett, who proved eager to cooperate. She told them how much Nelson paid in rent, kept them abreast of his travel plans, and told them all about Betty—she dyes her hair, Corbett said, and she wears long skirts because she thinks her legs are too thick.

Corbett spoke with the FBI on six separate occasions while Nelson was overseas, but the call she placed in August of 1969 was the last. The FBI closed Nelson's file four days later, and never reopened it. They had been following him, on and off, for twenty-nine years, and in that time, they had amassed a six-volume file that totaled 886 pages—all without proving he had done a thing to warrant their scrutiny.

The Last Carousel

(September 1969–November 1973)

Nelson spent the first six decades of his life trying, and mostly failing, to balance a long list of competing and contradictory desires. He wanted respect and accolades from the literary establishment, and the freedom to express controversial ideas. He wanted fame, and money enough to avoid writing for pay alone. He wanted to go out and hear music whenever he pleased, and he wanted to see the world—but he also yearned for devoted friends and the stability and comfort of a home, a wife, and children.

Chasing those urges had left Nelson feeling lonely and regretful, and around the time he turned sixty, he reconciled with that fact and adjusted his expectations. After returning from Vietnam, he rejected accolades when they were offered, turned down money if he didn't absolutely need it, made peace with the fact that he was not meant to have anything resembling a traditional home life, and created a division of labor to satisfy his social and emotional needs.

For companionship, Nelson established relationships with several different women and arranged for each of them to visit him weekly on an agreed-upon night. Two of the women were sisters, and his relationships with them were either chaste or nearly so. Another was an editor who had two young children Nelson enjoyed spending time with. And one was a writer who stripped down every time she visited Nelson's apartment so he could bathe her and they could talk.

When Nelson craved more platonic attention, he went out. Sometimes, he visited the Three Corners—a local bar still frequented by the neighborhood's Polish residents. Other times, he joined the city's reporters and editors as they made their rounds after work. It was customary for the newspaper crowd to eat dinner at Riccardo's on Rush Street after they filed their last stories, move on to O'Rourke's Pub on North Avenue, and then visit the Old Town Ale House. Nelson routinely appeared at some point along that route and mixed into the crowd. He went to see Studs Terkel, Roger Ebert, and the columnist Mike Royko, but also to be around the generation of reporters that was just coming up. He befriended young local writers like Michaela Touhy, and the editors of an underground paper called the *Chicago Free Press*.

To stay in touch with the underworld, Nelson spent his summers in Belleville, Illinois, with a big powerful man named Stanley Kowalski— a former pimp who was married to a former prostitute everyone called Flat Top. Kowalski owned a share of Nelson's horse, Jellious Widow, and a large limestone ranch house that he safeguarded by chaining angry dogs in his front yard. He lived about fifteen miles from the Cahokia Downs racetrack, and Nelson spent about a month with him every year—looking after their horse, drinking in the bars frequented by local jockeys, getting high, and collecting stories.[*]

"Law & Order has never gotten a firm grasp on the natives" of Belleville, Nelson once wrote to a friend while at Kowalski's house. "A

---

[*]   Kowalski is one of the few real mysteries in Nelson's life. He had very little contact with the legitimate world and left a thin paper trail. It's unclear how Kowalski and Nelson met, but Nelson told Betty that Kowalski had been arrested for murder earlier in his life. He also liked to say Kowalski led a mutiny after being drafted into the Navy during World War II. I can't confirm either story, but I can report that Kowalski supplied the dynamite used in the 1981 assassination of a St. Louis mob figure named George Faheen. Details of his involvement are included in the Eighth Circuit Court of Appeals' decision *United States of America v. Raymond H. Flynn.*

youth who dropped in here Sunday is carrying a recently healed bullet-scar on his left cheek, inflicted during a robbery. He is seriously thinking of suing the victim because, he contends, 'there was no necessity of shooting me.' (*He* was doing the sticking-up.)"

And when Nelson wanted to feel the warm, steadying embrace of family, he visited Stephen Deutch and his wife, Helene. Deutch was a photographer and sculptor who spoke with a thick eastern European accent and rationed his words carefully. He had been born in Budapest in 1908, and left school after completing the eighth grade to become a wood-carver's apprentice. When he was twenty-three years old, he moved to Paris to make his name as a sculptor, and went broke. His work was featured in several galleries but never sold, and his only income came from selling faux antiques.

Deutch was poorer than most, but luckier, too, and before he starved, he had the good fortune to meet a young woman from Transylvania named Helene. She had studied photography at the Sorbonne and then gone to work shooting for *Vogue Paris*. She taught Deutch how to take photographs as well, and soon they married and had a daughter and named her Annick. They moved to Chicago in 1936, during the Great Depression, and then they had two more daughters— Katherine, and Carole.

At first, the Deutches were radicals. Stephen joined the Communist Party during the same period Nelson was active, and he considered fighting in Spain during the Civil War. He became friends with Studs Terkel and Ben Burns, the editor of the *Chicago Defender*, and once he was beaten by a group of men while he was handing out propaganda flyers—maybe because he was a Communist, or maybe because he was Jewish. Woody Guthrie sang in the family's living room, and they supported Henry Wallace for president during the Red Scare.

The Deutches started a commercial photography studio after the Depression, and soon it was among the most respected in the Midwest. Helene ran the business, and Stephen took the photographs. Their clients were newspapers, slick magazines, department stores, and advertising agencies. They worked long hours and operated without assistants to save money, and they were rewarded for their labor. They bought a house in the suburbs and a summer home in Sawyer, Michigan, and their two eldest daughters attended the private Francis W. Parker School in Lincoln Park.

Stephen Deutch never forgot the poverty of his childhood or lost touch with his radicalism, though, so he spent his spare time ensuring that his daughters understood what the world was like for people who couldn't afford to live where they lived. He drove them through Chicago's slums so they wouldn't think of them as foreign lands, and brought them to the stockyards so they would know what physical labor looked like. One time, he drove them into the forest and down a fire road until he reached a logging camp. Then everyone watched lumberjacks fell trees, turn them into logs, roll them down a hillside, and load them onto trucks.

All of the attention Deutch dedicated to his work and his family precluded him from making friends. So, when his daughters began to move away for college and marry, he grew lonely. That's when he met Nelson.

Deutch and Nelson were introduced in 1960, when a small publisher called Angel Island hired Deutch to take pictures for a new edition of *Chicago: City on the Make*. Nelson dropped by Deutch's studio to have his portrait taken, and while he was there, he inspected the photographs on display. In addition to his commercial work, Deutch was an experienced street photographer, and as Nelson walked by the prints produced by those sessions, he nodded his head approvingly and smiled. From that moment forward, the two men were bound to each other. I don't know "what made me feel a kind of warmth toward him," Deutch said later, "but that was instantaneous."

Nelson and Deutch went to lunch after the shoot, and continued doing so about once every month, provided Nelson was in town, for the next several years. They had little to say to each other at first because they had lived such different lives, but something bonded them and they began spending progressively more and more time together.

Sometimes, they met at Riccardo's for lunch and sat in the overstuffed booth seats and talked for hours—about family, politics, books, fighters, or horses. Other times, they met for dinner at one of their homes or the other, or made trips to the bar. Nelson started bringing Deutch along as his date when he made public appearances, and when he needed to relax, he went to the Deutches' house and spent an evening listening to opera, chamber music, or blues—drinking with Stephen, and trying to make Helene laugh. Eventually, their house became Nelson's second home, and when they vacationed at their place in Sawyer, Michigan, Nelson often tagged along.

Nelson and Deutch were brothers in every respect but blood by 1970, and they only grew closer with time. Over the course of the next few years, Nelson sold his horse, stopped visiting Belleville, and became a less frequent presence in the city's bars. Eventually, the women he had been seeing all married or moved away as well, and he filled the breach created by those losses with his relationship to Deutch. "My father loved" Nelson, Carole Deutch said. "They were soul mates," her sister Katherine agreed.

Nelson wrote to Kay Boyle at the end of 1971 to say that he was slowing down and slipping into routine. "What I'm doing is what *I* always do," he wrote. "Trotting to the supermarket, watching *Laugh-In*, going to movies, reading a few books, and patching up old short stories in the hope of selling something to *Playboy* so I can keep on going to the supermarket, watching *Laugh-In*, etc."

Nelson was sixty-two years old when he wrote that letter, and while it's true he was leading a quieter life than he had in the past, he was exaggerating the point for Boyle's benefit. In truth, the stories Nelson was "patching up" were part of the most significant writing project he had undertaken since he finished writing *A Walk on the Wild Side* in 1955.

Nelson still had two books left to write before his contract with Putnam was fulfilled—a novel and a collection of stories—and he wrote to his editor, Bill Targ, at the beginning of 1971 and said he was finally ready to begin putting the collection together. He asked for two years to complete it, and said he wanted it to be a big book—five hundred pages, at least. Targ agreed.

Over the course of those months, Nelson worked harder than he had in years, and when he was finished, his manuscript was more than two hundred thousand words long. It wasn't *a* collection of his short writings; it was *the* collection—it contained virtually every uncollected piece he had published in the past fifteen years, as well as his best unpublished work. He submitted the book to Putnam in early 1973, it was accepted, and its release date was scheduled for later the same year.

Nelson called his book *The Last Carousel*, and both its title and its content suggest it was intended as a farewell to the literary world. The writing is strikingly good compared to his two previous books. The bitter tone that had defined his recent work is almost entirely absent, and its most affecting characters, appropriately, are master craftsmen approaching the end of their careers and dwelling on their legacies.

"Dark Came Early in That Country" is the first standout piece. Its protagonist is a veteran boxer named Roger Holly, who, though only thirty-two years old, has been fighting professionally for thirteen years. He's a minor talent and knows it, so he employs cunning and stoicism to compensate for his lack of skill. He fights dirty enough to give himself an advantage in the ring, but not so dirty that he runs the risk of disqualifying himself from future work, and he has no compunction about taking a dive if the payoff makes it worthwhile.

Holly lives in Shawneetown, Illinois, with his wife and his ailing father, and though he's often on the road, he returns to them regularly and sends them money faithfully. Beth, Holly's wife, is tender and supportive, but never servile. She refuses to stroke Holly's ego, and on one occasion she reads an article about bush-league fighters who work without managers, sees Holly's name, and teases him. The story says he's "the best of a bad lot," and after reading it, Beth says, "I always knew you were a bad lot, but I never dreamed you were the *very best of it.*"

That article raises Holly's profile, and after its publication, he books the most lucrative fight he has had in years. He expects to win and earn a shot at the title, but instead, he takes a beating and returns home with nothing to "show for getting" his "face punched in for fourteen years" but a "swab stick, the cardboard core of a roll of gauze, the top of a Vaseline jar and a half a bottle of liquid adrenaline."

Holly's career ends with that fight, but unlike Nelson's other memorable protagonists, his life does not have a tragic conclusion. Instead, he and Beth use the last of his earnings to open a diner, and he spends the remainder of his years tending to customers and reminiscing. In his idle moments, he tries to recall the names of the men he fought during his boxing career, but can't, so instead, he recounts the names of the arenas he appeared in. "The Marigold in Chicago," he thinks, "and the Armory A.C. in Wilkes-Barre and the Valley Arena at Holyoke," he tells himself, "and Joe Chap's Gym in Brooklyn and the Grotto in Jersey City and . . ."

Unlike Nelson's earlier writing, "Dark Came Early in That Country" wasn't the product of intense research, but he drew on more than forty years of accumulated boxing knowledge, and it's as detailed and confident as anything he produced before. Its style is distinct though. He wrote the story using spare, journalistic prose that looks forward toward the work of writers like Richard Ford, Denis Johnson, and Raymond Carver instead of employing the lyrical, poetic flourishes he was known for during his heyday in the 1950s.

Two other stories in the collection share those qualities. The first is a long short story called "Bullring of the Summer Night," whose protagonist is a jockey named Hollis Floweree—a tiny man with two criminal convictions in his past, two recent falls on the track, and a fast-fading career. He rides a horse called Red's Big Red that races at a short, steeply banked "bullring" track, and he lives in a trailer with a woman named Kate Mulconnery who is both his employer and his lover.

Floweree and Mulconnery barely get along, mostly because of Floweree's ego. He resents working for a woman and gives her steady reminders of his dissatisfaction. When he wakes in a foul mood, she knows what to expect. "He'll be pecking at me now for my Ozark talk . . . ," she thinks, "or for being a head taller and half again his size. Or for looking years younger while being years older. Or for being born in the mountains or raised on a river." And she knows, just as surely, that he'll never mention the thing that bothers him most: the fact that she bedded his fiercest competitor before she bedded him. "A touchy group, these riders," she thinks, "whose need of proving themselves could be felt in their mounting of women as well as of horses."

Floweree is set on getting away from Mulconnery, so he buys an electrified whip off another jockey, bets on himself, and cheats by using the whip during his next race. As a result, he injures another rider by running him off the track and fails to place. "You'd fuck up a one-car funeral, mister," Mulconnery says after the race. They never speak again, and Floweree never rides again.

The next story in the collection, "Moon of the Arfy Darfy," provides a glimpse of his future. Floweree has moved to Chicago and been reduced to earning his keep by collecting discarded betting slips in the hope of finding a winner someone forgot to claim. But like all Nelson's best protagonists, he still has his pride. "It's a big comedown," he thinks, "from parading in front of the clubhouse in your pretty-day silks, to stooping for tickets people throw away by mistake. But I never stooped until the stands were empty. And nobody I used to know—at Waterford and Evangeline and Ozark Downs—had any idea that Sportsman's was my playground now."

"I'd had my picture in *The Form* once," he recalls, "—but who remembers that? I didn't really care anymore, one way or another. When you come to the end it's the end, that's all."

Several of *The Last Carousel*'s less ambitious pieces also hold their own. "Watch Out for Daddy" feels like Nelson's older work—it's a dark, tightly focused story whose protagonists, a couple, are junkies bound to each other by their shared addiction and their isolation. It dates back to the period when Nelson was still working on the novel he began about Paula Bay's life, and the world it describes is governed by contradictory and self-defeating passions. "Poor useless boy," the wife thinks, "—I'd rather have his hate than some fat square-fig's love. Love or hate, whatever, it don't matter so long as it's real."

"The Last Carousel," the title story, fictionalizes Nelson's time at the Sinclair station in Texas and his stint working for the traveling carnival. "What Country Do You Think You're In?" is set in Vietnam and features an American protagonist who becomes so comfortable in Saigon, he forgets he's in a war zone and nearly dies in a bombing. "I Never Hollered Cheezit the Cops" is a racetrack story about an illiterate jockey named Rusty de John that's written with a light, comic touch, and "Ballet for Opening Day" is a deeply researched essay about the Chicago Black Sox scandal.

The collection has flaws as well. Nelson makes no distinction between nonfiction and fiction, so there's no way to tell which pieces are supposed to be truthful, and the stories are arranged without any discernable logic. Three pieces included for spiteful reasons—one each insulting Otto Preminger, Simone de Beauvoir, and Alfred Kazin—are bitter and ill conceived.* Two essays that appear sequentially contain overlapping material, and the Vietnam stories are politically astute but marred by stereotypical and dismissive descriptions—the Chinese in Vietnam have "class," Nelson says, while the Vietnamese have a "listless, dispirited air."

But when *The Last Carousel* was released in November 1973, most

---

* This sounds like an exaggeration, but it's not. A friend of Nelson's suggested that these three pieces should not have been included in the collection, and Nelson responded by saying, "You're right about the Kazin and de Beauvoir and a couple other pieces—also the Preminger, being spiteful. You're also wrong about omitting them. You're [sic] feeling is based upon a false assumption: namely, that the writer is a literary dude of great detachment, intent upon producing *Literature*. . . . So the point of those stories wasn't to impress the reader but to knock the smile off Kazin, Preminger, et al. . . . The cost in literary reputation is trivial."

reviewers were willing to overlook the book's faults. "It's about time!" the *New York Times* review begins. "When we've got a living American writer as sure-footed and as fast off the mark as Nelson Algren, it's almost criminal not to have something of his in hard covers at least once a year, to heft and roar at and revel in." The reviewer lavished praise on the collection's best work, told readers not to take everything in the book seriously, and concluded by saying, "Anyone daring to review Nelson Algren today stands in grave danger of being a 'past-poster'—a party who puts down a heavy bet on a horse that has already won."

"What an exhilarating experience it is to read Nelson Algren's new collection of stories!" Max Geismar began his review in the *Chicago Sun-Times*. "I lived it all day long and could not wait to get back to it the next day and read and reread the best in it with a great sense of pleasure and delight."

"[O]nce you begin reading it," the *Tribune*'s reviewer said, "you will not be able to put it aside."

Those were the best reviews Nelson had received in years, and they were accompanied by other promotions as well. The *Chicago Daily News* profiled him, and so did the *Pacific Sun* and *Publishers Weekly*. All that attention for a collection of stories made Nelson hopeful, and he began to think the book might really sell—unlike his last two—so he contacted Bill Targ and asked about Putnam's promotional strategy. That's when he learned that there was none. The publisher had low expectations, and had not budgeted for a launch party or an advertising campaign.

One of Nelson's fans—a man from Detroit that he had never met— heard about the situation and offered to pay for a signing party. He hired Nelson's friend Van Allen Bradley to organize it, and Bradley coordinated with Nelson, rented a space, and ordered books. But when the appointed date arrived, Bradley had no books to sell because they were never delivered. Putnam had delayed *The Last Carousel*'s release date by three weeks without telling Nelson, Bradley, or the local papers. The best reviews the book was going to receive had already been published, but there wasn't a store in Chicago with a copy to sell.

Nelson, alerted to the situation by Bradley, arrived for his signing carrying fifty copies of *The Last Carousel* taken from his personal store of author's copies. He sold every one of them, and believed he could have sold twice as many if there had been enough on hand.

Putnam began distributing the book in December—a month after reviews began appearing—but bungled that as well. They printed a small batch of books, it sold out before Christmas, and they didn't get more on the shelves until early the following year.

The following spring, while Nelson was still seething over the botched release of *The Last Carousel*, Kurt Vonnegut nominated him for the Award of Merit for the Novel from the American Academy of Arts—a prestigious prize only presented once every five years. At the time, six writers had received it: Theodore Dreiser, Thomas Mann, Ernest Hemingway, Aldous Huxley, John O'Hara, and Vladimir Nabokov.

Nelson hadn't written a novel in almost twenty years, but the other members of the academy welcomed the nomination. There was no campaigning necessary, Vonnegut said; everyone agreed.

The academy announced that Nelson had been granted the award in March. It was among the greatest honors a writer could ask for at the time, and the greatest Nelson would ever receive, but accolades meant little to him by then—he was just a journalist, or so he said, and he didn't think any honor, presented so belatedly, could save his career.

The awards ceremony was scheduled for May, in New York City, and Nelson told Vonnegut not to expect him. He wrote a terse acceptance speech for Vonnegut to read in his stead, but when Vonnegut suggested it was in bad taste, Nelson agreed to cut it.

When Vonnegut stepped on stage to accept the award on Nelson's behalf, he said simply, "Thank you."

"The Sanest Man I've Ever Met"

(December 1973–March 13, 1975)

Nelson traveled to New York City in December 1973, checked into the Chelsea Hotel, crossed beneath the Hudson River by train, and stepped off in Newark, New Jersey, where he met an investigator named Fred Hogan.

Hogan was young, pugnacious, inquisitive, and a little wild. He drank hard and he could become manic when he was excited, but he took his work seriously and he held faith with quaint ideas about right and wrong, good and bad. He had grown up in Bayonne, graduated from high school, and then served in the army. He joined the police force in a small town called Atlantic Highlands after he left the service, and when he grew bored of a beat cop's routines, he went to work for the office of the public defender.

Hogan often found himself inside Rahway State Prison after he switched to the defense side—a massive red-brick complex with a domed roof, and miles of chain link and razor wire surrounding it. He went there to interview clients and witnesses, and sometimes, before he left for the day, though it had nothing to do with his job, he asked the prison's guards to produce Rubin "Hurricane" Carter as well.

Carter was a short, thickly built black man who wore a neatly trimmed beard and kept his head shaved clean. From 1961 to 1966, he had been a professional boxer best known for his glower and his unrelenting offense. He was a masterful intimidator in the ring, a hard man to catch with a punch, and a tenacious brawler—and that combination propelled him to the top of the rankings.

Carter even fought for the middleweight title once, in 1964. That match went the distance—fifteen rounds, all told—and when it went to the judges, they gave the victory to Carter's opponent, Joey Giardello. Many fight watchers believed Giardello had been allowed to keep his title because he was white and Carter was black. It was presumed that Carter and Giardello would fight again, but then Carter got arrested.

Early in the morning of June 17, 1966, Carter and a young man named John Artis were driving through Paterson, New Jersey, in a white Dodge sedan when the police pulled them over. Earlier that morning, two men had entered the Lafayette Bar and Grill on East Eighteenth Street in Paterson, pulled out a gun each—one shotgun, one pistol—began firing, and hit four people. Two of their victims died that night, one held on for a month before succumbing, and one survived, even though he had been shot in the head.

The police released Carter and Artis, but soon afterward, they were stopped a second time and brought to the scene of the shooting for identification. No one recognized them, but the police brought them to the station anyway, questioned them extensively, and then released them without charges.

Months passed. Then two men who admitted they were near the Lafayette Bar and Grill on the night of the shooting because they intended to rob a nearby warehouse—Alfred Bello and Arthur Dexter Bradley—told the police that Rubin Carter was one of the shooters.

The police arrested Carter and Artis and charged them with murder. They went to trial the following year, in 1967. The fact that Carter was a professional fighter and had a juvenile criminal record helped the district attorney's case, and the jury ultimately found both men guilty of triple murder.

None of that—not Carter's reputation as a fighter, and not his life sentences—intimidated Fred Hogan. He had been an amateur boxer in high school, and he had met Carter at a training camp one summer. He had looked up to the older man then, and when he heard that Carter had been found guilty of murder many years later, he presumed Carter had been wrongfully convicted.

So, when Hogan found himself inside Rahway Prison, he asked to meet with Carter. At first, they just got to know each other, but eventually, they began discussing Carter's case and the evidence that had been used against him. Carter and Artis both maintained their innocence, and soon Hogan was convinced they were telling the truth and began investigating the case on his own time.

That investigation was the reason Nelson visited Newark. *Esquire* magazine had offered him $1,250 to write a profile of Carter, and said they wanted something Algrenesque—maybe a psychological portrait of a boxer turned killer. Nelson knew little about Carter's trial and was excited to write the piece *Esquire* had commissioned—but then he met Fred Hogan.

By the time Nelson reached New Jersey in 1973, Hogan was spending all of his free time immersed in the minutiae of Carter's case. He had been sifting through the evidence used during the trial, and had recently heard rumors that both of the men who testified against Carter—Bello and Bradley—later told acquaintances that they lied on the stand. Hogan was sure, he told Nelson, that he could get them to admit that they had perjured themselves because the statute of limitations for that crime had passed. He just needed to find them.

Nelson was intrigued, and before he returned to Chicago, he visited Carter at a hospital in Newark. Carter had just had an operation on his right eye, so he was lying in bed and wearing a robe when Nelson arrived, but he looked dignified nonetheless. He had recently completed a memoir called *The Sixteenth Round* that was due to be released the following year, and he seemed like a warrior-scholar to Nelson— intense, brooding, concise in his speech, and self-assured.

Nelson closed the door to Carter's room after he entered, without thinking, and a guard soon appeared and opened it.

"Sorry, Rubin," the guard said, "the door has to stay open."

Carter stood up and walked toward the guard, and when he was close enough to reach out and touch him, he said, "We're on the fourth floor, man. Do you think I can fly out of here?" Then he closed the door.

The guard was silent, and Carter turned toward Nelson. "I've had this trouble before," he said. "What they do now is phone the Bureau of Institutions and Agencies to find out what they're supposed to do. Don't worry. The door will stay closed. What can they do?"

Then he answered his own question. "They can kill me, that's all."

Nelson left New Jersey with a copy of Carter and Artis's trial transcript, and his own nascent doubts about Carter's guilt. He didn't think Carter was the sort of person who would throw his life away for the thrill of killing strangers in a bar, and by the time he finished reading the trial transcripts, he was convinced that Carter had been framed.

Nelson returned to New Jersey in March 1974, to interview Carter a second time. This time, they met in the visiting area of Rahway State Prison, and Carter looked even more dignified. He was wearing frameless eyeglasses, and though everyone else was wearing state-issued uniforms, he was dressed in civilian clothes.

"I don't wear prison dress," Carter told Nelson. "Why should I? I'm not supposed to be here." When they tried to put me on a work detail, Carter said, I turned it down flat. "I love work," he said. "But for 80 cents a day? Not on your life."

Nelson left Rahway Prison that day more impressed by Carter than he had been after their first meeting. He's "the sanest man I've ever met," he wrote to a friend soon afterward. He refuses to allow himself to be dehumanized by the prison, but he doesn't openly challenge authority or cause trouble, so the "guards just let him alone. He sleeps during the day and does his own work at night. He doesn't fuck with anybody, black or white, in the joint, and they're content to stay out of his way. If he doesn't like somebody's approach he tells him to fuck off, that's all."

Nelson spent the remainder of that spring writing about Carter. *Esquire* had commissioned him to write something lyrical and character-driven, but instead, he composed a straightforward piece of journalism that drew heavily on trial transcripts and interview material. He laid out the facts and tried to make the case that Carter and Artis deserved a new trial.

Nelson submitted his article sometime that summer, and *Esquire* rejected it soon afterward. Jim Ryan, the editor who commissioned the story, was impressed by the effort Nelson put into it, but didn't want to print it. "It wasn't Nelson Algren at all," he said later. "It was a reporter reporting all kinds of goddamn facts that hadn't been properly presented before, but for our purposes it wasn't a story."

Ryan asked Nelson to start over from scratch, but Nelson declined. I'll do it if you pay me twice, he said. And when Ryan refused, Nelson said, "Well, to hell with you then."

Esquire's rejection didn't faze Nelson. He sent his story to *The New Yorker* next, and when *they* rejected it, he began to think of Carter's case as a long-term project. By then, Fred Hogan had found Alfred Bello and Arthur Dexter Bradley and convinced them to sign statements confirming that they had perjured themselves on the stand during Carter's trial because they had been pressured by the Paterson police. The *New York Times* had just reported on the recantations, and it seemed inevitable that Carter and Artis would receive a new trial. If they did, it would be a sensation and Nelson would be in an ideal position to write about it.

Nelson spent the fall as an instructor at the University of Florida, in Gainesville, and then he traveled to Paterson by train, checked into a downtown hotel, and began searching for an apartment. A few days later, he found one on the first floor of 38 Quinn Street and moved in with nothing but a suitcase, his typewriter, and the research he had been collecting on Carter's case. He spent Christmas on the Jersey Shore with Fred Hogan, and by January, he had decided to move east permanently. He was hoping to earn enough writing about Carter and Artis to finance his retirement, but he had kept that ambition to himself—maybe because it was such a far-fetched plan.

Nelson told Steve Deutch that he was moving to Paterson in February, but did so casually. He said that he would return home soon to wrap up his affairs and clear out his apartment, but that he didn't intend to stay. Leaving Chicago—the city he had been raised in, lived in for decades, loving and hating it in equal measure the entire time, and helped define through his writing—was a monumental decision, but Nelson acted as if it was of no consequence. He said that Chicago hadn't had any use for him in years, and joked that his impending move made perfect sense. "I don't know why you, or anyone, should be surprised at my moving to Paterson," he wrote. "I've been telling you, for at least a decade, that I planned to move to San Francisco, and Paterson is directly on the way."

Nelson had been complaining about Chicago publicly for a very long time by 1975. He had been referring to the city as a "great gray subcivilization" for more than a decade, and accusing it of being shallow and conformist for far longer. The year *The Last Carousel* was released, he even told a reporter, "I don't see Chicago ever becoming a city that is fun to live in. That's out of the question. It's a money city, a city to make money in, it's not an Athenian city, it's a Spartan city, which is why almost everybody leaves here, you know, if they're interested in writing or the theater."

But even so, no one had seriously considered the possibility that Nelson would ever leave, and when he announced that he was moving to Paterson, New Jersey, the response was overwhelming. The day after the news broke, the *Tribune* ran an article entitled "GOLDEN ARM" AMBIENCE GONE, AUTHOR GOES, TOO. The *Daily News* followed five days later with a story headlined ALGREN HITS THE OPEN ROAD and a quote of Nelson saying, "There's nothing left for me in Chicago. I'm not involved with anything here. Chicago is gone." The *Tribune* ran a second story about Nelson's departure the same week, its gossip columnist reported that he had been spotted eating lunch at the Corona Café, and then it ran a third story. Not to be outdone, the *Chicago Sun-Times* published a column calling Nelson's departure "tragic."

Then Nelson announced he would be auctioning off the contents of his apartment, and the city's papers spent days chasing each other to report on the sale. Before Nelson escaped, Chicago's readers had been subjected to thirteen articles about his decision to leave—and heard about it on the radio and seen it reported on TV.

When Nelson's auction began at noon on March 8, 1975, there was a crowd of people waiting outside 1958 West Evergreen Street. They were each holding a number that guaranteed them admission to his apartment, and when the front door opened, twenty people climbed the unlit stairs that led to the third-floor flat. For the remainder of the day, the apartment remained full.

Nelson had shipped seventy-five boxes of books, collages, and pictures to Paterson, but he was hoping to sell everything else—and very nearly did. Writers, admirers, academics, gadflies, and reporters all visited the auction, and every one of them seemed to walk away with something. A *Sun-Times* reporter bought an old card table—with a rip in its felt—that Nelson had once used as a writing desk. A political consultant bought an unwashed frying pan for fifty cents. Nelson's friend Louis Szathmary bought the cookbook manuscript Nelson wrote for the WPA Writers' Project back in 1937—and someone unscrewed a hook from the inside of the bathroom door and pocketed it.

On the second day, Nelson sold his refrigerator and was forced to clean it out. There was butter inside, and frozen sausages, and he carried them downstairs and knocked on his neighbor's door.

"Hi, it's me," he said when she answered. He tried to place the food in her hands, but they didn't know each other well and she didn't speak

English, so she backed away. "No, no," he said. "It's okay, it's fresh. You see, I just sold my fridge and—" The woman accepted the food then, and closed the door.

Nelson climbed the stairs and grabbed half a loaf of bread and some meatloaf from the kitchen and carried them to the back porch so that no one would buy them. He might get hungry later, and there was nothing else to eat. There was a reporter following him, and when they got outside, Nelson turned to him and said, "This is all worthwhile. For the first time in my life—now that I'm leaving—Chicago is finally saying some nice things about me. You know, the kind of praise I wouldn't be getting unless I had just died."

Part V

EXILE

You know, Hemingway said that the main point
is to last. And I guess I'm still here.

—*Nelson Algren, March 1981*

Paterson, New Jersey

(March 14, 1975–July 1977)

*Nelson and Rubin "Hurricane" Carter discussing Carter's conviction and
pending legal appeal inside the Trenton State Prison library in 1975.*

Photo by Linda Kay

Nelson embraced Paterson after his move, and at first, he felt the
city was charming and quaint. His neighbors hung their laundry
on clotheslines in their yards, and his block was clean and quiet. There
was a little park near his house, and a bakery whose owner greeted him
warmly each morning, and one day he checked his mailbox and discovered a book written by a local poet named Louis Ginsberg—Allen
Ginsberg's father—that had been signed and delivered by its author.

The *New York Times* called Nelson for an interview that same week, and found him at ease in his new home. He hadn't even unpacked yet, but he was already thinking about retiring in Paterson. It's a "pleasant little country town," he said. "I have no plans beyond this. I like the climate. . . . I like the water tank on the hill. I'll just stay here and review books."

By then, Nelson's project had expanded. He had already written several hundred pages about Carter and his trial and knew he wanted to turn them into a series of articles, but he didn't know how many yet, or how long they would take to write. Work "proceeds slowly," he told a friend. "Mostly a matter of chasing down facts." Luckily, time was on his side. Carter and Artis had appealed their convictions after Bello and Bradley recanted their confessions, but their appeals had been denied. Their case was heading for the state supreme court, but it would be months before it was heard.

The Carter story dominated Nelson's life that spring and summer. He invested hundreds of hours in sorting through his research materials and trying to shape the police reports and courtroom testimony he had gathered into a narrative. He also interviewed witnesses and visited locations important to the case. Once, he went to the Lafayette Bar and Grill and tried to talk his way into a second-floor apartment—one of the witnesses at the trial had been living there on the night of the shootings, and Nelson wanted to see the street from her perspective—but the building's owner wouldn't allow him inside.

Over the course of his first months in Paterson, Nelson made himself more knowledgeable about Carter's life and legal case than anyone except Carter, Fred Hogan, and Carter's lawyers, and in that process, his understanding of the events surrounding the murders at the Lafayette Bar and Grill evolved. As his investigation progressed, he became more certain that Carter and Artis had been railroaded, but also more convinced their case could only be understood in the context of Paterson's history.

Paterson had once been an industrial hub—the country's first manufacturing capital. Industry thrived along the banks of the Passaic River for more than a century, and the city's factories and mills made silk, guns, beer, and aircraft engines—but after World War II, manufacturers moved to larger cities with busier ports, and Paterson began to decline.

Black southerners began arriving in Paterson around the same time as part of the Great Migration, and the city's white residents—Italians, mainly, whose forebears had been discriminated against when they immigrated decades earlier—responded by fleeing to the suburbs, or holding fast and growing paranoid and angry. The city's new black residents felt embattled as well, but with good reason. By the 1960s, they constituted almost one-fifth of the population, but weren't represented anywhere in government—not on the police force, not in City Hall, and not in the management of the remaining factories.

Inevitably, there was conflict. Urban uprisings and riots swept through the country in 1964, and over the course of a few months, people fought against police and National Guard troops in the streets of Harlem, Philadelphia, Chicago, Jersey City, and Rochester, New York—and then Paterson. That August, black residents smashed windows and threw Molotov cocktails, and in return, the police fired live rounds and tear gas. The riots dragged on for two days and didn't stop until Frank X. Graves—the city's mayor—appeared downtown in a police helmet, grabbed a radio, and announced that officers were free to "meet any violence with total force."

The fighting ended soon afterward, but white flight intensified in the months following. People abandoned their homes or sold them at discount, and the city never recovered.

Nelson could still feel the tension created that summer, and he soon realized that, beneath its quaint veneer, Paterson was seething with rage and riven along racial lines. Even for someone from Chicago, the level of vitriol and distrust he sensed was shocking. He never saw any black faces in his neighborhood or in the Italian restaurants he frequented, and when he hired a black man to install a phone line in his apartment, his landlady objected and barred the man from entering the building's basement to complete his task.

By summer, Nelson had begun calling Paterson an apartheid city and thinking of Rubin Carter's conviction as part of a larger story. Carter's case was so controversial, he realized, because it distilled the city's racial anxieties. Carter was an archetypal angry black man, and the Lafayette Bar and Grill was a redoubt of racial privilege—the neighborhood surrounding it had recently become majority black when the murders took place, but its bartender only served white patrons. Worse yet, Carter was defiant, so a reversal of his conviction would be understood as a challenge to the authority of the police department that had arrested him, the court that convicted him, and the newspapers that had denounced him.

People were scared of Carter even though he was in prison, and because Nelson was involved with Carter's case, they were worried about him as well. Fred Hogan thought Nelson's life was in danger while he was in Paterson, and he called every day to check on him.

One morning in September, a precocious young journalist named Linda Kay met Nelson at his apartment so they could visit Rubin Carter in Trenton State Prison.

Nelson welcomed Kay inside, led her into his kitchen, offered her a glass of water, and then dumped a dozen rolls onto a table and said, "Let's eat." She picked one up to be polite, though she wasn't hungry, and watched Nelson. He ate hurriedly, while standing, and tore at his rolls and chewed them with his mouth open. He barely looked at her during his meal, and didn't speak.

Nelson finished eating after a few minutes, and then he and Kay got into her car and began driving. The trip took about an hour, and Nelson was silent the entire time.

Kay had known Nelson for five months by then, and had never seen him act so oddly. She had first knocked on his door four days after he moved into the apartment on Quinn Street. She asked him for an interview that day, and he politely declined, but a few weeks later, he called her desk at the *Paterson News* and said he was ready to talk. He told her that he had read some of her articles and been impressed, and they had been in touch ever since. She wrote a story about his move to Paterson, and afterward he introduced her to Fred Hogan and convinced Rubin Carter to grant her an interview.

Nelson and Kay were separated when they reached the prison, and they were searched in different rooms. When they met afterward, Nelson was even more agitated. He still wasn't speaking, and there was a pained expression on his face. Later, he told Kay he couldn't tolerate confinement, and that even the thought of it terrified him.

Guards led Nelson and Kay to the prison's library, where they were supposed to meet Carter, and Nelson began pacing nervously. Then he looked up, noticed an oil painting of Richard Wright hanging high on a wall, and relaxed. "We were great friends in Chicago," Nelson told Kay. Then he posed beneath Wright's portrait, smiling rakishly, and Kay snapped a picture of him.

When Carter entered the library, he and Nelson greeted each other with smiles and a bear hug. Then they dragged two stools close together and conferred about Carter's appeal in quiet voices. Kay took a picture of them looking relaxed and conspiratorial, and when they were finished speaking, she interviewed Carter.

After she returned from the prison, Kay wrote a series of articles about Carter for the *Paterson News*. The first one ran on the front page beneath a picture of Nelson and Carter, and a few days later, Nelson was in court.

Nelson's landlady had been giving him trouble since she realized he was in Paterson to write about Carter, and after Kay's story was published, she served him with eviction papers. He was sixty-six years old at the time and went to bed at ten o'clock every night, but she claimed his lifestyle was incompatible with the neighborhood. Nelson refused to leave, but on October 6, 1975, a judge ordered him to vacate the premises.

Nelson's landlady claimed she had evicted Nelson because she wanted to occupy his unit herself, but Kay suspected Nelson's association with Carter was the real reason. Years later, she reflected on Nelson's brief tenure in Paterson, and wrote, "The police chief didn't want [Nelson there]. The county sheriff didn't want him there. Even the *Evening News* didn't want him there. Very few people in Paterson cared about his literary credentials ... They knew he was in Paterson to write about Rubin 'Hurricane' Carter, and that meant digging around for clues that might prove Carter didn't shoot three people in a bar in 1966. Nelson Algren was trouble."

Nelson moved into an apartment in a two-family home at 82 Maple Avenue in Hackensack, New Jersey, after his eviction. His new block was quiet and tree-lined, as Quinn Street had been, but his landlord was a history professor and his next-door neighbor was black, so he felt more at ease being a friend of Rubin Carter's there than he had in Paterson.

Nelson resumed his work after settling in, and in early 1976, he finally came to terms with the fact that he was writing a book, not a series of articles. His manuscript included a detailed account of Carter's childhood and boxing career by then, as well as the killings at the Lafayette Bar and Grill, the trial, and Carter's time in prison. It was already four hundred pages long and kept growing, and so did Nelson's ambition. Sometime that year, he began saying that he wouldn't sell his story for less than a hundred thousand dollars.

There was good reason for Nelson to think his book would become a sensation. Rubin Carter and John Artis had been obscure figures when Nelson began writing about them, but they, and their case, had since become famous. Bob Dylan had recently recorded a protest song called

"Hurricane," and Muhammad Ali, William Friedkin, Harry Belafonte, and Johnny Cash had all joined an organization called the Hurricane Trust Defense Committee. Interest in Carter and Artis's case peaked in March 1976, when the Supreme Court of New Jersey overturned its convictions and granted them a new trial. Both men were released on bail, and there was a general consensus among their supporters that a second jury would clear their names.

Henry Kisor, the book editor of the *Chicago Daily News*, visited Nelson in Hackensack just after Carter and Artis were released, and found him excited about his book and its prospects.

"Do you prefer this kind of work to fiction?" Kisor asked.

"Yes, I like this sort of job very well," Nelson said, "because it's a living job. I mean, you don't know where the end is going to be. You see, two years ago, when I came in, Hurricane wasn't known, except to old time fight fans. They were the only ones who knew about him. So it's interesting because the scene keeps changing. The situation keeps changing."

I hope the book comes out before the trial, Nelson said. He explained that Putnam had rejected the manuscript, but he was happy they had. He had been trying to void his contract with the publisher since they botched the release of *The Last Carousel*, and now that they had taken a pass on his book about Carter, he was free to sell it to anyone he pleased.

Random House will publish the book, Nelson told Kisor. I haven't sent it to them yet, but I know they will.

N elson arrived in Paterson at 8:45 a.m. on October 5, 1976, and made his way to the courthouse to observe the start of Carter and Artis's second trial. He remained in the building until the court adjourned, and then returned the next morning, and the next, and the next, through October, and then November, and into December.

The atmosphere in Paterson was poisonous during the trial. The local papers had published more than three hundred stories and editorials about Carter and Artis in the lead-up to the trial, all negative—"Murderer," they said. "Assassin." "Killer of white people." The trial itself only made things worse. The prosecutors had not been able to establish any real motive that could explain why Carter and Artis would have murdered strangers, so they advanced the theory that the shootings at the Lafayette Bar and Grill had been undertaken to exact "racial revenge" for the murder of a black bar owner earlier that night.

But Nelson still felt confident Carter and Artis would be acquitted. There was no physical evidence linking them to the crime, and the only witness who placed them at the scene was Alfred Bello—maybe the least credible man in New Jersey. He had testified at the first trial, recanted his testimony under oath several years later, and then, during the second trial, he recanted his recantation and swore he had been telling the truth during the first trial.

The state rested its case in December, and the jury began their deliberations. They reached a verdict on December 22, 1976, and when they filed into the room to announce their decision, Nelson was present and waiting anxiously. Once the court had come to order, the foreman said: We find that Rubin Carter and John Artis are guilty of murder.

Nelson was dumbstruck. "The verdict was a stunner," he wrote to a friend, "not only to me. Everyone around there, who wasn't in uniform, assumed it would be for acquittal."

Nelson visited Carter at the New Jersey State Prison at Trenton after the trial. He was carrying a magazine and a copy of one of his books when he arrived, but the guards said he wasn't allowed to give either to Carter. He entered the visiting area after passing through security, poured himself a cup of water, and waited.

There was no bear hug when Carter arrived this time, no smiles. The two men sat facing each other, and Nelson told Carter about his hassle with the guards and made fun of the prison's rules. He was trying to get a laugh, but none was forthcoming.

"They're crazy," Carter said flatly. "This is an insane asylum where the patients have taken over the management."

Nelson changed the subject. He had come to discuss the case so he could give his book an ending. Your expensive New York lawyer, he said, didn't do you any good. He turned everyone off because he was an outsider. "But the man who lost your case for you was yourself."

"How?" Carter asked.

"After ten years of proclaiming your innocence," Nelson said, "you failed to say it to the jury. It might have made all the difference."

Carter demurred. He said declining to testify had been the smart move. If he had taken the stand, the prosecution would have been able to impeach him and bring in new witnesses to testify to his character and truthfulness. "It was my own decision, to fall or stand by," he said. "I'd do it the same way again."

They talked about the case some more, and Carter's troubles. He had been accused of assaulting a woman while out on bail, and lost many of his celebrity supporters as a result. Nelson had interviewed the woman, and she told him the attack was unprovoked. He asked Carter for a response, and Carter called it a lovers' quarrel. She tried to slash my eye with her nails, he said, so I punched her.

Then Nelson moved on. In *The Sixteenth Round*, he reminded Carter, you wrote about consulting different aspects of your personality while in your cell—"Rubin, Hurricane and Carter. Hurricane was the one who wanted to throw it all up for grabs. Have you talked to Hurricane lately?"

Carter grinned, and leaned toward Nelson. "Look, man," he said. "I *am* Rubin 'Hurricane' Carter. It's all one man. It's *me*. You understand?"

Nelson returned to Hackensack and added a scene describing his final visit with Carter to the end of his manuscript. Then he began revising, but with no sense of urgency.

A *Chicago Tribune* reporter named Jim Gallagher visited Nelson for an interview three months later, and noticed that Nelson's typewriter looked like it had not been used in some time. There was a sheet of yellow paper wound around the platen, but it was drooping uselessly.

Gallagher questioned whether there was any chance of selling a book that argued for Carter's innocence, and Nelson insisted he would see his project through.

"I've gone this far with it so I'll finish it," he said. He had received a grant from the National Endowment for the Arts so that he could afford to continue writing, but he allowed that his book might never see print. "It's possible, I suppose, that I'll never publish another book," he said, "but so what? That'll mean just one less book in the world."

Nelson completed his manuscript later that year, and gave it the title *The Other Carter*. He sent it to Candida Donadio so she could try to sell it, and then he visited Chicago and spent six weeks with Stephen and Helene Deutch. Donadio began shopping the book while Nelson was on vacation and continued doing so for more than a year, but never received any offers. As Gallagher prophesied, no one was interested in publishing a book that cast doubt on the guilt of a man who had been convicted of murder not once, but twice.

The Devil's Stocking

(August 1977–August 1980)

Nelson lived alone on a dead-end street in Hackensack and made no effort to establish himself in the city. He was friendly with his landlord and said hello to his neighbors. He joined the YMCA and knew the regulars at the OTB downtown, but that was the extent of his contact with Hackensack.

That sounds like a lonely way to live, but it wasn't. Fred Hogan and Stephen Deutch called regularly, and every few months, Nelson threw a party, and friends from New York City crossed the Hudson River to attend. The painter Richard Merkin came to one, and the actors Geraldine Page and Rip Torn dropped by another.

Nelson and Page had known each other since 1955, when she was visiting Chicago to appear in a play and he was trying to divorce Amanda. They met in Page's hotel room regularly for the length of Page's run, but they never became lovers because Nelson never tried. She had the impression that he believed it was louche for a man to make the first move on a woman, and she was too shy to take charge. Page had felt close to Nelson since, and she was happy to find him in good spirits at his party—smiling while everyone cavorted, and occasionally silencing the room to tell a joke or a story.

Two men in particular kept a close watch on Nelson in the aftermath of the Carter case: Roger Groening and Roy Finer.

Groening was the owner of a bookstore in Saratoga, New York. He had written a fan letter to Nelson in the early 1960s and they had been corresponding since. It was a casual friendship for about a decade, but then Groening's wife left him and took their child, and he attempted suicide, and was confined to a psychiatric hospital.

When Nelson learned where Groening was, he visited—and after he returned to Chicago, he called the hospital every day. I tried to kill myself once too, he told Groening. I survived, and you will too. He hadn't admitted as much to anyone in decades.

Groening did recover, and afterward, he was devoted to Nelson. The two men wrote to each other regularly for years, and when Nelson moved east, Groening made a habit of driving to New Jersey to make sure Nelson was safe and had everything he needed. He invited Nelson to Saratoga as well, and introduced him to Roy Finer.

Finer was a New York City homicide detective whom Nelson referred to as "the big cop." He was more than six and a half feet tall, but looked even larger because his hair was a jumble of thick black curls and his body was broad and powerful. He carried a gun on his waist and another on his ankle, and he walked with a lumbering kind of swagger.

Finer and Groening had been friends since grade school. They were almost family, and when Groening told Finer what Nelson had done for him, Nelson became family too. Finer visited Nelson in Hackensack, and sometimes he allowed Nelson to shadow him at work, or brought him to the medical examiner's office to observe autopsies.

Nelson boarded a bus in downtown Hackensack in May 1978 and rode it into Manhattan. He got off at the Port Authority Bus Terminal and walked north and east until he reached the Mansfield Hotel at 12 West Forty-fourth Street, where he paid twenty dollars for a room without a television.

The next morning, he woke early, put on a dark red shirt without buttoning it all the way, draped a blue jacket over his shoulders, and walked outside. It was 8 a.m., and when he left the hotel and stepped onto the sidewalk, an Irishman with graying hair and thick dark eyebrows approached him. "You owe us another one," he said, meaning a book.

"I don't owe anything," Nelson said.

The Irishman was a *Daily News* columnist named Jimmy Breslin, and after he and Nelson greeted each other, they walked across the street, entered a coffee shop, and sat down at an uncleared table.

Breslin was planning to write a feature about Nelson for the next day's paper, so he began interviewing. "When was the last time you were in Chicago?" he asked. "How long have you been around here?" For a while, they just chatted, but before the interview was over, Breslin pressed Nelson hard on the one question he was really interested in: "So, why don't you sit down and start a fiction book, use Carter as a basis, use anybody? Why don't you start an Algren novel?"

Nelson squirmed. "People say to me," he said, "'When are you going to give us the big one?' I say, 'When you start reading the little ones.'"

Breslin's *Daily News* column the following day was maybe the kindest thing ever written about Nelson. "When you say today that Nelson Algren is a great American writer," it read, "there are not enough people, particularly young people, who have heard of that name. This is something that should not be." To make his point, Breslin quoted the first two paragraphs of *The Man with the Golden Arm* in full.

Then Breslin proclaimed, "He should be a wealthy man. Fifty years from now, he will be studied in schools as perhaps one-two-three in his time, and a student will wonder how this man lived with all his riches."

Nelson had given up on his book about Carter by then, but a few weeks after he sat down with Breslin, he returned to his manuscript and began to fictionalize Carter's story—just as Breslin suggested, and contrary to his promise that he would never write another novel. Nelson applied for a Guggenheim fellowship in July to finance the project, and used Breslin as a reference. The book, he said, will be called *The*

Fighter. He changed the title to *Chinatown* later, and later still, he settled on *The Devil's Stocking.*

Nelson devoted the next year and a half of his life to that project. At first, he made minor changes to the text. He changed Rubin Carter's name to Ruby Calhoun, and changed Fred Hogan's name to Barney Kerrigan. The Lafayette Bar and Grill became the Melody Bar and Grill—but much of the chronology, some of the dialogue, and most of the settings remained the same.

Eventually, Nelson began to break away from his source material, and he developed the novel so that it was related to the story of Carter's conviction and incarceration, but distinct from it. He removed John Artis's character from the book, and created two new ones—Dovie-Jean Dawkins and Red Haloways. He moved a portion of the novel's action to Times Square, and he wrote a prison riot into the plot and based it, in part, on the Attica prison uprising in 1971.

In some ways, the book is the most conservative Nelson ever wrote. It is tightly plotted, and the prose is restrained. The cast of characters is small, there are few lengthy sociological digressions, and more words are spent rendering dialogue than creating atmosphere. Though Nelson had first become famous for the lyricism of his prose, he tells Carter's story using economical, journalistic sentences that propel the narrative without drawing attention to themselves. Lines like these, describing Ruby Calhoun's prison: "The hundred-odd men who report every morning for sick call don't get physical examinations. Chronic physical or emotional disabilities are not assessed. If a prisoner appears seriously ill, he is sent back to his cell. If not quite sick to death, he is given a pill. He retains the privilege of complaining loudly and bitterly. So long as he does not sustain his complaint too long, too loudly, or too bitterly, he is tolerated."

In other respects, though, the novel is incredibly bold. Though written by a white man nearing seventy, its protagonists are black and its subjects are race, the criminal justice system, and dislocation. After Nelson broke from the constraints of nonfiction, he created characters that embody the fear and bigotry he observed in Paterson and used them to give voice to hateful ideas no one had been willing to express when he interviewed them. The white man who shot and killed the black bartender on the same night that the murders in the Lafayette Bar and Grill were committed, for instance, describes his actions this way in *The Devil's Stocking*: "I went down there and I took my shotgun. Oh yeah. Just one crack out of that redheaded nigger and he's going to get it. Oh yeah.

"The redhead ain't there. So I shoot the old man instead. One is as good as another, they're all alike, makes no difference which one you shoot. You think I won't talk to a jury the way I talk to you now? The jury will love me."

Similarly, Nelson used Red Haloways—one of the purely fictitious characters in the book—to comment on the racial stereotypes that had made it so easy to demonize and convict Rubin Carter.

Ruby Calhoun is a serious, disciplined man who speaks in a straightforward manner in *The Devil's Stocking*. He's very much the person Nelson perceived when he spoke to Rubin Carter, but Red Haloways, in contrast, is the man that people who read the Paterson newspapers imagined Carter was—angry, irrational, and so damaged by racism that he has been driven mad and become violent.

Haloways has an almost pathological hatred of white people, and by the end of the novel, he's been committed to a psychiatric institution, where he structures his days around receipt of the newspaper. "He spread the paper's section out on his bed," Nelson wrote, "and sat in his armchair before them. He began stripping the business section first, into long, neat strips. When it was done he gathered the strips and put them into the waste basket. And took another glass of water.

"It was slow work, because each section had to be stripped neatly and scissors were not allowed."

In the novel, Calhoun is convicted of murder twice, but Haloways— a real killer—escapes serious punishment. The irrational fear Calhoun has engendered in the city's police and white residents blinds them to the real threat—a man who has become a killer after being subjected to that same irrational fear and bigotry for years.

Maybe most presciently, Nelson used the novel to comment on the fear and anger demographic change had created in Paterson. In the novel's final scene, the character based on Fred Hogan visits the site of the murders Calhoun was convicted of. He goes into the bar alone and looks around. It had once been an all-white establishment in a black neighborhood, but it had since become black-owned. After that change, it was impossible to imagine what the neighborhood's white residents had been so fearful of.

"The tavern that once was the Melody Bar and Grill is now the Aquarius Lounge," Nelson wrote.

"The changes have been great. There had been no change at all.

"The pool table remains in the middle of the room; but the players now are black. Budweiser ads still border the walls but the handsome young marrieds in them are, again, black."

Hogan's character sits at the bar, and asks the bartender, with faux innocence, "Isn't this the place that got into the papers some years back?"

"The bartender was a black woman who had read Frantz Fanon," Nelson wrote.

"'Maybe it is. Then again maybe it isn't,' she replied, concealing her hostility beneath the guise of courtesy. 'We don't know anything about this place when it was a white bar. I'm sure I couldn't tell you.'"

"I heard there was a triple homicide here," Hogan's character says.

"'Mister,' the woman came close to her white customer, 'I don't know what you're after but you won't find it here.'"

And Nelson ends the book: "All, all is changed.

"And everything remains the same."

Nelson sent his manuscript to Candida Donadio in April 1979, and eventually the publisher at Arbor House, Donald Fine, showed interest in it. He liked the book, but thought it was still too faithful to its source material—too similar to Carter's story—so he sent Nelson several pages of suggestions.

Nelson began revising his manuscript, and submitted a new draft in October. Fine offered Nelson fifteen thousand dollars for the book but asked for more changes, and Nelson agreed to continue revising, but told Fine he would have to come up with more money.

When Christmas arrived, Nelson was still writing. He was alone for the holidays that year, and before the night ended, he was having trouble breathing and was sweating heavily. He remained in his apartment for a long time, trying to muscle through his anxiety and fear, but eventually, he called his downstairs neighbor for help.

An ambulance picked Nelson up the next morning and brought him to the hospital, where he was admitted for observation and informed that he had suffered a minor heart attack.

Roy Finer called Nelson's house that morning. He let the phone ring for a long time, but Nelson never answered, so he drove to Hackensack and knocked on Nelson's door. There was no answer there, either, so Finer asked a child he saw playing in the street if they had seen anything out of the ordinary.

A few minutes later, Finer entered the local hospital and located Nelson's room: 461-1.

"How the hell did you find me?" Nelson asked, surprised.

"I'm a detective," Finer said.

Roger Groening drove down from Saratoga when he heard about Nelson's heart attack, and when he arrived, Nelson swore him to secrecy. Roy Finer was in the room as well, and Nelson made them both promise to keep his illness to themselves. If anyone learns that I had a heart attack, he said, Arbor House won't buy my book. They'll just wait for me to die so they can get it for nothing.

Nelson returned home in January and went back to work. He sent the final version of his manuscript to Candida Donadio the following month, and she sent it to Arbor House. When he received it, Donald

Fine offered Nelson fifteen thousand dollars—the same amount he'd offered the year before— and Nelson turned him down flat.[*]

The novel wasn't Nelson's best—some of the transitions between scenes were jarring, and there was too much courtroom drama—but it was the best book he had written in twenty years, and he wanted a hundred thousand dollars for it—anything less, he felt, was an insult. The following year, Nelson saw Donald Fine at a party and called him a "cheap SOB" in front of a room full of people.

Nelson turned seventy-one a few days after he rejected Donald Fine's offer, and he began thinking seriously about how he wanted to spend the time he had remaining.

Mortality had been the subtext of Nelson's life for a while by then. Friends had been dying at a steady pace for years—first Jesse Blue, and then Bud Fallon and James Blake—and journalists had begun asking him retrospective questions about his life and work. And though he still received letters from young writers, lately, their senders addressed him as a veteran, not a soldier. "You," Cormac McCarthy had written a few months earlier, "were one of the people who influenced me in becoming a writer."

In May, Nelson decided he had had enough—of writing, of caring about his legacy, and of city life. He had always wanted to live by the sea, so he bought a map of Long Island, brought it home, and allowed his eyes to drift down the coastline—Oyster Bay, Cold Spring Harbor, Southampton. He didn't know a soul in any of them, and didn't care.

The year before, a young journalist named Jan Herman had interviewed Nelson for the *Chicago Daily News*, and afterward, he and Nelson developed a friendship. Herman, Nelson learned, had led a fascinating and idiosyncratic life—he had hung around with Allen Ginsberg and William Burroughs, worked at City Lights Books in San

---

[*] That would be about forty-five thousand today.

Francisco, started a little magazine called *Earthquake*, and had been the editor-in-chief for a small publisher called Something Else Press.

One of Herman's many literary friends was a translator named Carl Weissner, who lived in Mannheim, and because Nelson's work had always been popular in Germany, Herman put Nelson and Weissner in touch. Soon, that connection proved lucrative for both men. Weissner helped Nelson place two stories in the German edition of *Playboy*, found a publisher interested in having him translate *The Man with the Golden Arm* and *The Last Carousel* for publication, and then began soliciting offers for a German edition of *The Devil's Stocking*.

Money from those deals began arriving in the spring of 1980, and when it did, Nelson rented a small house in Southampton, sight unseen, and hired a moving company to pack his books into one hundred boxes and drive them to Long Island.

Nelson moved into his new home and lived there peacefully for several days, but when the movers arrived and began unloading his things, his landlord appeared. She looked at the truck, and Nelson's many boxes, and announced he was no longer welcome to rent her home. She said his things would never fit inside the house, and told him to leave—immediately.

Nelson found a payphone and began placing calls. He had nowhere to live, and his possessions were scattered across a stranger's lawn.

Eventually, Nelson reached Joe Pintauro, a playwright and novelist he had met only once. Pintauro lived a few miles away, in Sag Harbor, so he drove to Southampton, picked Nelson up, and brought him home. Then he gave Nelson a change of clothes and put a drink in his hand.

The next day, Pintauro found Nelson a small apartment, and by August, Nelson had moved into a house on Glover Street—just a block from Upper Sag Harbor Cove.

"The End Is Nothing, the Road Is All"

(September 1980–May 1981)

In his prime, Nelson was a solitary creature—a man most at ease in his goat's nest, a flat that looked down onto an empty lot and a trash-strewn alley. He forswore luxury, scoffed at chasing status, trained like a boxer to keep his mind sharp, and avoided the company of writers—because writers who spend time with writers write books about writers who spend time with writers, so that their work will be read by other writers. He was never interested in that, so instead, he wandered the neon wilderness by night, and stalked people who lived behind billboards or slept in cage hotels. They were the story no one saw, and he believed it was possible to forecast the future by reading their scars.

But by the time he reached Sag Harbor, Nelson was a jolly old man with a big, round belly, and he had had enough of abstention. He lived a block from the ocean in a wood-framed house with a peaked roof and a fireplace, and in the mornings, he slipped into the frigid Atlantic and swam a little, but not a lot. He liked to laugh and to make people laugh, and when he found himself in uptight company, he let them know he had no patience for pretension. In expensive restaurants, he removed his dentures at the table and rinsed them in his water glass.

Solitude had also lost its appeal, so Nelson surrounded himself with friends and admirers. He invited Roger Groening and Roy Finer to visit, and he hosted Jan Herman, his wife, Janet, and their daughter, Olivia, for an entire week. Sag Harbor, Nelson soon learned, was thick with writers, and when his new neighbors Kurt Vonnegut, Peter Matthiessen, John Irving, and E. L. Doctorow sought him out, he welcomed their company. Betty Friedan had a house just across the street from Nelson's, and she often drove him around town because his only means of transportation was a used bicycle.

Nelson was no longer writing regularly by the time he reached Sag Harbor, but his mind was still sharp, and because there was nothing else to preoccupy him, he dwelled on the past and wondered how he would be remembered when he was gone. There was a debate about the merits of his life and work raging constantly in his mind, and no side ever claimed victory for long.

In the summer of 1980, a German film crew visited Nelson for an interview, and he swaggered for them. "I am a survivor," he said, ". . . the greatest taker of the mandatory eight-count who gets up and starts all over."

But by Christmas, Nelson was gripped by doubt. He spent the holiday at a party hosted by Gloria Jones—James Jones's widow, and mother to a young woman named Kaylie. Everyone drank heavily that night—martinis, and Stolichnaya—and when the festivities ended, Kaylie Jones, the best drunk driver in the house, volunteered to drive Nelson home.

Jones loaded Nelson into the car, got behind the wheel, and began driving toward Sag Harbor—her eyes locked on the twisting road. For a long time, she and Nelson were silent. Then he spoke. At dinner, Jones announced she had applied to Columbia's MFA program, and he wanted to know why.

"Why do you want to be a writer?" he asked.

"I don't know if I want to be a writer," she said.

"Good. Don't become a writer," he said.

"I'm just going to study writing," she hedged.

"Good," he said. "Study all you want, just don't become a writer. It's a lousy, stupid thing to do. You start out thinking people are going to admire you and love you and respect you but really nobody gives a shit. It's a terrible life."

Then, in February 1981, Nelson changed his mind again. That month, he learned that the American Academy and National Institute of Arts and Letters had decided to make him a full member. Donald Barthelme had nominated him, and Malcolm Cowley and Jacques Barzun seconded.

Nelson had been wary of awards for years, and was dubious about the intentions and integrity of the people who conferred them. When an arts organization presented him with a grant a few years earlier, he had refused to thank them because he didn't see why he should, and he had had Kurt Vonnegut accept the Award of Merit for the Novel in his stead. But this was different. Membership in the academy wasn't a bauble conferred by the literary establishment—it was an invitation to join.

On April 9, Nelson made his way into Manhattan wearing a pinstriped suit, a gravy-stained tie, and a rosette that indicated he was a member of the academy. He met a woman named Carolyn Gaiser that afternoon, and together they flagged down a cab and headed uptown.

Nelson and Gaiser met at the Bread Loaf Writers' Conference in 1968, and they had dated briefly. She knew him to be a cynical man, but that night was different. He seemed almost giddy. "You don't know how lucky you are," he said. He had just bet a horse and won, and he displayed his winning ticket proudly. "Tonight's on OTB," he said.

The cab pulled over on West 155th Street, and Nelson and Gaiser stepped out, climbed the academy building's wide, regal steps, and passed beneath an ornate wrought-iron gate. They went inside and found the bar and ordered drinks, but then a member of the staff interrupted them.

"Mr. Algren," she said, "You're *late*. You've missed the members' meeting." She took Nelson and Gaiser in hand and led them into a library, where the academy's members were seated. "Just a moment," she said. "I'd like to introduce another new member—who was late. Nelson Algren."

The room erupted in applause, and when it died away, people read tributes to Nelson and praised his body of work.

When they finished, Nelson turned to Gaiser and said, "Here we are. Meeting the elite."

"You're one of the elite yourself, how does it feel?" she asked.

"Joining this outfit can be very important for a writer," Nelson reflected. "For your work," he continued. "They start taking your work much more seriously." His novel about Rubin Carter was about to be released in Germany as *Calhoun*, and his other major works were also scheduled for publication there. He had been paid well for them, and if the book took off, it would mean better sales in Italy and France, and possibly an American edition of *The Devil's Stocking*. It seemed just possible that his writing could have a renaissance.

Nelson looked into his martini glass then, and told Gaiser, "Drink up, kid. These drinks are on the house."

Nelson's formal induction into the academy was scheduled for May 20, and he decided to throw himself a party to celebrate it on May 9. He invited all his friends to attend, and most said they would try. Jan Herman made plans to fly out from Chicago with his family so he could write about the party for the *Sun-Times*, and Roy Finer said he would take the train from the Bronx.

The afternoon before the party, a journalist named W.J. Weatherby dropped by Nelson's house for an interview and found him in good spirits. They sat in the living room, and Nelson joked about his nomination and reflected on his career.

"I didn't know I was running for office until they informed me I was elected," he said. "It puts you in the league of people who are 'distinguished,' so I'm told by my literary friends."

"If I had only written one book," he said, "I'd want it to be *A Walk on the Wild Side*. Or maybe this new one, *The Devil's Stocking*."

Weatherby shifted the conversation to Beauvoir, and Nelson became agitated. Almost two decades had passed, but he was still upset that she had written about their affair. "I've been in whorehouses all over the world," he said, "and the women there always close the door. . . . But this woman flung the door open and called in the public and the press."

Tension gathered in Nelson's chest as he spoke, and he became short of breath. Earlier that day, he had visited a doctor and been advised to check himself into a hospital, but he had refused. He was about to host a party, and people were flying in from out of state to attend.

Weatherby changed the subject, but Nelson was like a dog with a bone. She violated my privacy, he said, so I'll violate hers. He threatened to auction off her love letters. They were sitting nearby in a tin container, and he said, "If one half of a correspondence is made public, then the other half should be."

Weatherby, mindful of Nelson's health, said he should go—it was getting late. Nelson encouraged him to stay and talk some more, but Weatherby insisted.

Come to the party tomorrow, then, Nelson said. "I've already bought the liquor."

When Weatherby left, Nelson was alone in his little house by the sea. Everything he needed to do to prepare for the party had been done, so he went out. He got on his bike and pedaled around Sag Harbor, beneath the dark spring sky, until he tired of it, and then he returned home.

He entered his cottage after midnight, and sometime later he went to the bathroom on the second floor. His chest was feeling tight again, and while he stood there alone, his heart quivered, and then stopped.

He fell, and as he did, his left wrist smacked against something. The glass face of his wristwatch broke, and the hands froze in place. They read: 6:05.

Roy Finer arrived at Nelson's house a few hours later and tried the front door. It was locked, so he went around to the back door and let himself in. He climbed the stairs, and found Nelson supine on the bathroom floor. The phone was ringing, but Finer ignored it, kneeled down, and placed a hand on Nelson's belly. The flesh was cold, so he went downstairs and sat on the couch.

Jan Herman called a few minutes later. He had been trying to get through while Finer was upstairs, and when no one answered, he and his wife, Janet, and their daughter, Olivia, went to the store and bought a bottle of Chivas Regal. They left the store with their purchase, and Jan returned to the payphone he had used a few minutes earlier and called again.

This time, Finer answered. "Don't come," he said. "He's gone."

Nelson was buried in Sag Harbor's Oakland Cemetery on Monday, May 11, before a crowd of about thirty people. Stephen Deutch and his daughter Katherine were there, and so were Peter Matthiessen, Pete Hammill, Gloria Jones, and Linda Ronstadt. A woman with bright red hair and blue-green eyes arrived wearing all black, and began sobbing. She told the other mourners that she had read every word Nelson wrote, and intended to forswear novels for the remainder of her life now that he was dead.

When the ceremony began, Joe Pintauro stepped forward and read from one of Nelson's poems. A cold wind was blowing, and he said:

Again that hour when taxis start deadheading home
Before the trolley buses start to run
And snow dreams in a lace of mist drift down

When from asylum, barrack, cell and cheap hotel
All those whose lives were lived by someone else
Come again with palms outstretched to claim
What never rightly was their own.

Nelson's casket was lowered into the grave when Pintauro finished, and later, a headstone bearing an epitaph selected by Candida Donadio was installed at its head.

It read:

THE END IS NOTHING

THE ROAD IS ALL.

Afterword

On June 29, 1981, a group of Nelson's friends gathered at the Second City Theater in Chicago to remember him. Studs Terkel served as emcee, and began by saying, "This is in the nature of a celebration rather than a service." He was on stage with a piano player when the program began, and he said, "Nelson just loved the blues, so Fred is playing the blues; it's as simple as that."

The evening was dedicated to reminiscing, and over its course, friends from almost every period of Nelson's life paid their respects. Jan Herman spoke about Nelson's years in New Jersey and his work on *The Devil's Stocking*, and Stephen Deutch said Nelson was "the warmest human being" he had ever known. Then Dave Peltz told everyone about the time he helped Nelson cash a check for twenty-five thousand dollars.

Len Despres, a former Chicago alderman, walked on stage and said, "It was a great privilege to know Nelson Algren because you felt, when you were with him, that you were in the presence of an authentic genius." And the poet Gwendolyn Brooks took the microphone and explained that Nelson often brought out-of-town guests to her house, "saying," she recalled, that before his guests met "the devils," he wanted them to "meet something human." My husband and I "considered that a great compliment," she said.

The Second City memorial was an auspicious start to the creation of Nelson's legacy, and other encouraging events soon followed. Kay Boyle and Jan Herman raised funds for, and created, a literary award named for Nelson. Arbor House released an American edition of *The Devil's Stocking* in 1983, and around the same time, a young editor named Dan Simon read one of Nelson's short stories, fell in love with Nelson's writing, and released new editions of *The Neon Wilderness* and *Never Come Morning* through a publishing imprint called Four Walls Eight Windows.

But despite those promising developments, Nelson's legacy soon became warped by misunderstandings and inaccuracies. Though no one close to Nelson ever claimed he drank heavily, it became an accepted fact after his death that he had been an alcoholic— and though it seems Nelson only gambled problematically during two distinct periods of his life, it has long been understood that he lost everything he earned playing cards. Nelson maintained many of his friendships for decades, but people now say he was a loner who burned every bridge he crossed. And though Nelson's work was praised and admired by all the literary greats of his day, it is now most associated with the verdicts of the Red Scare–era critics who dismissed him as the "bard of the stumblebum."

Nelson laid the groundwork for some of these misunderstandings by distorting his life story in *Conversations with Nelson Algren*, but others deserve blame as well. The FBI damaged Nelson's legacy by failing to release his file in its entirety when first requested, therefore obscuring the cause of his career's decline. Doubleday denied Algren the opportunity to frame his body of work and explain his convictions when it declined to publish *Nonconformity*. And many people who spoke on the record about Nelson after his death made intentionally misleading statements, or spoke beyond their competence— Dave Peltz, for instance, told several interviewers that Nelson had no political convictions, and stopped writing novels because he had writer's block.

But now, almost four decades after his death, it is finally possible to tell Nelson's story in full—his complete FBI file has been released, his letters have been donated to more than fifty archives, and new interviews have been unearthed. His life and work can now be evaluated in their proper historical context for the first time, and it is my hope that his writing will find new readers as a result, his reputation will be repaired, and his ideas about literature will be debated anew.

ACKNOWLEDGMENTS

When my partner and I decided to have a child in 2011, I began wondering whether that child, when it grew old enough to ponder such things, would be proud to have me as a father. I was freelancing at the time, doing a little ghostwriting, and hiring out as a researcher, and I thought, *If I were that kid, I wouldn't be.*

So, I decided to change tacks. I found a day job, began writing primarily before dawn, and promised myself I would only take on projects I was passionate about—whether or not they paid.

Soon afterward, I came up with the idea of writing a profile of Nelson Algren, an author whose work I had recently fallen in love with. I pitched my idea to *The Believer*, and they said I was welcome to write the article on spec. So I did. After my essay was accepted for publication, Karolina Waclawiak and Andi Winnette, *The Believer*'s editors at the time, gave it a tough and thoughtful edit, and made it the lead feature of the magazine's January 2013 issue.

Then things began happening quickly. I sent a copy of *The Believer* to Algren's publisher, Dan Simon, and in return, he invited me out for a beer and introduced me to an agent named Ria Julien, who took me on as a client. Then Jan Herman emailed to say he had read my essay and liked it. He had spent a good chunk of the 1980s researching a biography of Algren that he never wrote, and he said I was welcome to all of the material he gathered during that time if I decided to write about Algren again.

Tom Mayer, an editor at W. W. Norton, was the next stranger to reach out. He had also read the *Believer* essay, and wanted to know if I was interested in writing a biography. I was. Over the course of the next few months, I wrote a book proposal, Mayer ushered it past the board at Norton, and I signed a contract to write the book you're holding.

If your name appears in one of the preceding paragraphs, you should know that this book would not exist without you, and that I owe you much more than "Thanks."

I owe many other people gratitude as well, of course. Nora Carroll—my partner when I began writing this book, now my wife—read every page of my manuscript several times, and provided invaluable editorial advice. My son, Dante—yet to be born when I began writing about Nelson Algren, and now seven years old—suffered through so many stories about Algren that he began calling him "Uncle Nelson."

Makis Antzoulatos, Nora Fussner, Michael Wolraich, and Geoff Fuller all read early drafts of my manuscript and provided valuable feedback. My friends from the Neptun Polish beer garden (RIP) were always encouraging and supportive. Christine Guilfoyle, an Algren scholar from the UK, was generous with her insights and information. Aaron Shulman offered himself as a sounding board for ideas, and whenever I needed to focus solely on my writing, Richard Wechsler let me hide out in his house on the Maryland shore.

Without the financial support of the Leon Levy Center for Biography, it's likely I would not have completed this book, and without the insights provided by the center's other 2015–16 fellows—Eric Washington, Gordana-Dana Grozdanic, Blake Gopnik, Jennifer Chancellor, and Daron Jabari Howard—this book wouldn't be as good as it is. The center's staff—Gary Giddins, Annalyn Swan, and Michael Gately—read a few of my early chapters as well, and provided a steadying presence in my life when I began rewriting my manuscript for the second time and started to wonder why I had ever wanted to write a book in the first place.

Warren Leming from the Nelson Algren Committee welcomed me to Chicago when I visited, and so did Michael Caplan, Nicole

Bernardi-Reis, and Gail Sonnenfeld—the team behind *Algren*, the feature-length documentary released in 2014. They were generous enough to share their research with me, and so were Denis Mueller, Mark Blottner, and Ilko Davidov—the team behind *Nelson Algren: The End Is Nothing, the Road Is All*.

By the end of my research process, I had retrieved material from almost fifty archives, and in every instance I found the archivists and librarians I interacted with to be helpful and professional. If you are one of them, thank you. Among their number, Rebecca Jewett and her team at Ohio State University stand out. They were incredibly accommodating and responsive to requests during the three weeks I spent with them.

I also owe a debt of gratitude to Bettina Drew, Algren's first biographer. After Drew's book was published in 1989, she deposited her research material at Ohio State University—including, most importantly, audio recordings of the interviews she conducted. After reviewing those interviews, I came to some very different conclusions about Algren's character and career than Drew did—but that is primarily because I was able to check the information she gathered against a virtually unredacted copy of Algren's FBI file, and material gathered from dozens of archives that did not exist when she wrote her book. Most of the people Drew spoke with are now long dead, and without access to her recordings, I would not have been able to tell Algren's story with the level of detail and accuracy it demanded. There's no way to write a responsible biography of Algren without reviewing Drew's interviews, and for that reason, every Algren fan is in her debt.

I am also indebted to the generations of Algren's champions who kept interest in his work alive so I could discover it, Dan Simon especially. After Four Walls Eight Windows, Simon founded Seven Stories Press in 1995. He took Algren's books with him, and since then he has, among other accomplishments, released a critical edition of *The Man with the Golden Arm*, edited and published *Nonconformity*, and released a collection of Algren's work called *Entrapment and Other Writings*. Brooke Horvath, who coedited *Entrapment* with Simon, also wrote an insightful work of criticism called *Understanding Nelson Algren*, and James R. Giles wrote one of the first books focused on Algren's writing: *Confronting the Horror: The Novels of Nelson Algren*. More recently, Carlo Rotella and Bill Savage (who coedited the critical edition of *Arm*) have been keeping Algren's ideas in circulation, and for that I am deeply grateful.

I owe thanks to everyone who granted me an interview as well, but Don DeLillo, Robert Gover, Roger Groening, Timothy Seldes, Chester Aaron, Fred Hogan, and Stephen and Helene Deutch's daughters—Kat, Carole, and Annick—deserve special mention. Unfortunately, Gover, Groening, and Seldes all died before I completed this book, so they'll never know how helpful they were. Neither will Art Shay, who died the day after he granted me permission to use his images in this book. RIP Robert, Roger, Timothy, and Art.

And now for some regrets: Several of the most important people in Algren's life appear in this book briefly, or have been written about with less feeling and depth than they deserve. Among their number are: Paula Bays, Jerome Hanock, Bud Fallon, Jesse Blue, Richard Majewski, Bill Hackett and his wife, James Blake, Stanley Kowalski, Joan Kerckhoff, and Studs Terkel. Each of these people should have played a larger role in this book, but didn't, because there was not enough information available about their relationship to Algren.

Bays, after marrying and changing her name to Larsen, virtually disappeared. She was interviewed by Bettina Drew briefly, but I was unable to find her, or her daughter, when I tried to track them down thirty years later. Hanock (one of Algren's high school friends), Fallon, Blue, and James Blake were each close to Algren for decades, but died before he did and were never interviewed about their friendships with him. Richard Majewski and Stanley Kowalski left very thin paper trails during their lives, and proved impossible to track after their (presumed) deaths. So did Bill Hackett and his wife. Studs Terkel and Joan Kerckhoff were each friends with Algren for decades, but both declined to be interviewed by Drew (or gave her cursory interviews), and died before I began this project.

NOTES

A NOTE ON SOURCES

Much of the material I used to compose this book can be accessed online, using print resources, or by querying university archives—but some cannot. Bettina Drew's interviews are one such source. Drew, Algren's first biographer, made audio recordings of the interviews she conducted, and later gave them to Ohio State University. When I reference her interviews in my notes, I am referring to her recorded interviews—not her book. Currently, though, those interviews can only be reviewed onsite at her archive at OSU. Jan Herman was another important source of interview material. He spent several years researching an Algren biography he never wrote, and when I began this book, he gave me all of his research—including letters, images, video recordings, and transcriptions of the interviews he conducted. Herman and I both possess copies of those materials, but they are not publicly available. Michael Caplan, the director behind the film *Algren*, also shared transcriptions of his interviews with me that are not publicly available. And finally, Christine Guilfoyle, an Algren scholar from the UK, shared several important documents with me, some of which are not publicly available.

Algren's FBI file was another important source. The FBI tracked Algren, on and off, from 1940 to 1969. After Algren's death, at least three people requested copies of his FBI file and received a stack of documents—approximately four hundred pages' worth—that are heavily redacted and nearly worthless. On September 23, 2013, I requested a new copy of Algren's FBI file. It had been transferred to the National Archives by then, and in response to my request, I received a file containing 886 pages that are, essentially, unredacted. Every reference to Algren's FBI file in this book is a reference to the more recent version.

My use of *Conversations with Nelson Algren* also deserves an explanation. This book is often used as a primary source for writing about Algren, but shouldn't be. I have discussed some of the distortions in its pages, but there are many I didn't get to, and everyone who knew Algren well was aware of them. Robert Joffe (Algren's nephew), Betty Algren, and H.E.F. Donohue all told Algren's first biographer that the book was partly fictional: "I knew he was fibbing," Donohue said. "I didn't care." *Conversations* "is crap," Betty Algren said. And yet, I do refer to it because it is one of the only available sources of information for several periods of Algren's life. I approach the book skeptically though. My rule is this: Material that added nuance to events I was able to verify through other means was included, and anything contradicted by the archival record was excluded. Material I was not able to corroborate in any way was also excluded. For instance, Algren's story about visiting a brothel in college made the cut because reporting by the *Daily Illini* established that Algren's story was plausible. I also use *Conversations* as a source for writing about Algren's time with the Luthers because Benton Curtis verified much of it. However, I do not use Algren's timeline because the archival record shows he distorted it by conflating his two trips south.

Due to space constraints, I had to source this book lightly. Consequently, I have not provided citations for easily verifiable historical facts or easily searchable texts. For instance, no citation is provided for the passage of legislation, Senator Joseph McCarthy's infamous speech in West Virginia, the Paterson riots in 1964, or quotes from the Bible or *Das Kapital*. I did not have the space necessary to provide citations for the atmospheric details that give Algren's story nuance, either—for instance, mentions of the weather, or the hermit who lived near the railroad tracks near Nelson's childhood home. In general, details about Chicago come from the *Tribune*, and references to national and international events come from the *New York Times*. Additionally, when quoting from Algren's published work, I have only provided citations when the source of the text is not clear from the narrative of this book.

SOURCE NOTES

Unless otherwise noted, all references to Algren's books are to the following editions, which I refer to using the abbreviations that appear in bold:

Boots—*Somebody in Boots*. Vanguard Press, 1935.
Morning—*Never Come Morning*. Harper & Brothers, 1942.
Wilderness—*The Neon Wilderness*. Doubleday, 1947.
Arm—*The Man with the Golden Arm*. Doubleday, 1949.
Chicago—*Chicago: City on the Make*. Doubleday, 1951.
Wild Side—*A Walk on the Wild Side*. Farrar, Straus & Cudahy, 1956.
Who Lost—*Who Lost an American?* Macmillan, 1963.
Conversations—Donohue, H.E.F. *Conversations with Nelson Algren*. Hill & Wang, 1964.
Sea Diary—*Notes From a Sea Diary: Hemingway All the Way*. Putnam, 1965.
Carousel—*The Last Carousel*. Putnam, 1973.
Stocking—*The Devil's Stocking*. Arbor House, 1983.
Nonconformity—*Nonconformity: Writing on Writing*. Seven Stories Press, 1996.

I quote from the following archives most frequently, and in these source notes, they are referred to using the abbreviations that appear in bold:

AK Collection: Nelson Algren Collection belonging to Amanda Algren, Rare Books and Manuscripts Library, The Ohio State University.

BD Papers: Bettina Drew Papers on Nelson Algren, Rare Books and Manuscripts Library, The Ohio State University.

DD Papers: Don DeLillo Papers, Harry Ransom Center, The University of Texas at Austin.

JC Papers: Jack Conroy Papers, Modern Manuscripts, The Newberry Library.

JCH Papers: John Clellon Holmes Papers, 1959–1968, Special Collections and Archives, Kent State University.

KB Papers: Kay Boyle Papers, 1914–1987, Special Collections Research Center, Southern Illinois University.

MG Collection: Maxwell Geismar Collection, Howard Gotlieb Archival Research Center, Boston University.

NA Collection: The Nelson Algren Collection, Rare Books and Manuscripts Library, The Ohio State University.

RW Papers: Richard Wright Papers, Beinecke Rare Book & Manuscript Library, Yale University.

The following people are referred to in these source notes by these abbreviations:

AA	Abraham Aaron
AK	Amanda Kontowicz (later, Amanda Algren)
BB	Betty Bendyk (later, Betty Algren)
BC	Benton Curtis
BD	Bettina Drew
CG	Christine Guilfoyle
DD	Don DeLillo
DP	Dave Peltz
EA	Edward Aswell
EH	Ernest Hemingway
FL	Frankie Lemon
JC	Jack Conroy
JCH	John Clellon Holmes
JF	James Farrell
JH	Jan Herman
KB	Kay Boyle
KMC	Kenneth McCormick
MC	Michael Caplan
MG	Maxwell Geismar
MGH	Martha Gellhorn (Hemingway)
NA	Nelson Algren
PF	Paul Forchheimer
RG	Roger Groening
RJ	Robert Joffe

RW   Richard Wright
SB   Simone de Beauvoir
SD   Stephen Deutch

INTRODUCTION

xi   **"The captain never"**: *Arm*, pp. 3–4.

xii   **"Those first hours"**: *Entrapment*, p. 169.

xiii **"Never has any"**: *Nonconformity*, p. 75.

xiii **earned a record sum**: Edwin McDowell, "Herbert Alexander, Pocket Books Editor . . . ," *New York Times*, 24 November 1988.

xiii **"the best writer of good"**: Algren's copy of *Native Son*, NA Collection.

xiii **Algren had topped Faulkner**: Letter from EH to KMC, NA Collection.

xiv   **"You were one of the people"**: Letter from Cormac McCarthy to NA, NA Collection.

xiv   **"I admired Algren"**: Beef Torrey and Kevin Simonson, eds., *Conversations with Hunter S. Thompson* (Jackson, MS: University of Mississippi, 2008), p. 50.

xiv   **BUDINTZ Coal**: *Arm*, p. 219.

xiv   **Budenz, without being prompted**: NA's FBI File.

xv   **"bard of the stumblebum"**: Leslie A. Fiedler, "The Noble Savages of Skid Row," *Reporter*, 12 July 1956.

xv   **"An underworld groupie"**: William Styron, *Havanas in Camelot* (New York: Random House, 2008), pp. 108–18.

xv   **"puerile sentimentality"**: Alfred Kazin, "Some People Passing By," *New York Times*, 20 May 1956.

xvi   **"was a tragic loss"**: "Amateur Night Way Out East," unpublished memoir by RG, courtesy of JH.

xvi   **"read, remembered, and admired"**: Catherine Meredith Brown, "Chicago without Tears or Dreams," *Saturday Review*, 8 February 1947.

xvi   **"a writer of parables"**: John Chamberlain, "Books of the Times." *New York Times*, 25 April 1942.

xvi   **"the whole contour of"**: Maxwell Geismar, *American Moderns* (New York: Hill & Wang, 1958), p. 190.

xvi   **"the dramatic sense of right"**: Citation from American Academy of Arts, NA Collection.

THE STORY OF ISAAC

3   **a German Mauser**: Eleanor Randolph, "Algren's House Sale . . . ," *Chicago Tribune*, 9 March 1975.

4   **"No, no novel"**: Letter from NA to JCH, JCH Papers.

5   **offered them bourbon**: Michael Edelstein and Robert Lamb, "No Room, No Time, No Breath . . . ," *Phoenix* (University of Chicago), spring 1962.

5   **"great gray sub-civilization"**: "Angry Author Scorns His City." *Chicago Daily News*, 17 June 1961.

5   **"I'm not second best"**: Interview of NA, David Ray Papers, University of Chicago Library.

5   **"The American way"** and **"I don't know of one writer"**: "No Room, No Time, No Breath."

6   **"My mother had"** and **My father "was a machinist"**: *Conversations*, pp. 3–4.

6   **paternal grandfather was named Nils**: NA routinely spelled his grandfather's name as "Nels," but I suspect the proper spelling is "Nils." A review of Swedish birth records from the period turns up many people with that name, and in every instance, it is spelled "Nils."

6   **he was born in Sweden around 1820**: US Census, 1880. NA routinely claimed (falsely) that his grandfather was born decades later, but the census established that Isaac was sixty years old in 1880.

7   **The manifest**: New York Passenger Lists, 1820–1957, *White Falcon*, 18 July 1854.

8   **chided them for lapses**: Unpublished memoir, NA Collection.

8   **entered the Minnesota Territory**: *Conversations*, p. 6.

9   **Rabbi Bernhard Felsenthal**: "Marriages Performed by Three Rabbis in Boston, Chicago and Massachusetts, 1861–1956," Ancestry.com.

10   **perpetual motion** and **he abandoned**: *Conversations*, p. 7.

11   **the Mount of Olives**: Descriptions of Jerusalem come from John Cramb, *Jerusalem in 1860: A Series of Photographic Views* (Glasgow: Collins, 1860).

11   **Jette was not** and **"Hey! I'm coming"**: *Conversations*, pp. 8–9.

12   **sixth child was Rosa**: US Census, 1880.

12   **any flavor of gospel**: Martha Heasley Cox, *Nelson Algren* (Boston: Twayne, 1975), p. 18.

15   **never claimed atheism**: Unpublished memoir, NA Collection.

15   **once referred to God ... "all our wars"**: *Conversations*, pp. 14–15.

15   **faced his opponents**: Interview of RJ, BD Papers.

15   **"There is no truth"** and **a streetcar arrived**: *Conversations*, p. 10.

15   **Isaac died a few years later**: US Census, 1900. Jette first listed herself as a widow on this census, and continued doing so for the remainder of her life.

16   **emigrated ... sights set on**: *Conversations*, p. 12.

16   **She married Gerson**: Marriage license, BD Papers.

17   **had another daughter**: Abraham family Bible, NA Collection.

17   **That child was born**: Birth certificate, NA Collection.

BETWEEN ST. COLUMBANUS AND THE WROUGHT-IRON GATE
OF OAK WOODS CEMETERY

18   **lost faith ... in 1912**: *Conversations*, p. 4. The year of the family's move is often listed as 1913, but NA consistently said he moved to Chicago when he

was three—meaning 1912, or the first three months of 1913. In some interviews, he said plainly that it was 1912.

18   **"no future" in cars:** Interview of RJ, BD Papers.

19   **A teenager delivered:** "Down Memory Lane with Ann Esch and Nelson Algren." *Chicago Tribune Magazine,* 18 June 1972.

20   **cross on the church's roof:** *Who Lost,* p. 232.

20   **He built a garage:** Unpublished memoir, NA Collection.

21   **She mixed up her *Ms*:** *Conversations,* p. 17.

23   **Allies and Huns:** *Who Lost,* p. 242, and unpublished memoir, NA Collection.

25   **"lucky cork or two":** Unpublished memoir, NA Collection.

25   **piano crate . . . he hid inside:** Interview of AK, BD Papers.

25   **toward the Warshawsky:** Unpublished memoir, NA Collection.

27   **McGuire's Ice Cream Kings:** *Who Lost,* pp. 243–44.

28   **trucks . . . loaded with barrels:** Unpublished memoir, NA Collection.

28   MAN SELLS WIFE: All references to *Blade* content come from the 2 February 1918 and 5 July 1919 issues.

29   **Nelson timed his sales:** *Carousel,* p. 229.

31   **"You've got him":** Unpublished memoir, NA Collection.

31   **"It's just a case" and "sort of city-wide sorrow":** ibid.

32   **"feminine modernists":** "Pastor Declares Movement Is Periled . . . ," *Chicago Tribune,* 21 March 1913.

32   **top scores in physics:** Notes from Bernice's diary, BD Papers.

32   **Bernice told Nelson to read:** *Who Lost,* p. 233.

32   **a broadsheet newspaper:** NA Collection.

34   **"*You* send Valentines to niggers":** *Who Lost,* p. 239.

34   **"Thousands of whites":** Letter from NA to RW, RW Archive.

34   **Bernice saw six:** Unpublished memoir, NA Collection.

34   **love for the game "was not shaken":** *Entrapment,* p. 292.

"TELL YOUR TIRE TROUBLES TO NELSON ABRAHAM"

35   **He raised the car:** Unpublished memoir, NA Collection.

37   **he sat on the back porch:** Unpublished memoir, NA Collection.

37   **"We were the kind":** Interview of BC, BD Papers.

39   **Seven people and "Abraham continues":** Uptown Arrows record book, NA Collection.

40   **met on the beach and people who knew him best:** Interview of RJ, BD Papers.

41   **"We felt life was":** Interview of BC, BD Collection.

42   **located in the building:** *Conversations,* p. 18, and Interview of BC, BD Papers.

43   **"pang of shame" and "I can't charge" :** Unpublished memoir, NA Collection.

44   **"Well, that's crazy":** *Conversations,* p. 18.

44   **forty dollars and "Are you going to open":** Unpublished memoir, NA Collection.

45   **"Now it's time":** *Conversations*, p. 21.

46   **earned the highest grades:** High School grade book, NA Collection.

46   **Civics Club and TELL YOUR TIRE TROUBLES:** Roosevelt High School Year Book, 1927, courtesy of CG and Stuart Simon.

STOIC. ACADEMIC. INK-STAINED WRETCH.

47   **He had fifty dollars:** *Nelson Algren*, p. 18.

48   **heavy load of classes:** College transcript, BD Papers.

48   **Marcus Aurelius, forsaking indulgences,** and **Chaucer, Shakespeare, and Byron:** *Conversations*, pp. 23–27.

50   **fewest number of words:** *Conversations*, p. 24.

51   **William Styron and Terry Southern:** *Havanas in Camelot*, pp. 108–18.

51   **Goldie's favorite** and **"Man is made":** *Conversations*, p. 9.

52   **"For the first time":** *Nelson Algren*, p. 18.

52   **"It was an interesting kind of struggle"** and **"It wasn't a passive":** *Conversations*, p. 26.

53   **A madam named Bess Maxwell:** "Bawdy House Operator Talks." *Daily Illini*, 28 February 1939.

53   **"think of nothing but"** and **"Well, I've got":** *Conversations*, p. 28.

54   **"Crime is an art":** "People Should Pay Attention to Crime. . . ," *Daily Illini*, 17 April 1930.

55   **"[S]ocial conditions may":** William Fielding Ogburn, *Social Change* (New York: B.W. Huebsch), p. 332.

55   **"a strange midnight dignity":** This quotation comes from the back cover of the 1961 Ace Books edition of *Arm*.

55   **"I fulfill my obligations":** *Arm*, p. 104.

56   **"I think I began":** *Conversations*, p. 29.

57   **nine journalism courses:** College transcript, BD Papers.

57   **stayed on campus:** *Daily Illini* masthead, 25 December 1930.

57   **his grades were good:** College transcript, BD Papers.

57   **capable "editor, columnist":** *Conversations*, p. 30.

57   **"I had tremendous faith":** "Break Through Myths of Our Time . . . ," *Daily Illini*, 6 April 1957.

THE PAST RECEDED LIKE A WAVE JUST SPENT

58   **Nelson entered:** "Early Chicago Journalism," *Chicago Free Press*, 15 September 1970.

58   **Its office was:** A.A. Dornfeld, *Behind the Front Page* (Chicago: Academy Chicago, 1983). The reference to the bottle of Scotch appears on page 151.

59   **I'm looking for a job:** "Early Chicago Journalism."

59   **he lost five thousand:** Interview of RJ, courtesy of JH.

60 the past had receded: *Boots* (Berkley Medallion 1965 edition), p. 7.

61 Two officers, "If there is shooting," and "A ruthless policy": Randi Storch, *Red Chicago* (Urbana: University of Illinois Press, 2009). Also, *Chicago Tribune*, 4 August 1931.

64 "We can't pay you": *Conversations*, p. 31.

65 "I began fancying" and "Somebody told me": Unpublished memoir, NA Collection.

67 Nelson saw a man lying: *Conversations*, p. 55.

68 bought a po' boy: *Nelson Algren*, p. 21.

69 a man from the sales crew: For all references to the Luthers, see the footnote.

71 Nelson asked for work: Letter of introduction, NA Collection.

72 "Jobs were absolutely," There was a letter, and "Don't ever show me": Interview of BC, BD Papers.

75 "I gave the whole Confederacy": Alston Anderson and Terry Southern, "The Art of Fiction," *Paris Review*, winter 1955.

76 "I remember going through": *Conversations*, p. 51.

"SO HELP ME"

77 He witnessed "thousands" and "Everything I'd been": *Conversations*, p. 55.

78 The youth had an outfielder's and a woman sitting "before a whiskey glass": *Boots* (Berkley), p. 6.

78 "the tens of thousands," "all the whores," and "sitting around": *Conversations*, p. 55.

79 The advertisement appeared: *Conversations*, p. 60.

79 "Well," he said and "You don't need": Interview of Murray Gitlin, BD Collection.

80 "A dollar woman": Nelson Algren, "So Help Me," *Story*, August 1933.

81 "vital, vigorous material": *Anvil* references come from the first issue of *The Anvil*, May 1933.

82 Conroy was a tall: Biographical references to Conroy are from Douglas C. Wixson, *Worker-Writer in America* (Urbana: University of Illinois Press, 1994).

83 "I am the bastard": Herman Spector, *The Bastard in the Ragged Suit* (San Francisco: Synergistic Press, 1977), p. 57.

83 "I was a little" and Gold was proud: Mike Gold, *Jews without Money* (New York: Public Affairs, 2009), pp. 37 and 11.

83 Farrell said he wanted: James T. Farrell, *Studs Lonigan* (New York: Modern Library, 1938), p. xi.

84 "Art is a class weapon": This was the motto of the John Reed Clubs.

84 He began corresponding: Letter from Milton Ellison, NA Collection.

85 "I believed the world was": *Conversations*, p. 87.

85 "We are interested in, and What would you, and Ten dollars, Nelson

said: *Conversations*, pp. 60–61, and Algren on *Book Beat*, WTTW-TV, 1974 [date unknown].

86 **"This letter will confirm"**: Vanguard Press contract, courtesy of JH.

87 **"At the Mexican line"** and **"He'll toss 'em"**: Notebook, NA Collection.

88 **Railroad bulls stopped Nelson's**: Letter from NA to Bill [?], NA Collection.

88 **a bulb attached** and **Eventually, a redhead named**: Interview of PF, BD Papers.

90 **"various eastern magazines"**: "Young Novelist to Speak . . ." *Skyline* (Sul Ross State Teachers College), December 1933, courtesy of CG.

90 **"I didn't have a novel"**: letter from NA to Bill [?], NA Collection.

91 **"American Diary"**: NA Collection.

91 **The meeting was held**: "Novelist Talks on Proletarian Culture." *Skyline*, 15 January 1934, courtesy of CG.

91 **"All night one night"**: Untitled poem, NA Collection.

92 **Nelson walked up**: Algren's deposition, courtesy of CG.

92 **Nelson hopped off**: *Conversations*, p. 38.

92 **"I wanted a typewriter"**: Algren's deposition, courtesy of CG.

"WHAT IS A CARPENTER WITHOUT HIS TOOLS?"

93 *I kissed her:* Notebook, NA Collection.

93 **He killed a Mexican man** and **A one-handed drifter**: *Conversations*, pp. 39–41.

94 **"Every man must wash"**: "Rules of the Court," NA Collection.

94 **Nelson wrote and drew**: Notebook, NA Collection.

94 **"I'm on my way to Huntsville"**: Interview of JC, BD Papers.

94 **"I've gotten myself into"**: Notebook, NA Collection.

94 **"It was a big event"**: *Conversations*, p. 43.

94 **"I don't think"**: Interview of PF, BD Papers.

94 **southern gentleman**: Account of NA's time in Alpine by J. Allen Briggs, BD Papers.

95 **"militant, defiant man"**: "'Taking Ways' Cause of Young Novelist's . . . ," *Skyline*, February 1934, courtesy of CG.

95 **on my way to hell**: Interview of JC, BD Papers.

95 **"a youth with a mysterious brain"**: "'Taking Ways' Cause of Young Novelist's . . ."

95 **"not stealing because of,"** **"You would not be hard on a carpenter,"** and **"What is a carpenter"**: Notes on NA collected from an interview of PF, courtesy of CG.

96 **"This young man claims"**: Account of NA's time in Alpine by J. Allen Briggs, BD Papers.

96 **"The defendant,"** he said: Judge's instructions, BD Papers.

96 **"We, the jury"**: Jury's verdict, BD Papers.

97 **"So long,"** he said: "'Taking Ways' Cause of Young Novelist's . . ."

SOMEBODY IN BOOTS

99   **He taught his grandson, he flinched,** and **"Long live"**: Interview of RJ, BD Papers.

99   **"You are going to"**: Letter from JC to NA, NA Collection.

100   **found a door bearing**: Richard Wright, *American Hunger* (New York: Harper & Row, 1977), chapter IV.

102   **He was "shy"**: Interview of Sam Ross, BD Papers.

102   **He had a "gangling, shuffling"**: Interview of AA, BD Papers.

102   **We were all "on the verge"** and **"He had a very conscious"**: Interview of Meridel Le Sueur, BD Papers.

102   **"Nelson was death"**: Interview of AA, BD Papers.

102   **Aaron was from**: Biographical details about AA are from Interview of AA, BD Papers. And a personal Interview of Chester Aaron, 30 December 2015.

104   **Wright was born**: Biographical details about RW are from Hazel Rowley, *Richard Wright* (New York: Henry Holt, 2001).

105   **"What on earth"**: *American Hunger*, p. 61.

105   **Nelson began dating**: Interview of AK, BD Papers.

106   **Farrell distilled their concerns**: Letter from JF to John Switalski, BD Papers.

107   **marry a "negress"**: Notes from JF's diary, BD Papers.

107   **"the Party line"**: Letter from JF to John Switalski, BD Papers.

107   **They arrived with an agenda** and **Richard Wright fought**: *Richard Wright*, pp. 85–87.

108   **"The club was my first contact"**: *American Hunger*, p. 69.

109   **"Censored by Commonwealth College"**: *Windsor Quarterly*, winter 1935.

113   **"Like it or not"**: H. W. Boynton, "'Somebody in Boots' and . . . ," *New York Times*, 7 April 1935.

114   **then seven hundred. Sixty more**: Royalty statement, NA Collection.

114   **heard that Nelson had hiked**: Interview of Mrs. William Jordan, BD Papers.

114   **"Had a letter from the guy"**: Letter from AA to JC, JC Papers.

THE CRACK-UP

115   **Lawrence Lipton's phone rang**: This account of Nelson's time with Lipton is from an interview of Lawrence Lipton, UCLA Library, Center for Oral History Research.

117   **Goldie called her "whore"**: Interview of AK, BD Papers.

118   **"The capitalist system"**: The open letter ran in the 22 January 1935 edition of *New Masses*.

118   **Two hundred and sixteen writers** and **I have traveled**: Henry Hart, ed., *American Writers' Congress* (New York: International Publishers, 1935), pp. 13–19.

119   **Le Sueur looked at Nelson**: Interview of Meridel Le Sueur, BD Papers.

119   **How embarrassing, Ross thought**: Interview of Sam Ross, BD Papers.

119   "You may not understand" and "Everything remains": *American Writers'*
       Congress, pp. 178 and 192.

120   He looked "malevolent" and "How does it feel": Interview of JC, cour-
       tesy of JH.

121   Richard Wright thought: Letter from JF to John Switalski, BD Papers.

121   "A going almost insane": Notes from JF's diary, BD Papers.

121   Dorothy Farrell met the men and "He wasn't doing anything": Interview
       of Dorothy Farrell, BD Papers.

121   "I have not had the chance": Letter from Ames to JF, BD Papers.

TWO FORLORN CHILDREN

125   Amanda Leocadia Kontowicz had: All biographical information about AK
       comes from an interview of AK, BD Papers, and an interview of AK, cour-
       tesy of JH.

127   the Workers' Center on Kedzie and "Ten Years of Workers' Literature":
       Scrapbook, NA Collection.

127   "Why," Amanda's friend asked: Interview of AK, BD Papers.

128   "It's hard to die": Unpublished memoir, NA Collection.

128   Eventually, she replied: Interview of AK, BD Papers.

129   "Unk," Robert Joffe said: Interview of RJ, BD Papers.

129   They found a basement room: Interview of AK, BD Papers.

130   "You're trying to do me in": ibid.

130   I "felt obliged": Guggenheim fellowship application, BD Papers.

130   "Frank Mears turned south": Nelson Algren, "American Obituary," *Parti-*
       san Review, October-November 1935.

131   a pair of suede oxfords: Interview of AK, BD Papers.

131   "We're here," they said: ibid.

131   "Jeezus," he teased and Nelson rarely drank: ibid.

TROTSKYISTS, COUNCIL COMMUNISTS, AND MATTICKITES

133   "strike a blow": *American Writers' Congress*, p. 83.

133   *Rise up, workers*: Nelson Algren, "Holiday in Texas," *Anvil*, May-June 1934.

134   write "without fear": Nelson Algren, "Do It the Hard Way," *Writer*,
       March 1943.

134   "Environment is a tremendous thing": Stephen Crane, "Maggie: A Girl
       of the Streets" in Barbara H. Solomon, ed., *The Haves and Have-Nots* (New
       York: Signet Classics, 1999), p. 219.

135   "a worse evil": "Yama: The Pit." Wikipedia. Retrieved 4 February 2017.

135   "born-to-be-doomed" and "a wedge for the inarticulate": Nelson Algren,
       "Remembering Richard Wright," *Nation*, 28 January 1961.

135   put down the "world of reality": "Do It the Hard Way."

135   "I was just going around" and "I went to a Walkathon": *Conversations*, p. 89.

136   "accurate description of" the city: Guggenheim fellowship application.

137   even "near writers" were welcome: Jerre Mangione, *The Dream and the Deal* (Syracuse: Syracuse University Press, 1996), p. 48.

138   "Galena, nestling against steep hills": Federal Writers' Project (Illinois), Works Progress Administration, *Galena Guide*, 1937.

138   feeling the "world was against them": *Conversations*, p. 64.

138   "The suicide rate": David A. Taylor, *The Soul of a People* (Hoboken, NJ: Wiley, 2009), p. 9.

138   Amanda had specific ideas, Nelson's ideal life, and "He refused to pay": Interview of AK, BD Papers.

140   took a few hours off work: NA claimed he married AK in 1936, but the records of the Chicago Bureau of Vital Statistics show the date was March 1, 1937.

140   Abe Aaron visited and Good paragraph: Personal interview of Chester Aaron, 30 December 2015.

141   "Most of the young artists": *Richard Wright*, p. 121.

141   The congress was: All references to the congress are from Henry Hart, ed., *The Writer in a Changing World* (New York: Equinox Cooperative Press, 1937).

142   "Directly or by implication": "Writers Spurred to Fight Fascism," *New York Times*, 6 June 1937.

142   News of the protest: Some accounts place NA at this congress, but I am confident he did not attend because AA, in a letter to RW, mentions that he allowed NA to read the news RW sent from the congress, and then describes his reaction. NA would not have had to read about the congress in a letter if he had been there.

142   "It was a quarrelsome situation": Interview of FL, BD Papers.

143   "I'm letting my Party membership": Letter from AA to RW, RW papers.

143   then so be it: *Richard Wright*, p. 127.

143   These will become "part of": NA's FBI file.

AT HOME IN RAT ALLEY

144   The buildings faced: Interview of AK, BD Papers.

145   young Marxists established: Interview of FL, BD Papers.

145   Two adjacent storefronts: Interview of AK, BD Papers.

146   Margaret Walker, the youngest: Interview of Margaret Walker, BD Papers.

146   secretary of the Chicago chapter: Letter from NA to J. Kerker Quinn, J. Kerker Quinn Papers, University of Illinois Archives.

147   Nelson sent Jack Conroy: Interview of JC, courtesy of JH.

147   Conroy had fallen: *Worker-Writer in America*, chapter 17.

148   "wounded gorilla": ibid., p. 5.

148   Conroy met a wild and "C-I-O, C-I-O": Douglas Wixson, "Jack Conroy and the East St. Louis Toughs," *New Letters* 57, no. 4 (summer 1991).

149   "One man'd go": Douglas Wixson, "Very Penniless If Fairly Philosophical Victim," *New Letters* 57, no. 4.

149   **"I've got a leanin'"**: "Jack Conroy and the East St. Louis Toughs."

149   **"I often reeled"**: *Worker-Writer in America*, p. 429.

149   **"just a lot of boxes"**: "The Jean Winkler Correspondence . . ."

150   **I rambled like**: Letter from JC to Wallie Wharton, Walter William Wharton Papers, State Historical Society of Missouri.

150   **He was in a "bad way," a large presence**, and **He started an affair**: Interview off AK, BD Papers.

151   *The Drunkard's Warning* and **"You Goldblatt"**: *Worker-Writer in America*, pp. 443–45.

152   **beat someone in the head**: Interview of JC, BD Papers.

152   **"I have heard very distressing rumors"**: Letter from Franklin Folsom to NA, NA Collection.

153   **casting "bad reflections"**: Interview of JC, BD Papers.

153   **"we were fighting the war against"**: *Conversations*, p. 88.

154   **the only white members** and **Marry me and my friend**: Interview of JC, courtesy of JH.

155   **"hipsters in artistic revolt"**: Frank Sandiford, "My Main Man," *New Letters* 57, no. 4 (summer 1991).

155   **called themselves "lost" men** and **raped a dog**: Interview of FL, BD Papers.

155   **"Tell all them kunts"**: Letter from Fallon to JC, JC Papers.

156   **"It got a little ridiculous"**: Interview of FL, BD Papers.

156   **"He was smart as a shit house rat"**: Interview of JC, courtesy of JH.

156   **"I don't have a Pulitzare"**: *Worker-Writer in America*, p. 434.

157   **"I . . . know you for what you are"**: Letter from Fallon to NA, Walter William Wharton Papers, State Historical Society of Missouri.

157   **"I hate to knock down"**: Letter from NA to RW, RW Archive.

157   **a weekly painting class** and **"It's very nice"**: Interview of AK, BD Papers.

158   **a tall Armenian man**: This account of AK's affair is from an interview of AK, BD Papers.

159   **cancer in her intestines**: Interview of RJ, BD Papers.

160   **haunting street carnivals**: Letter from NA to Granville Hicks, Granville Hicks Collection, Syracuse University Libraries.

161   **"I used to go by," "In 1937 I was,"** and **"The boys rolled a Jew"**: Notes for *Morning*, NA Archive.

162   **Nelson and Amanda went**: This account of the evening's events, and the following day, come from an interview of AK, BD Papers.

163   **Nelson attacked Finch**: ibid.

163   **nearly insensate, singing**: Interview of FL, BD Papers.

MORNING

164   **cutting his reviews out**: Postcard from NA to RW, RW Papers.

165   **"To my old friend"**: NA's copy of *Native Son*, NA Collection.

165   **"I haven't begun it"**: Postcard from NA to RW, RW Papers.

166   **"I really hadn't planned on writing"**: Letter from NA to RW, RW Papers.

168   **kept a pot on his stove**: Interview of Lil Frankel and Blanche Robbins, BD Papers.

169   **"I think the English"**: Letter from RW to NA, NA Collection.

169   **Abe Aaron wasn't as cavalier**: Letter from AA to RW, RW Papers.

169   **a Russian cossack gutted**: Personal interview of Chester Aaron, 30 December 2015.

169   **"I'm on the books"**: Letter from NA to RW, RW Papers.

169   **mentioned to the Dies Committee**: United States Congress, House of Representatives, Special Committee on Un-American Activities (1938–1944), *Investigation of Un-American Propaganda Activities in the United States*.

169   **Communist "antiseptic squad"**: NA's FBI file.

170   **"Better destroy this letter"**: Letter from AA to RW, RW Papers.

170   **"I feel pretty goddamn bad"**: ibid.

171   **"too many parties"**: Letter from NA to RW, RW Papers.

171   **"He is young, and he"**: Letter from RW to NA, NA Collection.

171   **keeping herself busy**: Interview of AK, BD Papers

172   **they drifted apart the moment**: Interview of RJ, BD Papers.

172   **"I read page after page"**: letter from RW to NA, NA Collection.

173   **Edward Aswell agreed** and **"Nothing remains"**: Letter from EA to NA, NA Collection.

174   **friend named Alexander**: Letter from Celia [?] to NA, NA Collection.

174   **minor operation in the spring**: Interview of RJ, BD Papers.

174   **She never shed a tear**: *Carousel*, p. 249.

175   **"Everyone [at Harper's]"**: Letter from EA to NA, NA Collection.

182   **"I consider Never Come Morning"**: Letter from JF to NA, NA Collection.

182   **The *Providence Journal*** and **"It is not too much"**: Jacket copy for the 1948 Avon edition of *Morning*.

182   **"an unusual book"**: Fred T. Marsh, "Poles in Chicago," *New York Times*, 10 May 1942.

183   **"Mr. Algren blends"**: John Chamberlain, "Books of the Times," *New York Times*, 25 April 1942.

183   **"not by instinct a novelist"**: Malcolm Cowley, "Chicago Poem," *New Republic*, 4 May 1942.

183   **"that if we did not"**: *Morning* (Berkley Medallion 1968 edition), p. xiii.

183   **"I protest strongly"**: Letter from John Olejniczak to EA, NA Collection.

183   **"It is contemptible"**: Letter from John Czech to EA, NA Collection.

183   **"Herr Goebbels's"**: Letter from A.J. Lukaszewski to EA, NA Collection.

184   **"You might care to"**: Letter from John Czech to NA, NA Collection.

184   **Fallon heard about Nelson's plight**: Interview of Dorothy Farrell, BD Papers.

184   **"I just want to tell you"**: Letter from MGH to NA, NA Collection.

185   **"*Never Come Morning* hasn't a dull"**: Letter from MGH to EA, NA Collection.

"DO IT THE HARD WAY"

186   **The military had a hard time:** George Sarka, "The Role of the United States Public Health Service in the Control of Syphilis during the Early Twentieth Century" (dissertation, University of California, Los Angeles, 2013), UCLA Electronic Theses and Dissertations.

187   **applied for the same position:** Interview of JC, BD Papers.

187   **Leads were often slim:** ibid.

187   **pimp came after Conroy:** ibid.

187   **"I was waitin' to see"** and **"Not sick":** Field notes, NA Collection.

187   **"He was very sympathetic":** Interview of JC, BD Papers.

188   **No tool at a writer's disposal:** "Do It the Hard Way."

189   **In the spring, Amanda:** The account of Amanda's return comes from an interview of AK, BD Papers.

191   **he rambled through:** Letter from NA to AK, AK Collection.

191   **"The fact of your being":** ibid.

191   **Nelson's induction form:** NA's army records.

THE ANONYMOUS MAN

193   **Private Abraham, serial number 36679611:** NA's army records.

193   **Nelson's unit woke:** Letter from NA to Geraldine Brooks, *Poetry: A Magazine of Verse* Records, University of Chicago Library.

193   **"[T]hey play for keeps":** Letter from NA to JC, courtesy of JH.

193   **"We put in so much time":** Letter from NA to Geraldine Brooks, *Poetry: A Magazine of Verse* Records, University of Chicago Library.

194   **The army reassigned Nelson:** NA's army records.

194   **Nelson tried to leave:** Letter from NA to Pete [?], *Poetry: A Magazine of Verse* Records, University of Chicago Library.

194   **"Not that I'm feeling particularly":** ibid.

194   **because he was Jewish:** Interview of AK, BD Papers.

194   **A judge seated on the Circuit Court:** NA's army records.

195   **he became apathetic:** NA's army records.

195   **"I have found this man":** ibid.

196   **"I'm Nelson Algren":** Robin D. G. Kelley, "Interview of Herbert Aptheker," *Journal of American History* 87, no. 1 (1 June 2000).

196   **Aptheker demurred:** ibid.

196   **boarded a train there:** This account of Amanda's visit comes from an interview of AK, BD Papers.

197   **You've been transferred:** Letter from NA to JC, JC Papers.

197   **Richard Wright called:** Letter from NA to RW, RW Collection.

197   **"I haven't hit the army":** ibid.

198   **His paperwork was stamped:** NA's army file.

198   publication of *Never Come Morning*: NA's FBI file.
199   agent named John Bowker: ibid.
199   According to Camp Maxey gossip: Interview of Irwin Glustoff, BD Papers.
199   The evacuation hospital received: NA's army file.
199   Some of the men in Nelson's unit: *Conversations*, p. 68.
199   "You're not going" and "I don't want to get left": ibid.
200   "Looking forward to": Letter from NA to JC, courtesy of JH.
200   Timid bay waves and Red Cross workers moved: 125th Evacuation Hospital Unit History.
200   soldiers in Nelson's unit disembarked: All reference to unit movements, ibid.
201   "There was no war near there": *Conversations*, p. 80.
201   "They were firing everything": *Conversations*, p. 81.
202   occupied the St. Francis hospital: 125th Evacuation Hospital Unit History.
202   made themselves at home: ibid.
202   "Don't worry . . . gotta golden arm": "The Art of Fiction."
202   The men in Nelson's unit: 125th Evacuation Hospital Unit History.
202   Nelson called him a "ghost": Letter from NA to Lou Gilbert, BD Papers.
203   Nelson was in Paris: *Conversations*, p. 82.
204   a campground for GIs: ibid.
204   "I just had a cot" and "The town was full": *Conversations*, pp. 82–83.
204   "Every morning I": Letter from NA to MG, MG Collection.
204   the "most isolated": ibid.
204   "It seemed like it was time": *Conversations*, pp. 91–92.

EXPLORING THE NEON WILDERNESS

207   The army delivered Nelson: NA's army file.
208   and accepted $160.60: ibid.
208   went looking for a flower shop: This account of this day's events comes from an interview of Dorothy Farrell, BD Papers.
210   In January, he found: Letter from NA to Mary Guggenheim, BD Papers.
211   "You're a jack roller": Show-up notes, NA Collection.
212   "failed before the radio commercials": *Arm*, p. 17.
212   "live out their hand-to-mouth": *Nonconformity*, pp. 35–36.
212   "Every day is D-Day": *Chicago*, p. 71.
212   "Never has any people": *Nonconformity*, p. 75.
213   Amanda arrived first: This account of Amanda's visit comes from an interview of AK, BD Papers.
213   "I'd like to see": Letter from MGH to NA, NA Collection.
213   Nelson offered Gellhorn: ibid., and an interview of AK, BD Papers.
213   "I love your Siberian country": Letter from MGH to NA, NA Collection.
214   "It occurs to me": Letter from NA to AK, AK Collection.
214   Kenneth McCormick arrived: "The Art of Fiction."

215 **I want enough to live on**: ibid.

215 **"I believe in you as a writer"**: Letter from EA to NA, NA Collection.

217 **Nelson finished assembling**: Letter from NA to AK, AK Collection.

217 **Mary Guggenheim arrived**: This account of Guggenheim's visit and biography come from an interview of Mary Guggenheim, BD Papers.

218 **"such a solitary person"**: ibid.

218 **"Did I ever tell you"** and **"Give my regards"**: Letter from NA to Mary Guggenheim, BD Papers.

219 **"I'd like to make it lighter"**: Letter from NA to AK, AK Collection.

219 **"[I]f you think la vie ici"**: Letter from NA to Mary Guggenheim, BD Papers.

220 **"Far from being ashamed"**: Letter from NA to Mary Guggenheim, BD Papers.

220 **Guggenheim flew to**: This account of Guggenheim's visit comes from an interview of Mary Guggenheim, BD Papers.

220 **"A writer of sociological slant"**: Kelsey Guilfoil, "Stories Bare Bitter Truth . . . ," *Chicago Tribune*, 26 January 1947.

221 **"the staccato precision"**: "Chicago without Tears or Dreams."

221 **"determined that we should . . . see"**: John Woodburn, "People of the Abyss," *New York Times*, 2 February 1947.

222 **"suggest the whole contour"**: *American Moderns*, p. 190.

222 **reputation as "one of the few"**: *Wilderness* (Four Walls Eight Windows 1986 edition), p. 7.

A BOY FROM THE PROVINCES

223 **he had been cooking**: *Conversations*, p. 180

223 **"Please be patient"**: Simone de Beauvoir, *America Day by Day* (Berkeley: University of California Press, 2000), p. 96.

224 **"That Simone Boudoir"**: Letter from NA to Mary Guggenheim, BD Papers.

225 **she could only understand**: *America Day by Day*, p. 97.

225 **French government was sponsoring**: This account of Beauvoir's travel comes from *America Day by Day*.

225 **"I told her all about the war"**: *Conversations*, p. 181.

225 **"Why did they build so many"**: *America Day by Day*, p. 91.

226 **fixated on a serial killer** and **I'm the only serious writer**: *Conversations*, p. 182.

226 **"I think you're the only sinister thing"**: ibid.

226 **The room thrummed** and **"It's beautiful"**: *America Day by Day*, pp. 97–98.

227 **The main room was almost**: This account of the scene in the saloon comes from *America Day by Day*, pp. 98–99.

227 **she and Nelson left** and **they began making love**: Deirdre Bair, *Simone de Beauvoir* (New York: Summit Books, 1990), p. 336.

228 **brought her to a private club**: *America Day by Day*, pp. 100–101.

229 **borrowed a government car**: This account of the afternoon comes from *Simone de Beauvoir*, p. 336.

229   **upset, and she refused to let go:** Simone de Beauvoir, *After the War: Force of Circumstance*, vol. I (New York: Paragon House, 1992), p. 125.

229   **"He seems to me":** *America Day by Day*, p. 103.

229   **"Before going to sleep":** Simone de Beauvoir, *A Transatlantic Love Affair* (New York: New Press, 1998), p. 12.

230   **picked up a copy:** Letter from NA to AK, AK Collection.

230   **"in recognition of his stories":** Citation from American Academy of Arts, NA Collection.

230   **two of Carl Sandburg's books:** Letter from NA to Carl Sandburg, Carl Sandburg Papers, University of Illinois at Urbana-Champaign.

230   **Mary Guggenheim returned** and **"He just let me go":** Interview of Mary Guggenheim, BD Papers.

231   **hotel called the Brevoort:** *Simone de Beauvoir*, p. 340.

231   **agreed she should write:** ibid., p. 353.

232   **"only a boy from the provinces":** ibid., p. 340.

232   **"If he was sometimes blunt":** *Force of Circumstance*, vol. I, p. 126.

233   **"[H]e believed me":** ibid.

233   **wanted to say goodbye** and **"*à Simone*":** *Simone de Beauvoir*, p. 341.

233   **"I feel you with me":** *A Transatlantic Love Affair*, p. 15.

234   **Nelson preferred the latter:** This account of NA's Clark Street haunts comes from *America Day by Day*, pp. 356–58.

234   **might be too big a word:** This account of Jack's apartment and the group of people associated with it comes from NA's *Paris Review* interview, NA's recollections in *Conversations*, Beauvoir's account of the apartment in *Force of Circumstance*, vol. I (pp. 154–56), and an interview of DP, courtesy of JH.

235   **"I consider myself properly":** Letter from R. Majowski to NA, NA Collection.

236   **scenes "in which human beings":** *Conversations*, pp. 93–94.

236   **"I even got rid of [Bud]":** Letter from NA to AK, AK Collection.

236   **"I'm reworking the first couple hundred":** Letter from NA to KMC, NA Collection.

237   **"Make it good":** *A Transatlantic Love Affair*, p. 29.

237   **"I have to find a way of saying the truth":** ibid., p. 35.

238   **"I can feel my love for you":** ibid., p. 36.

238   **"I could never give everything":** ibid., p. 52.

239   **"it is Nelson-seeing I want":** ibid., p. 58.

239   **Beauvoir's trip began:** This account of Beauvoir's visit comes from *Force of Circumstance*, vol. I (pp. 135–36), *America Day by Day* (pp. 361–64), and *Simone de Beauvoir* (pp. 352–54).

EXILE?

241   **"whiz us"** and **"jump off":** Notes on Division Street idioms, NA Collection.

242   **"Jesus, that's *dessert*":** "The Art of Fiction."

242 **"Jack is having trouble"**: ibid.

243 **Jack was an advocate**: ibid.

243 **drummer from Arkansas**: *Conversations*, p. 155.

243 **Bill Hackett, the card dealer**: *Conversations*, p. 104. Hackett is referred to as Acker.

243 **Paula Bays was also desperate**: This account of Bays's stay at Nelson's comes from a memoir entitled "Blanche Sweet under the Tapioca," *Chicago Tribune*, 30 April 1972. In it, NA refers to Bays as Margo and claims he met her shortly after his army service ended. The account appears to be accurate, except for the timeline. BD later interviewed Bays, Caesar Tabet, and DP, and the information provided by those interviews allowed me to confirm that Bays was Margo, to fill in Bays's biography, and correct the timeline of NA's account. JH also interviewed DP about Bays, and NA later testified at Bays' divorce hearing.

246 **"You think that, uh"**: "The Art of Fiction."

246 **"Well," the boy said**: ibid.

246 **"You gotta belong to somebody"**: *Conversations*, p. 104.

247 **"Well, you don't know what it's like"**: *Conversations*, p. 155.

247 **"The morphine was heated"**: Field notes, 15 April 1948, NA Collection.

248 **"[T]he committee is seeking"**: "Congress Investigates Communists in Hollywood," Universal Newsreel, 20 October 1947.

248 **Walt Disney was one**: HUAC Testimony. 24 October 1947.

248 **Gary Cooper went**: HUAC testimony. 23 October 1947.

249 **A rabbi named Schultz**: Rabbi Benjamin Schultz, "Communists Invade the Churches," *Pittsburgh Press*, 16 October 1947.

249 **the US Chamber of Commerce**: *A Program for Anti-Communist Action* (Washington: Chamber of Commerce of the United States, 1948).

250 **The Newberry Library**: Letter from Newberry Library to NA, NA Collection.

250 **Nelson spotted Beauvoir**: Shared diary, NA Collection.

250 **"Happened upon a strange"**: ibid.

250 **Nelson brought Beauvoir**: *Force of Circumstance*, vol. I, pp. 154–55.

250 **" . . . bank, traveler's checks"**: Shared diary, NA Collection.

250 **On their fifth morning**: This account of NA and SB's trip comes from *Force of Circumstance*, vol. I, pp. 156–60.

251 **"Went out to the bull park"**: Letter from NA to JC, courtesy of JH.

252 **I have to return to Paris**: *Force of Circumstance*, vol. I, p. 158.

253 **"I began to pay"**: ibid., p. 159.

254 **"I'm ready to marry you"**: ibid., p. 160.

254 **"I realized," she wrote later**: ibid.

254 **a letter from Ken McCormick**: Letter from KMC to NA, NA Collection.

255 **"I won't have an affair"**: *Force of Circumstance*, vol. I, pp. 166–67.

256 **He spoke at several**: "Writers for Wallace" flier, NA Collection.

256 **"Yours for Wallace"**: Letter from NA to Carl Sandburg, Carl Sandburg Papers, University of Illinois at Urbana-Champaign.

256   **an open letter:** "Moscow says 32 Artists . . . ," *New York Times*, 3 May 1948.

257   **BUDINTZ COAL:** *Arm*, p. 219.

258   **"'Aesopian' language":** Ellen Schrecker, *The Age of McCarthyism* (Boston: Bedford Books, 1994), p. 180.

258   **He used their apartment:** Interview of AK, BD Papers.

260   **Beauvoir was eager:** This account of NA's vacation with SB comes from *Force of Circumstance*, vol. I, pp. 178–84.

262   **"They know it is not out of kindness":** Letter from NA to Carl Sandburg, Carl Sandburg Papers, University of Illinois at Urbana-Champaign.

262   **Nelson and Wright met** and **"I'd be afraid":** Bettina Drew, *Nelson Algren: A Life on the Wild Side* (New York: Putnam, 1989), p. 206.

264   **"You have no right":** *Force of Circumstance*, vol. I, p. 180.

264   **Hassine Ameur Djemail:** Letter from NA to JC, courtesy of JH.

265   **"He went through the door":** *Force of Circumstance*, vol. I, p. 184.

"OK, KID, YOU BEAT DOSTOYEVSKY"

266   **began signing copies:** This account of the signing party comes from Stuart Brent, *The Seven Stairs* (Boston: Houghton Mifflin, 1962; New York: Touchstone, 1989), pp. 41–44, and Fanny Butcher, "The Literary Spotlight," *Chicago Tribune*, 16 October 1949.

267   **"I would crown":** Kelsey Guilfoil, "Novel of the Damned . . . ," *Chicago Tribune*, 11 September 1949.

267   **"are far outweighed":** A.C. Spectorsky, "Saloon Street, Chicago," *New York Times*, 11 September 1949.

267   **"Readers with queasy":** "The Lower Depths," *Time*, 12 September 1949.

277   **Book Find Club selected:** Letter from KMC to NA, NA Collection.

277   **Pocket Books paid:** "Herbert Alexander, Pocket Books . . ."

277   ***Time* magazine:** Letter from KMC to NA, NA Collection.

277   **"a run-of-the-mill Chicagoese":** Harvey Breit, "Talk with Nelson Algren," *New York Times*, 2 October 1949.

278   **"I think it's the strongest":** Letter from Ken Millar to NA, NA Collection.

278   **"I honest to God don't know":** Letter from Bob Lowry to NA, NA Collection.

278   **"Into a world of letters":** Letter from EH, NA Collection.

278   **"Algren is probably":** Carlos Baker, ed., *Ernest Hemingway: Selected Letters* (New York: Scribner, 1981), p. 681.

278   **"OK, kid, you beat":** Norberto Fuentes, *Hemingway in Cuba* (Secaucus, NJ: Lyle Stuart, 1984), p. 266.

278   **pressed Ken McCormick:** Letter from NA to KMC, NA Collection.

279   **"[P]lease don't consider":** Letter from KMC to NA, NA Collection.

279   **kept in touch with Richard Majewski:** Letter from Richard Majewski to NA, NA Collection.

279   **"Nelson, I'd like to say again":** Letter from John Bays to NA, NA Collection.

280 **A man named Bob Roberts:** This account of Nelson and Hackett's departure comes from *Conversations*, pp. 103–107. Roberts is referred to as Moxon.

282 **"a thousand merry-go-rounds":** Letter from NA to Ken Millar. The Morgan Library and Museum.

282 **Nelson and Hackett had nothing to do:** Letter from NA to JC, courtesy of JH, and Interview of AK, BD Papers.

282 **The problem was money:** *Conversations*, p. 108.

283 **trading insults freely:** This account of NA's negotiation with Roberts comes from *Conversations*, pp. 112–13, and Thomas F. Brady, "Metro Planning Sequel to Movie," *New York Times*, 16 February 1950.

284 **had been released after:** Interview of KMC, BD Papers.

284 **The award ceremony was held:** "Book Publishers Make 3 Awards," *New York Times*, 17 March 1950.

284 **largest group of "critics":** Frederic Babcock, "National Book Awards Go to . . . ," *Chicago Tribune*, 26 March 1950.

285 **"I'm going around thanking":** *Conversations*, p. 111.

"HOW LONG DOES THIS SORT OF THING GO ON?"

286 **taught a writing course:** Letter from NA to Ed Rolfe, Rolfe Archive, University of Illinois at Urbana-Champaign.

287 **writing a screenplay:** *Conversations*, p. 115.

287 **long essay about Chicago's history:** Letter from NA to KMC, NA Collection.

287 **photographer named Art Shay:** Personal interview of Art Shay, 3 January 2013.

287 **Nelson and Amanda had rekindled:** Interview of AK, BD Papers.

288 **We refused to testify:** *The Hollywood Ten*, Ironweed Films, 1947.

289 **a pamphlet called *Red Channels*:** *Red Channels* was published by the American Business Consultants, publishers of *Counterattack*, in June 1950.

290 **bring in about five hundred dollars:** Letter from NA to Ed Rolfe, Rolfe Archive, University of Illinois at Urbana-Champaign.

290 **"American artists are being":** "What Are You Doing Out There?" *New York Times*, 15 January 1951.

290 **"It looks like a year in the pokey":** Letter from NA to Ed Rolfe, Rolfe Archive, University of Illinois at Urbana-Champaign.

290 **afraid to leave Paris:** This account of Beauvoir's visit comes from *Force of Circumstance*, vol. I, pp. 224–30.

292 **The woman Beauvoir invited:** Interview of DP, courtesy of JH.

293 **"Because I gave you so little":** *A Transatlantic Love Affair*, p. 435.

293 **"One can still have the same feelings":** *Force of Circumstance*, vol. I, pp. 250–51.

294 **Marijuana grew wild:** Interview of AK, BD Papers.

294 **Amanda visited the month:** ibid.

294 **He was "wide-eyed":** *A Life on the Wild Side*, p. 223.

295   **Dave Peltz . . . moved:** Interview of DP, courtesy of JH.

295   **Jesse Blue—the toughest character, called the woman Shotsy, and James Blake, a writer:** Interview of DP, courtesy of JH.

296   **I just left prison:** James Blake, *The Joint* (Garden City, NY: Doubleday, 1971), p. 125.

296   **I had a black lover:** ibid., p. 317.

298   **account of Chicago's history:** All references to this essay's contents are derived from its final published version, *Chicago: City on the Make.*

300   **They pushed him:** Letter from Harry Sions to NA, NA Collection.

300   **Nelson submitted his manuscript:** Letter from Harry Nickles to NA, NA Collection.

300   **"seriously handicapped":** Letter from NA to Harry Nickles, NA Collection.

300   **"It is necessary to go back":** Emmett Dedmon, "Hustling Metropolis," *Saturday Review,* 8 December 1951.

301   **"work of genius":** This quote appeared in an advertisement in the *Chicago Tribune* on 18 November 1951.

301   **"Ra(n)t Control":** *Chicago* (University of Chicago Press, 2001 edition), p. 87.

301   **prose was "kaleidoscopic":** "Chicago: City on the Make," *Nation,* 10 November 1951.

301   **"an embarrassment":** "Books in Brief," *New Republic,* 4 February 1952.

NONCONFORMITY

302   **Paula Bays couldn't tolerate:** This account is based on interviews of Paula Bays and Caesar Tabet, BD Papers, and an interview of DP, courtesy of JH.

303   **He had recently joined:** NA's FBI file.

303   **"I would like to state":** ibid.

303   **mutual friend named Caesar Tabet:** Interview of Caesar Tabet, BD Papers.

304   **John, got to her:** Bays's divorce papers. Cook County General No. 53c-2733.

304   **"You hang on to":** Interview of Caesar Tabet, BD Papers.

305   **"The struggle to write":** "There's Going to be a Pile-Up on U.S. 66" [speech transcript], courtesy of JH.

307   **Nelson was sitting:** Van Allen Bradley, "Author Nelson Algren . . . ," *Chicago Daily News,* 6 September 1952.

308   **"When am I":** Letter from NA to AK, AK Collection.

308   **they started to plan** and **"[I]t strikes me":** ibid.

309   **Amanda flew into O'Hare:** This account of Amanda's arrival comes from an interview of AK, courtesy of JH, and an interview of AK, BD Papers.

311   **GREAT WRITING BOGGED DOWN:** *Chicago Daily News,* 18 December 1952.

311   **a reader ordered:** Note, written by Bradley, attached to *Nonconformity* manuscript, NA Collection.

311   **Bradley wanted to release:** Letter from Bradley to KMC, NA Collection.

311 **He decided Doubleday should:** Letter from KMC to Bradley, NA Collection.

312 **the State Department notified:** NA's FBI file.

312 **It "ruined him":** Interview of AK, BD Papers.

313 **"I wish you would stay out":** Letter from Blake to NA, JC Papers.

313 **Millar thought the portion:** Letter from NA to Ken Millar, Morgan Library and Museum.

313 **"[W]hatever I'm accused of":** ibid.

313 **An FBI agent visited:** This account of the FBI's scrutiny comes from NA's FBI file.

316 **Amanda opened the door:** This account of NA's second wedding to AK comes from interviews of AK, Caesar Tabet, and Paula Bays, BD Papers.

317 **Nelson wrote to Beauvoir:** *A Transatlantic Love Affair*, pp. 478–82.

317 **She retyped portions:** Interview of AK, BD Papers.

317 **The book begins:** All references to this essay are from *Nonconformity*.

320 **Nelson felt beset upon:** Interview of AK, BD Papers.

321 **he requested a thousand:** Letter from NA to MG, MG Collection.

321 **"Guess what happened?":** Interview of AK, BD Papers.

321 **Seldes's instructions:** Letter from NA to MG, MG papers.

321 **Nelson got him high:** Personal interview of Timothy Seldes and Susan Shreve, 8 March 2015.

322 **"I am so depressed":** Letter from MG to NA, NA Collection.

322 **Doubleday finally responded:** Letter from NA to MG, MG Collection.

322 **"I'll tell you what I think":** Letter from NA to Millen Brand, Millen Brand Papers, Columbia University Libraries.

"RIDING DAY-COACHES TO NOWHERE"

323 **he pressed the tip:** This manuscript, entitled *Angel's Trade*, can be found in the NA Collection.

324 **they offered to pay:** Letter from NA to MG, MG Collection.

325 **he started riding the train:** *A Transatlantic Love Affair*, pp. 491–92.

326 **"I think that the writers":** Letter from NA to MG, MG Collection.

326 **Le Sueur was waiting tables:** Interview of Meridel Le Sueur, BD Papers.

327 **The beach was:** Interview of AK, BD Papers.

327 **Nelson packed a bag in July:** This account of NA's trip to Texas and Mexico comes from a letter from NA to MG, MG collection.

329 **He returned to Gary:** Letter from NA to MG, MG collection.

329 **Nelson's last stop of the year:** ibid.

330 **"I can't tell you how right":** ibid.

331 **An employee of the:** Letter from NA to AK, AK Collection.

331 **"Mr. Preminger is coming":** This account of NA's meeting with Preminger comes from *Conversations*, pp. 118–19.

332   **Someone from Preminger's office and "politically clear":** Letter from NA to AK, AK Collection.

332   **Nelson began collecting rumors:** Letter from NA to JC, JC Papers.

333   **he passed a movie theater:** *Conversations*, p. 119.

333   **The letter said Hollywood:** Letter from NA to JC, JC Papers.

334   **"So little pages":** Letter from NA to JC, JC Papers.

334   **Nelson moved into:** Letter from NA to AK, AK Collection.

335   **"Trouble is that":** ibid.

335   **"Though your thoughtfulness":** Letter from NA to Preminger, JC Papers.

335   **Hackett called Nelson:** Letter from NA to AK, AK Collection.

336   **Hackett's "one big worry":** ibid.

336   **"Coming back to Gary":** ibid.

336   **The Linkhorns were "fierce":** All references to this text are from the published version of *A Walk on the Wild Side*.

340   **"For Christ's sake let's get":** Letter from NA to AK, AK Collection.

340   **"I don't do myself any good":** ibid.

341   **The newspapers were reporting:** Thomas M. Pryor, "Preminger Signs Sinatra . . . ," *New York Times*, 3 May 1955.

341   **presented him with a subpoena:** "No Room, No Time, No Breath . . ."

"THEY DON'T EXACTLY GIVE ME ANY MEDALS FOR CAUTION"

343   **two aspiring writers:** This account of the interview comes from "The Art of Fiction."

346   **Seldes ordered a martini:** This account of NA's meeting with Seldes comes from a letter NA sent to MG, MG Collection.

347   **Nelson's first stop was Baltimore:** This account of NA's stay in Baltimore and his road trip comes from a letter NA sent to MG, MG Collection.

349   **Ken McCormick had tried to call:** ibid.

349   **"I really do think":** Letter from Sheila Cudahy to NA. Farrar, Straus & Giroux, Inc. records, New York Public Library.

349   **"It is a hell of a novel":** ibid.

349   **Doubleday was claiming:** Letter from NA to MG, MG Collection.

350   **Jack Kirkland's theatrical:** Arthur Gelb, "Lindsay Comedy without a Home," *New York Times*, 21 November 1955.

350   **Preminger's film "has me breathing":** Letter from NA to Herman Kogan, NA Collection.

350   **Nelson left Jesse Blue:** This account of NA's trip to Miami and Cuba comes from "A Few Rounds with Papa and a Bottle of Scotch," *New York Times*, 29 March 1981, and a letter from NA to MG, MG Collection.

352   **she allowed him inside:** Interview of AK, BD Papers.

352   **At 5 a.m. on January 16:** Interview of AK, courtesy of JH.

352 **"Look," he said:** ibid.

353 **"I wish to affirm":** NA's FBI file.

A WALK ON THE WILD SIDE

354 **Nelson entered the University Club:** "The Literary Spotlight," *Chicago Tribune,* 3 June 1956.

354 **Nelson and Straus moved on:** "Authors Feted; 3 Parties . . . ," *Chicago Tribune,* 20 May 1956.

355 **"I think Madame de Beauvoir":** " 'Golden Arm' Author Has Mean Elbow," *New York World-Telegram and Sun,* 22 June 1956.

355 **"an ironical parody":** Maxwell Geismar, "Against the Tide of Euphoria," *Nation,* 2 June 1956.

355 **"the product of a distinguished":** James T. Farrell, "On the Wrong Side of Town," *New Republic,* 21 May 1956.

355 **"The Chicago School of Realism":** James Kelly, "Sin-Soaked in Storyville," *Saturday Review,* 26 May 1956.

355 **"The point Algren sought to make":** Victor P. Hass, "Algren Sees the World in Grain of Sand," *Chicago Tribune,* 20 May 1956.

356 **"puerile sentimentality":** "Some People Passing By."

356 **"human monsters":** "Books of the Times," *New York Times,* 23 May 1956.

356 **"is that we live in a society whose bums":** Norman Podhoretz, "The Man with the Golden Beef," *The New Yorker,* 2 June 1956.

356 **"a museum piece":** "The Noble Savages of Skid Row."

357 **labeled it "Paris":** Letter from NA to AK, AK Collection.

357 **"lights like candle-lamps":** Letter from NA to MG, MG Collection.

357 **Nelson was in the audience:** ibid.

358 **The news Nelson received:** This account comes from a memo summarizing the meeting held in Straus's office. Farrar, Straus & Giroux, Inc. records, New York Public Library.

359 **"When I began *that* one":** Letter from NA to MG, MG Collection.

360 **Nelson requested seven thousand:** Letter from Madeleine Brennan to Roger Straus. Farrar, Straus & Giroux, Inc. records, New York Public Library.

360 **so he met with the lawyer:** Interview of AK, BD Papers.

360 **Blue called Amanda:** ibid.

361 **he woke screaming:** Interview of DP, courtesy of JH.

361 **"What happened?" Peltz asked:** ibid.

362 **"Help me," he pleaded:** Interview of AK, BD Papers.

362 **The next morning, Amanda called:** Interview of DP, courtesy of JH.

362 **and began screaming:** ibid.

362 **and wrote: E:** ibid.

363 **"Dave," Nelson pleaded:** ibid.

363   diagnosed with "anxiety": NA's FBI file.

363   doctor who had been assigned to treat: Interview of AK, BD Papers.

364   The bureau decided to use the delay: NA's FBI file.

A LIGHTLESS CAVE OFF A LOVELESS HALL

366   Nelson went outside: This account of Nelson's walk across the ice comes from an interview of DP, courtesy of JH.

367   "I feel I may be able to": Letter from NA to Roger Straus. Farrar, Straus & Giroux, Inc. records, New York Public Library.

367   "playing around": Interview of DP, courtesy of JH.

368   Three brothers who shared: "Save Novelist from Lagoon," *Chicago Tribune*, 1 January 1957.

369   "The damn fool": Interview of DP, courtesy of JH.

369   "You see," he reflected later: ibid.

369   attended a New Year's Eve party: Letter from NA to J. Kerker Quinn, J. Kerker Quinn Papers, University of Illinois Archives.

369   The first thing Nelson did: Interview of Art Shay, BD Papers.

370   sold the film rights to: Film contract, NA Collection.

370   told a gossip columnist: Herb Lyon, "Tower Ticker," *Chicago Tribune*, 7 January 1957.

370   Paula Bays played a role: Interview of Paula Bays, BD Papers.

371   "most writers of the new school": "Break Through Myths of Our Time . . ."

371   Nelson couldn't make himself cash: This account of Nelson's trip to the bank comes from an interview of DP, courtesy of JH.

372   an unremarkable racehorse: Race program dated 10 May 1958, NA Collection.

372   purchased an apartment building: Herb Lyon, "Tower Ticker," *Chicago Tribune*, 23 May 1958.

372   Someone said they spotted: Interview of Frank Sandiford, BD Papers.

372   A friend reported: Interview of Sanka Gregoriev, BD Papers.

372   And Amanda claimed: Interview of AK, BD Papers.

372   *Sports Illustrated* asked him: "Prose for the Roses." *Sports Illustrated*, 28 April 1986.

373   Nelson arrived a week: ibid.

373   "The first thing I did": Unpublished transcript, NA Collection.

373   "Nothing comes easy to Silky": Whitney Tower, "Prose for the Roses," *Sports Illustrated*, 28 April 1986.

374   "[I]n a different age": ibid.

374   one of the three lawyers: "Author Nelson Algren Sued . . . ," *Chicago Tribune*, 13 May 1958.

374   he sold his house: Letters between AK and William Regan, AK Collection.

374   **"lightless cave off a loveless"**: Letter from NA to MG, MG Collection.
375   **I don't feel that I'm "coming back"**: ibid.

"NO, NO NOVEL"

379   **three strong men**: Letter from NA to MG, MG Collection.
380   **"No, no novel"**: Letter from NA to JCH, JCH Papers.
381   **"sucked and smiled"**: ibid.
382   **stopped writing or speaking to Maxwell**: NA's correspondence with MG
       stops abruptly around 1959, and BB later told BD that NA attributed their
       rift to MG's habit of writing brief letters.
382   **stopped speaking to the photographer**: Shay, though asked repeatedly,
       never spoke about the cause of his break with Nelson. This account is based
       on my conversations with JH. JH spoke to both NA and Studs Terkel about
       Shay decades later, and received the impression from both that Shay had
       been using NA.
382   **when he heard that Jack Conroy**: The cause of the rift between JC and NA
       has long been mysterious, and JC usually cast himself as the victim. NA did
       make insulting public statements about JC in 1959, but JC admitted to JH
       that they were preceded by a comment he made during a speech.
383   **"Your stance," he said**: *Conversations*, pp. 271–72.
383   **The State Department informed**: NA's FBI file.
384   **"So you could even"**: *A Transatlantic Love Affair*, p. 530.
384   **Beauvoir had been feeling**: *Simone de Beauvoir*, pp. 471–73.
385   **Nelson arrived at Beauvoir's**: This account of NA's vacation with SB comes
       from *Hard Times: Force of Circumstance*, vol. II (New York: Paragon House,
       1992), pp. 214–31.
386   **"The arrogance of the respectable"**: ibid., p. 216.
387   **"Once I used to live in America"**: ibid.
387   **"He had been promised one world"**: ibid.
388   **visited the US embassy**: NA's FBI file.
389   **"I can assure you"**: *Who Lost*, p. 152.
389   **"Not a single shadow"**: *Force of Circumstance*, vol. II, p. 231.
389   **"As if my body"**: ibid.
390   **After she left, he lingered**: *Simone de Beauvoir*, p. 482.
393   **"But it doesn't necessarily"**: Charles Purvis, "Life's Imperfections Seen in
       a Narrow Perspective," *Chicago Tribune*, 12 May 1963.
393   **"It would be fine to discover"**: Herbert Gold, "After All, Who Is the
       Enemy?" *New York Times*, 2 June 1963.
393   **"[Caught] between his own past"**: Hilton Kramer, "He Never Left Home,"
       Reporter, 20 June 1963.
394   **"Give me one," Goldie said**: *Conversations*, p. 328.

A CHARACTER NAMED NELSON ALGREN

395 **Someone was cheating:** This account of the card game and aftermath comes from an interview of DP, courtesy of JH.

398 **"its rusty heart would break":** Letter from NA to JCH, JCH Papers.

399 **a tramp steamer that operated:** ibid.

399 **he was a "broken" man:** *Sea Diary*, p. 169.

400 **Wright "came to Chicago":** "Remembering Richard Wright."

401 **"simply," he said, because:** *Conversations*, p. 175.

401 **Choryang-dong port in Busan:** *Sea Diary*, p. 47.

401 **Nelson followed a member:** *Sea Diary*, p. 69.

401 **found the Kamathipura district:** *Sea Diary*, pp. 133–52.

401 **"When a ship doesn't dock":** *Conversations*, p. 177.

402 **a stack of newspapers:** Letter from NA to JCH, JCH Papers.

402 **"Creative writing is dead":** "A Coffee Hour with Nelson Algren," *Chicago Daily News*, 3 March 1963.

403 **Donohue first stumbled:** *Conversations*, p. 331–33.

404 ***Notes toward a Biography*:** *Conversations*, p. 331.

409 **an "extraordinary book":** Kenneth Rexroth, "Innocence Observed," *New York Times*, 25 October 1964.

409 **"totally delightful, irreverent, mad":** "Nelson Algren Talks Shop," *Chicago Daily News*, date unknown.

409 **"a remarkably lively":** Francis Coughlin, "The True and Original Nelson Algren," *Chicago Tribune*, 25 October 1964.

409 **"I know he [Nelson] is behind":** Letter from Thomas Pynchon to Candida Donadio, NA Collection.

SEA DIARY

410 **"Boys," Bruce Jay Friedman told:** This account of NA's arrival comes from "On Nelson Algren," a talk delivered by Josh Alan Friedman on March 26, 2011.

411 **Nelson got up before dawn:** This account of NA's time with the Friedmans comes from an interview of Bruce Jay Friedman, courtesy of MC.

413 **"Conditions for writing":** Letter from NA to KB. KB Papers.

413 **a young man named Donald DeLillo:** This account of NA's time with DeLillo comes from a personal interview of DeLillo, 25 February 2016.

414 **just signed a three-book deal:** Putnam contract, NA Collection.

415 **"was the voice of a prophet":** Interview of Philip Kaufman, courtesy of MC.

416 **Banks, like DeLillo, wanted:** This account of NA's time with Banks comes from an Interview of Russell Banks, courtesy of MC.

416 **Nelson introduced DeLillo:** Personal interview of DeLillo, 25 February 2016.

416 **invited Nelson to live with him:** Personal interview of Robert Gover, 10 November 2013.

418 **"brilliant bursts"**: Lester Goran, "Nelson Algren—Promising Old Novelist," *Chicago Tribune*, 15 August 1965.

418 **"arch, arbitrary" tone**: Arno Karlen, "Hard Shell, Soft Center," *New York Times*, 22 August 1965.

419 **"back seat to nobody"**: "Nelson Algren on Hemingway . . . ," *Chicago Daily News*, 14 August 1965.

419 **the Putnam contract**: Putnam contract, NA Collection.

"ON THE HO CHI MINH TRAIL"

420 **Betty Ann Bendyk arrived**: Interview of BB, BD Papers.

421 **"the images, everything"**: Interview of BB, courtesy of JH.

421 **maybe five dates**: Interview of BB, BD Papers.

421 **"to hear her laugh again"**: Letter from NA to DD. DD Papers.

421 **"whirlwind romance"**: Interview of BB, BD Papers.

422 **Nelson and Betty were married**: "Nelson Algren Married," *New York Times*, 28 February 1965.

422 **he dripped gravy**: Interview of SD, BD Papers.

423 **"keep an eye on the opposition"**: Notes on meeting with NA, Matthew J. Bruccoli Papers, Kent State University.

423 **"It was like living in his studio"**: Interview of BB, courtesy of JH.

423 **He slept little**: ibid.

423 **about fourteen thousand dollars**: Notes on meeting with NA, Matthew J. Bruccoli Papers, Kent State University.

424 **"I loved his humor"**: Interview of BB, courtesy of JH.

424 **In exchange for twenty thousand**: Notes on meeting with NA, Matthew J. Bruccoli Papers, Kent State University.

424 **accepted—with one condition**: Letter from NA to KB. KB Papers.

425 **Betty rented a large**: Interview of BB, BD Papers.

425 **a book worth "rereading"**: *Carousel*, p. 77.

425 **Nelson's attitude in class**: This account of Nelson's behavior on campus comes from Burns Ellison, "The First Annual Nelson Algren Memorial Poker Game." *Iowa Review* 18, no. 1 (1988).

426 **"The longer I hang on here"**: *Carousel*, p. 77.

427 **an active poker scene**: This account of Nelson's poker playing comes from "The First Annual Nelson Algren Memorial Poker Game."

429 **"He was giving me leverage"**: Interview of BB, BD Papers.

429 **"Father Confessor and Listener"**: Letter from BB to NA, NA Collection.

430 **"Going on the Ho Chi Minh Trail"**: "The First Annual Nelson Algren Memorial Poker Game."

430 **"I'm scheduled to examine"**: "Myths and Mores" [speech transcript], Carolina Symposium Records, University Archive, University of North Carolina at Chapel Hill.

431 **"we are now in World War III"**: Letter from NA to DD, DD Papers.

433 **"I've had a bad operation"**: Letter from KB to NA, NA Collection.

433 **"Tough about losing"**: Letter from NA to KB, KB Papers.

433 **"Actually . . . I don't know"**: ibid.

433 **booked passage on a freighter**: Letter to Horizon Travel and Tours, NA Collection.

434 **"This is a mean, sick city"**: Letter from NA to RG, courtesy of JH.

434 **he made a series of forays**: ibid.

435 **he devised a scheme**: This account of NA's black market scheme comes from "Amateur Night Way Out East."

435 **"counting the days"**: Letter from NA to RG, courtesy of JH.

436 **"[I]t simmers down to"**: "Amateur Night Way Out East."

436 **Helen Corbett was one**: NA's FBI File.

THE LAST CAROUSEL

437 **Nelson established relationships**: Personal interview of Chris Chandler, 28 February 2014, and interview of SD, courtesy of JH.

438 **Kowalski—a former pimp**: Interview of BB, courtesy of JH.

438 **"Law & Order has never"**: Letter to RG, courtesy of JH.

439 **he visited Stephen Deutch**: This account of NA's friendship with SD, and the Deutches' biographies, come from personal interviews with Kat Tatlock, Annick Smith, and Carole Deutch on, respectively, 11, 13, and 19 February 2015.

441 **"What I'm doing"**: Letter from NA to KB, KB Papers.

441 **he wrote to his editor**: Letter from NA to Bill Targ, NA Collection.

446 **"It's about time!"**: James R. Frakes, "The Last Carousel," *New York Times*, 11 November 1973.

446 **"What an exhilarating experience"**: Maxwell Geismer, "Algren Shows Us How Good . . . ," *Chicago Sun-Times*, 25 November 1973.

446 **"[O]nce you begin reading"**: Cyrus Colter, "Algren Resurrected . . . ," *Chicago Tribune*, 25 November 1973.

446 **One of Nelson's fans**: Unpublished memoir, NA Collection.

446 **Putnam had delayed**: Interview of NA by Henry Kisor, transcript courtesy of JH.

447 **Kurt Vonnegut nominated**: *A Life on the Wild Side*, p. 348.

447 **"Thank You"**: ibid., p. 349.

"THE SANEST MAN I'VE EVER MET"

448 **Hogan was young**: All biographical details about Hogan are from a personal interview on 22 April 2014.

450 *Esquire* **magazine had offered**: Interview of Jim Ryan, courtesy of JH.

451   **"Sorry, Rubin," the guard:** Unpublished nonfiction Carter manuscript, NA Collection.

451   **"I don't wear prison dress":** ibid.

451   **"the sanest man I've ever met":** Letter from NA to RG, courtesy of JH.

452   **"It wasn't Nelson Algren at all":** Interview of Jim Ryan, courtesy of JH.

452   **traveled to Paterson by train:** Letter from NA to SD, BD Papers.

453   **"I don't know why you":** Letter from NA to SD, BD Papers.

453   **"I don't see Chicago ever becoming":** Interview of NA by Henry Kisor, transcript courtesy of JH.

454   **"There's nothing left for me in Chicago":** "Algren Hits the Open Road," *Chicago Daily News*, 8 February 1975.

454   **When Nelson's auction began:** "Old Card Table Is One of a Kind," *Chicago Sun-Times*, 9 March 1975.

454   **seemed to walk away with something:** "Algren's House Sale . . ."

454   **"Hi, it's me":** Rick Soll, "Nelson Algren Bids Final Farewell," *Chicago Tribune*, 10 March 1975.

455   **"This is all worthwhile":** ibid.

PATERSON, NEW JERSEY

460   **"pleasant little country town":** "Nelson Algren 'Settling In' in Paterson," *New York Times*, 15 April 1975.

460   **Work "proceeds slowly":** Letter from NA to SD, BD Papers.

462   **One morning in September:** This account of Linda Kay's time with NA comes from her book *The Reading List* (Lanham, MD: Hamilton Books, 2005).

464   **"The police chief didn't want":** ibid., p. 2.

465   **"Do you prefer this kind of work":** Interview of NA by Henry Kisor, transcript courtesy of JH.

465   **published more than three hundred:** Geoffrey Robertson, "Rubin 'Hurricane' Carter's Life Story Is . . ." *Guardian*, 21 April 2014.

466   **"The verdict was a stunner":** Letter from NA to Lyle Silbert, Lyle Silbert Papers, University of Chicago Library.

466   **Nelson visited Carter:** This account of NA's meeting with Carter comes from NA's unpublished nonfiction Carter manuscript, NA Collection.

468   **"I've gone this far with it":** Jim Gallagher, "Literary 'Exile' Is Pleasant for Algren," *Chicago Tribune*, 29 March 1977.

THE DEVIL'S STOCKING

469   **Nelson and Page had known:** Interview of Geraldine Page, BD Papers.

470   **learned where Groening was:** Personal Interview of RG, 2 August 2014.

470   **a New York City homicide detective:** Interview of Roy Finer, BD Papers.

470   **boarded a bus in downtown Hackensack:** This account of Nelson's meet-

ing with Breslin comes from "The Man in the $20 Hotel Room," anthologized in Jimmy Breslin, *The World According to Breslin* (New York: Ticknor & Fields, 1984).

471   **applied for a Guggenheim:** Guggenheim application, BD Papers.

474   **Nelson sent his manuscript:** Letter from NA to Candida Donadio, NA Collection.

474   **publisher at Arbor House, Donald Fine:** Letter from Donald Fine to Candida Donadio, BD Papers.

475   **He was alone for the holidays:** Interview of Roy Finer, BD Papers.

475   **Nelson's room: 461-1:** Hospital visitor's pass, courtesy of JH.

475   **"How the hell did you find me?":** Interview of Roy Finer, BD Papers.

476   **called him a "cheap SOB":** *A Life on the Wild Side*, p. 372.

476   **"You," Cormac McCarthy had written:** Letter from Cormac McCarthy to NA, NA Collection.

476   **Oyster Bay, Cold Spring Harbor:** "Respite from the Wild Side," *Newsday*, 22 January 1981.

477   **Herman put Nelson and Weissner in touch:** Letters from Weissner to NA, courtesy of JH.

477   **Nelson found a payphone:** This account comes from Joe Pintauro, "Nelson Algren's Last Year," *Chicago* magazine, 1 February 1988.

"THE END IS NOTHING, THE ROAD IS ALL"

479   **a German film crew:** *Algren in Sag Harbor*, directed by Wolf Wondratschek, courtesy of JH.

479   **But by Christmas:** This account comes from Kaylie Jones, *Lies My Mother Never Told Me* (New York: William Morrow, 2009), pp. 76–78.

480   **On April 9, Nelson made his way:** This account of NA's visit to the academy comes from "Nelson Algren Meets the Literary Establishment," *Newsday*, 7 June 1981.

481   **"I didn't know I was running":** This account of NA's interview of Weatherby comes from *The Devil's Stocking*, pp. 9–12.

482   **alone in his little house:** *A Life on the Wild Side*, p. 376.

483   **Roy Finer arrived:** This account comes from Jan Herman, *Ticket to New Jersey* (Impromptu Editions, 2014), pp. 22–24.

483   **Nelson was buried:** "Algren Burial among Old Whalers," *Chicago Sun-Times*, 12 May 1981.

483   **woman with bright red hair:** Personal interview of Kat Tatlock, 11 February 2015.

483   **Pintauro stepped forward:** "Nelson Algren's Last Year."

INDEX

Page numbers in *italics* refer to illustrations.
Page numbers after 492 refer to endnotes.